The Old South

BLACKWELL READERS IN AMERICAN SOCIAL AND CULTURAL HISTORY

Series editor: Jacqueline Jones, Brandeis University

The *Blackwell Readers in American Social and Cultural History* series introduces students to well-defined topics in American history from a socio-cultural perspective. Using primary and secondary sources, the volumes present the most important works available on a particular topic in a succinct and accessible format designed to fit easily into courses offered in American history or American studies.

The Old South

Edited by

Mark M. Smith

Copyright © Blackwell Publishers Ltd 2001; editorial matter and organization
copyright © Mark M. Smith 2001

First published 2001

2 4 6 8 10 9 7 5 3 1

Blackwell Publishers Inc.
350 Main Street
Malden, Massachusetts 02148
USA

Blackwell Publishers Ltd
108 Cowley Road
Oxford OX4 1JF
UK

Library of Congress Cataloging-in-Publication Data has been applied for.

ISBN 0-631-21926-9 (hardback); 0-631-21927-7 (paperback)

British Library Cataloguing in Publication Data
A CIP catalogue record for this book is available from the British Library.

Typeset in 10/12 Plantin
by Kolam Information Service Pvt. Ltd., Pondicherry, India
Printed in Great Britain by MPG Books, Bodmin, Cornwall

This book is printed on acid-free paper.

For Catherine, with love

Contents

Series Editor's Preface

The purpose of the Blackwell Readers in American Social and Cultural History is to introduce students to cutting-edge historical scholarship that draws upon a variety of disciplines, and to encourage students to "do" history themselves by examining some of the primary texts upon which that scholarship is based.

Each of us lives life with a wholeness that is at odds with the way scholars often dissect the human experience. Anthropologists, psychologists, literary critics, and political scientists (to name just a few) study only discrete parts of our existence. The result is a rather arbitrary collection of disciplinary boundaries enshrined not only in specialized publications but also in university academic departments and in professional organizations.

As a scholarly enterprise, the study of history necessarily crosses these boundaries of knowledge in order to provide a comprehensive view of the past. Over the last few years, social and cultural historians have reached across the disciplines to understand the history of the British North American colonies and the United States in all its fullness. Unfortunately, much of that scholarship, published in specialized monographs and journals, remains inaccessible to undergraduates. Consequently, instructors often face choices that are not very appealing – to ignore the recent scholarship altogether, assign bulky readers that are too detailed for an undergraduate audience, or cobble together packages of recent articles that lack an overall contextual framework. The individual volumes of this series each focus on a significant topic in American history, and bring new, exciting scholarship to students in a compact, accessible format.

The series is designed to complement textbooks and other general readings assigned in undergraduate courses. Each editor has culled particularly innovative and provocative scholarly essays from widely scattered books and journals, and provided an introduction summarizing the major themes of the essays and documents that follow. The essays reproduced here were chosen because of the authors' innovative (and often interdisciplinary) methodology and their ability to reconceptualize historical issues in fresh and insightful ways. Thus students can appreciate the rich complexity of an historical topic and the way that scholars have explored the topic from different perspectives, and in the process transcend the highly artificial disciplinary boundaries that have served to compartmentalize knowledge about the past in the United States.

Also included in each volume are primary texts, at least some of which have been drawn from the essays themselves. By linking primary and secondary material, the editors are able to introduce students to the historian's craft, allowing them to explore this material in depth, and draw additional insights – or interpretations contrary to those of the scholars under discussion – from it. Additional teaching tools, including study questions and suggestions for further reading, offer depth to the analysis.

Jacqueline Jones
Brandeis University

Acknowledgments

For her encouraging words during the formulation of this book, I thank Jacqueline Jones, and for their superb editorial guidance, I am grateful to Susan Rabinowitz and Ken Provencher. The anonymous readers for this book offered very helpful and constructive suggestions concerning the choice of essays and I remain in their debt. Cheryl Wells proved an excellent research assistant, and I remain in Jenny Tyler's debt for her stellar editing. I am grateful for permission to reprint the articles published here and I'd like to take this opportunity to thank the authors of the various essays. Walter Johnson in particular went beyond the call of duty in several respects and I thank him for his help.

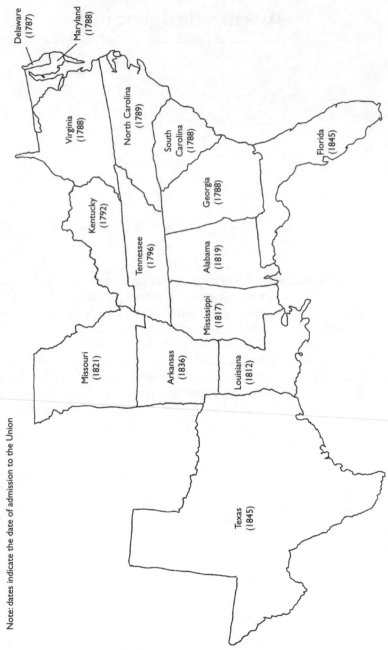

The Old South in 1860

Note: dates indicate the date of admission to the Union

Delaware (1787)

Maryland (1788)

Virginia (1788)

North Carolina (1789)

South Carolina (1788)

Florida (1845)

Kentucky (1792)

Georgia (1788)

Tennessee (1796)

Alabama (1819)

Mississippi (1817)

Missouri (1821)

Arkansas (1836)

Louisiana (1812)

Texas (1845)

Chronology

1776	Declaration of Independence
1783	Peace of Paris
1787	Constitutional Congress meets and submits the Constitution to the states for ratification
1788	Constitution ratified by states
1789	George Washington elected President
1790	Samuel Slater's cotton mill established in Rhode Island. In this decade, prices for prime field hands range between $300 and $400
1793	A practical gin for short-staple cotton is invented and cotton cultivation begins to spread westward as a result. With cotton go the enslaved, so that the next thirty or so years witness the spread of slavery into Alabama, Mississippi, Tennessee, and Texas
1801	Raw cotton output reaches roughly 100,000 bales per year
1803	Louisiana Purchase more than doubles the size of the United States
1808	Further importation of slaves banned by Congress. Number imported to date is roughly 660,000
1812	War with Britain
1815	Peace of Ghent
1815–19	War years difficult but peace brings a return to prosperity and even a brief boom in the cotton industry
1819–30s	The Panic of 1819 delivers a crushing blow to the southern economy. The region experiences a slow comeback in the

	1820s. Rice remains stable as does sugar cane. By the 1830s a new economic enthusiasm stirs the South, especially in the Southwest. Railroads begin to connect cotton economy with southern ports and the Midwest. This period also witnesses the rise of scientific agriculture among southern planters
1820	5.5 percent of southerners live in an urban area by this time. For New England, the figure is 10.5 percent
1820	Missouri Compromise. Maine is admitted to the Union as a free state, Missouri as a slave state. Slavery is banned north of the 36 degree, 30 minute line but allowed south of the line. The Compromise settles the question of slavery's expansion for the next quarter of a century
1822	Cotton mills open in Lowell, Massachusetts
1822	A slave insurrection planned by Denmark Vesey in Charleston, South Carolina, is foiled but leaves white South Carolinians in a state of heightened anxiety
1828	Andrew Jackson elected president. John C. Calhoun's *South Carolina Exposition and Protest* outlines the right of a state to nullify an act of Congress deemed unconstitutional by the state
1831	William Lloyd Garrison begins publication of *The Liberator* in which he calls for immediate emancipation of southern slaves. In the 1830s, prices for a prime field hand are $1,000–$1,300
1831	Nat Turner's Rebellion in Southampton County, Virginia. Turner and his slave allies kill fifty or so whites; the Virginia militia kills large numbers of slaves in putting down the revolt. Turner and his accomplices are hanged and white Virginians begin to debate the desirability of slavery in their society
1832	Building on Calhoun's 1828 *Exposition and Protest*, South Carolina issues an Ordinance of Nullification repudiating the tariff acts of 1828 and 1832 as unconstitutional. The crisis is resolved but the question of states' rights and the South as a conscious minority gain currency
1833	Chicago founded
1835	Raw cotton output reaches about 1 million bales a year
1837	Panic of 1837 strikes ferociously. This period represents the deepest and most prolonged depression in the antebellum period. In some places cotton goes below 5 cents per pound. Tobacco and rice also suffer although sugar cane holds on. Bitter political fights over fiscal policy erode optimism

1840	The percentage of the South's population living in an urban environment is 7.7; for New England, 19.4 percent; for the Mid-Atlantic states, 18.1 percent
1846	United States declares war on Mexico. The Wilmot Proviso attempts to ban slavery from any territory acquired as a result from the war with Mexico. The Proviso does not pass but in effect resurrects the debate that seemed to have been settled by the Missouri Compromise. Slavery and its expansion is once again a national political issue
late 1840s on	Across the South the 1850s are the most prosperous decade of the nineteenth century. Big increases in the production of most staples do not depress prices, which either rise or remain stable. The Panic of 1857 has little effect on the southern economy generally
1850	The Compromise of 1850 attempts to resolve the growing crisis between North and South over the westward expansion of slavery. A fragile agreement is reached with the compromise which admits California as a free state to the Union and offers southern planters an invigorated fugitive slave law in return. Neither section is particularly happy with the terms of the compromise but their commitment to the Union and the functioning of the two-party system enables the individual provisions of the compromise to pass. In the 1850s, prices for a prime field hand average \$1,500–\$2,000
1852	Harriet Beecher Stowe publishes *Uncle Tom's Cabin* which depicts slavery as a callous institution and manages to raise the ire of northern abolitionists and incense southern proslavery ideologues
1854	The Kansas–Nebraska Act in effect repeals the Missouri Compromise, thus destabilizing the sectional truce. The act leads to violence in Kansas and makes sectional compromise less likely than ever
1856	Preston S. Brooks of South Carolina canes Senator Charles Sumner of Massachusetts on the floor of the United States Senate for real and perceived insults leveled by Sumner against Brook's uncle, Senator Andrew P. Butler, and his native state. The episode is a microcosm of sectional animosity and serves to reinforce mutual stereotypes among northerners and southerners
1857	Dred Scott decision. Chief Justice Robert B. Taney rules that African Americans, even free ones, are not citizens and "have no rights which the white man is bound to respect." Taney also judges the Missouri Compromise

unconstitutional since Congress, by ruling that certain new territories could exclude slavery, had wrongly and unconstitutionally deprived citizens of property rights in slaves. This decision serves to reinforce the fear in the North that the government itself has become hostage to the designs of the southern Slave Power

1859   John Brown's Raid sends chills up the spines of southern slaveholders. Raw cotton output in the South reaches 5.4 million bales a year

1860   The South is home to 3.84 million slaves. 11.5 percent of the South's population lives in towns or cities. In New England, the figure is 36.6 percent; in the Mid-Atlantic states, 35.4 percent

1860   Republican Abraham Lincoln elected President

1860–1 Southern states secede from the Union

1861   Civil War breaks out

1863   Lincoln issues the Emancipation Proclamation

Introduction

Always enigmatic and not infrequently elusive, the Old South was a place and time whose intellectual, spatial, and temporal boundaries were characterized more by their elasticity and permeability than by their concreteness. The Old South was, in short, a society defined by many constituents and, as such, there were many historical realities that went to make up a region and period we call the "Old South." While these many realities do not prevent us from talking about the Old South generally, they do force us to think hard about, and be sensitive to, the variety of historical experiences of those who lived in the region.

Work by social and cultural historians of the past three decades or so has alerted us to the variety of experiences within the Old South. But cultural and social history does more than simply rescue the multiplicity of historical experience from the past. In addition, cultural and social historians generally, those of the Old South included, tend to eschew the older emphasis of political and economic historians whose work focused mainly on formal political events, dates, episodes, and figures, as well as economic growth and crises. Social and cultural historians usually tend to look less at the famous, well-known figures of history, and instead seek to recover the hidden and sometimes obscured pasts and experiences of average men and women. Using quantitative and qualitative data, cultural and social historians, while sometimes sensitive to the political and economic implications of their topics, seek mainly to examine the value systems of average people. That much said, cultural and social histories of the Old South not only analyze how average men and woman functioned, they also examine how they were influenced by historical events and how they in turn influenced those events, and in some instances consider the cultural values and set of social beliefs not just of average peoples but also of the elite. Consequently, some social and cultural historians of the Old South do not analyze, for example, formal, high politics but, rather, examine the formation of political culture that undergirded the political structure at the local and national levels. The distinguishing characteristic of social and cultural history, then, is not so much the constituency examined but the way the subject matter is explored. As a result, there are social and cultural histories of, for example, the theological beliefs of the master class as well as the world views of slave women. Moreover, in recent years social and cultural histories have attempted to relate the uncovering of hidden pasts to the larger developments of political and economic history. All of the essays in this volume reveal one or more of these characteristics of social and cultural history. Before introducing these essays and their accompanying documents, however, it is helpful to sketch the principal contours of the history of the Old South in order to understand how social and cultural history has furthered and enriched our knowledge of the region's history and, indeed, histories.

By the end of the American Revolution, the South was no longer a colonial society with slaves; rather, it was a maturing slave society – a society whose social and economic relations, political structure, intellectual life, and cultural values were, to varying degrees, touched and influenced by the presence of a legally entrenched and socially mandated system of chattel slavery. The gradual abolition of slavery in northern states both during and after the Revolution was paralleled by the consolidation of slavery in the South. Although some southern slaveholders questioned the legitimacy of human bondage in the revolutionary and early national periods, most did not, and came to see slavery as part and parcel of their social, political, and economic order. Conversely, some northerners took steps, sometimes gradual, to rid their society of slavery. Although some northern thinkers saw merit in the socially stabilizing features of bondage, many were able to institute emancipatory measures simply because their society had always been less dependent on slavery and because they embraced a growing humanitarian sentiment that slavery and the principles of freedom and equality expressed in the Revolutionary War were increasingly incompatible.

Post-revolutionary elite white southerners, by contrast, proceeded apace to further entrench slavery legally, politically, socially, and economically. Slavery had always held particular economic value to the southern colonies. Slaves had been used to cultivate indigo, tobacco, and rice in South Carolina, Georgia, Virginia, and North Carolina. In the 1790s, southern masters were presented with an additional economic incentive to preserve and, indeed, expand, their increasingly peculiar institution. Cotton, and the invention of the cotton gin, provided that incentive. Although cotton had been grown in the colonial South, the quantities were always small not simply because demand for the crop had to await British industrialization beginning in the 1750s (and, slightly later, the coming of northern textile mills), but also because the growing and processing of the crop was difficult. Before the Revolution, planters tried to process the hardy green-seed variety of cotton using a primitive "churka" gin. But because the gin was primitive and because the cotton lint clung doggedly to the seed, production of cotton remained small because seed and lint still had to be separated by hand. The invention in the 1790s of a cheap and effective gin, the ability of short-staple cotton to grow in a wide variety of soils, and Britain's increasing demand for the crop marked a revolution of sorts in southern society.

As the United States spread westward, so too did short-staple cotton (the cultivation of the highly profitable but delicate long-staple cotton remained confined primarily to the coasts of South Carolina and Georgia). And with short-staple cotton went slaves. By 1800, slave labor produced sugar in Louisiana, rice on the coasts of Georgia and South Carolina, tobacco in Virginia and North Carolina, and, everywhere, cotton. Unlike, for example, tobacco, cotton was not pushed west by soil depletion. Rather, it was pulled westward by the attraction of higher yields and profits.

The net effect of these developments measured in numerical terms is staggering. Raw cotton output, for example, expanded from about 100,000 bales per year in 1801 to 1 million bales in 1835 and reached a phenomenal 5.4 million bales per year in 1859. So too with the numbers of enslaved people in the Old South. From about 700,000 slaves in 1790, the region had a slave population of 3.84 million by 1860. A total of roughly 660,000 bondpeople were brought to the United States before the further importation of slaves was banned congressionally in 1808, a figure representing about 7 percent of all African slaves who were forcibly transported across the Atlantic. More than 4 million slaves, by contrast, were shipped to, for example, Brazil. And yet, by 1825, the United States was home to almost 36 percent of all slaves in the western hemisphere while Brazil, which had transported more than six times as many, had just 31 percent of all slaves in the Americas. Clearly, the American South had become distinctive among slave societies in the New World not least because it had managed to produce a self-sustaining slave society, one independent of further importation of African slaves. Not surprisingly, southern slave women bore, on average, more children than their counterparts in other slave societies in the Americas during the nineteenth century. And where slaves were lacking within the South, a sophisticated internal slave trade served to reallocate labor. Between 1820 and 1860, just over 800,000 slaves were traded to the new western slave states, principally from the Upper South.

Numbers, of course, can give false impressions, and it should be remembered that the Old South did not form suddenly at a particular moment in time, nor was the society monolithic. The place expanded and evolved through time and the legal entrenchment of slavery was quite fitful, with some southern states treating slaves simply as property while others kept more ambiguous laws on the books. Slavery, and by extension the Old South, evolved rather than crystallized. Following the ban on the importation of slaves in 1808, for example, planters were required to adopt new mentalities and strategies for dealing with their slaves in order to become, as it were, self-sufficient in the "production" of their labor force. Planters accordingly encouraged the formation of stable slave families not least by attempting to further strengthen their slaves' Christian values and by adopting a more paternalistic attitude toward their bondpeople.

Slaves hardly accepted these values *in toto* and instead incorporated them within their own culture in an effort to sustain themselves spiritually and sometimes to resist the institution physically, principally by running away and, on occasion, revolting. Still, the trend toward equalization of sex ratios among bondpeople helped in the formation of slave families throughout the South and produced slaves whose cultural values were an amalgam of African and American mores and beliefs. Perhaps more importantly still, the establishment of slave families helped the enslaved form more stable and enduring plantation communities. These communities were critical for the further formation of an African-American culture which manifested itself in myriad ways ranging from dress and food preparation to religious expression and material culture. These cultural values in turn shaped white value-systems and culture and, in effect, created a southern cultural and social identity that was a product of the braiding of white and black culture. It is the creation of these value systems among black and white, free and enslaved, men and woman that social and cultural historians have been particularly sensitive to exploring and interrogating.

Myriad, multiple, and plural though the Old South was, then, one institution stood at its center and defined virtually all social, economic, political, and cultural arrangements. That institution was black slavery and, in this sense, any history of the Old South is really, at base, a history of an aspect of slavery, broadly conceived. Of course, not every white southerner owned slaves. Few did, in fact. Of the 8 million white southerners in 1860, there were only 385,000 slaveowners. Half of these masters owned one to five slaves and only 12 percent belonged to the so-called planter class — those who owned twenty or more bondpeople. Only 13,000 masters owned more than fifty slaves in 1860, and three-quarters of white families owned no slaves at all. Moreover, slaveholding became concentrated in fewer hands as the Civil War approached. Roughly 30 percent of white families owned slaves in 1830; only 25 percent did by 1860. Similarly, not all black people in the Old South were slaves. In 1790, the South was home to just over 32,000 free blacks (almost 5 percent of the total black population); by 1840 they numbered 174,357 (8 percent). Although the next twenty years saw a relative decrease in the proportion of free blacks, they nonetheless remained an important constituency in the Old South.

Although relatively few whites owned slaves, the institution of slavery touched everything in southern society. The presence of enslaved African Americans helped whites define their own freedom. More obviously, slavery penetrated political discourse, both formal and informal, in many ways. At the national level, slavery was a question of property rights and constitutionality and, occasionally, morality. At the local level, slavery was often invoked to justify white freedom and superiority. Here, slaveholders made the case that all southern whites shared a degree of equality based on their skin color. In making this argument, the southern master class attempted to minimize differences of class within the southern white community by highlighting the importance of race. Some slaveless whites doubtless found solace in the distinction, although others probably accepted slavery for very different reasons, among them their own tenacious commitment to republican independence and freedom.

Slavery constituted the basis of the South's economy, making it at once a society tied intimately to the world market by virtue of its export of staples and an intensely local society in which southern planters, merchants, factors, yeomen, and poor whites were linked by the workings of the slave-based plantation economy. Even the leisure pursuits of the southern intelligentsia (at least those who owned slaves) were to some extent influenced by slavery: slave labor freed some planters to pursue the life of the mind by leaving manual labor to others, namely, black slaves. In short, slavery affected definitions of how one perceived self and others, cast shadows local and international in scope, and essentially made the South distinct from the North. Without slavery there would have been no Old South.

This is not to say, of course, that southerners were utterly distinct from northerners. In fact, they shared much in common. Elites from both sections were often wary of the proclivities of laboring classes, and one can find many statements by southern patricians echoed by their northern brethren concerning the proper place for women, immigrants, Native Americans, African Americans, and the laboring poor. Indeed, the similarities between the Old North and the Old South were striking. In both regions, a majority of people continued to make a living in agriculture by 1860. Although the South grew export staples, there were many southern farmers who, like their northern counterparts, strove for self-sufficiency.

It is also worth recalling that by mid-century, industrial workers in the South, as in the North, worked primarily in small shops and households, not in large factories. And while the North had more factories and large towns than the South, the functions of southern towns and factories were very similar. In terms of transportation, it should be noted that southern railroads, both in terms of total mileage and function, were roughly equal to northern ones by the 1840s. If we turn our attention to social structure, similarities between North and South become even more apparent. In both sections, for example, wealth was maldistributed and concentrated in the hands of a few. By 1860, about 50 percent of the free adult males in both North and South held less than 1 percent of the real and personal property; the wealthiest 1 percent owned 27 percent. Not only were the inequality levels similar, but, according to some observers, rates of vertical social mobility were parallel. Few people, north or south, apparently experienced rapid and significant upward social mobility in the antebellum period. A common belief in social hierarchy, Protestant Christianity, deferential republicanism, the ideal (if not always the reality) of democratic governance, the Constitution, and economic progress provided much of the glue that held the two sections together.

For all the similarities between the two regions, there were important, and growing, differences. In some respects, these differences were present in the colonial period. Although often simply a geographical designation, the word "southern" by the mid–eighteenth century came to mean something different from the word "northern," a difference measured primarily in the increasing reliance on slave labor in Virginia and South Carolina particularly. The differences became more acute after the nationalizing effects of the Revolution began to wear off. The North's gradual and fitful abolition of slavery after the Revolutionary War began to sharpen distinctions between the two regions. Although there were calls for the abolition of slavery, particularly in the Upper South (Maryland, Delaware, and Virginia), most slaveholders in the border states, and particularly in the Deep South, did not embrace the abolitionist cause. Indeed, in the Lower South especially, the rapid growth of a free black population following the Revolution eventually led to a stricter form of racial control even as the existence of free African Americans undermined the logic of race-based slavery. By the time of the Missouri Compromise in 1820, the South was on the brink of becoming a politically and socially conscious section which argued for the right not only to hold slaves but also to transport chattels into western territory.

In the forty years following the admission of Missouri as a slave state, the ability of the South and North to compromise on the question of slavery's westward expansion eroded. That the two sections managed to compromise for as long as they did is quite striking and explicable in large part by the existence of a two-party system (the Democrats and the Whigs) which operated in both sections of the country and thereby limited sectional political rivalry. But developments within each section served to heighten tensions. Most graphically, the anti-slavery sentiment among particular constituencies in the North during and after the 1830s offered a scalding critique of a supposedly inefficient and morally debased southern society that was good for neither slaves, slaveless whites, slaveholders, nor the American nation generally. In response to the critique, southern thinkers defended their society not so much by applauding slavery as a necessary evil (as had been the case in Thomas Jefferson's day) but, rather, by constructing an argument pointing out the supposed virtues of enslavement. This argument, which drew on scriptual, biological, and economic justifications for slavery, served to make the South a conscious minority – to distinguish the region and its people as qualitatively different from the liberal, democratic, industrial, urban, capitalist North. With the collapse of the two-party system in the 1850s and the emergence of the purely sectional (northern) Republican Party in 1854, these differences could no longer be minimized by the political system. Sectionalism reached its height in the late 1850s and war, to many contemporaries, seemed inevitable.

The foregoing description of southern history is not one with which cultural and social historians of the Old South are preoccupied. Rather than focusing their attention on the acts of major politicians or exploring the intricacies of economic trends, cultural and social historians, while situating their findings within the broader developments of southern and American history, tend to explore the cultural and social beliefs and values of the Old South's various constituencies. Interested in questions of cultural value, recent historical inquiry into the Old South tends to examine the interior lives of particular groups or constituencies, looking more to their construction of value systems, how they worked, and what they meant, rather than to the acts of the so-called Great Men of southern history which tend to tell us more about high-level political maneuvering and developments and less about the range and complexity of social and cultural values of the Old South. More conspicuously, recent work often (though not always) looks not at the South as a whole but, rather, examines particular aspects of southern history either from a sub-regional level – such as state or local history – or from the vantage of particular groups in particular locales. To be sure, some work still attempts to describe and characterize the Old South in meta-historical terms. This much is clear from part I of this book, in which two historians offer broad characterizations of the Old South's society, culture, and world view. In chapter 1, Raimondo Luraghi argues that the Old South, generally speaking, is best characterized as a quasi-feudal, certainly premodern society where the quest for honor and social status, a fascination with the conservatism of the past, and the social order reflected in the aesthetics of antebellum architecture combined to make the world of the planter class specifically, and the cultural and social texture of the entire society generally, something other than capitalist. In Luraghi's opinion, the Old South's master class was reminiscent of the old European feudal, seigneurial class. The slaveholders shaped their society around conservative values, appreciated the lessons, architecture, and strict hierarchy of classical antiquity, and did their best to preserve this world in the face of an emerging northern, alternative vision of society that stressed liberal capitalism, urbanization, and industrialism. Luraghi's article and the documents that accompany it certainly suggest that slaveholders embraced a world view that looked backward, not forward, that coveted the order of social conservatism, not the fluidity of liberal, democratic capitalism. Even if planters were profit-minded capitalists, suggests Luraghi, they were not successful ones because slavery, by virtue of its anti-industrial, anti-urban tendencies, hampered economic growth. For Luraghi, slavery was an inflexible economic institution, an economic arrangement in which labor could not be reallocated, expanded, or contracted efficiently or quickly. Moreover, planters' capital was tied inextricably to a system that fed consumption, not production. Based as it was, then, in a culture that scorned acquisitiveness, Luraghi's Old South was utterly premodern. Anchored as it was by non-wage labor, Luraghi's Old South could not be anything else but precapitalist.

Although the debate concerning the relative capitalist or precapitalist characteristics of the Old South no longer commands the attention among historians that it once did, this does not mean to say that historians interested in the social have abandoned the debate altogether. As the second essay and set of documents show, there have been some recent attempts to treat southern society as a whole and characterize it at a general level. By comparing the way southerners, black and white, used and understood time, to the ways in which clock time was applied and understood in modernizing, sometimes industrial, free-wage labor nineteenth-century societies, Mark M. Smith argues that the Old South may not have been as backward as Luraghi and others have suggested. For Smith, the presence or absence of free-wage labor in deciding how to characterize a particular society is not as important as it is for Luraghi. Indeed, according to Smith, slaveholders preferred the clock precisely because clock time – provided it was owned by the planter class and not made available to slaves – was both conservative and modern. Slaveholders embraced the clock because it satisfied their concerns regarding plantation efficiency and their political and social worries concerning the preservation of social order. In comparative perspective, argues Smith, the Old South's master class was among the most clock-conscious ruling classes of the nineteenth century and in some respects was more modern than its capitalist counterparts elsewhere. While the enslaved were not turned into time-disciplined workers (as in the North), they were made obedient to the clock not least because masters coupled clock time to the whip. This braiding of time and violence proved sufficient, argues Smith, to make the Old South's plantation economy efficient and orderly. Hence, the absence of wage labor in the Old South did not doom the region to premodernity. Rather, the master class was far more agile in modernizing its society on its own terms than some historians are inclined to think. Smith makes these points primarily because he uses comparative history, which still offers southern historians an important and useful analytic framework for understanding the Old South.

If Smith and Luraghi attempt to characterize the broad social values of the Old South, the documents and essays presented in the second part deal with specific aspects of that larger culture. In "The Appearance of Honor and the Honor of Appearance," Kenneth S. Greenberg examines the cultural phenomenon of duels among the Old South's elite. To explain why southern men dueled more often than their northern counterparts, Greenberg looks at the notion of southern honor. By tracing some specific disputes played out in newspapers, Greenberg shows that southern men were preoccupied with the preservation of their honor. In the context of the Old South, maintains Greenberg, honor was anchored mainly in appearances. To accuse a southern gentleman of falsehood, of telling a lie, was, in effect, to call into question his status as a gentleman and to doubt his honesty, his appearance, and, ultimately, his honor. Far less than northern men, southern gentleman understood their role and position in the world in terms of public character. Attacks on their character – suggestions that they were somehow not what they appeared – were considered slanders on a man's honor, attacks that demanded defense and redress, sometimes in the form of a duel. The public nature of the duel itself – ritualized, orchestrated, almost theatrical but, of course, potentially deadly – shows that dueling was designed to reassure onlookers of the true worth of the southern gentleman's appearance, that he was, in fact, who he purported to be. Northern men of similar social standing, points out Greenberg, could barely understand this world.

Men like P. T. Barnum, after all, made their living manipulating appearances, not preserving them intact. For northern men, the truth of the matter was the key; for southern men the appearance of the fact was preeminently important. "The man of honor does not care if he stinks," explains Greenberg, "but he does care that someone has accused him of stinking."

Honor was also used by southern gentlemen to differentiate themselves from slaves, says Greenberg. As he explains: "The words of the master had to be accorded respect and accepted as true simply because they were the words of a man of honor. The words of the slave could never become objects of honor. Whites assumed that slaves lied all the time – and that their lies were intimately connected to their position as slaves." Southern honor, then, was a cultural value, communicated and understood in a variety of cultural gestures and languages, that served to differentiate elite white southern men not only from their slaves but also from their northern counterparts. As such, southern honor was critical to the cultural identity of the Old South.

Or was it? If Greenberg is right, could non-elite white southern men also have "honor" as popularly conceived? Elliot J. Gorn answers this and many other questions in his essay on fighting among poor whites on the southern frontier and in the backcountry. Gorn's essay, and the documents that accompany it, not only depict in sometimes horrific and gory detail how and why poor white men on the frontier fought, but reveal how they were perceived by educated elites who witnessed the bloody gouging and stomping and seemingly gratuitous violence. Frontier men, according to elites, were uncivilized barbarians, men who had yet to be tamed by the discipline of the market. Although their behavior was in part due to their peripherality to market relations, Gorn suggests that we can understand this violence in other ways. First, he notes that violence among poor white southern men may well have been a product of their honor. Their sensitivity to the spoken word was legendary and not altogether different from the kind of touchiness apparent in elite white southern society. In an oral and aural culture like that of the southern backcountry, words carried the same weight as action. Insults could do terrible damage to a poor man's reputation, especially since his poverty meant that his reputation was usually all that he had by way of social status in very localized communities. "Men were so touchy about their personal reputations," says Gorn, "that any slight required an apology." And if one were not forthcoming, terrible violence could ensue. In this sense, then, Gorn adds an important dimension to our understanding of southern honor. Although the ways elite and poor whites resolved affronts to their honor differed, the fact remains that both groups were very sensitive to personal slights and attacks on their reputation. If Gorn is right, the coming of the market revolution to the southern frontier presumably altered the way poor whites defended that honor, turning, like elites, to revolvers instead of relying on fists and sharpened nails to resolve disputes.

If honor was central to southern white men's understanding of themselves and their society, so too was religion. Religion was also highly functional, for it provided a powerful glue uniting white southerners of all classes and genders. Such, at least, are the conclusions to be drawn from the documents and essays presented in part III. In "Slavery Ordained of God," Elizabeth Fox-Genovese and Eugene D. Genovese contend that the defense of slavery was grounded in a cogent articulation of scripture and theology. The Old South's preeminent thinkers, maintain Fox-Genovese and Genovese, "not merely persisted in the defense of slavery, they purposefully raised it to an abstract model of necessary social order" by drawing on a biblical defense of human servitude. At base, proslavery ideologues rejected the radical individualism of northern anti-slavery thought and instead justified the retention of slavery by making the theological argument that bondage was not only humane but, in fact, ordained by Christian values which emphasized the preservation of a conservative social order as the guarantee of collective freedom. Anxious to rescue the theological dimension of proslavery ideology from apparent historical amnesia, the authors, and the documents accompanying their essay, show not only that proslavery ideologues took their Christianity seriously but, and more importantly perhaps, that the theorists believed sincerely in God's endorsement of human bondage. The implication of the argument put forward by Fox-Genovese and Genovese is that the theological defense of slavery worked and that it was sufficiently powerful to offer southern slaveholders some justification that slavery was in fact correct. But did the argument persuade the nonslaveholding or yeoman majority of the Old South – those people who held few if any slaves?

Although Fox-Genovese and Genovese present some documentary evidence to suggest that it did, Stephanie McCurry's "Proslavery, Gender, and the Southern Yeomen" makes a fuller case that the argument worked not least because proslavery ideologues successfully linked the defense of slavery to the defense of ordered, conservative gender relations within yeomen households. As her essay and the documents preceding it show, evangelical Christianity, particularly the tracts written, published, and read by proslavery ideologues and heard by yeomen at church or, perhaps, read at home, managed to yoke the slave–master relationship to the husband–wife bond in a relatively seamless web which, ideologues contended, undergirded the entire set of southern social relations. "By equating the subordination of women

and that of slaves," writes McCurry, "proslavery ideologues and politicians attempted to endow slavery with the legitimacy of the family
and especially marriage and, not incidentally, to invest the defense of
slavery with the survival of customary gender relations." By looking at
what amounts to the permeability of public and private spheres in antebellum South Carolina, the importance of gender ideology, and the
defense of slavery, McCurry offers a powerful explanation of how
and why nonslaveholders in the region came to support the larger
slaveholding elite.

A principal concern of historians of the Old South over the past three
decades or so has been to recapture the lives of the historically inarticul-
ate. Nowhere has this attempt been more obvious and successful (and
still ongoing) than in the study of the lives of the enslaved. The material
presented in part IV speaks to a relatively recent debate among historians
of southern slavery. While earlier work on slavery concentrated on the
slave community by examining slave family formation, slave religious
practice, and slave resistance, recent attention has been turned to the
question of the economic lives and activities of southern slaves and
the social impact of these activities on the slave community. Although
some excellent and important work is still produced on, for example,
slave family and religion, the recent emphasis on the economic activities
of the enslaved – often coined the "slaves' economy" – has resulted in
some pathbreaking work.

Among the first historians to identify the existence of slaves' economic
activities was Philip D. Morgan. His essay, "Benefits of the Lowcountry
Slaves' Economy," offers two principal conclusions. First, the essay and
the attendant documents show conclusively that slaves in the South
Carolina and Georgia lowcountry did manage to acquire personal property, primarily because the task system under which they worked allowed
them time to grow crops for sale and to trade them for cash and property.
Second, Morgan's essay maintains that slaves' property was recognized
as such by slaveowners and that slaves' independent economic activity
actually helped bind the slave community together. Slaves' property,
maintains Morgan, was both individual and communal, and bondpeople
cooperated with one another in the production of their goods and
property. Moreover, the practice of bequeathing property from one
slave generation to the next indicates not only "the extent to which
slaves created autonomy for themselves while they were still enslaved"
but also shows how slaves' independent economic activities "in turn
strengthened the family unit."

Lawrence T. McDonnell agrees with much of what Morgan says, even
though McDonnell's analysis is of the slaves' economy outside of
South Carolina's lowcountry. He agrees, for example, that upcountry

South Carolina slaves, who tended not to work according to the task system, managed to accumulate personal property. But he disagrees with Morgan in characterizing the effects of the slaves' economy. For McDonnell, slaves' economic activities were deleterious to their community and instead of helping cement ties between bondpeople, the competition between sellers and buyers served to fracture the slave community and make them competitive, sometimes violent, petty capitalists who resorted to fighting over disputed debts and the idea of possessing property. The "individual slave's success," concludes McDonnell, "too often proved the slave community's disaster." Whatever their disagreements, though, both historians recognize the critical importance of studying the institution of slavery from the perspective of those who were enslaved.

After the ban on further importation of slaves in 1808, southern slavery could not have survived without the internal slave trade. The slave trade facilitated the westward expansion of cotton, slavery, and, therefore, the South. But who did the selling and trading of slaves, and how did the enslaved experience this most wretched of southern institutions? The answers to these questions are the focus of part V, "Selling Southern Bodies." In "The Slave Trader in Image and Reality," Michael Tadman (and the documents supporting his essay) explains how the slaveholding southern elite attempted to distance themselves from slave traders by constructing negative, largely literary, images of traders. Tadman, though, exposes the contradiction of masters' paternalist rhetoric concerning the beneficial aspects of the peculiar institution by showing that traders were, in fact, gentlemen of some standing in southern society. By selling slaves to traders, argues Tadman, putatively paternalist masters were themselves important agents in the enormity of trading human beings. Slaveholders' efforts to demonize slave traders, shows Tadman, belied their actual relationship with such men. Moreover, Tadman goes on to illustrate how and why traders did the job that they did. Profit was an important motive.

In "Asking Questions, Reading Bodies," Walter Johnson takes us into the very process of selling southern bodies. He shows the minute and critically important ways traders and buyers examined the bodies and characters of the enslaved in their efforts to ascertain price. He shows how buyers and sellers evaluated slaves and explores how the information and stereotypes that buyers and sellers brought with them to slave markets shaped their thinking and judgments about who they would buy, and why. But Johnson is also concerned to show that slaves were not passive agents in the process of the sale. They read and judged prospective buyers as much as the buyers read the slave. Johnson demonstrates that slaves could, in fact, shape the process of the sale and sometimes end it altogether by virtue of their behavior at a particular point in the process of the buyer's evaluation of the bondman or bond woman. Johnson, in other words, is inclined to see the process of selling southern bodies as a product of subtle negotiations between buyer and slave, a process where the smallest twitch, the gentlest of gestures, could and did alter the outcome of the transaction. His analysis is, then, "an important reminder about the extent to which the histories of domination and resistance are inextricably intertwined." Johnson's essay is a good example of the cultural historian at work, and read in conjunction with Tadman's piece it offers the student of southern history a subtle, rich, textured understanding of the process by which slaves were traded and sold in the Old South.

If cultural and social historians have done much to rescue the histories of slaves, they have also done much to uncover the histories of another traditionally marginal group, women. Although some of the other essays and documents in this collection touch on the history of southern women, slave and free, none deal with women exclusively, hence the subject matter of part VI, "Womanhood in Black and White." At first glance, the essay by Sally McMillen on breast feeding and elite white womanhood and the article by Brenda Stevenson, "Slave Women and Definitions of Womanhood," seem utterly unrelated. After all, McMillen and the supporting documents look at the breast-feeding patterns among privileged white women of the Old South while Stevenson's concern is to uncover the thoughts and value systems of slave women. Yet both historians seek not only to rescue the history of southern women generally but also to demythologize their pasts by attempting to show how the two groups of women, while radically different in many respects, showed agency in their fashioning of notions of self-identity, womanhood, and motherhood.

McMillen argues that the rather romantic image of the black wet nurse tending the elite white child is highly misleading, and her evidence shows that elite white women breast-fed their children whenever possible. They did so for many reasons ranging from concern for the child's health and character to the use of lactation as a contraceptive method. Preeminently, though, breast feeding helped white women establish bonds of female intimacy with their children and with one another and so served as a way for elite white women of the Old South to define their role as mothers and women. "Imbued with the crucial importance of their maternal duties," maintains McMillen, "southern women accepted breast feeding as an initial rite of motherhood."

Although less concerned with the question of motherhood per se, Brenda Stevenson's work also speaks to the way southern women, in this instance slave women, fashioned their definitions of womanhood. Stevenson's analysis of narratives by slave and former slave women shows that they exercised some control over how their womanhood and identity was constructed. Although they shared some of the values of white womanhood, slave women created counter-images to those imposed on them by masters and mistresses. In place of the stereotypes of promiscuity, passivity, and degradation, slave women constructed their own images which stressed strength, moral decency, support for the black family, and heroic acts. Through their tales, fantasies, and real life stories and experiences, maintains Stevenson, ostensibly powerless black women fashioned a durable and usable image of themselves that contributed to a distinct sense of womanhood and gave strength to the slave community.

Whatever their specific emphasis, then, all of the documents and essays presented here deal, in some fashion, with the creation, articulation, and shaping of social and cultural values among various constituencies of the Old South. All of the themes identify important areas in southern society and they all profile the everyday and ideological instead of the formally political or heavily economic.

A few words on the structure and contents of this collection of essays and documents. The essays and topics presented here hardly begin to exhaust the interests and work of cultural and social historians of the Old South, and of necessity much excellent and interesting work has been excluded. That much said, the subjects presented here do cover a fairly wide and representative range of issues that historians have tackled and analyzed in the past two or three decades. In every instance, the documents that accompany the selected essays have been selected from the notes of the essays themselves. By reading the documents first, students should be able to detect and identify the broad argument of the essay in each instance and see how historians select and use evidence to support their arguments. I have edited the documents when original spelling and word choice was confusing or unclear. For the most part, though, the documents have remained unchanged. The documents should also alert students to the range of sources the historian is often required to consult in the construction of an argument.

Ultimately, careful reading of the documents (primary evidence) and essays (secondary sources) will show students not only how an historical argument is constructed but illustrate that historical arguments are just that: interpretations of a past which are always changing and being revised. The suggested reading at the end of each chapter is not intended to be catholic. Rather, the works cited will give students the opportunity to engage some of the most pertinent literature on the particular topic under consideration. The study questions that follow each chapter are designed to prompt students to think about the sources under consideration and see connections and dissonances between the documents and essays.

Further Reading

Berlin, Ira 1974: *Slaves Without Masters: The Free Negro in the Antebellum South*. New York: Pantheon.
Berlin, Ira 1998: *Many Thousands Gone: The First Two Centuries of Slavery in North America*. Cambridge, MA: Harvard University Press.
Bertelson, David 1967: *The Lazy South*. New York: Oxford University Press.
Boles, John B. 1999: *The South through Time: A History of an American Region. Volume I*. Upper Saddle River, NJ: Prentice-Hall.
Boles, John B. and Nolen, Evelyn Thomas (eds) 1987: *Interpreting Southern History: Historiographical Essays in Honor of Sanford W. Higginbotham*. Baton Rouge: Louisiana State University Press.
Cash, W. J. 1941: *The Mind of the South*. New York: Knopf.
Cobb, James C. 1992: *The Most Southern Place on Earth: The Mississippi Delta and the Roots of Regional Identity*. New York: Oxford University Press.
Cooper, William J. Jr, and Terrill, Thomas E. 1990: *The American South: A History*. New York: Knopf.
Degler, Carl N. 1977: *Place Over Time: The Continuity of Southern Distinctiveness*. Baton Rouge: Louisiana State University Press.
Escott, Paul D., Goldfield, David R., McMillen, Sally G., and Turner, Elizabeth Hayes (eds) 1999: *Major Problems in the History of the American South. Volume I: The Old South*. New York: Houghton Mifflin.
Franklin, John Hope and Moss, Alfred A. Jr 1947: *From Slavery to Freedom: A History of African Americans*. New York: Knopf.
Freehling, William W. 1990: *The Road to Disunion: Secessionists at Bay, 1776–1854*. New York: Oxford University Press.
Kolchin, Peter 1993: *American Slavery 1619–1877*. New York: Hill and Wang.
Miller, Randall M. and Smith, John David (eds) 1997: *Dictionary of Afro-American Slavery*. Westport, CT: Greenwood Press.
O'Brien, Michael 1995: Finding the outfield: Subregionalism and the American South. *Historical Journal*, 38, 1047–56.
Parish, Peter J. 1989: *Slavery: History and Historians*. New York: Harper.
Perman, Michael (ed.) 1993: *The Coming of the American Civil War*. Lexington, MA: D. C. Heath.
Pessen, Edward 1980: How different were the antebellum North and South? *American Historical Review*, 85, 1119–49.
Roller, David C. and Twyman, Robert W. (eds) 1979: *The Encyclopedia of Southern History*. Baton Rouge: Louisiana State University Press.
Smith, Mark M. 1998: *Debating Slavery: Economy and Society in the Antebellum American South*. Cambridge: Cambridge University Press.
Wilson, Charles Reagan and Ferris, William (eds) 1989: *Encyclopedia of Southern Culture*. Chapel Hill: University of North Carolina Press.
Woodward, C. Vann 1993: *The Burden of Southern History*, 3rd edn. Baton Rouge: Louisiana State University Press.

Part I
A Modern Old South?

Introduction to Documents and Essays

Among the many long-running debates in southern history, none has generated such controversy as the question: Was the Old South a modern or precapitalist society? Presented here are two answers to that question. By examining southern literature, architecture, urbanization, and agricultural production, Raimondo Luraghi argues emphatically that the antebellum South was a quintessentially precapitalist society. Mark M. Smith agrees that premodern impulses were apparent in the Old South but argues that a comparative analysis of slaveholders' use and understanding of clock time suggests that the Old South was one of the most modern of all nineteenth-century societies.

I

An "Old" Old South

Sketches of the South Santee, 1797–1798

Insights into the nature of the American South may be gleaned from the diaries and observations made by numerous travelers to the region. Here is one such travel account by a visitor to South Carolina at the beginning of the antebellum period. The account was subsequently published in 1836. (From G. S. S., "Sketches of the South Santee," *American Monthly Magazine*, 8 (October, November 1836), pp. 313–19, 431–2)

An acquaintance with the characters, habits, and manners of different and remote sections of a common country goes far to correct local prejudices, and may be considered essential to its amicable relations. . . . With these views, the writer of this paper enters upon the following sketches – and, if in connexion with the *scenes* which they present, notices of *individuals* appear, which may be deemed unnecessarily minute, they will have been admitted in order to furnish a *generic* description of a *particular class of society*.

It was in the winter and spring of 1797–8 that the following incidents and scenes made an impression upon my mind, ...

I spent those seasons at the country-seat of Mr. B., [John Bowman] in South Carolina, about forty miles north of Charleston; and was placed upon terms of intimacy with his amiable and accomplished family. . . .

From the insalubrity of the climate during the summer and autumn, arising principally from long-continued heat and the inundation of the

Rice lands (the latter being essential to that grain through the period of its growth), those of the white inhabitants, who could meet the expense, were in the habit of quitting their estates in the month of June, and repairing, for the preservation of their health, through the warm season, either to Charleston, or the sea-board, or the hilly country of the interior, and did not deem it prudent to return until the frost had extinguished the noxious exhalations which had been generated during the summer. . . .

The mansion of Mr. B., which was the ancestral residence of the L – s, was pleasantly situated on the right bank of the South Santee, twenty-five miles from its confluence with the ocean. In its architectural style and general appearance – the massy materials of which it was composed – its spacious halls and polished oaken pannels – its furniture (a portion of which, and of the family plate, though rich and expensive, was of the fashion of other days), and in its numerous and well-appointed retinue of household attendants, there was something of Baronial grandeur. For more than one generation it had been known as the abode of opulence, refinement, and hospitality.

It stood upon one of those elevated bluffs which are much prized in that champagne country, and presented opposite fronts, which were ornamented with spacious Grecian porticos.

One of them looked out upon a grassy lawn of eighty or a hundred acres, decorated with stately oaks, apparently almost coeval with the alluvial soil in which they had vegetated. On the right were gardens, in which were domesticated many of the flowers and fruits, and culinary productions of northern and tropical climates. At a convenient distance, on the right and left of the mansion, out-offices were tastefully arranged; and the lawn itself was terminated by a forest, from which, in their proper season, the honeysuckle, the sweet-scented jessamine, and the magnolia-grandi-flora sent forth their perfumes.

The other front presented an extensive view upon the river; on the opposite side of which, during the summer months, the Rice crops waved over fields of thousands of acres in extent, and upon a surface so level and unbroken, that in casting one's eye up and down the river, there was not for miles, an intervening object to obstruct the sight. These were bounded by morasses, covered with wood, in which the cypress-tree, rooted in a soil of unrivalled fertility, flourished with gigantic luxuriance; and in whose lofty branches the timid and beautiful wood-duck built its nest, and hatched its young, and ruffled its plumage, in its occasional alarms at the splash of the alligator in some pool beneath.

Here, too, within the limits of a few miles upon the banks of the South Santee, South-Carolina, still in the days of her chivalry, could point to many of both sexes as amongst the flower of her population: the Pinkneys, the Middletons, the Lynches, the Motts, the Shulebreads, the Horrys, and others; where wealth, hereditary distinction, and educated talent, and services in the military field or the councils of the nation, gave them a consideration which few parts of the country had excelled. . . .

At the distance of a mile or two to the north, is the North Santee. A few miles up the country, the river known as the Santee, and which is formed by the waters of the Wateree and Congaree, divides itself into two branches, and again unites below, including between the two an island of several miles in length, and of various width; constituting, perhaps, one of the most valuable tracts in the world for the cultivation of Rice. . . .

The agricultural improvements are found, almost exclusively, upon the rich alluvial river bottoms, or upon the fertile savannahs, when the latter are supplied with sufficient water to form a head for overflowing the rice-fields; the water being, as we have already remarked, essential to the crop.

With the exception of now and then a small stream, there called a branch, whither the deer resort to drink, and whose borders are margined with different kinds of grasses and shrubs, upon which they love to browse, the country, aloof from the river bottoms and savannahs, seems as if it were one interminable forest of pine-barren. It is threaded by narrow avenues through the tall pines, whose branches frequently unite at the top, and form a canopy over the head of the traveller; and these avenues are so straight, and level, and unvaried, that he wearies his eye in looking forward through, what appears to him, an endless trail. Should but a deer or wild turkey flit across his track, he can descry them as far as the eye can reach. Occasionally he diverges to the right or left, through some narrower defile; and arriving at a gateway, suddenly leaves the wilderness behind him. He finds it the residence of a planter; and in the days of which I am speaking, was sure of a welcome; and hospitality, the more cordial in proportion to the length of the visit.

A Georgia Planter on the Classical South, 1835

The following letter was written by a planter-politician, John Basil Lamar, of Georgia, to his sister in 1835. The letter is rich in detail and deserves careful reading. In it, Lamar alludes to classical images, the treatment of slaves, and proper conduct among men and women in the Old South. (From John Basil Lamar, Athens, Georgia, to his Sister, Miss Mary Ann Lamar, Athens, Georgia, January 27, 1835, Howell Cobb Papers. Reproduced courtesy of the Hargrett Rare Book and Manuscript Library, University of Georgia Libraries, Athens, GA)

My Dear Sister

Yours dated 18th inst' is now before me, on an old walnut side table (which from its antique appearance would warrant the belief that it commenced its career of usefulness in the Lamar family, at an early period, and as it successively groans under my nascent "bulletins," & "daily bread" (hog fowl, turnips &c) seems proud, that its last days, like its first, are to be spent, in the same family.) I took your letter from the office in Macon yesterday, & should have answer'd it forthwith, but prefering the calm of Swift Creek [plantation], to the boisterous crowd of the Central hotel, for that purpose, I deffer'd it until now.

I am more happy, Sister, than words can express, to learn, that you pass your time pleasantly in Athens. You have "floated, so long upon the tide of circumstances," and without having a home, you have had too many, made from convenience and broken up from necessity. What I am extremely gratified to learn, that at length you are settled to your satisfaction, & that your new associates are to your taste & your visiters are pleasing.

I very much admire a sentiment, you let fall once, in speaking of your Scottsboro' school associates, that you were friendly to all but intimate with very few. That is a good rule to act by through life. I have experienced the inconvenience of over-intimacy. A person (and especially a female) should observe closely & mark well the conduct of an associate, before she is taken as an intimate, – a constant associate.

However – do not construe me to advise, a stiff, abrupt deportment. Far from it. You know I am a great admirer of sociability, altho' I practise it so rarely.

Neither would I dissuade you from a discreet intimacy, with a congenial soul, a young lady of good family, polished manners, amiable, *discreet* – et cetera &c&c. Such can be *selected* from the *select* community of Athens, doubtless.

Tell the Gen[eral] [Lamar's brother-in-law?] I am glad he is so devoted to his studies. I infer this from his being so much engaged that he could not find time to fill out the space you assigned him at the bottom of the page with a half dozen lines. I think when he receives (among the other *sundries* which I have sent in his trunk) the paper, quills, steel pens, inkstand &c, he will take the hint, and not be so reserved in future.

I shall visit you when the sale is over, on uncles return. I bought a neat little Chariotte from Craft, yesterday, and the blacks being in fine order I shall travel in some style. A very amusing incident occurred last night which has made me busy all this morning in having a carriage house built. A young mule, which I purchased at the Cedar shoals sale, took such a fancy to my vehicle, that by morning I found the drop cloth, under the front seat, torn into tatters. I was wrathy at this mulish way of showing admiration, at first, and if I had caught his mule-ship at his pranks, might have given him a shower of buck-shot. But when I saw where he had torn out pieces of broadcloth, as if to try its strength & texture, and after chewing awhile, left it on the ground, I was somewhat appeased & have sent the carriage off to Macon to be fixed My new carriage house, like an Arabs stable, is a part of my dwelling. I have converted one of my nice little shed rooms into that purpose, by sawing out a large door. My kitchen is in another shed room, I keep my ploughs, axes, hoes &c in the third. My overseer occupies one of the tenements of the main building, and I the hall. I have to regret that there are no more shed rooms to my house, if there were Rob-roy, Redgauntlet & Koscius should have a berth among us. Also, I have a garret to my house it is true but it would incommode the rats, (who are lords paramount) overhead, as well as be somewhat inconvenient to the four footed gentry in getting up and down stairs.

My house is a log castle of the first order & I am as happy in it as feudal baron ever was, ensconced in walls of stone. I will at some other time give you the geography & natural curiosities of my domain, they are interesting, I do assure you.

I am at present having my negro cabins refitted, and new ones built. Having consolidated my force on the north side of Swift Creek, I have an idea of *locating*, permanently on the South bank of that stream, where I have a snug white house, the house that father occupied, when one visits to the plantation.

Yours affectionately
John Basil Lamar

A Georgia Planter Bemoans the Cost of Slavery, 1846

Many planters considered their plantations more of an economic drain than a blessing. Here, John Basil Lamar explains why to his brother-in-law, Howell Cobb. (From John Basil Lamar, Macon, Georgia, to Howell Cobb, May 23, 1846, Cobb-Erwin-Lamar Papers. Reproduced courtesy of the Hargrett Rare Book and Manuscript Library, University of Georgia Libraries, Athens, GA)

Dear Howell

Understanding a short times since that Benj S Jordan of Baldwin intended investing a large amount of ready money in negroes, I addressed him a letter proposing to sell him mine at 350$ each, if he would take the land at a fair valuation. He answered that he would meet me on the 15th June & examine the property.

I do not know what will come of it, but if he is disposed we shall trade. I have long decided to get out of the business & have my means invested in government or other good securities that would yield me a genteel support, without having to slave myself after scoundrelly overseers & all to no profit. After paying expenses there is not enough left at raising cotton to compensate a man for his trouble. One who lives at home, raises his own meat, makes his own clothing & spends nothing but for sugar & coffee can make money at planting no other sort can. Absentees can do little over support themselves now, & the fact stares me in the face that before many years negroes will be an expense to an absentee.

There is a stir in the market now & I feel disposed to avail myself of it & sell out & be done with it.

Will you find out for me what Government bonds can be bought for? What interest they pay? & how long time they have to run? If I sell I wish to know all these things so as to invest as soon as possible. . . .

I wish to have a certain income that will not fluctuate, & that will give me no trouble in its management. I am tired of being bedevilled with overseers, and making nothing. And then the abolitionists are gaining ground every year & a paper constitution is a poor safeguard against a furious majority.

Please write me soon on the above questions. . . .

An "Old" Old South

Raimondo Luraghi

Slavery, transplanted to the New World by capitalism as a ready-made tool for putting immense stretches of land to cultivation, with its pre-capitalist labor arrangement (it seems necessary to stress once again that where there is no wage labor, there is no capitalism), powerfully fostered the rise of the seigneurial class. Slavery developed the seigneurial habit of exercising a paternal yet absolute power, made of the seigneur not only an entrepreneur like the bourgeois industrialist, but also – and more – an

From Raimondo Luraghi, *The Rise and Fall of the Plantation South* (New York: Franklin Watts, 1978), pp. 148–51, 64–82. Excerpts reprinted by permission of Grolier Publishing.

absolute master, very like the feudal lord of the Middle Ages. Slavery created and fostered the patriarchal family, wholly different from the bourgeois family we are acquainted with; made of the seigneur a person who preferred to reveal his wealth, culture, and magnificent life, rather than to conceal money under plain clothes as the bourgeois did. It gave him, as an ideal, not profit (which, however energetically seigneurs sought it, was a means, not an end in itself), but status, political power, military service, and glory, so that the seigneur considered bearing arms and serving the state natural rights, to be exercised with moderation and statesmanship, almost like hereditary kings. Slavery impoverished the internal market and thus forestalled the industrial revolution, which can be based only upon mass production to cover a continuously increasing and highly dynamic market. It even allowed the seigneur to create an old-fashioned industry, wholly dependent on agriculture, in order to provide for immediate needs, and built – in the very center of the modern world – the last civilization in which country dominated over town.

Nowhere did this peculiar kind of seigneurial civilization achieve such a high development as in the United States and Brazil; but it was the Old South that soon fell into conflict with bourgeois, capitalist America, generated by Calvinist Dutch and Puritan New Englanders. In the beginning, the centers of capitalist power in the Americas were very small and limited, but the tremendous driving force of capitalism spelled doom for the old-fashioned seigneurial civilizations from the very start of the struggle.

However, the more the pressure grew on the Old South, the more self-conscious it became; the harder it tried to save its particular way of life and scale of values, the more it committed itself to the crucial experiment of trying to build its own "ideal state," wholly separated, based for the first time upon a seigneurial agrarian civilization *per se*. It was clear from the very beginning that it would mean war. War is really, for any kind of society, the "moment of truth." The war would measure the South's ability to accept the huge industrial conflict that the capitalist civilization was now able to wage.

Mercantile capitalism had coexisted reasonably well with seigneurial civilization (although the Canadian seigneurial society was swept away by the joint efforts of bourgeois New and Old England). As frequently observed, the growth of merchantilism in many cases was followed by an extension of slavery, and capitalist merchants made handsome profits in the slave trade. Newport, Rhode Island, for example, " ... has been, in a great measure, built upon the blood of the poor Africans...."[1] even if the bringing of thousands of slaves into America often met with stubborn resistance from seigneurial slave owners.

After the industrial revolution, capitalism began everywhere to over-throw the old-fashioned agrarian civilizations. It needed open markets, masses of "free" laborers, and an agrarian society to pay the expenses of industrialization. In other words, it needed contemporary colonialism. The industrial revolution, which prompted such expansionism, had even given tremendous destructive weapons to the modern, industrial nations; it had made possible the mobilization of millions of men and armed them with new, terrible engines of destruction on a heretofore unseen scale.

The South chose to accept battle on northern terms, the only choice it had, not only to resist aggression, but also to establish its own state founded on its own *Weltanschauung*. This seems to be the stumbling block for many historians who, unable to see the real essence of seigneur-ial civilization, insist on the South's being "capitalist." Capital usually moves toward the investment that looks more lucrative. Why did south-ern "capitalism" not rush into industrial production, thus making the South equal to the North in military terms, considering that war usually provides enormous profits? The fact was that southern "capital" (or better, southern money, which is far different) was mainly invested in slaves. To whom should southern slaveholders have sold their slaves in order to retrieve their money and so invest it in industrial production? This thought should suffice to show that southern civilization was not capitalist, as one of the basic characteristics of capitalism is high mobility of capital . . . .

As for black slaves, if they, as it has been alleged, were accustomed to working as efficiently as modern workers on assemby lines, why were they not sent to "assemble" cannon, ironclads, submarines, locomot-ives, railroad cars? Why had the South to fight so painfully against a shortage of manpower? Assemblying, after all, does not require much skill, only automatic work, as Charlie Chaplin showed so well in *Modern Times*. The fact was that slavery was tied down to plantations; planta-tions were not "plants," but living units, not to be reckoned in purely economic terms, but more in social, human, psychological values. At any rate, this is another indication that plantation economy was not capital-ist, as mobility of labor is another requisite of capitalism . . . .

Whereas the North was following . . . puritan ideologies, the southern ruling class was still sticking to its classical Renaissance origins. Classi-cism had, in the South of the late eighteenth and nineteenth centuries, a splendid revival. When Georgia decided to establish its university, the hill where it was to be built was christened "Athens": there the sons of planter aristocracy were to go to study the humanities, Latin, history. Immedi-ately thereafter, a series of such institutions – completely state-sponsored and free from any religious affiliation – spread all over the South.

So high was the consciousness of cultivated southerners as learned representatives of classic culture, that John Randolph of Roanoke contemptuously said that he had never seen "a yankee who knew anything about the classics." And the bare fact that a most hated northern politician, William Henry Seward, rejected anything Roman as an example worthy of imitation by America made Southerners even more proud of their classic heritage. Higher education in the South was rarely pursued without a deep study of Latin and Greek; classic culture (it was openly said) was what distinguished a true gentleman. George Fitzhugh underlined the similarity between his own ideas and Aristotle's, and, even more, between Aristotle's and John C. Calhoun's....

Culture, classic and humanistic culture, always loomed large in the southern aristocracy. It represented a true means of fulfillment, an individual and social achievement in itself. Planters were proud of attending classical schools. On December 22, 1860, the very moment when the United States was on the edge of being drawn into the whirlpool of secession and war, Robert Allston, a great rice planter of South Carolina, a refined lover of fine arts, received a letter from his son, Charles, in which he discussed at length Plutarch's *Lives*, which he was then reading. This interest was well in line with family traditions. One of his family's most prominent members, Robert himself was a deeply cultivated and widely traveled man who liked to write verses on classic and heroic subjects, such as a poem on Hannibal, "the Carthaginian hero." His accounts of travels in Europe still make for delightful reading.

Plutarch's *Lives* was a favorite book among planters. Mary Ann Lamar, sister of a prominent Georgia planter and wife of Howell Cobb, read it frequently and her knowledge was more than casual. Her brother, John Basil Lamar of Milledgeville, Georgia, was another very cultivated and refined man, who liked to live "in the quiet enjoyment of a large fortune, of foreign travel, the gratification of elegant and literary tastes."[2] Writing to his sister, he once said he was sitting at an old table "covered by the most classic confusion of volumes of Shakespeare, History of Greece and Decline of Roman Empire...".

But the most symbolic episode, revealing the deep roots of the classic mentality, was perhaps to be found once again in the Allston "dynasty." Adele Allston, wife of Robert Allston, writing to her son Charles, who was far from home in the Confederate Army fighting the War for Independence, showed it in a clear, almost dramatic way. It was April 1862; in the West, the bloody battle of Shiloh had just been fought; Farragut was ready to enter the Mississippi and take New Orleans; in Virginia, McClellan was nearing Yorktown, there to advance on Richmond; from the Sea Islands, the federals were threatening the very hearts of South Carolina and Georgia, and the sound of their guns may have been heard in the Allston family "big house." In such a tragic moment, in the midst of the very nightmare of war, Adele Allston strove to ensure that her son would not become only a man who-killed-not-to-be-killed. She (like Boethius in his death cell) remembered the *Consolatione Philosophiae*, how much spiritual life and culture may help a sensible soul to wade across the miseries of life at war. So, she exhorted her son to learn the ancient Greek language, explaining to him the marvelous aspects of that unperishable civilization. It was a moving but chilling letter; these members of the old southern civilization *knew* (even if they did not dare to confess it, not even to themselves), or they at least *felt*, in the depth of their unconscious, that their civilization, their whole world, their way of life, their class, all was doomed. In such a moment they felt the need to go back to their beloved classical world, which, if long since dead as a body, was still alive as a soul, still able to speak to them, still sending through innumerable ages its mild, warm light, to encourage them and give them comfort.

Planters liked well-furnished libraries, this is certain, but nowhere was their classical culture more evident than in southern architecture. Their mansions struck the northern traveler immediately with "something of Baronial grandeur." Indeed, for any agricultural civilization, the country mansion was of great importance; it was the cultural pivot of their world. Since the very beginning of the Old South, everything in the "big house," as in the hacienda, had been homemade, "from cutting down the pine trees to hanging the window blinds."[3] The "big house," however, had attained its most magnificent – classical – style when southern civilization had reached its maturity....

At the same time another change was taking place. Southern aristocracy was beginning to spend more and more of its time in the small cities of the Old South. As in Brazil, in the South the seventeenth century had been mainly an era of isolated country houses; this situation went on, in part, during the early decades of the eighteenth century. In that period some of the most beautiful aristocratic mansions were built, either in the "Peninsula" of Virginia or in lower South Carolina, from Shirley to Carter's Grove to Hampton, although South Carolina would soon boast a "major" city, Charleston (which, in the beginning, was mainly a seaport with warehouses and trade buildings). Then, a noticeable shifting toward cities began. This era witnessed the building of fine houses on Charleston's Battery. At the same time, to the south, Brazilian owners of large plantations were shifting from old-fashioned, country *casas grandes* toward urban *sobrados*, which, strange to say, were characterized by great verandas, similar to Charleston's famous "piazzas" and intended to permit, even inside towns, some life *en plein air*. Beautiful, unforgettable small cities were then growing or rising: Charleston and Georgetown, South Carolina; new residential areas in Richmond, Virginia; and several others, south through Georgia, Alabama, and Mississippi, to the very shores of the "Father of Waters."

This kind of urbanization was, however, *sui generis*. There is a remarkable difference between cities in agrarian civilizations and cities in industrial areas. In the first case, the center of production was in the country; cities were only places for aristocrats to meet (how to forget, here, the splendid, fascinating Meeting Street, in Charleston, South Carolina, true seigneurial *boudoir*?), to give parties, to exchange ideas, to go to balls, theaters, etc. Cities, in such civilizations, were not places where income was produced, but places where it was consumed. This should not be construed to mean that such cities had no artisans or manufacturers; they, indeed, had several. But their first and foremost economic activity was not in itself enough to characterize them as industrial cities. Except for the famous Tredegar Iron Works of Richmond, Virginia, factories in southern cities were small; even Tredegar was small in comparison with factories in the North. In the second place, many a manufacturer was also (and mainly) a planter, and his manufacturing activity was subordinated to his agrarian interests. Thirdly, the planter class showed a remarkable tendency to absorb persons from different activities. In the eighteenth century, merchants like Robert Pringle and Henry Laurens turned planters well before the ends of their lives. In this way the planter class showed its hegemony and also asserted the real essence of its society. James Hammond saw this very clearly and stated it outspokenly.

As Brazilian planters did when they passed from *casas grandes* to urban *sobrados*, southern planters, too, gave their city mansions a distinctly agrarian character, by means of gardens, trees, etc. Something like this is still to be seen in Italian Renaissance cities, which developed when rural aristocrats went to live in them for political reasons. A number of delightful cities (like Ferrara, Mantova, Urbino, Cortona, Città di Castello) still preserve such charming features: everywhere, concealed by walls, are small or large gardens, clumps of trees, even kitchen gardens, which contribute to city life a rural character, like the deep roots that still link those cities to their agricultural background, the real source of their wealth and power.

In the South the era of the cities was doomed to be brief, of course; and the Old South had no large cities, except New Orleans, and by 1860, it was already well into its decline. As far as customary urban life is concerned, southern cities had very little of it. Plantations were self-sufficient, and the population of towns was almost totally composed of planters and slaves. Eugene D. Genovese has stressed the fact that about 37 percent of the population in Mobile, Alabama, Savannah, Georgia, and Charleston, South Carolina, were either slaves or free blacks with very little purchasing power. Because of this, urban markets for food-stuffs almost did not exist.[4] In other words, such centers, more than cities in the modern sense of the word, were agglomerates of rural mansions, with as much of industry and trade as suited the interests of the planters and mainly owned and controlled by the planters them-selves. In the South the country still prevailed over the city and domin-ated it.

The country did not mean only the planters; it also meant the black slaves, who were the country laborers. The cultural influence of black Africans on the Old South is now, at last, being seriously studied. Such scholars as John W. Blassingame, George P. Rawick, and Orlando Pat-terson, among others (and, first among them all, Eugene D. Genovese), have stressed in a masterful way how a black culture not only existed and continued to develop under the almost prohibitive conditions of slavery, but also influenced widely and deeply the white culture, thus producing a complex southern culture in which original African elements are blended in an inextricable way, having fully disappeared as such in order to reemerge in a completely original and new blend.

It still remains to be studied more closely *how much* the characteristic culture of the seigneurial society was affected by the black culture. Such an inquiry will certainly demonstrate that the Afro-American contribu-tion to the culture of the planter civilization was enormous. In the particular case of the Old South, its innermost culture was a very com-plex blend of the Italian classicism of the Renaissance (in large part through its derivation, Elizabethan classicism); the Spanish seigneurial system, from Ponce de León to Ayllón and the Georgia missions; the French-American seigneurial system and culture through the Creole society of Louisiana; Amerindian culture, and African culture. All these elements cooperated to make the southern culture original and distinctive, more complex, spicy, and colorful than, for instance, the capitalist culture of the northern United States. It was less akin to the northern culture than to those of other plantation regions, which com-posed with the South the large and protean area of "tropical civiliza-tion." As Frank Tannenbaum wrote: "The institution of slavery had logic of its own. Wherever it existed in this hemisphere it worked its way into the social structure and modified the total society. The slave system was broader in its impact than might be discerned from a reading of the slave laws. The law itself was but evidence of the influence of slavery as an institution upon the *mores*.... Wherever we had slavery, we had a slave society, not merely for the blacks, but for the whites, not merely for the law, but for the family, not merely for the labor system, but for the culture – the total culture."[5]

Perhaps, among the several influences that molded the southern civilization, the most important (even if the least understood) was the black element. Prominent anthropologists have already begun to study both the rich essence of African cultures and the derived Afro-American culture; I firmly believe that, in this field, historians will never be able to make serious progress without wide and deep interdisciplinary work with anthropologists. It will be necessary to study the individual links between the treasures of southern popular culture and the black heritage. For instance, an intriguing subject is the rich lode of southern popular proverbs and the wonderful wealth of proverbs of the Mande, from the African Gold Coast, the starting point of so many slaves on the infamous "middle passage." It will be necessary to discover the connections between the peculiar genius of the South for short stories and tall tales and of the Bété of West Africa for folktales. As far as music is concerned, everybody acknowledges the basic, fundamental contribution to southern music (and not only to popular songs) of the Afro-American musical culture.

But the African heritage inside the southern seigneurial culture is by far wider and deeper. It permeates many habits and ways of living, even in less obvious areas: a certain tendency toward good-humored leisure; styles of cooking; even accent. As far as the last is concerned, the African influence on southern English is becoming more and more the subject of study by philologists. . . .

Perhaps the major consequence of the presence of black slaves was their effect on the image that planters began to form of themselves. It may be supposed that the slave idea of the paternal "Massa" helped the planter aristocracy to feel as they felt. This does not mean only that they were encouraged to look at themselves as naturally endowed with power, and, in some cases, to feel arrogant and overbearing, but refers to something less simple. Planters began to "individualize" themselves, to "understand" themselves from a peculiar standpoint, to live up to their "social function" of quasi-feudal seigneurs. It must be true that the serf makes the seigneur, at least as much as the seigneur makes the serf. African slaves, it must be stressed, "helped" planter aristocrats to think of themselves as "that particular kind of seigneur." The African civilizations from which the slaves came to America were all precapitalistic and agrarian, and any society of this kind is soundly based on patriarchalism, paternalism, and (in many cases) even true seigneurial classes with a strong hierarchical sense. African culture, therefore, would have played a prominent part in shaping the slaves' expectation of the kind of seigneurs they would find. Black slaves contributed in this way to giving the planter aristocracy its image of itself. After the destruction of slavery, planters with this mentality became "displaced persons" in the new context of a capitalist society that was totally extraneous to their "ethos." ...

The relations master-to-slave and white-to-black were far more morbid, pathological, and twisted than they appear if taken only at face value. The dominant position of slaveholders was weakened by the fact that their intercourse with the slaves had a hidden side that always lay buried deep inside their unconscious and was never allowed to emerge to light.

In the early nineteenth century, this patriarchal, paternalistic civilization was reaching its height. *Pari passu*, the sense of guilt was increasing inside the slaveholders' souls. Certainly, slavery was an evil (as is any exploitation); however, the justifications that the slaveholding class brought forth were not completely destitute of any foundation. It is true that, just before the Civil War era, southern slavery had reached possibly the most mild and humane (or least inhumane) level compatible with such a cruel institution. One is surprised to see planters (who should have been "shrewd businessmen") going directly against their economic interest, which they are supposed to have pursued like "able moneymakers," in order to respect the personality of their slaves. In 1835, John Basil Lamar, an important planter of Georgia, selling the slaves belonging to his father's unwilled property, purchased four of the old blacks and a deformed boy himself, because he thought they were unwilling to leave their old homes. Although they were no longer capable of any valuable work, he decided to disburse money in order to keep them with their relatives. There were many cases like this on nineteenth-century plantations; and this certainly did not contribute, from a purely economic viewpoint, to making the plantations "very efficient" enterprises, as Fogel, Engerman, and their school allege them to have been.

There was no better witness of this situation than Charles Francis Adams, Jr. Answering a letter from his father, who, as was true of many northerners, mainly abolitionists, had a kind of contempt toward black slaves, the younger Adams wrote: "I'm getting to have very decided opinions on the negro question ... I note what you say of the African race and 'the absence of all appearance of self-reliance in their own power' during this struggle. From this, greatly as it has disappointed me, I very unwillingly draw different conclusions from your own. The conviction is forcing itself upon me that African slavery, as it existed in our slave states, was indeed a patriarchal institution under which the slaves were not, as a whole, unhappy, cruelly treated or overworked. I am forced to this conclusion. Mind, I do not because of it like slavery any better. ..."

Very recently, a distinguished historian, Ludwell H. Johnson, reviewing the collection of the Jones family letters, and quoting an older one, the Fleet family letters collection, the first from Georgia, the second from Virginia, observed that those letters are "a compelling evidence" that the Old South, as depicted by writers like Thomas Nelson Page or Margaret Mitchell "did exist, that it is not the product of weak-minded romanticizing."[6] The same impression, I must add, is received by anybody going carefully and at length through the letters of many southern planter families.

All the vital elements coming from Africa blended, as already noted, with Elizabethan, Spanish, French, and even Italian aspects into southern culture. This rich background gave the planter class a consciousness of possessing a mentality of its own, which had almost nothing to do with the northern mentality. Perhaps, it should be stressed once more, it was more akin to other American cultures. I remember having been struck, when in Mexico City, by a new mural in the Hotel Colon, representing countries all around the Gulf of Mexico and the Caribbean. All these countries clearly represented parts of a sea-oriented world, their rivers running toward the same seas, and they turning, so to speak, their backs to the interior of the continent. All appeared characterized by very similar patterns of agrarian economies and cultures: the Old South, with its stately mansions, its cotton and rice fields, its towering steamboats moving like floating palaces down the Mississippi, its colorful quarters in Mobile and New Orleans; Mexico and Central America, with their haciendas, big houses, folkloristic dances, colorful cities; the sunburnt Caribbean islands, with their quasi-African folklore, lovely colonial cities, and large plantations producing sugar and coffee. This was, it seems, the world to which the Old South really belonged; and it is still to be discovered how much of this consciousness lay deep at the bottom of the so-called Southern dream of a Caribbean empire.

Pondering the distinctive shape of mind of the seigneurial class of the South, one is irresistibly drawn into thinking of the agrarian "senatorial" class of the Roman Republic. The Romans were frequently good administrators, even shrewd "businessmen," as far as the development of their properties was concerned; however, to them, business was always *vile negotium*. What gave human life its taste and its meaning were the so-called *otia*, or cultural, literary, even scientific pursuits, entertaining lavishly, cultivating friendships. Here perhaps is to be found the key to understanding why and how southern gentlemen, however concerned about their business (and in many cases managing it very adroitly), never had a capitalist *Weltanschauung*. And this, incidentally, in the economic war to come, would represent their chief "inferiority" in comparison to businessmen from the North. So one obtains the impression that money was to them only a means: the true aim of their lives was leisure, culture, and status. Increasing production was just a method to reach the true end: consumption.

Among the most important pursuits of the southern seigneurial class were military and political careers. A close scrutiny of the most prominent generals and officers in the Confederate army during the Civil War shows clearly that a military career was usually the choice of cadets from impoverished seigneurial families, very much as it was in the feudal noble class of Europe. Robert E. Lee is the most remarkable instance. As far as politics is concerned, to understand the aristocrat-politicians of the Old South, it is necessary to dismiss any idea we may have of politicians from our own bourgeois world. The "professional" politician was scarcely, if ever, to be found in the Old South. In our bourgeois societies, politics may represent a career in itself, frequently a business. After all, in capitalist society everything has been transformed into a commodity, to be bought and sold, whose value is to be reckoned in terms of money. So, politics, too, has become a business....

In the Old South, as in any aristocratic society, this was not usually the case. There were, of course, exceptions, but what matters here is the rule. Politicians were usually important planters with large estates. Studying their biographies closely, one gets the impression that they were not politicians at all, but planters who participated in politics. The South was no democratic society; it was an oligarchy, governed by a very intelligent, mild, shrewd, benevolent, and tolerant paternalistic class. However, poor whites very rarely became prominent politicians, and those who did fight their way up against the "plantocracy" succeeded only in jumping, in many cases, to "the other side of the river," as Andrew Johnson did.

As far as planters are concerned, one has only to peruse the papers of Thomas Jefferson, John Randolph, John C. Calhoun, Howell Cobb, Robert Toombs, and Jefferson Davis to see what kind of politicians they made. Ambitious they were – no man can go through life and accomplish anything without having a just ambition; but, climbers of the social ladder they almost never were. And what had they to climb for? They were already on the top, looking down from aloft on "inferior" classes. A remarkable member of the planter aristocracy, suggesting a social behavior to a younger member of the family, underlined that the best procedure was to be friendly to all but intimate with very few. The suggestion (a true Horatian *Odi profanum vulgus et arceo*) went to a lady, but gentlemen did not behave differently.

Frequently, through political life, such planter-politicians lost money. Going to Washington, taking seriously their political duties, meant neglecting their plantations; frequently left in the hands of unreliable people, their planter's business went completely astray. In

1842, Howell Cobb of Georgia and his brother-in-law, John Basil Lamar, both prominent members of the seigneurial class, were nominated for Congress. Immediately John B. Lamar wrote Howell Cobb a letter in which, without even mentioning the real motives that prompted his resignation, in a *grand seigneur* way, he declared that he would not accept the nomination. Lamar wrote that he had wanted to show that he would not have passed "through the world as a perfectly obscure individual," but, having won the nomination, he did not care to be a politician.

However, the real motives that prompted Lamar were deeper. He knew that his brother-in-law, a very generous and prodigal man, would soon have been completely bankrupt because of his plunging into politics. So Lamar, without breathing a word to his brother-in-law, decided that one politician in the family was enough; he would resign in order to dedicate himself completely to administering the estate and the interests of the family, so that his sister and his nephews would not starve and his brother-in-law would not be completely ruined. We know this only from his confidential letters, as Lamar was too generous and magnanimous, and even too proud, to confess to relatives what he was doing and why.

Perhaps the most striking example of this mentality was Jefferson Davis. When he reached the required age, he entered, as a cadet, upon a military career, leaving the estate to his older brother. One is struck by the truly magnificent sacrifice; but what was most wonderful was the political career he entered afterward. He chose it, objectively, as the right thing to do; he duly resigned from service in the Mexican War; and when the Confederacy, at the Montgomery Convention, elected him its provisional President, he accepted against his will, as a duty. He did not want to become President; he saw in front of him a way with many thorns and very few roses, if any, but he would never have turned away from a duty. To do his duty was the substance of his life, and he did it, truly embodying the iron will of the South. However criticized, abused, even slandered, he did not care to apologize or to give explanations. Why such an aloof and proud behavior? I believe that it was because he never considered politics as a career, but as a duty (or, better, as both a duty and a right for a man of his class).

A politician is, in a sense, an actor, whose audience is the whole world. So, like an actor, he has to care about what his audience thinks of him in the present, and what history will say of him in the future. Master politicians, like Napoleon, Cavour, and Lincoln, began very soon building up their legends and myths for the use of future generations. Augustus, on his deathbed, even asked rather cynically if he had played his part well. When answered in the affirmative, he said: "So, please, clap your hands, friends," and died. But Augustus was the most prominent member of a new, cynical, imperial class. Once again, southern seigneurs were very similar to members of the "senatorial" class of the Roman Republic, whose exponents were the Catos, not the Augustuses. Such men never had any idea of a political "career"; they simply considered politics as a duty – and an obvious right – of their class, like a great king who considered his duty that of being "the first servant of *his* people." That to rule was his right, he did not even bother to say – this was a matter of course. . . .

[A]ny social class produces sooner or later an elite, which is what I call a "political class." Such a "political class" must be understood in a very wide and complex sense. For instance, in the Old South, it did not only include such men as Thomas Jefferson, John C. Calhoun, Jefferson Davis, and Howell Cobb, but also others, such as Edmund Ruffin, Henry Sidney Lanier, William Gillmore Simms, John Mercer Brooke, Edgar Allan Poe, and Matthew Fontaine Maury. Others might call it an "intellectual class." Or, as Gramsci wrote: "Any social group, having been born upon the original ground of a specific attribution in the sphere of economic production, gives birth, organically, to one or more intellectual classes which give it solidity and self-consciousness, not only as far as its economic activity is concerned: but even concerning the political one."[7] Others, drawing upon Gramsci, might use the term "intellectual class." I prefer to follow Giovanni Mosca and adopt the definition of "political class" in a wider sense. I understand that the word "intellectuals" might be more precise, but it is also likely to create more misunderstandings.

By what is a political class characterized? First, it constitutes, as already stressed, the "self-consciousness" of its ruling class as a whole. Secondly, its members distinguish themselves from other components of the social ruling class by their capacity for considering any problem on the highest possible level: the purely political one, without allowing any narrowly economic and egotistic residual consideration to intrude. This, in turn, means that members of the political class are capable of seeing not only the present interests of the social class they belong to but even the future concerns, so that they are able to "persuade" their social class to sacrifice present interests for future, and more valuable, objectives. Thirdly, they are capable of taking into consideration not only the limited and egotistic interests of the social class to which they belong, but even, and more, those of the dependent classes, so that they are able to "persuade" their social class to act as a defender of such subordinate interests. In this way the ruling class is transformed from a barely dominating group into a leading one, that is, able to rule not only by clumsy and brute force (which does not create any lasting or successful order), but, to a certain extent, by the consensus of subordinate groups. In other words, capable of exercising hegemony.

What matters here is that it can be reasonably maintained that the old southern civilization produced one of the most remarkable political classes in history. As Georg Weber wrote, "In their opinions and tendencies, they were inspired by an high-mindedness superior to that of European aristocrats."[8] What was most admirable was the way in which they succeeded in understanding and interpreting the interests of the most dependent classes, even, in part, of black slaves. In a wonderful way they succeeded in giving to the slave subconscious a fair, lasting image of the "paternal master," making them feel like members of the "family" and, as a rule, treating them this way. Witness, for instance, a letter in which a planter, Mr. A. R. Wright, asked Howell Cobb to concede the hand of one of his slave girls to a black boy named Reuben, describing him as "honest, faithful and industrious." They even succeeded in giving the slaves the ideal figure of the white planter as a kind of "social ideal," a true "ideal model." This is, perhaps, why, during the Civil War, the slaves never revolted, even when white women, children, and old people were almost completely in their hands – and any attempts from the North to raise such revolts were, in the main, dismal failures. . . .

[But] Southerners felt more and more their fast worsening colonial status. John B. Lamar observed how indebted planters were, and later, in 1849, told his brother-in-law, Howell Cobb, that the South, after paying the costs of subsistence for white planters and black slaves, turned the whole balance of its income over to the North to build cities, factories, ships, and palaces, and said without any circumlocution: "We occupy virtually the same relation to the Yankees that the Negroes do to us."

Incidentally, this may be a response to the observations of Robert W. Fogel and S. Engerman that the cotton South "netted handsome profits." Yes, certainly. But where did those profits go? This is the question. It seems that they paused very briefly in southern pockets before finding their way north. It was like Menenius Agrippa's tale about the hands revolting against the stomach. Certainly, should the hands allow the stomach to starve, they would starve in turn; but it seems more difficult to prove that the hands do strengthen their body by feeding the stomach of somebody else. Clement Eaton rightly stressed that "the most striking characteristic of Southern economy was that although the colonial connection with England had been broken, a new colonialism arose with respect to Northern business."[9]

This dependency was obviously increased by the wastefulness of the southern economy. When somebody wonders how this was, since planters in most cases administered their properties carefully, even with a shrewd sense of business, he simply ignores the fact that the wastefulness lay not in men but was intrinsic to the system. It was intrinsic not to the system in absolute, but only in comparison with modern capitalism. For the most part, planters cared for their estates well; though one cannot miss the impression that this was not because they were "businessmen" or "money-makers" (as, in some cases at least, they actually were), but because it was *their* life, what gave their lives a meaning, a sense. For capitalists, business *is* life. It was different with plantations, because they (as Ulrich Bonnel Phillips rightly observed) were, in fact, more: they were a life, a civilization, and a civilization based only in part (unlike capitalism) on business. So, in plantation civilization, money was not an end in itself, as in capitalist ethos; it was a means. Ends were very different and more complex.

Notes

1   M. E. Massey, *Ersatz in the Confederacy* (Columbia University of South Carolina Press, 1952).
2   M. L. Rutherford, *The South in History and Literature* (Atlanta, GA: The Franklin-Turner Company, 1907).
3   P. H. Wood, *Black Majority* (New York: W. W. Norton and Company, 1974).
4   E. D. Genovese, *The Political Economy of Slavery* (New York: Pantheon Books, 1965).
5   F. Tannenbaum, *Slave and Citizen* (New York: Vintage Books, 1947).
6   In *Civil War History*, 19 (3) (September 1973).
7   Antonio Gramsci, *Gli Intellettuali e l'Organizzazione della Cultura* (Torino, Italy, 1958).
8   Georg Weber, *Storia Universale*, vol. 2 (Milan, Italy, 1881).
9   C. Eaton, *The Growth of Southern Civilization* (New York: Harper, 1961).

2

An Old South by the Clock

The Importance of "Early Rising," 1851

During and after the late 1820s, southern planters attempted to improve the efficiency of their plantations. Several agricultural journals were established in an effort to communicate labor-and time-saving ideas and methods to other slaveholders. The *Southern Planter* was but one of several southern agricultural periodicals in which planters and reformers counseled one another on plantation efficiency. Not infrequently, though, southern periodicals simply reprinted advice previously published by northern periodicals. Such is the case with the following excerpt, published originally in the *Boston Cultivator* and reprinted in the *Southern Planter* in 1851. (From "Early Rising," *Southern Planter*, 11 (January 1851), pp. 21–2)

Are you poor? you will probably forever remain so, if you habitually waste the precious hours of the morning in bed. Who will seek the labor or services of him who sleeps and doses in the morning until seven or eight o'clock? If such a person is poor, he must remain poor. "He that would thrive must rise at five." The poor can ill afford to lose daily two or three hours of the best portion of the day. Economy of time and diligence in business, are virtues peculiarly appropriate to those who depend upon their earnings for the means of subsistence. Allowing twelve working hours to a day, he who by rising at eight instead of five o'clock in the morning, thereby loses three hours' daily labor, parts with one-fourth of his means of supporting himself

and family: ten years' labor lost in the course of forty years! – *Boston
Cultivator.*

Clock Time and Southern Railroads, 1834

Southern railroads were important for helping to bring clock-consciousness
to the plantation and for heightening the notion that the clock was a true and
legitimate arbiter of time. Here we see glimpses of how the operations of
South Carolina's Charleston and Hamburg Railroad affected southern notions
of regularity and punctuality. (From Horatio Allen, "Report of the Chief
Engineer," in Elias Horry, comp., *Annual Report of the Direction of the South
Carolina Canal and Rail Road Company, to the Stockholders, May 6th, 1834*
(Charleston, SC: J. S. Burges, 1834), pp. 5, 12)

The Company now sends an express daily from one commercial city to
another, distant 136 miles, in 12 hours, and that in the day time. The
daily papers of this city, are sent by this conveyance, but merchants'
letters of the utmost importance to them in business, are not less than 2
days going under contract . . . .

    With the view of attaining the greatest possible regularity in the time of
running of the passenger Engines, regulations have been established
fixing the hour of departure, from the 6 more important points on the
line, as well as that of the earliest time, at which they are permitted under
a penalty of five dollars, to arrive at the following one. One of the printed
cards, containing the particulars of this arrangement, is sent herewith.
The only difficulty that has been found in carrying this into practice, has
arisen from the want of a uniform standard of time at the different
points. This we have removed by placing clocks at the Depositories at
Charleston, Summerville, Branchville, Blackville, Aiken and Hamburg
which being well regulated and readily accessible, to the Engineer and
Agent, will enable them to regulate their movements on the road with
great accuracy.

    The agents at these six places are required to transmit daily to the
clerk at Charleston the time of arrival and departure, with statements of
number and description of cars with each Engine that passed their
Depository on the day previous. From these returns a register is kept
which presents at one view the degree of regularity with which the road is
travelled. The Abstract from the daily register, (embracing from the 6th
to 30th April) herewith presented, exhibits a degree of regularity that
could scarcely have been anticipated, ...

Plantation Time, 1851

Presented here is strong evidence, again from a southern agricultural journal, that the concern to save time was not simply an abstraction. Rather, it was a real need to southern slaveholders and one that encouraged them to arrange their slave labor accordingly. Note the role of sound in communicating time on plantations. (From the *Southern Cultivator*, Tattler, "Management of Negroes," *Southern Planter*, 11 (February 1851), pp. 39, 41)

Mr Editor, – As the proper management of our negroes is a subject not second in importance to any discussed in your columns, I hope it will not be deemed amiss if, in giving my views, I enter somewhat into detail....

To make one negro cook for all is saving of time. If there be but ten hands, and these are allowed two hours at noon, one of which is employed in cooking their dinner, for all purposes of rest that hour had as well be spent in ploughing or hoeing; and would be equal to ten hours' work of one hand: whereas the fourth of that time would be sufficient for one to cook for all....

It is expected that servants should rise early enough to be at work by the time it is light.... One of the most important regulations on a farm is to see that the hands get plenty of sleep. They are thoughtless, and if allowed to do so, will set up late of nights. Some of them will be up at all hours, and others instead of going to bed will set on a stool or chair and nod or sleep until morning. By half past nine or ten o'clock, all hands should be in bed and unless in case of sickness or where a woman has been up with her child, if any one is caught out of bed after that hour, they should be punished.

A large sized cow bell that could be heard two miles, and would not cost more than three or four dollars, would serve not only as a signal for bed-time, but also for getting up of a morning, for ceasing work at noon, and resuming it after dinner. Where the distance to be heard is not great, a common bar of cast steel hung up by passing a wire through one end, may be struck with a hammer and will answer in place of a bell.

Timing Slave Labor by the Watch, 1843

Sometimes, short, scribbled notes in plantation journals reveal much about slaveholders' mindsets. The following brief extract from an unknown South

Carolina planter proves the point. (From Anon., Plantation Journal, Barnwell District, South Carolina, August, 1843. Reproduced courtesy of the South Caroliniana Library, University of South Carolina, Columbia, SC)

Work timed by watch

Summer House Field. It takes exactly 5 minutes to run a furrow from one end of the cotton rows to the other that is to say *from the S. H. thicket [d]own to the bay.*
From S. House thicket down to Jackson Branch, next [to] Charleston road = 15 minutes.
Planted the *Alligator* [field] in Corn 6 by 4, 1 hand to drop & 2 hoes to cover – in 3 days – commencing on the 1st day about 8 o'clock.
Alligator. Time taken to run round a row with shovel 14 minutes this allows for stopping, turning. &c.

Plantation Time from a Slave's Perspective, 1847

Slaves who managed to escape bondage during the antebellum period related details about the nature of plantation labor often over looked by visitors to the South. Here, William W. Brown, who had been born into slavery in Kentucky but subsequently escaped, gives us some idea of the nature of time-regulated labor on his plantation and the way masters enforced slaves' obedience to the sound of time. (From [William W. Brown], *Narrative of William W. Brown, A Fugitive Slave. Written by Himself* (Boston: Published at the Anti-Slavery Office, 1847), pp. 13–16).

My master owned about forty slaves, twenty-five of whom were field hands. He removed from Kentucky to Missouri, when I was quite young, and settled thirty or forty miles above St. Charles, on the Missouri, where, in addition to his practice as a physician, he carried on milling, merchandizing and farming. He had a large farm, the principal productions of which were tobacco and hemp. The slave cabins were situated on the back part of the farm, with the house of the overseer, whose name was Grove Cook, in their midst. He had the entire charge of the farm, and having no family, was allowed a woman to keep house for him, whose business it was to deal out the provisions for the hands.

A woman was also kept at the quarters to do the cooking for the field hands, who were summoned to their unrequited toil every morning at four o'clock, by the ringing of a bell, hung on a post near the house of the overseer. They were allowed half an hour to eat their breakfast, and get to the field. At half past four, a horn was blown by the overseer, which was the signal to commence work; and every one that was not on the spot at the time, had to receive ten lashes from the negro-whip, with which the overseer always went armed. The handle was about three feet long, with the butt-end filled with lead, and the lash six or seven feet in length, made of cowhide, with platted wire on the end of it. This whip was put in requisition very frequently and freely, and a small offence on the part of a slave furnished an occasion for its use. During the time that Mr. Cook was overseer, I was a house servant—a situation preferable to that of a field hand, as I was better fed, better clothed, and not obligated to rise at the ringing of the bell, but about half an hour after. I have often laid and heard the crack of the whip, and the screams of the slave. My mother was a field hand, and one morning was ten or fifteen minutes behind the others in getting into the field. As soon as she reached the spot where they were at work, the overseer commenced whipping her. She cried, "Oh! pray—Oh! pray—Oh! pray"—these are generally the words of slaves, when imploring mercy at the hands of their oppressors. I heard her voice, and knew it, and jumped out of my bunk, and went to the door. Though the field was some distance from the house, I could hear every crack of the whip, and every groan and cry of my poor mother. I remained at the door, not daring to venture any farther. The cold chills ran over me and I wept aloud. After giving her ten lashes, the sound of the whip ceased, and I returned to my bed, and found no consolation in my tears. It was not yet daylight.

An Old South by the Clock

Mark M. Smith

[M]ainly because they have seldom considered the question of time consciousness, historians of the American slave South have suggested that antebellum masters and bondpeople, caught as they were in the webs of seasonal agriculture and non-wage economic and social relations, were necessarily peripheral to the emergence of clock time. But viewed and evaluated in comparative perspective, it seems that rather

From Mark M. Smith, "Old South time in comparative perspective," *American Historical Review*, 101 (1996), pp. 1432–69. Excerpt reprinted by permission of the American Historical Association.

than constituting a place on the edge of modern time consciousness, the post-1830 slave South was very much in and of it. In fact, the Old South, though a society nurtured in nature's womb, was possibly more clock conscious than many nineteenth-century free wage labor industrial societies. This possibility has eluded not only historians of the Old South but also those committed to the historical study of time generally. With few exceptions, historical analyses of time consciousness have concentrated on the evolution of clock consciousness and time discipline in wage-labor, urban-industrial, conventionally capitalist societies. Even on those occasions when historians of slave societies have ventured to consider the relationship between clock consciousness and slavery, they have done so by borrowing a conceptual lens from historians who have examined the emergence of time discipline under industrial, free wage labor capitalism.

Drawing on a growing and relatively recent historical literature, this essay questions the importance of free wage labor industrial capitalism in promoting a modern time consciousness. It compares the evolution of clock consciousness in the American antebellum South, a society that was neither industrial nor capitalist in the free wage labor sense, to the emergence of time discipline in more typically capitalist societies, where industrialism and free wage labor particularly are seen as important agents in inaugurating and cementing a modern consciousness of the clock. This article argues that southern slaveholders were motivated by forces both similar to and distinct from those that propelled British, North American, Australian, and South African capitalist managers toward the use of clock time and suggests that American slaves, as much as industrial-urban wage laborers, were forced to acquiesce to clock-regulated plantation labor. These findings have some important implications not only for our understanding of the Old South's mode of production but also for a historical appreciation of the relationship between capitalism and time consciousness generally.

As most historians of time consciousness have recognized, the way a society perceives and uses time is mediated both through its dominant cultural values and, simultaneously, the prevailing mode of production. Yet, it seems fair to say, because historians have for the most part examined the emergence of clock consciousness in free wage labor, industrializing societies, they have tended, if only tacitly, to emphasize the importance of the economic and industrial aspects of the capitalist mode of production in shaping and promoting clock consciousness....

The success of Western capitalism in transmitting time discipline to its colonial outposts was due to its two-pronged nature: Western capitalism emphasized the intellectual and cultural legitimacy of rational, orderly time and the economic necessity and logic of work time. According to

Adam, "all work relations touched by clock time are tied up with hegemony and power."[1] A varied body of work suggests there are times "that are constituted as the shadows of the time economy of employment relations, times not calculable in monetary terms yet evaluated through the mediating filter of both the rationalized time of the Protestant ethic and the commodified time of the market."[2] Non-free labor modes of production and non-wage-based economic and social relations, like those prevailing under antebellum southern slavery, then, could theoretically harbor and promote a modern clock consciousness, without necessarily embracing traditional capitalist wage-labor relations. In other words, a society's cultural evaluation of time may be as important as the economic imperatives of its mode of production in determining how time is to be constructed and used. If we grant that a particular mode of production stresses efficiency in work and the strict regulation of labor, but it is one that is not premised on wage labor, and if we acknowledge that this same society places a premium on clock time, then this society could, in theory, embrace a clock consciousness not appreciably different from that present under a free wage labor mode of production. . . .

[T]he clock consciousness of nineteenth-century urban and industrial Britain, Natal, Australia, and the American North was modern. The secondary literature on these regions suggests that the evolution of clock consciousness and the proliferation of clocks and watches was a product of, and handmaiden to, the emergence of wage-labor capitalism, industrialism, urbanism, and the work ethic associated with Protestantism. Although it probably entertained a work ethic not appreciably different from the Puritan one, the antebellum South shared few of these structural features, but it nevertheless developed an equally modern clock consciousness. The slave mode of production, in its antebellum southern configuration at least, managed to introduce a refined and potent clock consciousness to its urban and rural environs without embracing wage labor or industrialism. Similarly high levels of timepiece ownership aside, what united antebellum southern slaveowners and nineteenth-century industrial capitalists was a mutual understanding that their particular class and social (hence political) interests were in some way served and bolstered by regulating labor and behavior by the clock. Industrial capitalists needed the clock to coordinate and discipline nascent wage laborers; slaveowners needed the clock to satisfy their own imperatives, which, from the 1830s on, centered on acquiring the title of "modern" while retaining strict control over, and promoting efficient work practices among, a potentially volatile slave labor force. Both classes subscribed to what Gregory Clark has termed the "coercion theory" of factory discipline, in which "[d]iscipline was designed to *coerce* workers into doing more than they would have freely chosen if

they had maintained control over their hours of work and work intensity."[3] Working slowly, horseplay, tardiness, and similar behavior
deemed inappropriate to either the factory floor or plantation field
could be modified by the clock in both instances. In some respects,
planters were more effective than some industrial capitalists at imposing
clock order on their environment. Surprisingly, the fact that the modes
of production of plantation master and factory manager differed matters
less than we might think, for both used the clock in remarkably similar
ways and produced two classes of workers who held much in common in
their understanding of, and obedience to, clock time. . . .

It is probably no accident that Britain was both the first country to
industrialize and among the first to have its shift from natural to clock
time scrutinized by historians. In his pioneering 1967 essay, "Time,
work-discipline and industrial capitalism," E. P. Thompson asked a
deceptively simple but incisive question: was the emergence of industrial
capitalism in eighteenth and nineteenth-century Britain "related to
changes in the inward notation of time" among managers and especially
workers?[4] Thompson contrasted pre-industrial Britain, which he considered to be characterized by a basic "disregard for clock time," the
structuring of work by task, and an appeal to natural cues as legitimate
arbiters of time, with industrial-era time discipline. Although he was
aware that naturally derived, task-oriented time "has by no means lost
all relevance in rural parts of Britain today," Thompson discerned a
protracted but real shift in conceptions of time in industrializing Britain.
Increasing ownership of watches by Britain's working classes and the
general diffusion of public, aural time through church clocks coincided
"at the exact moment when the industrial revolution demanded a greater
synchronization of labour." Public clocks and private watches, argued
Thompson, were the instruments "which regulated the new rhythms of
industrial life" and energized the advance of industrial capitalism. The
shift to time discipline was most apparent in urban and industrializing
areas, although non-urban or industrial arenas such as schooling and
domestic manufacturing also came under the sway of the clock.

The efforts of managers to introduce a respect for the clock among their
employees were not uncontested. "In the first stage," according to
Thompson, "we find simple resistance. But in the next stage, as the new
time-discipline is imposed, so the workers begin to fight, not against time,
but about it." Thompson made clear that this battle took place in industrial urban environments: "It was exactly in those industries – the textile
mills and the engineering workshops – where the new time-discipline was
most rigorously imposed that the contest over time became most
intense." Mark Harrison has elaborated on Thompson's ideas and suggests that it was not simply industrial but also non-industrial urban

environments such as nineteenth-century Bristol that shared a heightened consciousness of time, not least because public time in the form of civic clocks was easily communicable in an urban environment.[5]

Whatever the emphasis, though, it appears that a sharpened clock-based time consciousness evolved, in the British instance, primarily in urban and industrial environments. Thompson concluded that nineteenth-century British factory workers eventually internalized the time discipline demanded by their employers and, in the process, came to legitimize the very notion of clock time as a true measure of work. But if the larger thesis was pessimistic, Thompson did point out that pre-industrial conceptions of time remained strong in quite unexpected places, such as city ports, where time schedules were contingent on the natural phenomena of tides and weather. And there were other enclaves that resisted, often successfully, the intrusion of the Protestant ethic and the industrial clock, "the unenclosed countryside" especially. Thompson believed that nineteenth-century British agriculture was too contingent on nature for clock time to be of much importance. In all likelihood, the rural church clock did help introduce a sense of mechanical time into the British countryside and the efforts of nineteenth-century agricultural reformers helped make farm laborers more aware of the idea of time-thrift. As was the case for the British rural housewife and urban port worker, however, Thompson argued that naturally defined and task-oriented time were to remain the predominant ways of conceptualizing time and its passage, even as the clock took hold in urban and industrial nineteenth-century Britain.

Historians of the antebellum American North in particular have been indebted to Thompson and have often applied his insights to the northern experience with industrialization. And naturally so perhaps: the rise of the industrial American North was similar, at least in trajectory, to the British experience, since both societies embraced free wage labor and capitalist economic and social relations relatively quickly. Glancing back to the eighteenth-century North, Richard D. Brown, for example, found that "[t]ime-thrift and broader considerations of efficiency played a minor role" in peoples' lives and that clock time and punctuality were "alien" values to this pre-modern society.[6] Given this emphasis, labor historians of the nineteenth-century North such as Herbert G. Gutman and David Brody could reasonably posit a scenario in which the factory clock wrestled with nature and the task to produce the kind of protracted battle in the North over time that Thompson found in industrializing Britain. The patterns of workers' resistance to factory clock time were, apparently, similar. Both British and American workers invoked appeals to natural time and contested the amount of time to be worked in their efforts to combat managers' imposition of time discipline in the factories.

Recent work on the evolution of a modern time consciousness in colonial and antebellum New England, however, suggests that the factory was not solely responsible for the shift to time discipline: Puritanism and urbanization had important roles to play, too. "New Englanders," writes Paul Hensley, "bore the imprint of time long before the emergence of the factory."[7] Yet, it should be pointed out, much of what Hensley argues had been prefigured by Thompson, who was also cognizant of the importance of Puritan culture and urbanization in laying the foundation for industrial time discipline. Hensley's evidence, for example, points to the rise of an urban New England time consciousness, and, like Thompson, he notes the Puritan fascination with time-thrift in an urban context. So, for basically the same reasons that Thompson gave, Hensley concludes: "Whether working or resting, New England townspeople had become accustomed, long before the advent of [private] clocks, to heeding the sounds that marked public time." But Hensley's remarks on the time conceptions of rural New England are fewer and point to the absence of mechanical time consciousness in the northern countryside.... Hensley found little evidence to suggest that pre-eighteenth-century rural New Englanders shared the conception of time that was to take over New England's industrial urban centers. As he puts it, "In spite of the important relationship between time and labor in seventeenth-century New England, work was characteristically elastic and relaxed, attributes influenced by seasonal rhythms, the blending of farming and craft activities, and frequent shifts from one task to another." Hensley suggests that the stimuli for New England's time consciousness rested primarily with merchants and townspeople, not with New England farmers.

Certainly, as other work has made clear, there were some efforts in eighteenth-century New England to introduce time-saving innovations to both industry and agriculture. Hensley identifies several farmers from the late eighteenth century who fractionalized their work time to the hour. The non-industrial impetus here was, according to Hensley, deliciously simple and quintessentially American: "Toward the end of the eighteenth century, the republican concept of virtue, including its emphasis on working hard and husbanding time, was being combined with new ideas associated with technology...Factories would instill organization and discipline," and obedience to the clock was presumably an important ingredient in the republican cocktail. Here, Hensley's essential thesis is clear:

> Long before factory bells began to compete with church and public bells as arbiters of local time, family clocks well placed in hallways augmented communal time... Out of this family environment New England sons and

daughters moved to nineteenth century factories. Having been trained in time discipline within their communities and at home, they now encountered mill owners and managers who were demanding time obedience.

The victory of the New England mill owners seems as complete as that won by their British counterparts, perhaps more so in light of the limited infiltration of clock time into the northern countryside. What New England mill workers lamented most was not the intrusion of clock time itself but rather "their lack of control over their own time." Here, as in Thompson's England, there was resistance not to time as a category of work, as a measurement of labor, but rather to the perceived unfairness of managers' manipulation of workers' time.

Still more recent work, however, has gone beyond the idea that time discipline in the North was predominantly urban or industrial. In a thoughtful essay, Martin Bruegel argues that antebellum rural northerners, those in New York's Hudson Valley at least, were time-conscious clock users by the mid-nineteenth century.[8] ... By the 1840s, when almost three-quarters of the valley's rural inhabitants owned a clock or watch, rural time consciousness was becoming more pronounced. And it was during the 1830s and 1840s that rural and urban northerners began to demand louder public clocks to coordinate their increasingly punctual schedules. It was a trend that, according to Bruegel, expressed "[t]he need for more precise temporal definitions [which] was both a sign and a result of the changing social relations in the countryside where time evolved into a more precious resource." Ultimately, when clocks and watches became cheap enough so that a majority of rural and urban dwellers could afford them, "their utility as timekeepers superseded their role as markers of social hierarchies." Consequently, Hudson Valley farm laborers began recording the number of hours they worked and calculated how much time the use of plank roads would save them in transporting their goods to market. ...

If Bruegel is right in identifying the evolution of a rural time consciousness in the American North, then, by nineteenth-century standards at least, the region was quite exceptional. In the similarly sprawling Australian countryside, for example, mechanical time remained alien and largely irrelevant to its inhabitants. Attempts by Thompson's eighteenth-and nineteenth-century British colonists to introduce clock time to the bush failed. This is not to say that Aborigines had no sense of time. As Graeme Davison explains in his penetrating study, *The Unforgiving Minute: How Australia Learned to Tell the Time*, "Aborigines were not strangers to ideas of divided time. In some ways, their ideas of time were more precise than those of the Europeans. They were more alert to the subtle changes in foliage, wind direction, tidal movement and bird migration that marked the passage of the year." "In their own terms," Davison argues, emphasizing the cultural and social function of time, "Aborigines were a punctual people, for they were obedient to the time-signals that mattered to them." "Their way of life," he concludes, "which was essentially seasonal and nomadic, created neither the means, nor the creed, for [Western] calendars or clocks."[9]

Efforts by colonizing and proselytizing European capitalists to inculcate rural Aborigines and settlers to the clock notwithstanding, many still operated on natural time in the 1870s: "In the bush, then, clock-time was largely subordinated to the natural cycles of the sun, moon and the seasons." ... As long as these natural time cues predominated, as long as rural inhabitants' needs were met by such cues and not subject to particularly coercive and potent external forces, the clock remained largely irrelevant to bush settlers. The absence of industrial wage incentives in the bush (Davison sees them mainly confined to the towns) meant that the clock had little cultural, social, or economic currency in a rural environment that contained its own, relatively punctual, form of time reckoning. "It was only toward the end of the century," notes Davison, "as the railway and the telegraph began to set the standard of time for the whole society, that the time notations in the farmers' journals became more consistently precise." And even when Protestant missions and schools peddled "whitefellas" time to Aborigines, they proved woefully ineffective in persuading them that the clock was a fair or even useful arbiter of time. Martin Bruegel's Hudson Valley, then, seems a world away from the Australian bush.

So, too, in Natal province, South Africa, nineteenth-century colonizing European capitalists failed to instill their own sense of time discipline among rural Zulus. Keletso Atkins has recently argued, "Like most preindustrial people, the Zulu used the moon and stars to keep track of time."[10] European capitalists found it impossible to impose anything like a modern time consciousness ... on rural Zulu laborers. Efforts to convert rural Natal Africans to Western time amounted to little because, as Atkins explains, they were able to draw on their own, entrenched culture of time, which had long recognized nature as its legitimate arbiter. Yet if nineteenth-century rural Zulus were able to reject Western ideas about time, those who moved to Natal's urban enclaves found their cultural assumptions about time subjected to different and more potent forces. "The situation," observes Atkins, "developed somewhat differently in the urban areas." She continues: "As these people came into contact with more industrialized societies, they became isolated from time cues in the natural environment ... Man-made signals replaced this natural performance and aided town workers in determining their temporal bearings." While "[i]nfluences of the weekly rhythm ran shallowest in remote country districts . . ., [t]he reverse of this can be seen in the towns where the growing experience was toward an outward conformity to these new points of temporal references." Colonial urban public clocks and the insistence on wage labor had, it seems, the effect of shaping those Zulus who ventured to the province's cities into time-conscious workers, workers not so different from those in industrial-urban Britain, Australia, and the rural and industrial American North. "[A]t least by 1872, and perhaps well before that date," argues Atkins, "segments of the cities' black labouring population were perceiving time in discrete market as well as noneconomic terms – namely, regular work time, overtime, and leisure time."

How, then, did the time consciousness of Australia's rural peoples, British agricultural laborers, and rural Natal Zulus remain relatively independent of colonial Western time discipline? . . . Aborigines and white rural settlers in Australia, British agricultural laborers, and rural Natal Zulus were all nominally free laborers, and they were laboring in their own social and economic context, a context too grounded in its geographic, social, and cultural specificity for Protestant ethnic industrial-capitalist constructions of time to be of much potence, relevance, or persuasion. . . .

Collectively, then, this literature on the evolution of time consciousness identifies several broad historical forces promoting a clock consciousness among eighteenth-and nineteenth-century rural and, especially, industrial-urban managers and workers. If we accept the basic point that the larger forces of time's religious and economic rationalization and commodification provided the essential impetus behind the rise of time discipline, then the specific historical developments that created a modern time consciousness among workers and managers in the nineteenth century probably consisted of the following: first, the dilution of God's time and its articulation with a mercantile work ethic stressing that time was money and that, as such, it should be saved, not wasted; second, the concomitant rise of urban clocks to regulate and coordinate personal and public temporal activity; third, the increase in the number of clocks and watches in any given population; fourth, the emergence of industrial wage-labor time discipline; and, lastly, the advent of technologies such as the railroads, which disseminated urban and industrial time to the countryside and helped heighten a preexisting idea that punctuality and time-thrift were forms of religious, civic, and personal virtue.

If we agree with Babette M. Levy, Edmund S. Morgan, and Perry Miller that "the Puritan Ethic" embodied "the values that all Americans held," southerners included, and if some of the aforementioned agencies

behind the nineteenth century's drive toward clock time can be found in
the antebellum South, were these forces in and of themselves sufficient
(plainly, they appear to have been necessary) to push the non-wage
antebellum slave South toward the adoption of clock time?[11] If not,
what was it about slavery that rendered wage-labor industrialism unimportant while nevertheless encouraging planters to adopt clock time?

A brief examination of the activities and attitudes of southern merchants helps answer these questions. Because of their place in the Atlantic marketplace, eighteenth-and nineteenth-century southern merchants
appear to have developed a keen sense that time was money, that
punctuality in business transactions was a virtue and necessity, not
only from the requisites of their own trade but from their dealings with
northern and European merchants. Yankee merchants throughout the
colonial period, for example, coached their southern counterparts in the
need for punctuality in business. As Boston merchant Jonathan Johnson
advised Edward Telfair's Georgia mercantile firm in 1775, "let me
however request of you to execute this order with the utmost punctuality
& Expedition." By 1802, however, the situation was reversed. Charleston merchant Thomas Aiton complained to his firm's parent company,
William Stanley and Company of New York: "Three mails have arrived
since we received yours by Post informing us of your intention to Send
us by next Mail 2,000 dollars. We have neither received money nor
letter." Aiton then warned: "Such Conduct may be attended with very
serious circumstances if repeated. You know as well as us that the most
strict punctuality is necessary in money matters." Similarly, punctuality
with credit payments became a point of pride, indeed, of virtue, for
southern merchants. When Virginian George Carter failed to pay the
credit on a note signed by Landon Carter in 1806, the latter complained
that "you [have] done more injury to the respectability of my punctual
habits in Fredericksburg than any I have ever had before." While no
doubt influenced by the presence of public, church-based time, the
South's urban merchants, then, like their medieval forebears, developed
their own partially secularized notion of time. Atlantic merchants, in
short, bequeathed an important legacy to the antebellum South as, in
fact, they had to the nineteenth-century Western world.

The most conspicuous source of this mercantile and civic time consciousness in the South was in its urban environs. Eighteenth-and nineteenth-century southern towns constituted the physical space where
secular and sacred time meshed. Although southern industry was woefully undeveloped in both centuries, its absence does not seem to have
made the region's urban areas any less clock conscious. Few cities
though there were in the South, those that did exist seem to have
embraced and promoted an urban awareness of time that was little

different from northern, British, Natalian, or Australian urban time. Charleston's St. Michael's clock, installed in the 1760s, for example, was "a strong 30 Hour Clock, to show the Hour Four Ways, to strike the Hour on the largest Bell." In the antebellum period, civic authorities expanded the function of the church's time: "It will be noticed that it is 'to show the *Hour* Four Ways,' and this is all it showed till 1840, when, with the consent of the vestry, the City Council added minute hands." One should not underestimate the aural and temporal power of these and similar church bells. The bells in London's St. Mary-le-Bow, for example, can be heard for six miles above ambient twentieth-century London noise, and presumably the South's church bells could perforate a quieter colonial and antebellum soundscape at least as far.

In trying to evaluate the importance of urban church bells in promoting clock consciousness in the South, let us return to the significance and function of clock time. Certainly, bells had been important regulators and communicators of time in many societies, modern and pre-modern. But whereas medieval European monasteries had used aural time mainly (though not exclusively) for the express purpose of announcing God's time, clock bells in the eighteenth and nineteenth centuries were employed for additional, increasingly profane, purposes. The difference, of course, is best measured in degrees, not absolutes. In the urban environs of the American North, Natal, and Australia, particularly in the nineteenth century, aural time was used to announce not just God's time but increasingly to regulate the time of schools, markets, and factories.

The South's use of aural time was no different. In the 1740s, for example, Charleston's church clocks were enlisted to announce and coordinate the city's market times. The aural dimension of this sacred-secular urban time was often recorded by contemporaries. It was said of Charleston's St. Philip's clock and bells in 1828, for example, "truly nothing can be more awe-inspiring than at the silent midnight hour to hear St. Philip's clock with deep funeral knell tolling another day." For this observer, it was the clock that was heard. . . . Although never to lose its religious significance completely, aural church clock time, then, helped govern and coordinate the secular activities of the southern city and its inhabitants.

Added to the mercantile and urban forces promoting a clock consciousness in the South was an increasing disposition on the part of white southerners, both rural and urban, slaveholding and non –, to own timepieces, especially in the nineteenth century. The increasing availability of clocks and watches, combined with a reduction in their relative costs in the early antebellum period, had an impact on southern rural and urban areas just as it did on northern ones. And the basic reasons for increased watch and clock ownership in the South were the same as elsewhere. If we agree with Martin Bruegel that antebellum northern timepiece ownership was in part a result of heightening personal time discipline, the same was true in the South. By 1851, three entries in one southerner's diary could speak for the South generally: "Am to send for my carriage today at 5 PM... Mitchell & Allen family arrive from Glenroy a little before 2 PM... Am to call Board of Medical College to meet on Saturday 1 PM at Courthouse."

Similarly, if the railroads were primarily responsible for the diffusion of the North's urban time consciousness, the same process is in operation in the antebellum South. In 1834, for example, the Charleston & Hamburg railroad in South Carolina, at the time the world's longest railway under single management, achieved "the greatest possible regularity in the time of running Passenger Engines" by placing clocks at six of its stations. The chief engineer stipulated fines for unpunctual drivers: "regulations have been established fixing the hour of departure,... as well as that of the earliest time, at which they are permitted under a penalty of five dollars, to arrive at the following [station]." The engineer acknowledged that "[t]he only difficulty that has been found in carrying this into practice, has arisen from the want of a uniform standard of time at the different points," but by 1845 the railroad had improved enough to persuade the postal service that it could deliver the mail punctually. Trains failing "to arrive within the contract time" specified by the Post Office, after all, incurred hefty fines. The net effect of such time-specific forces as the railroad, not to mention the telegraph and mail, was to heighten southerners' awareness of clock time and need for punctuality.

The antebellum South, however, was not like everywhere else in one important respect: the peculiar institution. But rather than a fetter on clock consciousness and time-thrift, slavery proved to be a powerful stimulant in pushing southern planters toward the clock. The South's shift to clock time in the last thirty or so years of the antebellum period was undoubtedly due to railroads, urban time, mercantile time, and the other forces noted above. But there were also forces created by late antebellum slavery that helped master and slave adopt the clock. Whereas early experiments with the timing of hired labor in the rural North and the emergence of free wage industrial-urban labor elsewhere promoted clock consciousness, southern slaveowners' bid for slave-based modernity provided a similar catalyst. The notion of pre-modern impulses in southern slavery is, thanks to the pioneering work of Eugene D. Genovese, well known and probably true.[12] But when it comes to conceptions of time, it appears that different impulses applied, impulses from both inside and outside the South's putatively non-capitalist slave regime. These forces were equally conducive to the planters' embrace of a time discipline that was not only just as sophisticated as the North's but actually more successful in transmitting clock time to the countryside than wage labor and industrialization had proven in Britain, Natal, and Australia.

. . . [T]he fundamental push toward time discipline among the South's master class came in the 1830s. With their time consciousness heightened by railroads and the postal service, and drawing on a long familiarity with the imperatives of mercantile and urban time, slaveholders of the 1830s began to push for more efficient agriculture and a better ordering of their slave work force. Surrounded by a world moving toward free wage labor capitalism, slaveholders were at once repulsed by the dangerous rise of a landless and politically volatile proletariat and eager to garb themselves in modern clothes. The answer to this dilemma, or at least one part of it, was in the use of clock time. The nineteenth century's most obvious icon of modernity, the clock and the time it kept, was simultaneously modern but controlling, at once an engine for economic efficiency and a tool of social discipline. In the context of the late antebellum period, when slaveowners aimed to modernize slavery without threatening its fundamentally conservative social relations, the clock proved particularly attractive. Not only could clock time be spliced with more traditional forms of social control like the whip and the old, even revered, urban practice of sounding time, not only was clock time perceived to be in harmony with that arbiter of southern agriculture, nature, but the clock could be recruited to help create a modern, efficient, and disciplined slaveholders' regime. It would, ideally, be a regime that borrowed the discipline of the factory – a free wage labor clock without importing wage labor's associated, essentially mobocratic, tendencies. In a society that coveted profit and enslavement, efficiency and order, clock time – owned and controlled exclusively by masters – proved irresistibly alluring.

As Bertram Wyatt-Brown has pointed out, in their efforts to "modernize, to improve the 'home system,' so that its foundations were no less secure, no less progressive than those on which free labor rested," masters looked, of all places, to the free but materialist North.[13] Specifically, they turned to northern agricultural societies and scientific journals, they noted Benjamin Franklin's counsel that time is money, and then they reinterpreted this advice in the context of their slave society. A reprint from the *Boston Cultivator* in the *Southern Planter* for January 1851, for example, suggested that all agriculturalists, southern ones included, should allow "twelve working hours to a day," for "he who by rising at eight instead of five o'clock in the morning, thereby loses three hours' daily labor, parts with one-fourth of his means of supporting himself and family: ten years' labor lost in the course of forty years!" The careful harvesting of this time was essential for profit, and the responsibility rested, in the first instance, with the planter. Moreover, efforts to inculcate an internal time discipline among some planters appear to have succeeded. "My plan for working," revealed one small slaveholder in 1836, "was formed by necessity." Owning few slaves, he was obliged to organize his own time efficiently: "As soon as it was light enough to see, I hitched up and drove briskly until breakfast time – took out and fed while I ate, and for which I only allowed forty-five minutes – worked till one o'clock – rested an hour and a half when cool, two hours when warm."

If such examples failed to persuade planters, sarcasm was employed: "The old adage, that 'time is money,' may do well for the face of a Yankee clock, but it is altogether beneath the philosophy of *Young America. Therefore, lie in bed til your breakfast is ready, and be sure to go a fishing every Saturday evening.*" Those who did follow the Yankee way in their use of time were applauded publicly. One Alabama planter, for instance, was lauded not just because he "enforces a strict discipline among his negroes" but because the principles of progressive farming were "carried out with the most perfect clock-like precision, to the great benefit of master and servant." And one reason why punctuality was considered a good thing in the South was probably the same reason nineteenth-century Americans generally considered it healthy – it was virtuous and essentially republican....

Practically, this advice [on how to save time] was translated at the plantation level in a variety of ways. In some instances, planters bought time-saving machinery, especially cotton gins, which promised to clean five hundred pounds "in 31 minutes." Equally, planters tried to import factory methods directly to the plantation. Again, the aping of the North was obvious. Lowell mills, for instance, became models of efficiency, and planters were encouraged to emulate the factory's use of clock-regulated labor. The *Southern Agriculturalist*, for example, published one southerner's account of a visit to Lowell in 1845 and advised "all those who are politically or otherwise unfriendly to the factory system, to read the following article." The visitor, from Kentucky, was impressed by the fact that "[t]he very few persons that were occasionally seen at all, hurried to and fro, as if their time was precious," enthused over "the most perfect order, system, and regularity... everywhere exhibited," and praised the factory's use of aural time control: "At 12 o'clock, M., the factory bells chimed merrily, and the whirl of the spindles, the clatter of the looms, and the hum of the drums and wheels all ceased." In their efforts, then, to realize the ideal of time discipline and precise temporal coordination on their plantations, masters turned to the watch and the clock. Plantation clock time often mimicked the southern urban and northern factory form: it was communicated through sound. Bells and bugles, for instance, were rung or blown "at 9 o'clock, P.M.," when "every servant is required to return to his own cabin."

Sometimes, to be sure, nature intruded, but not as much as might be expected. Natural time and clock time did, of course, coexist on plantations; slaveowners' journals are eloquent on this point. Virginia planter George Llewellyn Nicolson, for example, took his temperature readings by the sun in one journal entry ("Thermometer 18 [degrees] at Sunrise") but also measured work done by the clock: "Filled ice House by 11 Oclock." Certainly, nature could be cruel and rush frazzled planters. William Fanning Wickham of Virginia could on one day in June 1828 congratulate himself that "[t]he corn is I think forward for the time of year," and four days later complain: "Finished the harvest early this morning – We should have been done some days sooner, but the weather this week has been so intensely hot that the reapers could make little progress." Nature proved difficult the next year, too. In January 1829, Wickham lamented, "The wheat in general is very backward." In March, he moaned, "Nearly a weeks work has been entirely lost by rain & bad weather." Yet Wickham did his best to minimize the impact of nature's unkind vagaries, and he often recruited the clock to regulate the work and time that he could control. In July 1830, he used clock time to describe his agricultural operations: "Began yesterday at eleven O Clock to thresh wheat." On other occasions, lost time to nature was minimized by forward planning and time harvesting: "We are later to sow wheat this year than I have ever been before – but by continuing to plough in the cornfield we shall be forward in our preparation – & no time shall be lost." When circumstances looked propitious, when it seemed as though he could exploit the window of time granted by nature, Wickham made the most of time and measured his tasks, in this case sowing wheat, to the hour: "Last night we had sown 588 bushels of wheat – we have got on better than ever before & the season has been most favorable to sowing – we have not lost an hour's work!" When nature could cost time, when it could expand and contract it, planters believed that agricultural operations were more likely to be completed in time if they paid close attention to time, its passage, and the clock.

In some respects, in fact, the vagaries of nature and the strictures they placed on planters' time were important for heightening masters' desire to make the most of time. Planters respected nature and its merciless control of time and, rather than trying to control it, looked instead to natural rhythms for inspiration. Even the most ardent scientific reformers of the 1830s agreed and counseled that "if we would catch the true spirit of improvement, we must bow at nature's shrine, and consult her oracles." The seasons still, as they always would, dictated planting and harvesting cycles, and planters deemed this proper and correct. But within these larger rhythms, the clock could be recruited, not to supplant nature but rather to complement and exploit its sometimes frenetic rhythms.

For some planters, the rhythm of the agricultural year, with its slack times, harried periods, and seasonal variations, did require a work schedule that was more flexible than that provided by a clock-defined, standard working day. But significantly, when planters most needed efficiency in slaves' labor, they invoked the clock and rendered all time into masters' time. Among the rules and "Priveleges" on Richard Eppes's Hopewell, Virginia, plantation, for example, was the following fiat issued to his bondpeople in 1857: "You will work from sunrise until sunset but when a press longer. Three quarters of an hour will be allowed you to breakfast and one hour and a quarter to dine from the month of October until April. One hour to breakfast and one hour and three quarters to dine from April until October." In other words, during the busiest but hottest seasons, when Eppes needed intensive and efficient labor the most, he seemed to give his slaves more time off, measured to within fifteen minutes. Yet these "apparently long breaks for meals and rest, especially during the summer," ought not, as one econometrician has recently contended, "be attributed to the philanthropic instincts of the planters." The effect of giving longer, clock-regulated recuperative breaks in the South's sweltering months actually increased slaves' efficiency at precisely the time when masters needed their people to labor most intensively. Moreover, that Eppes awarded his slaves an additional forty-five minutes to eat in the summer is hardly testimony to paternal magnanimity when we bear in mind that southern summer days were, on average, over three hours longer than winter ones. Eppes, in short, could afford to allow his hands more time to breakfast and lunch in the summer not only because it made economic sense but simply because there was more daytime to bestow. Plainly, then, all hands were primed for efficiency at all times, literally. And even if those times changed marginally during the year, they were still measured by the clock. All time was Eppes's time, and that time was clock regulated. Rule VI of Eppes's regulations reads: "You will be allowed to have half of every Saturday leaving your work at 12 O.C. except when a press then it will not be allowed you." When nature hindered the completion of one agricultural task, plantation labor could be reallocated in order to save time. As William Fanning Wickham noted in 1861: "The interruptions from the weather cause us to get on slowly with the wheat, but not much time is lost, as the ploughs are running when we cannot thresh."

The time spent cultivating some crops had to be more carefully monitored than when growing other staples. Tobacco, for instance, "requires a great deal of labor and attention to produce it of a fine quality." And quality tools were essential in the tobacco planter's fight against losing time:

> how much labor is often lost by giving a hand an indifferent axe or worn out hoe, . . . How much time is often lost in sending to a neighbor's to borrow a spade, or to grind axes for want of a grindstone at home. Half the time lost in this way in the course of a year would if employed in some useful labor more than purchase a spade and grindstone.

But whatever the crop, time lost was a pressing worry for masters. While individual planters were certainly free to impose their own temporal parameters and devise their own work regimes to suit their crop and labor force, all shared in an appeal to the clock as an arbiter of plantation order. In other words, while certain crops demanded particular work hours at particular points in the year, all crops, because they were cultivated by slaves, were clock regulated to some extent. It was more the labor and to a lesser extent the crop that was being timed and regulated. . . .

The introduction of the clock to the plantation field made temporal coordination and regulation under southern slavery very similar to that being enforced in free wage labor, industrializing societies. Clock-regulated bells and bugles especially were one way to regulate the work times of laborers, slave and free. Compare, for example, the following two statements, the first by a southern slaveowner in 1860, the second depicting the regulation of work time in English factories in 1833. The southern slave, apparently, was "not overworked; . . . He goes out when it is light enough to work, at 8 o'clock takes his breakfast, at 12 o'clock his dinner, at 2 o'clock goes to his work again, . . . [at] 9 or 10 o'clock goes to bed." Similarly, child laborers in Leeds "commenced at six o'clock; at nine, half an hour for breakfast; from half past nine till twelve, work. Dinner, one hour; from five till eight, work; rest for half an hour. From half past eight till twelve, (midnight,) work; an hour's rest."

If aural clock time was one weapon in the masters' arsenal to fight for progress, regulated slave behavior, and increased productivity, the watch was another. It was especially suited to gauging the economic productivity of labor. Because antebellum "laborlords," as Gavin Wright has called Old South planters, sought to maximize output per hand rather than yield per acre, the saving and manipulation of slaves' labor time was of great importance.[14] Although, as John F. Olson has pointed out, slaves worked fewer clock-time hours per year than free laborers,

North and South, slaves nevertheless "worked more intensively per hour" because their masters were able to regulate their productivity with the watch backed by the whip.[15] According to Olson, "slaves on plantations using the gang system worked 94 per cent more (harder) each hour than did free men." This level of intensity was achieved because slaveholders, like nineteenth-century managers elsewhere, came to recognize that work and leisure regulated by clock time was a means to increase and maintain the productivity of labor. Of course, if slaves did work so much harder per hour than free workers who were similarly regulated by the clock, one must assume that the whip *coupled* with the clock or watch was a better regulator of productivity than the watch and wage incentive. But planters, while undoubtedly linking the two in their discourse, tended to emphasize the role of the clock alone in maintaining productivity. Georgia planter James Thomas, for example, described how he gave his bondpeople a five-minute break every thirty minutes because he found that such respites from labor increased the amount of work performed by his slaves 15 percent. Other planters also devised procedures to "ascertain the actual cost of any specific work," when "the time it occupies being known." Examples were disseminated in southern agricultural journals. "The *daily labor of a team*," reported the *Farmers' Register* in 1834, "must necessarily be regulated by the manner in which it is employed, as well as by its strength." "In some southern and midland counties," the writer explained, "the carters who generally sleep in the house, rise at four in the morning, feed, clean, and harness the horses, get breakfast, and are ready to go a-field at six-'clock, or after seven in the winter, when they work till two, thus making at the utmost a yoking of eight hours." Some antebellum plantation journals had sections like "Work Timed by Watch" and entries detailing that "[i]t takes exactly five minutes to run a furrow," as well as notations documenting that a particular piece of plantation work "took Josey & Adam about 1/2 hour." The avowed ideal that clock-regulated plantations would render the coordination of plantation labor "like clock-work" was more often than not realized.

We need not rely solely on planters' records to verify that clock time was an important arbiter of work and life on antebellum southern plantations. Slaves remembered the clock and watch and testified that they had come to accept, albeit grudgingly, timed agricultural labor under slavery. Although they originally came from societies where natural time was predominant and that same reliance on natural time remained important to them, southern slaves, like nineteenth-century urban-industrial workers, found their reliance on sun and stars as exclusive arbiters of time attacked and, ultimately, undermined. Whereas rural workers in nineteenth-century Natal, Britain, and Australia were either slow to accept the legitimacy of the clock or able to reject it, American slaves appear to have succumbed more readily to their masters' admonitions concerning clock-regulated plantation labor. On the one hand, this is surprising because, some black slave drivers excepted, very few slaves actually owned a mechanical timepiece, something E. P. Thompson and others believe to have been important for the inculcation of clock consciousness among workers. But, on the other, it is of little surprise, especially when one considers how masters enforced slaves' obedience to the clock and how potent the aural power of time had proven in all societies, the South's included. Masters' two-pronged method to foist time obedience on their bondpeople, aurally communicated clock time backed up by the discipline of the whip, suggests that wage incentives, fines for lateness, and industrialization were not always necessary for the successful inculcation of clock time....

Because of the ubiquity of the clock in plantation affairs, slaves of the antebellum period as well as former slaves interviewed in the 1930s recalled clearly that clocks and watches were used to regulate their labor. Slaves who were timed in the field by their master's watch, for example, remembered the time pressure of work. A fugitive slave of the 1850s, Moses Grandy, acknowledged that on his North Carolina plantation, work and work breaks were watch regulated: "The overseer stood with his watch in hand, to give us just an hour; when he said, 'Rise,' we had to rise and go to work again." Moreover, being hectored by the timepiece in this way seems to have made slaves punctual. If other masters were anything like Lue Bradford's Texas owner, slaves' compulsion was understandable. "They would have to work until the horn sounded before they could stop for noon. In the morning the field boss would have the record book and each person was supposed to report before starting for work and all were punished who were late." The rationale for such a practice was clear to her: "This encouraged punctuality." Others, like John Washington of Virginia, recalled that during the 1850s if he "had any desire to go out again in a reasonable time," the time specified by his master on his "permission" slip enabling him to leave the plantation "must be punctually obeyed." According to Lu Lee of Texas, the slave knew when to return: "[The] nigger would get a pass and come over and stay with he gal and then he would say, 'I am sorry but it is that certain time and I got to go.'"

Born of their own experience with public, urban time, planters realized the power of communicating time through sound and so regulated plantation operations with clock-governed bells and horns. Cole Thomas of Texas explained at some length the system of rising by bugle on his plantation and the method his master used to ensure that it would be heard:

We has ter git up early every day in de year, rain or shine. De slaves was woke up every mornin at four thirty by a slave blowin a horn it was his job ter gits up and blow a bugle and den he would go ter work in de fiels wid de rest of de slaves. Dar was no danger of you not wakin up when de bugle blowed cause he blows it long and loud. He allus gits up of a mornin and gits his bugle down and comes out and climbs up on a platform wintah and summah and blows his bugle. Dis platform was about eight or ten feet tall.

"All the stock men worked in the field also – so many hours," remembered Cora Carroll of Mississippi. She explained: "They had a bell for them to go to work in the morning, a bell for them to get up by, and another one for noon, and another in the evening when they would knock off for dark." And it was through the constant reinforcement of time through sound that planters developed in their slaves a keen understanding of the precise time at which plantation affairs occurred: "[At] half-past eleven they would send the older children with food to the workers in the field," recalled one South Carolina ex-slave.

Slaves' obedience to the sound of plantation time was a product not simply of the imperious quality of the bell; it had just as much to do with the way masters ensured obedience to their sounding of the times. Former slave Bill Colins felt that the "large plantation bell which rang every morning at four o'clock" had a despotic quality, because "[t]he bell called and said, get up I'm coming to get you," and he understood that if slaves "did not answer the call the overseer would whip them." Controlling both the tools of time and of violence, planters ensured bondpeople's obedience to the sound of time with the whip. Jerry Boykins of Texas hinted at such a connection. "A big ole brass bell rang every mornin' at four o'clock on the plantashun," recalled Boykins, adding, "an' when that bell begin its racket, every darky roll out his bed, don't you forget!" John Barker was more explicit: "Maybe dey puts you on a task dis mawnin' and dat dere task got to be finished by seben o'clock dis evenin' an' if it ain't, dey whip you." Indeed, William Brown's 1847 testimony accords with later recollections by ex-slaves. On his tobacco and hemp Missouri plantation, field hands "were summoned to their unrequited toil every morning at four o'clock, by the ringing of a bell, hung on a post near the house of the overseer. They were allowed half an hour to eat their breakfast, and get to the field." Once there, aural plantation time, like the factory bell, signaled the beginning of work. The whip substituted for the free wage labor fine for those who were dilatory: "At half past four, a horn was blown by the overseer, which was the signal to commence work; and every one that was not on the spot at the time, had to receive ten lashes from the negro-whip, with which the overseer always went armed." Lateness was measured in minutes. "My mother was a field hand," explained Brown, "and one morning was ten or fifteen minutes behind the others in getting to the field." The punishment was as predictable to Brown as wage docking was to tardy industrial workers: "As soon as she reached the spot where they were at work, the overseer commenced whipping her." Plantation clock time and physical violence, then, went together.

What differentiated slaves from Thompson's industrial laborers was that bondpeople succumbed more readily to the dictates of clock time. Unlike free laborers, slaves could not engage fully in a debate over the worth and sanctity of their time. Certainly, they resisted masters' efforts to regulate their work by clock and watch. Some ran away, thus depriving masters of their labor time; others, most notably house hands, feigned ignorance of clock time altogether; and many attempted to carve out their own niches of free time. At most, some slaves negotiated with their masters over how much time was theirs to have. But even this kind of negotiation does not appear to have been widespread, and when it did occur it is surely testimony to the fact that slaves, like Thompson's industrial workers, were debating masters on their own terms, that is, negotiating about time as masters defined it. Most slaves' efforts to resist plantation clock time were unsuccessful because the master could always resort to the whip to enforce punctuality to the clock. The slaves' inability to enter the protracted battle over the legitimacy of the clock as an arbiter of work and rest is revealed most graphically in their almost frenetic responses to the sound of the plantation clock. While it is unlikely that this sense of time was ever internalized to the degree that nineteenth-century industrial-urban workers internalized time, it is nevertheless true that slaves' obedience to the clock was remarkably similar to the time discipline of northern, British, Australian, and Natalian urban-industrial workers. Slaves' obedience to plantation time, for example, appears especially heightened when compared to the behavior of rural Natal Zulus and Australians, who appear to have been able to rely on their own measures of time. In comparative perspective, slaves as clock-conscious workers ranked alongside northern rural farmers and industrial workers rather than with British agricultural laborers, rural South African Zulus, or Australia's rural inhabitants, not least because their masters proved among the most effective, if ruthless, enforcers of clock time in the nineteenth-century world.

There are several ways to interpret the above evidence. First, one might argue that if the South-as-non-capitalist scenario is correct, then the rise of clock time in any historical context is not an accurate indicator of modernity. This I am inclined to reject, not least because I am unwilling to refute Weber and Marx so cavalierly. A second interpretation that is rather more convincing raises some very interesting possibilities. If we agree that an emphasis on clock time, time-thrift, and punctuality is a legitimate and accurate talisman of a modern time consciousness, then we can argue for one or more of several conclusions. First, it seems that antebellum planters were more successful than British, Australian, and Natalian nineteenth-century capitalists in achieving a modern clock consciousness in a rural environment. In the British instance, this is rather hard to swallow, and it may well be that we simply do not yet know enough about the presence of a rural time consciousness in nineteenth-century Britain to say with any real authority that planters and slaves were comparatively more clock conscious than their rural British counterparts. Second, it seems that African-American slave culture was less able to resist the imposition of clock time than was rural Australian or Zulu culture. This interpretation, however, should not be overemphasized, since it is likely that, as recent studies have suggested, southern white culture was not external to African-American culture; rather, the two evolved in a complex, symbiotic relationship, living off of and shaping one another. And yet, with regard to the culture of antebellum time consciousness, this is one area where African-American culture was transformed by Euro-American attitudes toward time. Because colonial planters were themselves just beginning to appreciate the regulatory power of the clock, Euro-American time conceptions had not always prevailed, as Sobel has demonstrated for eighteenth-century Virginia. By the 1830s, however, the situation had changed. Although the slave mode of production was still in place, southern masters were trying to fulfill new cultural and economic imperatives. The specific forces promoting clock consciousness in the antebellum South rendered slaves more American than African and masters more modern than premodern. Once planters in their bid for slave-based modernity had embraced the clock, slaves found themselves more susceptible to masters' insistence, backed as it was by the whip and aural time obedience, on the legitimacy of clock time. What varying degrees of free wage labor failed to do to rural Australian, Zulu, and British workers, the whip and clock-regulated plantation bell succeeded in doing to southern bondpeople. Had these forces been less powerful, had African conceptions of time been less diluted by a comparatively long association with white culture, which, by the late eighteenth century, was beginning to move toward the use of the clock, then southern slaves would probably have been able to resist clock time more effectively. The main factor in converting slaves to clock time, however, was not so much their long and intimate contact with whites compared to that experienced by Natalian and Australian natives. Rather, it was due in larger part to the redoubtable power of the slaveholders' late antebellum regime in forcing the conversion. . . .

Viewed in comparative perspective, then, the slave South was evidently one of the few rural regions in the nineteenth-century world to be affected by a modern clock consciousness. The reasons for this are twofold. First, the slave South either shared or imported most of the forces that had promoted time discipline in other nineteenth-century societies. Second, what it refused to import, free wage labor in factory or agricultural form, mattered less than we have sometimes been led to believe. The slaveholders' drive for a qualified, clock-defined modernity was sufficient to impel both masters and their chattel toward a clock consciousness that was little different from, and in some ways more advanced than, the northern or British form. The whip coupled with the sound of clock time proved as effective in the South as the Protestant work ethic/free wage labor/industrial combination had in the North. Just as the capitalist time consciousness apparent on Martin Bruegel's antebellum northern farms accompanied and in some ways preceded northern industrialism, so the Old South's time-based plantation capitalism foreshadowed the coming of southern nominally free wage labor after the Civil War. Nor should this be considered especially unusual . . . If the time consciousness of the antebellum South is considered modern, then we may add to these formulations by suggesting that the postbellum South's transition to free wage labor was in some ways prefigured by a clock consciousness both nurtured from without and nourished from within the Old South's slave regime.

Notes

1   Barbara Adam, *Timewatch: The Social Analysis of Time* (Cambridge: Polity Press, 1995).
2   Ibid.
3   Gregory Clark, "Factory discipline," *Journal of Economic History*, 54 (March 1994).
4   E. P. Thompson, "Time, work-discipline and industrial capitalism," *Past and Present*, 38 (December 1967).
5   Mark Harrison, "Time, work and the occurrence of crowds 1790–1835," *Past and Present*, 110 (February 1986).
6   Richard D. Brown, *Modernization: The Transformation of American Life, 1600–1865* (New York: Hill and Wang, 1976).
7   Paul Hensley, "Time, work, and social context in New England," *New England Quarterly*, 65 (December 1992).
8   Martin Bruegel, " 'Time that can be relied upon': The evolution of time consciousness in the mid-Hudson Valley, 1790–1860," *Journal of Social History*, 28 (Spring 1995).

9   Graeme Davison, *The Unforgiving Minute: How Australia Learned to Tell the Time* (Melbourne: Oxford University Press, 1993).

10   Keletso E. Atkins, *The Moon is Dead! Give Us Our Money: The Cultural Origins of an African Work Ethic, Natal, South Africa, 1843–1900* (Portsmouth, NH: Heinemann, 1993).

11   Babette M. Levy, "Early Puritanism in the southern and island Colonies," *Proceedings of the American Antiquarian Society*, 70(1) (April-October 1960); Perry Miller, *Errand Into the Wilderness* (Cambridge, MA: The Belknap Press of Harvard University Press, 1956); Edmund S. Morgan, "The Puritan Ethic and the American Revolution," *William and Mary Quarterly*, 3rd series, 24 (January 1967).

12   Eugene D. Genovese, *The Political Economy of Slavery: Studies in the Economy and Society of the Slave South* (New York: Pantheon Books, 1965); *Roll, Jordan, Roll: The World the Slaves Made* (New York: Vintage, 1976); and with Elizabeth Fox-Genovese, *Fruits of Merchant Capital: Slavery and Bourgeois Property in the Rise and Expansion of Capitalism* (New York: Oxford University Press, 1983).

13   Bertram Wyatt-Brown, "Modernizing southern slavery: The proslavery argument reinterpreted," in *Region, Race, and Reconstruction: Essays in Honor of C. Vann Woodward*, ed. J. Morgan Kousser and James M. McPherson (New York: Oxford University Press, 1982).

14   Gavin Wright, *Old South, New South: Revolutions in the Southern Economy since the Civil War* (New York: Basic Books, 1986); and *The Political Economy of the Cotton South: Households, Markets, and Wealth in the Nineteenth Century* (New York: W.W. Norton and Company, 1978).

15   John F. Olson, "Clock time versus real time: A comparison of the lengths of the northern and southern agricultural work years," in *Without Consent or Contract: The Rise and Fall of American Slavery: Technical Papers*, ed. Robert William Fogel and Stanley L. Engerman, vol. 1 (New York: W. W. Norton and Company, 1992).

Study Questions and Further Reading for Part I

1   What do you think Luraghi means when he describes southern slaveholders as "the seigneurial class"?
2   Why, according to Luraghi, should Old South planters not be characterized as "capitalists"?
3   Why did the Old South's master class use clock time and to what effect?
4   Is it possible to reconcile the interpretations of the Old South advanced by Luraghi and Smith? Where are there areas of agreement between the two historians?

Anderson, Ralph V. and Gallman, Robert E. 1977: Slaves as fixed capital: Slave labor and southern economic development. *Journal of American History*, 64, 24–46.

Bateman, Fred and Weiss, Thomas 1981: *A Deplorable Scarcity: The Failure of Industrialization in the Slave Economy*. Chapel Hill: University of North Carolina Press.

Blassingame, John W. 1972: *The Slave Community: Plantation Life in the Antebellum South*. New York: Oxford University Press.

Bowman, Shearer Davis 1980: Antebellum planters and Vomarz junkers in comparative perspective. *American Historical Review*, 85, 779–808.

Coclanis, Peter A. 1989: *The Shadow of a Dream: Economic Life and Death in the South Carolina Low Country 1670–1920*. New York: Oxford University Press.

Dunaway, Wilma 1996: *The First American Frontier: Transition to Capitalism in Southern Appalachia, 1700–1860*. Chapel Hill: University of North Carolina Press.

Fogel, Robert William 1989: *Without Consent or Contract: The Rise and Fall of American Slavery*. New York: W. W. Norton and Company.

Fogel, Robert William and Engerman, Stanley L. 1974: *Time on the Cross: The Economics of American Negro Slavery*. 2 vols. Boston: Little, Brown and Company.

Genovese, Eugene D. 1965: *The Political Economy of Slavery: Studies in the Economy and Society of the Slave South*. New York: Pantheon.

Metzer, Jacob 1975: Rational management, modern business practices, and economies of scale in the ante-bellum southern plantations. *Explorations in Economic History*, 12, 123–50.

Oakes, James 1982: *The Ruling Race: A History of American Slaveholders*. New York: Knopf.

Oakes, James 1990: *Slavery and Freedom: An Interpretation of the Old South*. New York: Knopf.

Patterson, Orlando 1969: *The Sociology of Slavery: An Analysis of the Origins, Development, and Structure of Negro Slave Society in Jamaica*. Rutherford, NJ: Fairleigh Dickinson University Press.

Rawick, George P. 1972: *From Sundown to Sunup: The Making of the Black Community*. Westport, CT: Greenwood Press.

Shore, Laurence 1986: *Southern Capitalists: The Ideological Leadership of an Elite, 1832–1885*. Chapel Hill: University of North Carolina Press.

Smith, Mark M. 1997: *Mastered by the Clock: Time, Slavery, and Freedom in the American South*. Chapel Hill: University of North Carolina Press.

Wade, Richard C. 1964: *Slavery in the Cities: The South, 1820–1860*. New York: Oxford University Press.

Wahl, Jenny Bourne 1998: *The Bondsman's Burden: An Economic Analysis of the Common Law of Southern Slavery*. New York: Cambridge University Press.

Woodman, Harold D. 1963: "The profitability of slavery: A historical perennial." *Journal of Southern History*, 29, 303–25.

Wright, Gavin 1978: *The Political Economy of the Cotton South: Households, Markets, and Wealth in the Nineteenth Century*. New York: W. W. Norton and Company.

Part II
Southern Honor, Southern Violence

Introduction to Documents and Essays

Was the Old South a place where gentlemen decorously defended their honor in "civilized" duels? Or was it a place where men ripped eyes from one another and sharpened their fingernails in an effort to inflict damage on opponents who had insulted them? Here, we catch glimpses of the Old South's notions of honor and how different men of different classes – poor whites and affluent slaveholders – defended that honor. The essays invite comparison, for there were plainly differences in how men responded to slights, perceived and real. But there were also similarities for, as both essays suggest, the Old South was a touchy society where even small slights could cause great affront.

3

The Appearance of Honor and the Honor of Appearance

Affronts to Honor in a Southern Newspaper, 1843

The import of this document will become clearer once the accompanying essay on the Feejee [or Fejee] mermaid has been read. However, even in isolation, the document – part of an exchange between two men published in the Charleston, South Carolina, *Courier* in 1843 – is suggestive of the import-ance southern gentlemen attached to words and their public reputation and appearance. (From the Charleston *Courier*, Feb. 1, 1843)

The Mermaid, and "No Humbug" – As we have been entirely without apprehension of the ability of the *Mercury* writer, signing himself "No Humbug," to rob us of that which would not enrich him but would make us poor indeed, we have taken our leisure for reply to his unprovoked and uncivil assault upon us, giving preference and precedence to the weightier matters of the law, and other graver calls on our time and attention. Before grappling with our antagonist, how-ever, it may be proper to explain how we got involved in this *Mermaid* scrape. We were, bona fide, on our way to engage in the duties and enjoy the pleasures of Odd Fellowship, when, journeying with this intent, we were arrested or intercepted at the very foot of the stair-case, which we were about ascending, by the varied and attractive exhibition of which the Mermaid constituted one of the *charms*. Entering the room, we were soon in full sympathy of wonder and enjoyment, with adults and children, at the skill with which the ductile glass was blown or moulded into forms of exquisite beauty and grace; at the success in illusion and humor of ventriloquial comedy and farce; . . . and, "last, not least," at the Fejee Mermaid and its associate curiosities. The superintendent of the varied show, a gentleman of exceedingly bland and prepossessing countenance, carriage and deportment, hearing that a representative of the press was in the room, sent for us, and, voluntarily removing the glass from the Fejee beauty, placed her in our hands, and invited us and two other gentlemen present to give her the closest scrutiny; and after the best examination that the eye and the touch enabled us to give the curious object, we all agreed, whatever may have been our varying degrees of faith or scepticism, that if there was deception, it passed the ken of our senses. We were somewhat taken by surprise, at the readiness with which the Fejee lady was submitted to our handling and inspection, in consequence of the appearance of an article in the *Mercury*, signed "No Humbug," in which the writer undertook to pronounce the Mermaid "a smoke dried affair," "a clumsy affair," "the seams not sufficiently covered to conceal the point of union between fish and monkey, even through a glass case," out of which he intimated the proprietor would not permit it, and finally "a contemptible hoax" – and ever carrying his imprudence and injustice so far as to denounce the exhibitor, as an impostor, advising him to give leg bail. . . . Finding matters differing so much from what we had expected, we penned a hasty paragraph that very night, succinctly stating the facts: attacking nobody, and not assuming to speak *ex cathedra* or scientifically on the subject; but modestly expressing the opinion that the strange object was not, as had been supposed, a compound of monkey's head and fish's tail, but was either altogether the work of nature or altogether the production of art – adding at the same time our *inclination* to have faith on the occasion, and assigning certain analogical reasons, drawn from the animal and vegetable kingdoms, for the incipient belief that was in us. For such presumption on our part, we have incurred it seems, the displeasure of Mr. "No Humbug"; and he has assaulted us whip in hand, but we mean to take it from him and lay it, and that smartly, on his own shoulders. But may not the secret of our assailant's indignation be found, less in our modest difference of opinion, than in our refusal to give place to his original lucubration in our columns, on the express ground that it was grossly unjust to denounce one as an impostor, when the previous and obvious courtesy of requesting submission to a test had been confessedly omitted?

> "Sweet thing it is to see one's name in print –
> A book's a book, although there's nothing in't."

We confess we set down much to the spleen of the disappointed author in this matter; he wished his opinions to be widely circulated by a swift *Courier*, and was obliged forsooth, to put up with a half fledged or one winged *Mercury*.

Public Accusations of Falsehood, 1833

Here, the public attack against a man's character, the reasons for the charges, and the accused's reaction to the slighting of his name and public reputation are presented in clear profile. This time, the evidence is from Virginia's Richmond *Enquirer* in 1833. (From the Richmond *Enquirer*, May 14, 1833)

We lay before our readers a statement made by R. B. Randolph, late a Lieutenant in the Navy of the United States, from which he has been recently dismissed by the President, relative to his accounts as acting purser, in the room of Mr. Timberlake, together with the decision of the President in relation to the report of the court of enquiry, appointed to investigate his accounts. These documents contain a statement of the principal facts connected with the case; and with a few explanations taken from a statement made by the forth auditor relative to the causes which led to an examination into the case, after the account had been closed by his predecessor, and from the report of the court of enquiry, both of which are published in the Globe, will afford a clear insight into the subject. There has been so much said upon this subject that the public will naturally, we presume, be anxious to know something about the facts of the case; and the late assault made by Randolph upon the President, on account of his dismissal, will, we presume, increase the desire in the public mind to know more about the matter. With the view, therefore, of gratifying the curiosity of our readers upon the subject, we lay before them such a statement as will give them a full view of the matter.

The documents . . . show in what manner Mr. Randolph came into the situation of acting pursur [sic], and from those statements it will clearly appear that, to say the least of it, there was a gross neglect on the part of Mr. Randolph with regard to conforming to the rules of the Navy, in taking upon himself the discharge of the important duties of purser. Taking his own statement, it appears that he grossly violated those rules, by taking possession of the money and property which was left by Mr. Timberlake before an inventory had been taken of them. But from the statement of Captain Patterson, whose statement we have certainly as much right to believe as that of Randolph, (particularly as the former is given upon oath, and by one who has no direct interest in the matter, and the other is the mere naked assertion of one deeply interested,) it would appear that the inventory was directed to be taken, and that Randolph declared to him that it had been transmitted to the proper accounting officer at Washington, but it was never received there, and is now alleged never to have been taken. This omission, if we suppose it to have been an omission, was so highly improper that the court of enquiry, composed of Randolph's friends, condemn it in decided terms. But it seems that he not only neglected an attention to the rules of the Navy in this particular, but omitted to charge himself with the property thus received, or to give to the accounting officer any account respecting it; and for this he is also condemned by the court. It appears moreover that by taking receipts for money paid on Mr. Timberlake's account, as if they had been paid before his death the accounts were so blended that it was almost impossible to separate them, and for this he is condemned by the court; besides various other matters. Mr. Randolph pretends to justify himself for his neglect in relation to the taking of an inventory by asserting that the rules of the Navy did not require it, but gives an extract from the rules which clearly commands it to be done. . . .

In the statement of Mr. Kendall we are informed, that the large amount of the defalcation which was charged to an enquiry into the manner in which the money and other property left him at the time of his death had been disposed of, and the amount of money which had been received and expended by Mr. Randolph as his successor; and from the statement of the accounts of the latter it appears that he had received in slops at Port Mahon $742.50, and $11,000, at Gibraltar, and is credited with $20,729.98, for money paid and stores returned, being an excess over his receipts of near $9,000, which amount was paid to him on the settlement of his account, by the accounting officers under Mr. Adams. Being at a loss to conceive where the funds were received from which this large excess were made, Mr. Kendall requested of Mr. Randolph an explanation. This, however, he either could or would not give; but met the request with a violent display of temper, on the ground of its indicating on the part of the Auditor a disposition to injure him. On this subject the court of enquiry remark that the large amount of this excess ought to have suggested to Mr. Randolph the propriety of asking for an examination into the situation of his accounts without waiting to be called upon for an explanation; and Mr. Randolph's display of temper, so far from deterring Mr. Kendall from pressing the subject, seems only to have had the opposite effect, until the examination was made; and the result is now laid before the public.

Codes of Honor and Dueling, 1858

If honor and codes of everyday practice were highly ritualized, so was the process of identifying affronts to honor and redressing the grievance. Among the several handbooks on the subject published in the antebellum period, John Lyde Wilson's 1858 *The Code of Honor* defined when, precisely, an affront to honor was indeed an insult and how gentlemen should go about seeking redress. (From John Lyde Wilson, *The Code of Honor; or Rules for the Government of Principals and Seconds in Duelling* (Charleston, SC: James Phinney, 1858), pp. 11–12, 32–3)

Chapter I.
The Person Insulted, Before Challenge Sent.
1. Whenever you believe that you are insulted, if the insult be in public and by words or behavior, never resent it there, if you have self-command enough to avoid noticing it. If resented there, you offer an indignity to the company, which you should not.
2. If the insult be by blows or any personal indignity, it may be resented at the moment, for the insult to the company did not originate with you. But although resented at the moment, you are bound still to have satisfaction, and must therefore make the demand.
3. When you believe yourself aggrieved, be silent on the matter, and see your friend, who is to act for you, as soon as possible.
4. Never send a challenge in the first instance, for that precludes all negotiation. Let your note be in the language of a gentleman, and let the subject matter of complaint be truly and fairly set forth, cautiously avoiding attributing to the adverse party any improper motive. . . .

Chapter VIII.
The Degrees of Insult and How Compromised.
1. The prevailing rule is, that words used in retort, although more violent and disrespectful than those first used, will not satisfy, – words being no satisfaction for words.
2. When words are used, and a blow given in return, the insult is avenged; and if redress be sought, it must be from the person receiving the blow . . . .
4. Insults at a wine table, when the company are over-excited, must be answered for; and if the party insulting have no recollection of the insult, it is his duty to say so in writing, and negative the insult. For instance, if a man say: "you are a liar and no gentleman," he must, in addition to the plea of the want of recollection, say: "I believe the party insulted to be a man of strictest veracity and a gentleman."

The Appearance of Honor and the Honor of Appearance

Kenneth S. Greenberg

Sometimes, white men of the antebellum South pulled, or tweaked, one another's noses. Slaves never pulled anyone's nose; neither did white women. Nose pulling was a meaningful gesture that appeared almost exclusively in the active vocabulary of white men. To pull a nose was to communicate a complex set of meanings to an antagonist and an audience. What did the act mean to the men who performed it and witnessed it? For Southern white men, nose pulling was an action embedded in a larger system of signs – a "language" of honor. One must reconstruct the system in order to understand the meaning of its parts.

To understand the system of meanings that surrounded nose pulling in the South, it is necessary to interpret and to connect parts of white male language that may at first appear to be unrelated. En route to an analysis of nose pulling, this chapter explains why P. T. Barnum was less popular in the South than in the North; how scientific and market activities were connected to each other but not to the world of honor; why men of honor dueled over disagreements that people outside their tradition regarded as trivial; why practical jokes had a different meaning for men of honor than for men of trade; why many antidueling laws required the multilation of men who dueled; why abolitionists and proslavery apologists read the meaning of scars on the backs of slaves differently; and why the nose was more important than the genitals to Southern gentlemen. One thread runs through and around each of these cultural phenomena. Each demonstrates that Southern men of honor were "superficial." They were concerned, to a degree we would consider unusual, with the surface of things – with the world of appearances.

One good way to approach the language of white men of honor is through an analysis of a dispute occasioned by the exhibition of the Feejee Mermaid to the people of Charleston, South Carolina, in early

From Greenberg, Kenneth S., "The nose, the lie, and the duel," in his *Honor and Slavery: Lies, Duels, Noses, Masks, Dressing as a Woman, Gifts, Strangers, Death, Humanitarianism, Slave Rebellions, the Proslavery Argument, Baseball, Hunting, and Gambling in the Old South.* (Princeton, NJ: Princeton University Press, 1996), pp. 3–23. Copyright © 1996 by Kenneth S. Greenberg. Published by Princeton University Press. Excerpt reprinted by permission of Princeton University Press and the author.

1843. This event contains no explicit mention of noses (or lies or duels), but it harbors many oblique references. The story begins with a collaboration between Moses Kimball of Boston, the owner of the mermaid, and P. T. Barnum, who arranged for its exhibition. Barnum, that quintessential Connecticut Yankee, that master of deceit, showmanship, and humbug in nineteenth-century America, undoubtedly was aware from the start that the mermaid was a fake – the upper torso of a dead monkey skillfully joined to the lower body of a fish. Nevertheless, he hired a manager to take it on tour and arranged for an elaborate publicity campaign to herald its arrival in Philadelphia and New York. The exhibit met with such an enthusiastic reception in these cities that Barnum decided on a tour of the South that began in Charleston, South Carolina, early in 1843.

The mermaid stirred more than wonder upon its arrival in the South. It became the object of a controversy that threatened to break into violence. The disturbance began in the newspapers of Charleston just after the mermaid arrived. Richard Yeadon, a local lawyer and one of the three editors of the *Charleston Courier*, wrote an unsigned review of the exhibit, venturing his opinion that the mermaid was probably a natural object and that he could detect no seam to indicate that it was an artificial combination of ape and fish. "We were permitted to handle and examine it as closely as could be effected by touch and sight," he wrote, "and ... if there be any deception, it is beyond the discovery of both those senses." But, at almost the same time, a very different article appeared in the rival *Charleston Mercury*. Writing under the name "No Humbug," the respected naturalist and Lutheran minister John Bachman declared the mermaid to be a fraud, "a fishes tail attached to the head and shoulders of a Baboon," "a clumsy affair," "a smoke dried affair" created by "our Yankee neighbors." He suggested that the naturalists of Charleston should be allowed to examine it, and if they found it to be a hoax they should "throw the creature into the fire" and the exhibitor should "clear himself from the city as fast as his heels can carry him." The debate initiated by these notes led to the publication of more than two dozen letters during the next few months – some of considerable length, occasionally occupying more than a quarter of all the article space in the major South Carolina newspapers.

Among the dispute's many interesting features was Bachman's contention that the editors of the *Courier* had failed to treat him with respect. He had originally gone to them with his letter denouncing the exhibit as a fraud. They refused to publish it because they found the language of the letter "too severe." He then brought it to the *Mercury*, whose editors promptly printed it – only to discover that the *Courier* had not only rejected his letter but also published an editorial review in support of the mermaid. "Who was the writer of this anonymous communication [the editorial] I am not prepared to say," Bachman wrote with barely concealed fury, "and I leave the public to judge both of the author and the motives of its insertion in the very nick of time to serve as a foil to protect an Impostor [the exhibitor of the mermaid] from public indignation."

At the same time, Bachman raised the question of who was competent to pass judgment on the mermaid. Joined by other South Carolina scientists, he wondered why the lawyer and editor, Yeadon, felt qualified to make statements about matters scientific. Bachman had seen a seam at the juncture of fish and monkey, and if Yeadon did not detect one, it was only because he was "untrained in such observations." Yeadon conceded that he was no scientist and emphasized that he had not made an unequivocal claim about the authenticity of the mermaid – he had stated only that, when he took it from the case, he could neither see nor feel a seam. He cared "not a whit, not a stiver, whether the Mermaid is real or not." He only demanded that his observation be treated with respect. "Mr. No Humbug," Yeadon claimed, had unfairly attacked him: "he has assaulted us whip in hand, but we mean to take it from him and lay it, and that smartly, on his own shoulders."

Another theme in the dispute involved the use of names and pseudonyms. The original articles were either unsigned editorials or pieces signed with noms de plume such as "No Humbug" and "The Man Who Exhibits the Mermaid." But after February 6, the real names began to appear in print. This was an important transition. Yeadon apparently had long felt that, as editor of the *Courier,* he could not maintain anonymity as easily as could Bachman. An inequality had developed. He objected to his opponent's practice of addressing his letters to "the editor of the *Courier."* There were three editors, and it was offensive, Yeadon felt, to single out one by not using the plural form of address. The singular form of address had begun to move the dispute to a more dangerous and personal level. Moreover, Yeadon believed that Bachman had mentioned his name to other people, and he objected that "it [his name] was a common subject of conversation out of doors promiscuously," with the result that he had been "frequently met with the taunt that Mr. – has given it to you well."

In fact, the moment of transition from anonymity to names was so delicate that it required the intervention of "a mutual friend" to prevent the dispute from ending in an exchange of pistol shots. The mutual friend negotiated an agreement that allowed for the simultaneous public use of real names by each party. In the February 6 issue of the *Courier* Yeadon wrote that "an explanatory interview and consequent cessation of hostilities" had been effected, "the *amende honorable* has been made us, and mutual explanations were given." Both men then began to sign their names to their articles. But the anonymity issue would not die. When Yeadon later reverted to singing his initials – a tactic that did not really hide his identity but indicated a slight movement away from the open assertion of names that had become characteristic of the dispute – Bachman complained to the editor of the *Courier* (who of course was Yeadon), "I trust I am not making an unfair request that when any of your correspondents undertake to correct my statements in your Journal, you require them to give their names in full. In these matters I prefer seeing something beyond initials." Clearly, some important maneuvering was involved here.

What is most startling about the debate over the Feejee Mermaid is the remarkable lack of interest in the mermaid itself. While in another context the scientists might have had a desire to discover whether or not this was a natural mermaid, neither they nor Yeadon devoted much of their newspaper discussion to that topic. More important were such matters as whether Bachman had been handled with dignity by the *Courier*, whether Yeadon's observation that he could see no seam had been treated with proper respect by the scientists, and whether the parties had properly or improperly used and treated pseudonyms supplied by the writers. It was not a debate about whether the Feejee Mermaid was a real mermaid or a hoax. Yeadon himself had said so unequivocally. He "care[d] not a whit, not a stiver, whether the Mermaid is real or not." Although the mermaid had left town by the end of January, the dispute continued to rage until late March. The central concern of these men was to have their words, names, and pseudonyms treated with respect. Honor was at stake. Penetration into the secrets of nature was of little interest.

If the dispute over the Feejee Mermaid had been an isolated event in antebellum Southern history, it could be dismissed as trivial, but it was not. The lack of interest in the Feejee Mermaid and in other secrets of nature was characteristic of the antebellum South. The incident may clarify why scientists and other intellectuals in this culture felt unappreciated. Historians have long been aware of the complaints of neglect by the intellectuals of the South. Some have attributed the problem to the absence of cities and the consequent lack of a reading public concentrated in urban areas. Others have suggested that intellectuals play a marginal role in most societies. While these explanations offer some insight into the problems of Southern thinkers, the Feejee Mermaid episode points in another direction.

A central concern of nineteenth-century scientific and intellectual activity was to penetrate into the secrets of nature, to move from the level of superficial appearance to a deeper, hidden reality; it therefore may have involved a sensibility alien to antebellum Southern white male culture. Many cultures concerned with honor value appearance highly. Their members project themselves through how they look and what they say. They are treated honorably when their projections are respected and accepted as true. The central issue of concern to men in such a culture is not the nature of some underlying reality but the acceptance of their projections. They "care not a whit" about the reality of the mermaid. The men who achieve the most honorable positions in such a culture are statesmen – men whose vision of themselves and their world is confirmed by popular acclamation. Intellectuals, who conceive of their activity as exposing hidden levels of reality, are engaged in work of peripheral interest.

The Feejee Mermaid episode also echoed the world of Southern dueling. This connection is significant because the duel was a central ritual of antebellum Southern life, embodying many core values of white society. Evidence of its centrality exists everywhere. Large numbers of public figures participated in duels as principals or seconds; the South maintained a tenacious attachment to the institution even as it died in the North. Even more revealing of its importance in Southern life are the many examples of men who achieved great political success after they dueled, and men who feared that to refuse a duel was to become an outcast in the culture, and the almost complete absence of any successful prosecution of the substantial number of men who killed others in duels.

The Feejee Mermaid dispute resembled the duel in several striking ways. First, the form of the dispute was remarkably similar to the form of typical nineteenth-century dueling encounters. In both cases the conflict originated in insulting words or actions. Then came a carefully worded exchange of letters in which each party tried to describe how he had been injured – how he had not been treated with the kind of courtesy due him as a social equal. There was the intervention of another party whose job it was to bring about a reconciliation through a carefully constructed understanding in which each party explained his language and acknowledged his equality with the other. Even the publication of the details of the Feejee Mermaid dispute paralleled a practice typical of dueling encounters. A duel was a theatrical display for public consumption, and the parties expected descriptions of the events to be widely circulated. The Feejee Mermaid episode did not lead to an exchange of pistol shots, but neither did the vast majority of conflicts that were part of the world of dueling.

Second, participants in dueling encounters and in the Feejee Mermaid case expressed similar conceptions of what constituted an insult. At the heart of both encounters was the accusation of lying. Consider the importance of lying as an insult in a typical dueling dispute. Although white men of the South came in conflict with each other over many issues, they did not always duel. Only certain kinds of insulting language and behavior led to duels. The central insult that could turn a disagreement into a duel involved a direct or indirect attack on someone's word – the accusation that a man was a liar. To "give someone the lie," as it was called, had always been an insult of great consequence among men of honor. As one early-seventeenth-century English writer noted, "It is reputed so great a shame to be accounted a lyer, that any other injury is canceled by giving the lie, and he that receiveth it standeth so charged in his honor and reputation, that he cannot disburden himself of that imputation, but by the striking of him that hath so given it, or by chalenging him the combat."

It is easy to underestimate the importance of "giving the lie" as a reason for Southern duels without a broad understanding of what Southern white men had in mind by "lying." Sometimes, people would say it quite directly: "I hold Francis H. Welman a Liar, Coward and Poltroon," wrote John Moorehead in an 1809 issue of the *Savannah Republican*. But to search for the actual word "liar" in Southern insults is to miss the pervasive presence of the charge. "Giving the lie" to someone meant announcing that his appearance differed from his true nature – proclaiming as false his projection of himself. Thus the charge of being a coward or a poltroon was another form of the charge of lying: the accuser unmasked the accused. The goal of this unmasking was not to discover the real character underneath but to expose and shame an opponent. It was to identify an image as falsely projected and to show contempt for it. This was a charge made not by a scientist in search of hidden truths but by a gentleman intending to dishonor someone. For example, one man implicitly made the accusation of the lie as he pointed out his enemy to an audience. "Citizens," he announced, "this is not the profile of a man; it is the profile of a dog!" Similarly, when Charles A. Luzenberg woke up one day in antebellum New Orleans, opened his morning newspaper, and read a note accusing him of being a "puppy" who had "long humbugged the community with false ideas of his courage," he understood that someone was trying to unmask him – someone was accusing him of lying.

The Feejee Mermaid episode also involved the charge of lying. Yeadon worried that his words in support of the mermaid had been discounted. He had run his hands over the surface of the creature and detected no seam. His projection of the truth and thereby of himself had become connected to the appearance of the mermaid. Bachman, after having his own words rejected for publication in Yeadon's paper, exposed the humbuggery of the mermaid as a "clumsy affair" and thus came close to accusing Yeadon of lying. The dispute over the use of pseudonyms was actually another, even more complicated conversation about the relationship between asserted appearance and reality. The discussion touched on the dangerous issue of the connection between a man's real character and the character projected by a pseudonym. As the dispute moved from pseudonyms to names, Yeadon and Bachman each had to avoid the public perception that he had been unmasked and thereby shamed by his opponent. To avoid a confrontation that could only end in a duel, they had to move from pseudonyms to real names simultaneously; each had to unmask himself and have his new projection immediately accepted by his opponent.

Both the duel and the Feejee Mermaid episode evidence a world that placed a high value on appearances as asserted and projected through the words of honorable gentlemen. Many Northern men, the type who shared the values of the mermaid-exhibitor P. T. Barnum, could never fully understand this world. This is not to suggest that men like Barnum failed to appreciate the value of self-promotion and the manipulation of appearances. Barnum, after all, was the great showman of the nineteenth century. He was the virtual founder of modern American print advertising. He transformed Joice Heth, an elderly and nearly blind black woman, into "the most astonishing and interesting curiosity in the world," the 161-year-old former nurse of George Washington; he turned Tom Thumb from a very short person into a world celebrity; he elevated a large mammal into Jumbo the Elephant and then used him to advertise thread and baking powder – how could such a man not value the world of appearances? Yet it was precisely because he could manipulate such a world and simultaneously make money from it that he could never really see it as worthy of serious respect or disrespect. Words were his instruments in pursuit of gain; they were not linked to honor or dishonor. Perhaps nothing so clearly sums up Barnum's attitude toward the surface of images and language as his description of his first business experience in a Connecticut country store: "The customers cheated us in their fabrics, we cheated the customers with our goods. Each party expected to be cheated, if it was possible. Our eyes and not our ears, had to be our masters. We must believe little that we saw, and less that we heard." No nineteenth-century merchant could have expressed the core assumptions of this worldview with greater clarity. The world of trade was a world full of liars. People constantly unmasked each other, but at stake were profit and loss rather than honor and dishonor. When Bachman called his mermaid a fake, Barnum did not reach for his gun but instead thought of ways to turn the charge to his profit. . . .

Just as one can connect Barnum's experience of trade to his ideas about appearance, one can relate the white Southern experience of slavery to the white Southern attitude toward the surface of the world.

Masters and potential masters distinguished themselves from slaves in many ways, but one of the most important distinctions involved the issue of lying. The words of the master had to be accorded respect and accepted as true simply because they were the words of a man of honor. The words of the slave could never become objects of honor. Whites assumed that slaves lied all the time – and that their lies were intimately connected to their position as slaves. Masters articulated these beliefs when they argued that it was absurd for slaves to engage in duels and that the testimony of blacks could never be used in legal cases involving whites. Moreover, for many masters, the lie was at the heart of their problems with slave labor. Instead of engaging in the open confrontation expected of men of honor, slaves seemed to resist their masters by stealth and deceit. They stole food, ran away, burned buildings, broke tools, feigned illness or laziness, and sometimes even poisoned their masters' or mistresses' food. Masters repeatedly expressed exasperation about the deceitful behavior of their slaves. But in another sense, masters welcomed the chance to catch their slaves in lies. Their own honor and the respect accorded their words could then stand in favorable contrast to the dishonored condition of their slaves.

The clash between the lie as expressed in the world of the duel and the lie in the world of P. T. Barnum recurred in other places in nineteenth-century American culture. For example, men of honor and Barnum reacted quite differently to lies as expressed in practical jokes, a form of play Barnum loved. In a way, his entire career was based on a series of practical jokes – lying to the public in order to make money. But Barnum also enjoyed practical jokes outside the world of show business. In an echo of many market transactions, he especially enjoyed tricking a man who was trying to trick him. In his autobiography, Barnum proudly told the story of the "whole shirt" trick. A noted joker named Darrow used to frequent the barroom of a Bridgeport hotel and prey on unsuspecting guests. A favorite trick of Darrow's was to taunt a man with the declaration that he was probably wearing tattered clothes and did not have a whole shirt on his back. Darrow would persuade the man to bet that he did have a whole shirt on his back and then triumphantly point out that all men wore only half their shirts on their backs. One day, Barnum deliberately allowed himself to be drawn into the bet, then produced a whole shirt that he had carefully folded onto his back beneath his vest. Darrow was furious, but he paid what he owed, and the entire barroom had a good laugh and a round of drinks. Like the tricks played in the marketplaces frequented by men of trade, this joke did not make Barnum feel his life was in danger. Barnum had tricked Darrow this time. Darrow would trick Barnum and others the next time. That was life in the world of the market.

But a different set of meanings attended practical jokes among men of honor. J. Marion Sims describes one incident that parallels Barnum's joke except in its markedly different consequences. While he was at South Carolina College, Sims roomed with a group of other young Carolina gentlemen, including James Aiken and Boykin Witherspoon. One day at dinner, Aiken playfully pulled Sims's chair away just as Sims was about to be seated. Sims, however, seeing the motion out of the corner of his eye, did not sit down but reached over and pulled Witherspoon's chair away from him. Witherspoon fell on the floor. Unlike the men in the barroom with Barnum, however, no one thought this was funny. This was a moment of danger, not of laughter. One man had manipulated the world of appearances in order to humiliate another man. Sims immediately understood the seriousness of what had happened. As he later described it, "I apologized in the humblest manner that I possibly could. I assured him that I did not intend to throw him down, that I regretted it then, and that I was not ashamed to say that I was heartily sorry and should regret it always." Witherspoon said he was not satisfied. After dinner, he confronted Sims again. Sims repeated the abject apology, yet Witherspoon was still not satisfied. At this point, Sims believed he had humbled himself as much as was possible for a gentleman. "Now, Sir, help yourself," Sims finally blurted, meaning that he was willing to give Witherspoon satisfaction in a duel. Sims would apologize no more for fear that his friends, witnesses to the entire series of events, might think he was humbling himself in order to avoid risking his life in a duel. Everyone understood that this kind of joke in South Carolina did not end in laughter and a round of drinks. It was likely to end in death....

Conflicting conceptions of the lie between men inside and outside the culture of honor are apparent in the failure of many critics of the duel – frequently men outside Southern culture – to make sense of the world of the duelists. Benjamin Franklin, for example, wrote to a friend in 1784 that he could not understand the logic of the duel: "A man says something which another tells him is a lie. They fight, but whichever is killed the point in dispute remains unsettled." Franklin continued with an illustrative anecdote. A famous French duelist, St. Froix, was sitting at a cafe and turned to a stranger, asking him to move away because he smelled. "This is an affront," exclaimed the stranger. "You must fight me." "I will fight you if you insist on it," St. Froix replied, "but I do not see how that will mend the matter, for if you kill me I shall smell too, and if I kill you, you will smell, if possible, worse than you do at present." Whether or not the anecdote is true, men of honor would not have gleaned from it the point made by Franklin. For him, the duel seemed a pointless activity because it could not determine whether a man had really lied or whether he really smelled; it had no practical result. If Franklin had been involved in the Feejee Mermaid dispute, he probably would have used the same logic to push for an internal examination of the mermaid, rather than lingering over seemingly trivial insults. But men of honor "care not a whit" about real mermaids or real lies or real smells. What is central to their disputes is that someone has given expression to an insult. When the man of honor is told that he smells, he does not draw a bath – he draws his pistol. The man of honor does not care if he stinks, but he does care that someone has accused him of stinking.

Some critics of the duel did understand the causes of these encounters. One can see this in some of the laws designed to eliminate duels. No antidueling law ever worked to repress the institution; most people refused to treat men of honor in the ways demanded by such laws. But many of these laws at least show an understanding of the nature of the duel. For example, one law provided that the dead duelist should be "buried without a coffin, with a stake drove through the body." The survivor should be executed and similarly buried. A later revision offered an alternative to burial with a stake. The body could be delivered to "any surgeon or surgeons to be dissected and anatomized." Other laws ordered gibbeting – hanging the dead bodies to rot in public. But in the United States, by the nineteenth century the most common antidueling penalty was a disqualification from holding office. This may seem a rather strange development, a break from past punishment practices. But there are similarities among the stake through the heart, the gibbet, and the disqualification from office: all are ways of dishonoring a person in a culture of honor. Moreover, all involve the same technique: they prevent an individual from creating an image of himself that might become an object of public honor. To withhold office from a statesman is to prevent the public from confirming his vision of himself. To mutilate his dead body is to turn his physical projection into an ugly object worthy of scorn and shame.

The antidueling laws that struck at the body of the duelist show that some legislators understood the nature of men of honor. What was important to a man of honor was respect for the parts of a man that were visible to the public. These visible parts included his words and his version of the truth. They also included the visible surface of his body. This concern for the body can be seen in many different contexts in the culture of honor. To gouge out an eye or otherwise mutilate the face of an enemy was the most common objective of men involved in fistfights. With the possible exception of wounds received in battle, the mutilation itself was a dishonor no matter how it was actually acquired. In a sense, all mutilations were equal because men read the character of other men through the external physical features of their faces and bodies. This attitude toward appearance was given expression in the many letters of reference and descriptions of great men that mentioned their noble features. One can also see it in the way white Southerners used skin color as a way of determining the character of a man.

The same attitude toward the external appears in the masters' interpretation of scars on the backs of their slaves. For white Southerners, the mark of the whip on the back of a slave was a sign of the slave's bad character and "vicious temper." When the abolitionists disagreed, interpreting the scars on a slave as a sign of the bad character of the master or as an expression of the evils of enslavement, they were clashing with white Southerners in a fundamental way. This dispute involved not simply a difference of interpretation over the sign of the scar but also a different conception of the nature of reading signs. The abolitionists read for meaning beneath and beyond the surface. They found it important to imagine the scene behind the scar, and they recreated it endless times in word and woodcut. But men of honor did not linger over the scene that gave rise to the scar; it was irrelevant. The scar, in a sense, spoke for itself – or rather spoke about the man whose body carried it – regardless of the process or the larger set of relations that brought it into existence. Men of honor "care not a whit" if the mermaid is real.

This brings us to the nose. For Southern men of honor, the nose was the part of the face that preceded a man as he moved in the world. It was the most prominent physical projection of a man's character, and it was always exposed to the gaze of others. Little wonder that men of honor should regard the nose as the most important part of their bodies. As one antebellum Southern writer described it in a humorous, but also deadly serious, article on noses, "No organ of the body is so characteristic as the nose. A man may lose an eye or an ear without altering his features essentially. Not so with the nose." He went on to describe a man with "a most extravagantly protuberant nose" – a nose that "moved to and fro like a pendulum" – who had decided to have it trimmed by a doctor. "I saw him afterwards," he wrote, "and did not recognize him. I do not recognize him now, nor do I intend to. His individuality, his whole identity is lost. . . . The features do not fit; they become incongruous; he is himself no more; for, in truth, the individuality of a man is centred in his nose. Hence it is that nature, to indicate its great importance, has granted us but one nose, while all other organs are supplied in pairs." That this writer had it wrong – not all organs come in pairs – is another illustration of the focus of a man of honor. Clearly, he was comparing the nose to the eyes and the ears. The liver, the heart, the penis, and the stomach were not even considered. A man's character was expressed in what could be publicly displayed, not in what was hidden under clothes or skin. And the man of honor demanded respect for this display. Men of honor do not trim their noses. If P. T. Barnum, a man outside the tradition of honor, had a nose that drew laughs, he might have charged admission; Cyrano de Bergerac, on the other hand, fought duels with those who mocked his protuberance.

One of the greatest insults for a man of honor, then, was to have his nose pulled or tweaked. Actually, nose pulling was just another, more aggressive form of accusing a man of lying. It was the ultimate act of contempt toward the most public part of a man's face, an extreme expression of disdain for a man's projected mask. The meaning of nose pulling for men of honor is clear in one well-documented incident of the 1830s: when Thomas Walker Gilmer pulled the nose of William C. Rives.

The pulling of Rives's nose had its origin in a friendship and political alliance gone sour. Rives and Gilmer had long been close associates in Virginia politics as well as neighbors who frequently met socially. During the 1820s, they worked together as opponents of the administration of John Quincy Adams, and Rives had hopes that Gilmer might one day succeed him in Congress. Rives helped advance Gilmer, and Gilmer did the same for Rives. With the enthusiastic support of Gilmer in the state legislature, Rives returned home in 1832 after serving as ambassador to France and was immediately elected to the United States Senate. When other legislators raised doubts about Rives's soundness on the tariff issue – they feared that he might not take the position that it was unconstitutional, and that he might not support South Carolina's attempt to nullify the law – Gilmer assured his skeptical colleagues that they could rely on his friend.

But relations began to deteriorate within a few months when it became clear that Rives would not live up to the expectations created by Gilmer. Contrary to what Gilmer had indicated, Rives did not view the tariff law as unconstitutional. Moreover, he voted for the much hated Force Bill – Andrew Jackson's heavy-handed attempt to coerce the South Carolina nullifiers into submission. This betrayal became intertwined with more-specific grievances detailed in letters exchanged between the two men. Gilmer had several complaints. First, he had given his word to other men that Rives could be trusted on the tariff issue. Rives's vote on the Force Bill meant that these men had come to regard Gilmer as a liar. "I have been taunted more than once," Gilmer wrote Rives, "of having abused the confidence of those who listened to my appeal on your behalf." In fact, shortly after he pulled Rives's nose, Gilmer tried to show the public that he had legitimate grievances against Rives by publishing all the relevant correspondence. He included letters solicited from his colleagues in the legislature attesting that they "distrusted" him because his words about Rives had been shown to be false. In short, Gilmer stood in the same relation to Rives as Richard Yeadon did in relation to the Feejee Mermaid. Both men became identified with the object for which they spoke.

Gilmer had a second major grievance. Rives himself, like his colleagues in the legislature, had begun to denounce Gilmer as a liar. Rives accused Gilmer of appearing to be a friend on the surface while actually working against him in devious and hidden ways. Rives believed (erroneously, it turns out) that Gilmer was the author of an anonymous and highly critical article sent to the *Richmond Enquirer*; that, writing under the name "Buckskin" in the *Charlottesville Advocate*, Gilmer had viciously attacked him in print; and that Gilmer was behind a legislative attempt in Virginia to instruct Rives on how to vote on the Force Bill when it came before the Senate. Gilmer defended himself by acknowledging that he and Rives disagreed over the tariff issue but maintained that he had never tried to give any other impression. In other words, while Rives said that Gilmer's appearance differed from his reality, Gilmer argued that the two were in complete conformity. Gilmer claimed he had always been open and honest about their differences, and that these differences existed within the context of their friendship.

Rives had parallel grievances against Gilmer. He was disturbed that Gilmer pretended friendship and yet betrayed him behind his back. Rives also objected to Gilmer's insinuation that it was Rives who was the liar in the dispute – that he had misled Gilmer about his position on the tariff issue in order to win his support in the Senate election, and that he had secretly joined with his brother in a conspiracy to destroy Gilmer's reputation and career. Rives singled out for special mention Gilmer's accusation that "he had betrayed the principles of the party to which he *falsely* professed to belong."

After months of festering distrust and hatred, the Rives–Gilmer dispute reached its climax at the courthouse in Charlottesville, Virginia, in early July 1833. The two men's deteriorating relations up to that point could be followed in the salutations Rives used in his letters to Gilmer: first "Dear Gilmer," then "Dear Sir," then "Sir." By the time Rives began to call Gilmer "Sir" it must have looked as if they were close to some violent outbreak – perhaps even on the edge of fighting a duel. In Virginia in the 1830s, a duel was a logical result of this kind of dispute. By shooting at each other, men accused of lying could show the world that they would rather die or kill than allow the charge to stand.

But the Rives – Gilmer dispute did not reach the stage of a duel. Instead, Gilmer approached Rives on the terrace of the tavern next to the courthouse in Charlottesville. They began to go over their charges and countercharges, deciding first to move into the public room of the tavern and then into a more private back room. They could agree on nothing. Words between the two men became increasingly heated. Gilmer called Rives a "hypocrite," and Rives retorted that Gilmer was a "scoundrel." There are two versions of what happened next. As Gilmer described it:

> I then applied my right hand gently to his nose. He instantly disengaged himself from me, either by drawing back or pushing me from him, and having a horsewhip in his hand, struck me several times with the butt end of it. While I parried these blows with my right arm, I attempted to catch him by the collar of his coat with my left hand, and in this effort the forefinger of my left hand got into his mouth and was severely bitten. In the attempt to extricate it, my right thumb was painfully injured. While my finger was thus in his mouth I struck him two blows in the face with my right hand.

Gilmer then pulled the whip from Rives and used the "smaller end" to inflict "several stripes with it on his legs and shoulders and . . . one on his forehead." At that moment a crowd rushed in and separated the two struggling men.

The account of the fight offered by Rives and his supporters agreed with this description in all respects but one. The pro-Rives account emphasized that Rives was attacked completely by surprise and that he was seated while Gilmer stood and assaulted him. Gilmer denied this version of the attack. He preferred to portray himself and Rives as equals in combat. He also stressed that it was not his intent to draw blood or to hurt Rives in any way. He meant to apply his right hand "gently" to Rives's nose. The rest of the scuffle was in self-defense. As he stated, "My purpose throughout has been to vindicate myself – not to injure Mr. Rives."

Several features of this nose-pulling incident are worthy of emphasis here. Just as in the Feejee Mermaid episode, the dispute that led up to the attack was essentially about the proper treatment to be accorded the word of a gentleman. At its heart were accusations of lying. It is easy to miss this point. One might be tempted to say that the conflict was really a disagreement about the tariff issue or nullification. In one sense this would be correct, because it is impossible to imagine this series of events without the political dispute that gave rise to it. Similarly, it is impossible to imagine the Feejee Mermaid incident without a mermaid. But it is also clear from the angry letters in both cases that, at least in this context, the men involved did not focus on the substance of the matter that gave rise to the dispute. In the same way that Yeadon "care[d] not a whit" about the mermaid, Gilmer and Rives never discussed the substance of the tariff issue or nullification in their correspondence that led to the nose pulling. Many men disagreed over the tariff and nullification, but those disagreements did not lead to nose pullings or duels unless a man's character came under attack. This point is essential if one is to understand why the pulling of a nose seemed the appropriate remedy here. Gilmer had been accused of lying – of putting forth a projection of himself that was false. He pulled Rives's nose to show his contempt for the projection of his accuser. It was his way of invalidating the words of his enemy. The nose pulling was not primarily part of a conversation about the merits of the tariff or nullification. It was part of a conversation about lying. . . .

Although men who cared about noses no doubt also dreamed about them, few recorded their nightmares. But one Southern man's nose nightmare did reach print in an 1835 issue of the *Southern Literary Messenger*. It is the tale of a man who lay awake and restless, unable to sleep while crowded in with other bodies on a steamboat. Men with large noses snored loudly all around him as he pondered the prophecy of his aunt Deborah that unless he learned to practice prudence and economy "his nose must come to the grindstone." Suddenly two slaves (men he recognized as workers from a local tobacco factory) grabbed him by his arms and dragged him to the deck of the ship toward a grindstone being turned by a "black urchin." The slaves "forced my head downward, until my proboscis rested upon the revolving stone, and I felt its horrid inroads upon that sensitive member." While the wheel did its work the slaves began to sing:

> De man who hold his nose too high
>   Mus'be brought low:
> Put him on de grinstone
>   And grind him off slow.

> Wheel about, and turn about,
>   And wheel about slow;
> And every time he wheel about
>   De nose must go.

The man of honor, held down by black slaves, slowly felt his nose disappear. "The friction of the stone upon my cheeks," he wrote, "gave fearful evidence that what had been a nose, existed no longer, and brought the horrid reflection that I was noseless! That the pride of my countenance was gone, and forever." Here was a nightmare well understood by those who spoke the language of honor. It gave expression to their worst fears. To deprive a Southern man of honor of his nose (with the added humiliation of having it removed by slaves) was to threaten his appearance and thus his very self.

We who live in a post-Freudian age smile knowingly at these men who dreamed about the loss of their noses. We think we know what they really feared to lose. But if we are to explain why they acted as they did we must dig deeper and recognize the importance they attached to the most "superficial" and visible part of their bodies. We must move beyond their genitals – to their noses.

4

Poor, Violent Men in a Premodern World

A Traveler's Comments on the "Barbarity" of the Southern Frontier, 1816

Travelers to the southern frontier often associated the physical wilderness with the supposed barbarity of its inhabitants. Timothy Flint – Principal of the Seminary of Rapide, Louisiana – makes such associations here in his recollection of a trip in 1816 down the Mississippi River. (From Timothy Flint, *Recollections of the Last Ten Years, Passed in Occasional Residences and Journeyings in the Valley of the Mississippi, from Pittsburg and the Missouri to the Gulf of Mexico, and from Florida to the Spanish Frontier; in a Series of Letters to the Rev. James Flint, of Salem, Massachusetts* (Boston: Cummings, Hilliard, and Company, 1826), pp. 97–8)

The inhabitants on this portion of the river are what the French call "petits paysans," or small planters. They fix themselves on beautiful bottoms, of a soil of extreme fertility. The weeds, the trees, the vegetation generally, indicate a fertility still greater than that of the Ohio bottoms. There is by no means the same degree of enterprise, as there. The inhabitants seem indolent, yawning as if under the constant influence of fever and ague; which, in fact, they often have. Their young men, and too often their young women, are but too ready to take passage in the ascending or descending boat. They arrogate to themselves the finish and the entireness of the Mississippi character, of which they aver the Kentuckians have but a part. They claim to be the genuine and original breed, compounded of the horse, alligator, and snapping turtle. In their new and "strange curses," you discover new features of atrocity; a race of men placed on the extreme limit of order and civilization. I heard them on the bank, entering into the details of their horrible battles, in which they talked with a disgusting familiarity about mutilation, as a common result of these combats. Indeed I saw more than one man, who wanted an eye, and ascertained that I was now in the region of "gouging." It is to be understood, that it is a surgical operation, which they think only proper to be practised upon black-guards, and their equals. They assured us that no "gentlemen" ever got gouged. I heard them speaking of a tall, profane, barbarous, and ruffian-like looking man, and they emphatically pronounced him the "best" man in the settlement. I perceived that according to their definition, the question about the "best" man had been reduced to actual demonstration. I found, on farther inquiry, that the "best" man was understood to be the best fighter, he who had beaten, or, in the Kentucky phrase, had "whipped" all the rest.

A Traveler Observes Techniques of Fighting, 1807

Here, the English traveler, Charles William Janson, both describes and judges violence among poor southern whites in the early national period. (From Charles William Janson, *The Stranger in America: Containing Observations Made During a Long Residence in that Country, on the Genius, Manners and Customs of the People of the United States* (London: Albion Press, 1807), pp. 303–5)

... *gouging* is a barbarity still continued in America; ... I shall relate a few recent instances of its existence, and a painful description of an ocular demonstration of the horrors of its execution.

Passing, in company with other travellers, through the state of Georgia, our attention was arrested by a gouging-match. We found the combatants ... fast clinched by the hair, and their thumbs endeavoring to force a passage into each other's eyes; while several of the bystanders were betting upon the first eye to be turned out of its socket. For some time the combatants avoided the *thumb stroke* with dexterity. At length they fell to the ground, and in an instant the uppermost sprung up with his antagonist's eye in his hand!!! The savage crowd applauded, while, sick with horror, we galloped away from the infernal scene. The name of the sufferer was John Butler, a Carolinian, who, it seems, had been dared to the combat by a Georgian; and the first eye was for the honor of the state to which they respectively belonged.

The eye is not the only feature which suffers on these occasions. Like dogs and bears, they use their teeth and feet, with the most savage ferocity, upon each other.

A brute, in human form, named John Stanley, of Bertie county, North Carolina, sharpens his teeth with a file, and boasts of his dependence upon them in fight. This monster will also exalt in relating the account of the noses and ears he has bitten off, and the cheeks he has torn.

A man of the name of Thomas Penrise, then living in Edenton, in the same state, attempting at cards to cheat some half-drunken sailors, was detected. A scuffle ensued; Penrise knocked out the candle, then gouged out three eyes, bit off an ear, tore a few cheeks, and made good his retreat.

Near the same place, a schoolmaster, named Jarvis Lucas, was best by three men, one Horton, his son, and son-in-law. These ruffians beat the unfortunate man till his life was despaired of, having bitten, gouged, and kicked him unmercifully. On the trial of an indictment for this outrageous assault, a Carolina court of justice amerced them in a small fine only....

An American pugilist is equally dexterous with his feet, which are used, not only against his antagonist's shins, but are applied, with the utmost violence, against those parts which the contending beasts of the field never assail. Hence ruptures, loss of eyes, mutilated noses, and indented cheeks so frequently surprise and shock the traveller. A fellow named *Michie*, in my presence, boasted "that he could kick any man, six feet high, under the chin, and break his jaws."...

No such practices would be endured by an English mob; no such disgraceful revenge ever entered the breast of a Creek, a Cherokee, or a Kicapoo Indian.

The lower classes in this gouging, biting, kicking country, are the most abject that, perhaps, ever peopled a Christian land. They live in the woods and desarts and many of them cultivate no more land than will raise them corn and cabbages, which, with fish, and occasionally a piece of pickled pork or bacon, are their constant food.... Their habitations are more wretched than can be conceived; the huts of the poor of Ireland, or even the meanest Indian wig-wam, displaying more ingenuity and greater industry. They are constructed of pine trees, cut in lengths of ten or fifteen feet, and piled up in a square, without any other workmanship than a notch at the end of each log, to keep them in contact....

Amid these accumulated miseries, the inhabitants of log-houses are extremely tenacious of the rights and liberties of republicanism. They consider themselves on an equal footing with the best educated people of the country, and upon the principles of equality they intrude themselves into every company.

"Tall Talk" among Ruffians, 1843

This account of a particularly violent fight is revealing not simply of the observer's sarcasm and contempt for the participants but, more importantly, the role and value of "tall talk" as well as physical action between the two combatants. (From "An Arkansas fight," *New York Spirit of the Times*, Feb. 18, 1843, p. 611)

Once upon a time we were coming down the Mississippi river, on our way to this city. Bunyan has written about a certain delectable spot, situated somewhere in Utopia; but had the pilgrim seen the Arkansas landing we are just now speaking of, he would have thrown down his scallop shell and staff, and cut dirt as if the gentleman in black, on a streak of double-milled electricity, was after him. Two flat boats constituted the wharf, and they were continually butting their heads together. Such was the energy and regularity of their movement against each other, that for a moment we fancied the doctrine of Pythagorus was true, and that the departed spirits of two antagonistic rams had entered the timbers of the flatboats, and thence the combative symptoms spoken of. As soon as the steamboat was moored alongside this floating wharf, the rush to board her was tremendous. One man, dressed in a hunting shirt of coarse homespun, and a coonskin cap, with a knife, something like that which sailors wear, sticking in his girdle, was the first to get on the plank that led from the flatboat to the steamer, and in his hurry to get on board, he was pushed in the water, by a gigantic fellow in a bear skin coat, a coarse wool hat, and a pair of green baize leggings. The immersion of the gentleman in the hunting shirt was altogether accidental, but it was sufficient foundation, in the estimation of the cavaliers of Arkansas, for the tournament ground to be marked off, and the trumpets of blow "*largesse*" to the knights of the coonskin cap and the green baize leggings.

As soon as the ducked man arose from the top of the mulatto colored river, he clenched one hand above his head, and hallowed, "Hold on there – you thin milk livered skunk! Hold on till I get on shore, and may I be cut up for shoe pegs if I don't make your skillet-faced phizcymahogany look like a cabbage made into sour krout!"

"See here stranger," replied the offender, "your duckin' was axesighdental; but if you want a tussel I am har – just like a fin on a cat-fish's back!"

"The plank was mine by seniority, as the doctors say, old cat skinner, and may I be ground into gunpowder, if I don't light on to you like a bull bat on a gallinipper," remarked the dripping man, as he shook himself like a Newfoundland dog, and stepped on shore.

"Stranger," said the causer of the accident, while his eye gleamed like that of an enraged panther, and his fists clenched so forcibly that his nails were driven into the palms of his hands, "perhaps you don't know that I'm the man that fought with Wash. Coffeee [sic], and dirked wild Jule Lynch?"

"May I run on a sawyer, and may my brains fall down into my boot heels as I am walking up a stony hill, if I care if you had a rough and tumble with the devil. You pushed me off the plank and you must fight," was the peaceable reply of the wet gentleman.

"See here man," said the opponent of Wash. Coffee, as he bared his breast and pointed to a large scar that ran across three or four of his ribs, "Wild Jule done this, but I laid him up for a time – these big scratches on my face was got through my trying to hug a young b[e]ar – and this arm has been broken twice. I'm a cripple, but if you will fight, why strip and let's be at it."

In an instant a ring was made, and the two combatants, when doffed of their clothing, looked like middle aged Titans, preparing for battle. The youngest, who had fallen into the water, was about twenty-eight years of age, and his opponent was about thirty-four or five. With eyes made fiery by anger, and lips quivering with intense passion, the youngest dealt his adversary a tremendous blow in the breast. Until this affront the elder man had maintained a strange coolness, and manifested a disposition rather in favor of an apology than anything else; but the instant he felt the blow his nostrils became white, and twitched like a steed's scenting the battle. Closing his teeth hard together, he planted himself for the attack, and as his adversary approached him, he dealt him a fierce lick on the side of the face with his iron-bound knuckles, that laid his cheek bone as bare as though the flesh had been chopped off by an axe. Smarting with rage the other returned the compliment, and as the blood gushed in a torrent from his mouth, he turned around and spit out one or two of his teeth that were hanging by the gums, and with a "rounder" as it is technically termed, he hit the younger man a blow on the temple that laid him on the beach with a dead, heavy sound, like that of a falling tree.

"Thar, I hope he is got enough," said the elder of the two, at almost every word stopping to spit out some fragments of his broken jaw. One of his companions handed him a flask of brandy, and with a long deep drawn swallow, like that of a camel at a spring on an oasis, he gulped down enough of the fiery liquid to have made a common man mad.

"Enough," cried the other party, who had been in a like manner attended by his friends, "yes, when I drink your heart's blood. I'll cry enough, and not till then. Come on you white wind –"

"See here, stranger, stop thar. Don't talk of my mother. She's dead –
God bless her! I'm a man from A to izzard – and you – you thin gutted
wasp, I'll whip you now if I dies for it!"

With a shout from the bye-standers, and passions made furious by
hate and deep draughts of liquor, with a howl the combatants again went
to work. Disengaging his right hand from the boa constrictor gripe [sic]
of his opponent, the younger brute buried his long talon-like nails
directly under the eye-lid of his victim, and the orb clotted with blood
hung by a few tendons on his cheek! As soon as the elder man felt the
torture, his face for an instant was as white as snow, and then a deep
purple hue overspread his countenance. Lifting his adversary in the air as
though he had been a child, he threw him to the earth, and clutching his
throat with both hands, he squeezed it until his enemy's face became
almost black. Suddenly he uttered a quick sharp cry, and put his hand to
his side, and when he drew it away it was covered with blood! The
younger villain while on his back, had drawn his knife, and stabbed
him. As the elder of the combatants staggered up, he was caught by
some of his friends, and holding him in their arms, with clenched fists
they muttered curses towards his inhuman opponent, who being
shielded by his own particular clique, made for the river and plunged
in. When about half way across, he gained a small island, and rising to
his full height, he flapped his hands against his sides and crow'd like a
cock.

"Ruoo-ruoo-o! I can lick a steamboat! My finger-nails is related to a
saw mill on my mother's side, and my daddy was a double breasted
catamount! I wear a hoop snake for a neck-handkerchief, and the brass
buttons on my coat have all been boiled in poison. Who'll Ru-oo-ru-
ooo!!"

Poor, Violent Men in a Premodern World
Elliott J. Gorn

"I would advise you when You do fight Not to act like Tygers and Bears
as these Virginians do   Biting one anothers Lips and Noses off, and

From Elliot J. Gorn, "'Gouge and bite, pull hair and scratch': The social significance of
fighting in the southern backcountry," *American Historical Review*, 90 (1985), pp. 18–43.
Excerpt reprinted by permission of the author.

gowging one another – that is, thrusting out one anothers Eyes, and kicking one another on the Cods, to the Great damage of many a Poor Woman." Thus, Charles Woodmason, an itinerant Anglican minister born of English gentry stock, described the brutal form of combat he found in the Virginia backcountry shortly before the American Revolution. Although historians are more likely to study people thinking, governing, worshiping, or working, how men fight – who participates, who observes, which rules are followed, what is at stake, what tactics are allowed – reveals much about past cultures and societies.

The evolution of southern backwoods brawling from the late eighteenth century through the antebellum era can be reconstructed from oral traditions and travelers' accounts. As in most cultural history, broad patterns and uneven trends rather than specific dates mark the way. The sources are often problematic and must be used with care; some speculation is required. But the lives of common people cannot be ignored merely because they leave few records. "To feel for a feller's eyestrings and make him tell the news" was not just mayhem but an act freighted with significance for both social and cultural history.

As early as 1735, boxing was "much in fashion" in parts of Chesapeake Bay, and forty years later a visitor from the North declared that, along with dancing, fiddling, small swords, and card playing, it was an essential skill for all young Virginia gentlemen. The term "boxing," however, did not necessarily refer to the comparatively tame style of bare-knuckle fighting familiar to eighteenth-century Englishmen. In 1746, four deaths prompted the governor of North Carolina to ask for legislation against "the barbarous and inhuman manner of boxing which so much prevails among the lower sort of people." The colonial assembly responded by making it a felony "to cut out the Tongue or pull out the eyes of the King's Liege People." Five years later the assembly added slitting, biting, and cutting off noses to the list of offenses. Virginia passed similar legislation in 1748 and revised these statutes in 1772 explicitly to discourage men from "gouging, plucking, or putting out an eye, biting or kicking or stomping upon" quiet peaceable citizens. By 1786 South Carolina had made premediated mayhem a capital offense, defining the crime as severing another's bodily parts.

Laws notwithstanding, the carnage continued. Philip Vickers Fithian, a New Jerseyite serving as tutor for an aristocratic Virginia family, confided to his journal on September 3, 1774:

> By appointment is to be fought this Day near Mr. *Lanes* two fist Battles between four young Fellows. The Cause of the battles I have not yet known; I suppose either that they are lovers, and one has in Jest or reality some way supplanted the other; or has in a merry hour called him a *Lubber*

or a *thick-Skull*, or a *Buckskin*, or a *Scotsman*, or perhaps one has mislaid the other's hat, or knocked a peach out of his Hand, or offered him a dram without wiping the mouth of the Bottle; all these, and ten thousand more quite as trifling and ridiculous are thought and accepted as just Causes of immediate Quarrels, in which every diabolical Strategem for Mastery is allowed and practiced.

The "trifling and ridiculous" reasons for these fights had an unreal quality for the matter-of-fact Yankee. Not assaults on persons or property but slights, insults, and thoughtless gestures set young southerners against each other. To call a man a "buckskin," for example, was to accuse him of the poverty associated with leather clothing, while the epithet "Scotsman" tied him to the low-caste Scots-Irish who settled the southern highlands. Fithian could not understand how such trivial offenses caused the bloody battles. But his incomprehension turned to rage when he realized that spectators attended these "odious and filthy amusements" and that the fighters allayed their spontaneous passions in order to fix convenient dates and places, which allowed time for rumors to spread and crowds to gather. The Yankee concluded that only devils, prostitutes, or monkeys could sire creatures so unfit for human society.

Descriptions of these "fist battles," as Fithian called them, indicate that they generally began like English prize fights. Two men, surrounded by onlookers, parried blows until one was knocked or thrown down. But there the similarity ceased. Whereas "Broughton's Rules" of the English ring specified that a round ended when either antagonist fell, southern bruisers only began fighting at this point. Enclosed not inside a formal ring – the "magic circle" defining a special place with its own norms of conduct – but within whatever space the spectators left vacant, fighters battled each other until one called enough or was unable to continue. Combatants boasted, howled, and cursed. As words gave way to action, they tripped and threw, gouged and butted, scratched and choked each other. "But what is worse than all," Isaac Weld observed, "these wretches in their combat endeavor to their utmost to tear out each other's testicles."

Around the beginning of the nineteenth century, men sought original labels for their brutal style of fighting. "Rough-and-tumble" or simply "gouging" gradually replaced "boxing" as the name for these contests. Before two bruisers attacked each other, spectators might demand whether they proposed to fight fair – according to Broughton's Rules – or rough-and-tumble. Honor dictated that all techniques be permitted. Except for a ban on weapons, most men chose to fight "no holts barred," doing what they wished to each other without interference, until one gave up or was incapacitated.

The emphasis on maximum disfigurement, on severing bodily parts, made this fighting style unique. Amid the general mayhem, however, gouging out an opponent's eye became the sine qua non of rough-and-tumble fighting, much like the knockout punch in modern boxing. The best gougers, of course, were adept at other fighting skills. Some allegedly filed their teeth to bite off an enemy's appendages more efficiently. Still, liberating an eyeball quickly became a fighter's surest route to victory and his most prestigious accomplishment. To this end, celebrated heroes fired their fingernails hard, honed them sharp, and oiled them slick. " 'You have come off badly this time, I doubt?' " declared an alarmed passerby on seeing the piteous condition of a renowned fighter. "'Have I,' says he triumphantly, shewing from his pocket at the same time an eye, which he had extracted during the combat, and preserved for a trophy."

As the new style of fighting evolved, its geographical distribution changed. Leadership quickly passed from the southern seaboard to upcountry counties and the western frontier. Although examples could be found throughout the South, rough-and-tumbling was best suited to the backwoods, where hunting, herding, and semisubsistence agriculture predominated over market-oriented, staple crop production. Thus, the settlers of western Carolina, Kentucky, and Tennessee, as well as upland Mississippi, Alabama, and Georgia, became especially known for their pugnacity.

The social base of rough-and-tumbling also shifted with the passage of time. Although brawling was always considered a vice of the "lower sort," eighteenth-century Tidewater gentlemen sometimes found themselves in brutal fights. These combats grew out of challenges to men's honor – to their status in patriarchal, kin-based, small-scale communities – and were woven into the very fabric of daily life. Rhys Isaac has observed that the Virginia gentry set the tone for a fiercely competitive style of living.[1] Although they valued hierarchy, individual status was never permanently fixed, so men frantically sought to assert their prowess – by grand boasts over tavern gaming tables laden with money, by whipping and tripping each other's horses in violent quarter-races, by wagering one-half year's earnings on the flash of a fighting cock's gaff. Great planters and small shared an ethos that extolled courage bordering on foolhardiness and cherished magnificent, if irrational, displays of largess.

Piety, hard work, and steady habits had their adherents, but in this society aggressive self-assertion and manly pride were the real marks of status. Even the gentry's vaunted hospitality demonstrated a family's community standing, so conviviality itself became a vehicle for rivalry and emulation. Rich and poor might revel together during "public times," but gentry patronage of sports and festivities kept the focus of power clear. Above all, brutal recreations toughened men for a violent social life in which the exploitation of labor, the specter of poverty, and a fierce struggle for status were daily realities.

During the final decades of the eighteenth century, however, individuals like Fithian's young gentlemen became less inclined to engage in rough-and-tumbling. Many in the planter class now wanted to distinguish themselves from social inferiors more by genteel manners, gracious living, and paternal prestige than by patriarchal prowess. They sought alternatives to brawling and found them by imitating the English aristocracy. A few gentlemen took boxing lessons from professors of pugilism or attended sparring exhibitions given by touring exponents of the manly art. More important, dueling gradually replaced hand-to-hand combat. The code of honor offered a genteel, though deadly, way to settle personal disputes while demonstrating one's elevated status. Ceremony distinguished antiseptic duels from lower-class brawls. Cool restraint and customary decorum proved a man's ability to shed blood while remaining emotionally detached, to act as mercilessly as the poor whites but to do so with chilling gentility.

Slowly, then, rough-and-tumble fighting found specific locus in both human and geographical landscapes. We can watch men grapple with the transition. When an attempt at a formal duel aborted, Savannah politician Robert Watkins and United States Senator James Jackson resorted to gouging. Jackson bit Watson's finger to save his eye. Similarly, when "a low fellow who pretends to gentility" insulted a distinguished doctor, the gentleman responded with a proper challenge. "He had scarcely uttered these words, before the other flew at him, and in an instant turned his eye out of the socket, and while it hung upon his cheek, the fellow was barbarous enough to endeavor to pluck it entirely out." By the new century, such ambiguity had lessened, as rough-and-tumble fighting was relegated to individuals in backwoods settlements. For the next several decades, eye-gouging matches were focal events in the culture of lower-class males who still relished the wild ways of old.

"I saw more than one man who wanted an eye, and ascertained that I was now in the region of 'gouging,'" reported young Timothy Flint, a Harvard educated, Presbyterian minister bound for Louisiana missionary work in 1816. His spirits buckled as his party turned down the Mississippi from the Ohio Valley. Enterprising farmers gave way to slothful and vulgar folk whom Flint considered barely civilized. Only vicious fighting and disgusting accounts of battles past disturbed their inertia. Residents assured him that the "blackguards" excluded gentlemen from gouging matches. Flint was therefore perplexed when told that a barbarous-looking man was the "best" in one settlement, until he learned that best in this context meant not the most moral, prosperous, or pious but the local champion who had whipped all the rest, the man most dexterous at extracting eyes.

Because rough-and-tumble fighting declined in settled areas, some of the most valuable accounts were written by visitors who penetrated the backcountry. Travel literature was quite popular during America's infancy, and many profit-minded authors undoubtedly wrote with their audience's expectations in mind. Images of heroic frontiersmen, of crude but unencumbered natural men, enthralled both writers and readers. Some who toured the new republic in the decades following the Revolution had strong prejudices against America's democratic pretensions. English travelers in particular doubted that the upstart nation – in which the lower class shouted its equality and the upper class was unable or unwilling to exercise proper authority – could survive. Ironically, backcountry fighting became a symbol for both those who inflated and those who punctured America's expansive national ego. . . .

And yet, it would be a mistake to dismiss all travelers' accounts of backwoods fighting as fictions born of prejudice. Many sojourners who were sober and careful observers of America left detailed reports of rough-and-tumbles. Aware of the tradition of frontier boasting, they distinguished apocryphal stories from personal observation, wild tales from eye-witness accounts. Although gouging matches became a sort of literary convention, many travelers compiled credible descriptions of backwoods violence.

"The indolence and dissipation of the middling and lower classes of Virginia are such as to give pain to every reflecting mind," one anonymous visitor declared. "Horse-racing, cock-fighting, and boxing-matches are standing amusements, for which they neglect all business; and in the latter of which they conduct themselves with a barbarity worthy of their savage neighbors." Thomas Anburey agreed. He believed that the Revolution's leveling of class distinctions left the "lower people" dangerously independent. Although Anburey found poor whites usually hospitable and generous, he was disturbed by their sudden outbursts of impudence, their aversion to labor and love of drink, their vengefulness and savagery. They shared with their betters a taste for gaming, horse racing, and cockfighting, but "boxing matches, in which they display such barbarity, as fully marks their innate ferocious disposition," were all their own. Anburey concluded that an English prize fight was humanity itself compared to Virginia combat.

Another visitor, Charles William Janson, decried the loss of social subordination, which caused the rabble to reinterpret liberty and equality as licentiousness. Paternal authority – the font of social and political order – had broken down in America, as parents gratified their childrens' whims, including youthful tastes for alcohol and tobacco. A national mistrust of authority had brought civilization to its nadir among the poor whites of the South. "The lower classes... are the most abject that, perhaps, ever peopled a Christian land. They live in the woods and deserts and many of them cultivate no more land than will raise them corn and cabbages, which, with fish, and occasionally a piece of pickled pork or bacon, are their constant food... Their habitations are more wretched than can be conceived; the huts of the poor of Ireland, or even the meanest Indian wig-wam, displaying more ingenuity and greater industry." Despite their degradation – perhaps because of it – Janson found the poor whites extremely jealous of their republican rights and liberties. They considered themselves the equals of their best-educated neighbors and intruded on whomever they chose. The gouging match this fastidious Englishman witnessed in Georgia was the epitome of lower-class depravity:

> We found the combatants... fast clinched by the hair, and their thumbs endeavoring to force a passage into each other's eyes; while several of the bystanders were betting upon the first eye to be turned out of its socket. For some time the combatants avoided the *thumb stroke* with dexterity. At length they fell to the ground, and in an instant the uppermost sprung up with his antagonist's eye in his hand!!! The savage crowd applauded, while, sick with horror, we galloped away from the infernal scene. The name of the sufferer was John Butler, a Carolinian, who, it seems, had been dared to the combat by a Georgian: and the first eye was for the honor of the state to which they respectively belonged.

Janson concluded that even Indian "savages" and London's rabble would be outraged by the beastly Americans.

While Janson toured the lower South, his countryman Thomas Ashe explored the territory around Wheeling, Virginia. A passage, dated April 1806, from his *Travels in America* gives us a detailed picture of gouging's social context. Ashe expounded on Wheeling's potential to become a center of trade for the Ohio and upper Mississippi valleys, noting that geography made the town a natural rival of Pittsburgh. Yet Wheeling lagged in "worthy commercial pursuits, and industrious and moral dealings." Ashe attributed this backwardness to the town's frontier ways, which attracted men who specialized in drinking, plundering Indian property, racing horses, and watching cockfights. A Wheeling Quaker assured Ashe that mores were changing, that the underworld element was about to be driven out. Soon, the godly would gain control of the local government, enforce strict observance of the Sabbath, and outlaw vice. Ashe was sympathetic but doubtful. In Wheeling, only heightened violence and debauchery distinguished Sunday from the rest of the week. The citizens' willingness to close up shop and neglect business on the slightest pretext made it a questionable residence for any respectable group of men, let alone a society of Quakers.

To convey the rough texture of Wheeling life, Ashe described a gouging match. Two men drinking at a public house argued over the merits of their respective horses. Wagers made, they galloped off to the race course. "Two thirds of the population followed: – blacksmiths, shipwrights, all left work: the town appeared a desert. The stores were shut. I asked a proprietor, why the warehouses did not remain open? He told me all good was done for the day: that the people would remain on the ground till night, and many stay till the following morning." Determined to witness an event deemed so important that the entire town went on holiday, Ashe headed for the track. He missed the initial heat but arrived in time to watch the crowd raise the stakes to induce a rematch. Six horses competed, and spectators bet a small fortune, but the results were inconclusive. Umpires' opinions were given and rejected. Heated words, then fists flew. Soon, the melee narrowed to two individuals, a Virginian and a Kentuckian. Because fights were common in such situations, everyone knew the proper procedures, and the combatants quickly decided to "tear and rend" one another – to rough-and-tumble – rather than "fight fair." Ashe elaborated: "You startle at the words tear and rend, and again do not understand me. You have heard these terms, I allow, applied to beasts of prey and to carnivorous animals; and your humanity cannot conceive them applicable to man: It nevertheless is so, and the fact will not permit me the use of any less expressive term."

The battle began – size and power on the Kentuckian's side, science and craft on the Virginian's. They exchanged cautious throws and blows, when suddenly the Virginian lunged at his opponent with a panther's ferocity. The crowd roared its approval as the fight reached its violent denouement:

> The shock received by the Kentuckyan, and the want of breath, brought him instantly to the ground. The Virginian never lost his hold; like those bats of the South who never quit the subject on which they fasten till they taste blood, he kept his knees in his enemy's body; fixing his claws in his hair, and his thumbs on his eyes, gave them an instantaneous start from their sockets. The sufferer roared aloud, but uttered no complaint. The citizens again shouted with joy. Doubts were no longer entertained and bets of three to one were offered on the Virginian.

But the fight continued. The Kentuckian grabbed his smaller opponent and held him in a tight bear hug, forcing the Virginian to relinquish his facial grip. Over and over the two rolled, until, getting the Virginian under him, the big man "snapt off his nose so close to his face that no manner of projection remained." The Virginian quickly recovered, seized the Kentuckian's lower lip in his teeth, and ripped it down over his enemy's chin. This was enough: "The Kentuckyan at length *gave out*, on which the people carried off the victor, and he preferring a triumph to a doctor, who came to cicatrize his face, suffered himself to be chaired round the ground as the champion of the times, and the first *rougher-and-tumbler*. The poor wretch, whose eyes were started from their spheres, and whose lip refused its office, returned to the town, to hide his impotence, and get his countenance repaired." The citizens refreshed themselves with whiskey and biscuits, then resumed their races.

Ashe's Quaker friend reported that such spontaneous races occurred two or three times a week and that the annual fall and spring meets lasted fourteen uninterrupted days, "aided by the licentious and profligate of all the neighboring states." As for rough-and-tumbles, the Quaker saw no hope of suppressing them. Few nights passed without such fights; few mornings failed to reveal a new citizen with mutilated features. It was a regional taste, unrestrained by law or authority, an inevitable part of life on the left bank of the Ohio.

By the early nineteenth century, rough-and-tumble fighting had generated its own folklore. Horror mingled with awe when residents of the Ohio Valley pointed out one-eyed individuals to visitors, when New Englanders referred to an empty eye socket as a "Virginia Brand," when North Carolinians related stories of mass rough-and-tumbles ending with eyeballs covering the ground, and when Kentuckians told of battle-royals so intense that severed eyes, ears, and noses filled bushel baskets. Place names like "Fighting Creek" and "Gouge Eye" perpetuated the memory of heroic encounters, and rustic bombast reached new extremes with estimates from some counties that every third man wanted an eye. As much as the style of combat, the rich oral folklore of the backcountry – the legends, tales, ritual boasts, and verbal duels, all of them in regional vernacular – made rough-and-tumble fighting unique.

It would be difficult to overemphasize the importance of the spoken word in southern life. Traditional tales, songs, and beliefs – transmitted orally by blacks as well as whites – formed the cornerstone of culture. Folklore socialized children, inculcated values, and helped forge a distinct regional sensibility. Even wealthy and well-educated planters, raised at the knees of black mammies, imbibed both Afro-American and white traditions, and charismatic politicians secured loyal followers by speaking the people's language. Southern society was based more on personalistic, face-to-face, kin-and-community relationships than on legalistic or bureaucratic ones. Interactions between southerners were guided by elaborate rituals of hospitality, demonstrative conviviality, and kinship ties – all of which emphasized personal dependencies and reliance on the spoken word. Through the antebellum period and beyond, the South had an oral as much as a written culture.

Boundaries between talk and action, ideas and behavior, are less clear in spoken than in-written contexts. Psychologically, print seems more distant and abstract than speech, which is inextricably bound to specific individuals, times, and places. In becoming part of the realm of sight rather than sound, words leave behind their personal, living qualities, gaining in fixity what they lose in dynamism. Literate peoples separate thought from action, pigeon-holing ideas and behavior. Nonliterate ones draw this distinction less sharply, viewing words and the events to which they refer as a single reality. In oral cultures generally, and the Old South in particular, the spoken word was a powerful force in daily life, because ideation and behavior remained closely linked.

The oral traditions of hunters, drifters, herdsmen, gamblers, roustabouts, and rural poor who rough-and-tumbled provided a strong social cement. Tall talk around a campfire, in a tavern, in front of a crossroads store, or at countless other meeting places on the southwestern frontier helped establish communal bonds between disparate persons. Because backwoods humorists possessed an unusual ability to draw people together and give expression to shared feelings, they often became the most effective leaders and preachers. But words could also divide. Fithian's observation in the eighteenth century – that seemingly innocuous remarks led to sickening violence – remained true for several generations. Men were so touchy about their personal reputations that any slight required an apology. This failing, only retribution restored public stature and self-esteem. "Saving face" was not just a metaphor.

The lore of backwoods combat, however, both inflated and deflated egos. By the early nineteenth century, simple epithets evolved into verbal duels – rituals well known to folklorists. Backcountry men took turns bragging about their prowess, possessions, and accomplishments, spurring each other on to new heights of self-magnification. Such exchanges heightened tension and engendered a sense of theatricality and display. But boasting, unlike insults, did not always lead to combat, for, in a culture that valued oral skills, the verbal battle itself – the contest over who best controlled the power of words – was a real quest for domination:

> "I am a man; I am a horse; I am a team. I can whip any man *in all Kentucky*, by G-d!" The other replied, "I am an alligator, half man, half horse; can whip any man on the *Mississippi*, by G-d!" The first one again,

"I am a man, have the best horse, best dog, best gun and handsomest wife in all Kentucky, by G-d." The other, "I am a Mississippi snapping turtle: have bear's claws, alligator's teeth, and the devil's tail; can whip *any man*, by G-d."

Such elaborate boasts were not composed on the spot. Folklorists point out that free-phrase verbal forms, from Homeric epics to contemporary blues, are created through an oral formulaic process. The singer of epics, for example, does not memorize thousands of lines but knows the underlying skeleton of his narrative and, as he sings, fleshes it out with old commonplaces and new turns of phrase. In this way, oral formulaic composition merges cultural continuity with individual creativity. A similar but simplified version of the same process was at work in backwoods bragging. . . .

Tall talk and ritual boasts were not uniquely American. Folklore indexes are filled with international legends and tales of exaggeration. But inflated language did find a secure home in America in the first half of the nineteenth century. Spread-eagle rhetoric was tailor-made for a young nation seeking a secure identity. Bombastic speech helped justify the development of unfamiliar social institutions, flowery oratory salved painful economic changes, and lofty words masked aggressive territorial expansion. In a circular pattern of reinforcement, heroic talk spurred heroic deeds, so that great acts found heightened meaning in great words. Alexis de Tocqueville observed during his travels in the 1830s that clearing land, draining swamps, and planting crops were hardly the stuff of literature. But the collective vision of democratic multitudes building a great nation formed a grand poetic ideal that haunted men's imaginations. . . .

Foreign travelers might exaggerate and backwoods storytellers embellish, but the most neglected fact about eye-gouging matches is their actuality. Circuit Court Judge Aedamus Burke barely contained his astonishment while presiding in South Carolina's upcountry: "Before God, gentlemen of the jury, I never saw such a thing before in the world. There is a plaintiff with an eye out! A juror with an eye out! And two witnesses with an eye out!" If the "ringtailed roarers" did not actually breakfast on stewed Yankee, washed down with spike nails and epsom salts, court records from Sumner County, Arkansas, did describe assault victims with the words "nose was bit." The gamest "gamecock of the wilderness" never really moved steamboat engines by grinning at them, but Reuben Cheek did receive a three-year sentence to the Tennessee penitentiary for gouging out William Maxey's eye. Most backcountrymen went to the grave with their faces intact, just as most of the southern gentry never fought a duel. But as an extreme version of the common tendency toward brawling, street fighting, and seeking personal vengeance, rough-and-tumbling gives us insight into the deep values and assumptions – the *mentalité* – of backwoods life.

Observers often accused rough-and-tumblers of fighting like animals. But eye gouging was not instinctive behavior, the human equivalent of two rams vying for dominance. Animals fight to attain specific objectives, such as food, sexual priority, or territory. Precisely where to draw the line between human aggression as a genetically programmed response or as a product of social and cultural learning remains a hotly debated issue. Nevertheless, it would be difficult to make a case for eye gouging as a genetic imperative, coded behavior to maximize individual or species survival. Although rough-and-tumble fighting appears primitive and anarchic to modern eyes, there can be little doubt that its origins, rituals, techniques, and goals were emphatically conditioned by environment; gouging was learned behavior. Humanistic social science more than sociobiology holds the keys to understanding this phenomenon.

What can we conclude about the culture and society that nourished rough-and-tumble fighting? The best place to begin is with the material base of life and the nature of daily work. Gamblers, hunters, herders, roustabouts, rivermen, and yeomen farmers were the sorts of persons usually associated with gouging. Such hallmarks of modernity as large-scale production, complex division of labor, and regular work rhythms were alien to their lives. Recent studies have stressed the premodern character of the southern uplands through most of the antebellum period. Even while cotton production boomed and trade expanded, a relatively small number of planters owned the best lands and most slaves, so huge parts of the South remained outside the flow of international markets or staple crop agriculture. Thus, backcountry whites commonly found themselves locked into a semisubsistent pattern of living. Growing crops for home consumption, supplementing food supplies with abundant game, allowing small herds to fatten in the woods, spending scarce money for essential staples, and bartering goods for the services of part-time or itinerant trades people, the upland folk lived in an intensely local, kinbased society. Rural hamlets, impassable roads, and provincial isolation – not growing towns, internal improvements, or international commerce – characterized the backcountry.

Even men whose livelihoods depended on expanding markets often continued their rough, premodern ways. Characteristic of life on a Mississippi barge, for example, were long periods of idleness shattered by intense anxiety, as deadly snags, shoals, and storms approached. Running aground on a sandbar meant backbreaking labor to maneuver a thirty-ton vessel out of trouble. Boredom weighed as heavily as danger, so tale telling, singing, drinking, and gambling filled the empty hours. Once goods were taken on in New Orleans, the men began the thousand-mile return journey against the current. Before steam power replaced muscle, bad food and whiskey fueled the gangs who day after day, exposed to wind and water, poled the river bottoms or strained at the cordelling ropes until their vessel reached the tributaries of the Missouri or the Ohio. Hunters, trappers, herdsmen, subsistence farmers, and other backwoodsmen faced different but equally taxing hardships, and those who endured prided themselves on their strength and daring, their stamina, cunning, and ferocity.

Such men played as lustily as they worked, counterpointing bouts of intense labor with strenuous leisure. What travelers mistook for laziness was a refusal to work and save with compulsive regularity. "I have seen nothing in human form so profligate as they are," James Flint wrote of the boatmen he met around 1820. "Accomplished in depravity, their habits and education seem to comprehend every vice. They make few pretensions to moral character; and their swearing is excessive and perfectly disgusting. Although earning good wages, they are in the most abject poverty; many of them being without anything like clean or comfortable clothing." A generation later, Mark Twain vividly remembered those who manned the great timber and coal rafts gliding past his boyhood home in Hannibal, Missouri: "Rude, uneducated, brave, suffering terrific hardships with sailorlike stoicism; heavy drinkers, course frolickers in moral sties like the Natchez-under-the-hill of that day, heavy fighters, reckless fellows, every one, elephantinely jolly, foul witted, profane; prodigal of their money, bankrupt at the end of the trip, fond of barbaric finery, prodigious braggarts; yet, in the main, honest, trustworthy, faithful to promises and duty, and often picaresquely magnanimous." Details might change, but penury, loose morality, and lack of steady habits endured.

Boatmen, hunters, and herdsmen were often separated from wives and children for long periods. More important, backcountry couples lacked the emotionally intense experience of the bourgeois family. They spent much of their time apart and found companionship with members of their own sex. The frontier town or crossroads tavern brought males together in surrogate brotherhoods, where rough men paid little deference to the civilizing role of women and the moral uplift of the domestic family. On the margins of a booming, modernizing society, they shared an intensely communal yet fiercely competitive way of life. Thus, where work was least rationalized and specialized, domesticity weakest, legal institutions primitive, and the market economy feeble, rough-and-tumble fighting found fertile soil.

Just as the economy of the southern backcountry remained locally oriented, the rough-and-tumblers were local heroes, renowned in their communities. There was no professionalization here. Men fought for informal village and county titles; the red feather in the champion's cap was pay enough because it marked him as first among his peers. Paralleling the primitive division of labor in backwoods society, boundaries between entertainment and daily life, between spectators and participants, were not sharply drawn. "Bully of the Hill" Ab Gaines from the Big Hatchie Country, Neil Brown of Totty's Bend, Vernon's William Holt, and Smithfield's Jim Willis – all of them were renowned Tennessee fighters, local heroes in their day. Legendary champions were real individuals, tested gang leaders who attained their status by being the meanest, toughest, and most ruthless fighters, who faced disfigurement and never backed down. Challenges were ever present; yesterday's spectator was today's champion, today's champion tomorrow's invalid.

Given the lives these men led, a world view that embraced fearlessness made sense. Hunters, trappers, Indian fighters, and herdsmen who knew the smell of warm blood on their hands refused to sentimentalize an environment filled with threatening forces. It was not that backwoodsmen lived in constant danger but that violence was unpredictable. Recreations like cockfighting deadened men to cruelty, and the gratuitous savagery of gouging matches reinforced the daily truth that life was brutal, guided only by the logic of superior nerve, power, and cunning. With families emotionally or physically distant and civil institutions weak, a man's role in the all-male society was defined less by his ability as a breadwinner than by his ferocity. The touchstone of masculinity was unflinching toughness, not chivalry, duty, or piety. Violent sports, heavy drinking, and impulsive pleasure seeking were appropriate for men whose lives were hard, whose futures were unpredictable, and whose opportunities were limited. Gouging champions were group leaders because they embodied the basic values of their peers. The successful rough-and-tumbler proved his manhood by asserting his dominance and rendering his opponent "impotent," as Thomas Ashe put it. And the loser, though literally or symbolically castrated, demonstrated his mettle and maintained his honor.

Here we begin to understand the travelers' refrain about plain folk degradation. Setting out from northern ports, whose inhabitants were increasingly possessed by visions of godly perfection and material progress, they found southern upcountry people slothful and backward. Ashe's Quaker friend in Wheeling, Virginia, made the point. For Quakers and northern evangelicals, labor was a means of moral self-testing, and earthly success was a sign of God's grace, so hard work and steady habits became acts of piety. But not only Yankees endorsed sober restraint. A growing number of southern evangelicals also embraced a life of decorous self-control, rejecting the hedonistic and self-assertive values of old. During the late eighteenth century, as Rhys Isaac has observed, many plain folk disavowed the hegemonic gentry culture of conspicuous display and found individual worth, group pride, and transcendent meaning in religious revivals. By the antebellum era, new evangelical waves washed over class lines as rich and poor alike forswore such sins as drinking, gambling, cursing, fornication, horse racing, and dancing. But conversion was far from universal, and, for many in backcountry settlements like Wheeling, the evangelical idiom remained a foreign tongue. Men worked hard to feed themselves and their kin, to acquire goods and status, but they lacked the calling to prove their godliness through rigid morality. Salvation and self-denial were culturally less compelling values, and the barriers against leisure and self-gratification were lower here than among the converted.

Moreover, primitive markets and the semisubsistence basis of upcountry life limited men's dependence on goods produced by others and allowed them to maintain the irregular work rhythms of a precapitalist economy. The material base of backwoods life was ill suited to social transformation, and the cultural traditions of the past offered alternatives to rigid new ideals. Closing up shop in mid-week for a fight or horse race had always been perfectly acceptable, because men labored so that they might indulge the joys of the flesh. Neither a compulsive need to save time and money nor an obsession with progress haunted people's imaginations. The backcountry folk who lacked a bourgeois or Protestant sense of duty were little disturbed by exhibitions of human passions and were resigned to violence as part of daily life. Thus, the relative dearth of capitalistic values (such as delayed gratification and accumulation), the absence of a strict work ethic, and a cultural tradition that winked at lapses in moral rigor limited society's demands for sober self-control.

Not just unconverted poor whites but also large numbers of the slaveholding gentry still lent their prestige to a regional style that favored conspicuous displays of leisure. As C. Vann Woodward has pointed out, early observers, such as Robert Beverley and William Byrd, as well as modern-day commentators, have described a distinctly "southern ethic" in American history.[2] Whether judged positively as leisure or negatively as laziness, the southern sensibility valued free time and rejected work as the consuming goal of life. Slavery reinforced this tendency, for how could labor be an unmitigated virtue if so much of it was performed by despised black bondsmen? When southerners did esteem commerce and enterprise, it was less because piling up wealth contained religious or moral value than because productivity facilitated the leisure ethos.

Southerners could therefore work hard without placing labor at the center of their ethical universe. In important ways, then, the upland folk culture reflected a larger regional style.

Thus, the values, ideas, and institutions that rapidly transformed the North into a modern capitalist society came late to the South. Indeed, conspicuous display, heavy drinking, moral casualness, and love of games and sports had deep roots in much of Western culture. As Woodward has cautioned, we must take care not to interpret the southern ethic as unique or aberrant. The compulsions to subordinate leisure to productivity, to divide work and play into separate compartmentalized realms, and to improve each bright and shining hour were the novel ideas. The southern ethic anticipated human evil, tolerated ethical lapses, and accepted the finitude of man in contrast to the new style that demanded unprecedented moral rectitude and internalized self-restraint.

The American South also shared with large parts of the Old World a taste for violence and personal vengeance. Long after the settling of the southern colonies, powerful patriarchal clans in Celtic and Mediterranean lands still avenged affronts to family honor with deadly feuds. Norbert Elias has pointed out that postmedieval Europeans routinely spilled blood to settle their private quarrels.[3] Across classes, the story was the same:

> Two associates fall out over business; they quarrel, the conflict grows violent; one day they meet in a public place and one of them strikes the other dead. An innkeeper accuses another of stealing his clients; they become mortal enemies. Someone says a few malicious words about another; a family war develops.... Not only among the nobility were there family venegeance, private feuds, vendettas.... The little people too – the hatters, the tailors, the shepards – were all quick to draw their knives.

Emotions were freely expressed: jollity and laughter suddenly gave way to belligerence; guilt and penitence coexisted with hate; cruelty always lurked nearby. The modern middle-class individual, with his subdued, rational, calculating ways, finds it hard to understand the joy sixteenth-century Frenchmen took in ceremonially burning alive one or two dozen cats every Midsummer Day or the pleasure eighteenth-century Englishmen found in watching trained dogs slaughter each other.

Despite enormous cultural differences, inhabitants of the southern uplands exhibited charactersitics of their forebears in the Old World. The Scots-Irish brought their reputation for ferocity to the backcountry, but English migrants, too, had a thirst for violence. Central authority was weak, and men reserved the right to settle differences for themselves. Vengeance was part of daily life. Drunken hilarity, good fellowship, and high spirits, especially at crossroads taverns, suddenly turned to violence. Traveler after traveler remarked on how forthright and friendly but quick to anger the backcountry people were. Like their European ancestors, they had not yet internalized the modern world's demand for tight emotional self-control.

Above all, the ancient concept of honor helps explain this shared proclivity for violence. According to the sociologist Peter Berger, modern men have difficulty taking seriously the idea of honor.[4] American jurisprudence, for example, offers legal recourse for slander and libel because they involve material damages. But insult – publicly smearing a man's good name and besmirching his honor – implies no palpable injury and so does not exist in the eyes of the law. Honor is an intensely social concept, resting on reputation, community standing, and the esteem of kin and compatriots. To possess honor requires acknowledgment from others; it cannot exist in solitary conscience. Modern man, Berger has argued, is more responsive to dignity – the belief that personal worth inheres equally in each individual, regardless of his status in society. Dignity frees the evangelical to confront God alone, the capitalist to make contracts without customary encumbrances, and the reformer to uplift the lowly. Naked and alone man has dignity; extolled by peers and covered with ribbons, he has honor.

Anthropologists have also discovered the centrality of honor in several cultures. According to J. G. Peristiany, honor and shame often preoccupy individuals in small-scale settings, where face-to-face relationships predominate over anonymous or bureaucratic ones.[5] Social standing in such communities is never completely secure, because it must be validated by public opinion whose fickleness compels men constantly to assert and prove their worth. Julian Pitt-Rivers has added that, if society rejects a man's evaluation of himself and treats his claim to honor with ridicule or contempt, his very identity suffers because it is based on the judgment of peers. Shaming refers to that process by which an insult or any public humiliation impugns an individual's honor and thereby threatens his sense of self. By risking injury in a violent encounter, an affronted man – whether victorious or not – restores his sense of status and thus validates anew his claim to honor. Only valorous action, not words, can redeem his place in the ranks of his peer group.

Bertram Wyatt-Brown has argued that this Old World ideal is the key to understanding southern history.[6] Across boundaries of time, geography, and social class, the South was knit together by a primal concept of male valor, part of the ancient heritage of Indo-European folk cultures. Honor demanded clan loyalty, hospitality, protection of women, and defense of patriarchal prerogatives. Honorable men guarded their reputations, bristled at insults, and, where necessary, sought personal

vindication through bloodshed. The culture of honor thrived in hierarchical rural communities like the American South and grew out of a
fatalistic world view, which assumed that pain and suffering were man's
fate. It accounts for the pervasive violence that marked relationships
between southerners and explains their insistence on vengeance and
their rejection of legal redress in settling quarrels. Honor tied personal
identity to public fulfillment of social roles. Neither bourgeois self-
control nor internalized conscience determined status; judgment by
one's fellows was the wellspring of community standing.

In this light, the seemingly trivial causes for brawls enumerated as
early as Fithian's time – name calling, subtle ridicule, breaches of decorum, displays of poor manners – make sense. If a man's good name
was his most important possession, then any slight cut him deeply.
"Having words" precipitated fights because words brought shame and
undermined a man's sense of self. Symbolic acts, such as buying a round
of drinks, conferred honor on all, while refusing to share a bottle implied
some inequality in social status. Honor inhered not only in individuals
but also in kin and peers; when members of two cliques had words, their
tested leaders or several men from each side fought to uphold group
prestige. Inheritors of primal honor, the southern plain folk were quick
to take offense, and any perceived affront forced a man either to devalue
himself or to strike back violently and avenge the wrong.

The concept of male honor takes us a long way toward understanding
the meaning of eye-gouging matches. But backwoods people did not
simply acquire some primordial notion without modifying it. Definitions
of honorable behavior have always varied enormously across cultures.
The southern upcountry fostered a particular style of honor, which grew
out of the contradiction between equality and hierarchy. Honorific
societies tend to be sharply stratified. Honor is apportioned according
to rank, and men fight to maintain personal standing within their social
categories. Because black chattel slavery was the basis for the southern
hierarchy, slave owners had the most wealth and honor, while other
whites scrambled for a bit of each, and bondsmen were permanently
impoverished and dishonored. Here was a source of tension for the plain
folk. Men of honor shared freedom and equality; those denied honor
were implicitly less than equal – perilously close to a slave-like condition.
But in the eyes of the gentry, poor whites as well as blacks were outside
the circle of honor, so both groups were subordinate. Thus, a herds-
man's insult failed to shame a planter since the two men were not on the
same social level. Without a threat to the gentleman's honor, there was
no need for a duel; horsewhipping the insolent fellow sufficed.

Southern plain folk, then, were caught in a social contradiction.
Society taught all white men to consider themselves equals, encouraged

them to compete for power and status, yet threatened them from below with the specter of servitude and from above with insistence on obedi- ence to rank and authority. Cut off from upperclass tests of honor, backcountry people adopted their own. A rough-and-tumble was more than a poor man's duel, a botched version of genteel combat. Plain folk chose not to ape the dispassionate, antiseptic, gentry style but to invert it. While the gentleman's code of honor insisted on cool restraint, eye gougers gloried in unvarnished brutality. In contrast to duelists' aloof silence, backwoods fighters screamed defiance to the world. As their own unique rites of honor, rough-and-tumble matches allowed backcountry men to shout their equality at each other. And eye-gouging fights also dispelled any stigma of servility. Ritual boasts, soaring oaths, outrageous ferocity, unflinching bloodiness – all proved a man's freedom. Where the slave acted obsequiously, the backwoodsman resisted the slightest affront; where human chattels accepted blows and never raised a hand, plain folk celebrated violence; where blacks could not jeoparadize their value as property, poor whites proved their autonomy by risking bodily parts. Symbolically reaffirming their claims to honor, gouging matches helped resolve painful uncertainties arising out of the ambiguous place of plain folk in the southern social structure.

Backwoods fighting reminds us of man's capacity for cruelty and is an excellent corrective to romanticizing premodern life. But a close look also keeps us from drawing facile conclusions about innate human aggressiveness. Eye gouging represented neither the "real" human an- imal emerging on the frontier, nor nature acting through man in a Darwinian struggle for survival, nor anarchic disorder and communal breakdown. Rather, rough-and-tumble fighting was ritualized behavior – a product of specific cultural assumptions. Men drink together, tongues loosen, a simmering old rivalry begins to boil; insult is given, offense taken, ritual boasts commence; the fight begins, mettle is tested, blood redeems honor, and equilibrium is restored. Eye gouging was the poor and middling whites' own version of a historical southern tendency to consider personal violence socially useful – indeed, ethically essential.

Rough-and-tumble fighting emerged from the confluence of economic conditions, social relationships, and culture in the southern backcoun- try. Primitive markets and the semisubsistence basis of life threw men back on close ties to kin and community. Violence and poverty were part of daily existence, so endurance, even callousness, became functional values. Loyal to their localities, their occupations, and each other, men came together and found release from life's hardships in strong drink, tall talk, rude practical jokes, and cruel sports. They craved one another's recognition but rejected genteel, pious, or bourgeois values, awarding esteem on the basis of their own traditional standards. The glue that held men together was an intensely competitive status system in which the most prodigious drinker or strongest arm wrestler, the best tale teller, fiddle player, or log roller, the most daring gambler, original liar, skilled hunter, outrageous swearer, or accurate marksman was accorded respect by the others. Reputation was everything, and scars were badges of honor. Rough-and-tumble fighting demonstrated unflinching willingness to inflict pain while risking mutilation – all to defend one's standing among peers – and became a central expression of the all-male subculture.

Eye gouging continued long after the antebellum period. As the market economy absorbed new parts of the backcountry, however, the way of life that supported rough-and-tumbling waned. Certainly by mid-century the number of incidents declined, precisely when expanding international demand brought ever more upcountry acres into staple production. Towns, schools, churches, revivals, and families gradually overtook the backwoods. In a slow and uneven process, keelboats gave way to steamers, then railroads; squatters, to cash crop farmers; hunters and trappers, to preachers. The plain folk code of honor was far from dead, but emergent social institutions engendered a moral ethos that warred against the old ways. For many individuals, the justifications for personal violence grew stricter, and mayhem became unacceptable.

Ironically, progress also had a darker side. New technologies and modes of production could enhance men's fighting abilities. "Birmingham and Pittsburgh are obliged to complete ... the equipment of the 'chivalric Kentuckian,'" Charles Agustus Murray observed in the 1840s, as bowie knives ended more and more rough-and-tumbles. Equally important, in 1835 the first modern revolver appeared, and manufacturers marketed cheap, accurate editions in the coming decade. Dueling weapons had been costly, and Kentucky rifles or horse pistols took a full minute to load and prime. The revolver, however, which fitted neatly into a man's pocket, settled more and more personal disputes. Raw and brutal as rough-and-tumbling was, it could not survive the use of arms. Yet precisely because eye gouging was so violent – because combatants cherished maimings, blindings, even castrations – it unleashed death wishes that invited new technologies of destruction.

With improved weaponry, dueling entered its golden age during the antebellum era. Armed combat remained both an expression of gentry sensibility and a mark of social rank. But in a society where status was always shifting and unclear, dueling did not stay confined to the upper class. The habitual carrying of weapons, once considered a sign of unmanly fear, now lost some of its stigma. As the backcountry changed, tests of honor continued, but gunplay rather than fighting tooth-and-nail appealed to new men with social aspirations. Thus, progress and technology slowly circumscribed rough-and-tumble fighting, only to substitute a deadlier option. Violence grew neater and more lethal as men checked their savagery to murder each other.

Notes

1   Rhys Isaac, *The Transformation of Virginia, 1740–1790* (Chapel Hill: Published for the Institute of Early American History and Culture, Williamsburg, VA, by the University of North Carolina Press, 1982).
2   C. Vann Woodward, "Southern ethic in a Puritan world," in his *American Counterpoint: Slavery and Racism in the North–South Dialogue* (Boston: Little, Brown and Company, 1971).
3   Norbert Elias, *The Civilizing Process*, trans. Edmund Jephcott (New York: Urizen Books, 1978).
4   Peter Berger, Brigitte Berger, and Hansfried Kellner, *Homeless Mind* (New York: Random House, 1973).
5   J. G. Peristiany (ed.), *Honor and Shame* (Chicago: University of Chicago Press, 1966).
6   Bertram Wyatt-Brown, *Southern Honor: Ethics and Behavior in the Old South* (New York: Oxford University Press, 1982).

Study Questions and Further Reading for Part II

1   What does Greenberg mean when he calls southern honor "superficial"?
2   What was "appearance" and why was it so important to southern men?
3   To what extent did frontier rough-and-tumblers echo the sort of honor embraced by southern gentlemen?
4   What social, cultural, and economic functions did eye-gouging serve and what sort of society did it reflect?

Ayers, Edward L. 1984: *Vengeance and Justice: Crime and Punishment in the Nineteenth-Century American South*. New York: Oxford University Press.
Bruce, Dickson D., Jr 1979: *Violence and Culture in the Antebellum South*. Austin: University of Texas Press.
Franklin, John Hope 1956: *The Militant South*. New York: Beacon Press.
Greenberg, Kenneth S. 1985: *Masters and Statesmen: The Political Culture of American Slavery*. Baltimore, MD: Johns Hopkins University Press.
Hindus, Michael S. 1980: *Prison and Plantation: Crime, Justice, and Authority in Massachusetts and South Carolina, 1767–1878*. Chapel Hill: University of North Carolina Press.
Klotter, James C. 1982: Feuds in Appalachia: An overview. *Filson Club Historical Quarterly*, 56, 290–317.

McWhiney, Grady 1985: Ethnic roots of southern violence. In William J. Cooper, Jr, Michael F. Holt, and John McCardell (eds), *A Master's Due: Essays in Honor of David Herbert Donald*, Baton Rouge: Louisiana State University Press, 112–37.

Stowe, Steven M. 1979: The touchiness of the gentleman planter: The sense of esteem and continuity in the ante bellum South." *Psychohistory Review*, 8, 485–510.

Williams, Jack K. 1980: *Dueling in the Old South: Vignettes of Social History.* College Station: Texas A & M University Press.

Wyatt-Brown, Bertram 1982: *Southern Honor: Ethics and Behavior in the Old South.* New York: Oxford University Press.

Part III
Constructing and Defending Slavery

Introduction to Documents and Essays

How did slaveholders justify slaveowning? According to Elizabeth Fox-Genovese and Eugene D. Genovese, they defended slavery using biblical injunction and high-brow theology that, apparently, southern whites understood and endorsed. Stephanie McCurry agrees with much of this argument and focuses on how the proslavery argument – common among the elites – was communicated to poorer yeomen and nonslaveholders in South Carolina. Gender, for McCurry, is the key to understanding how the social order of the Old South generally, slavery in particular, was preserved and maintained.

5

Slavery Ordained of God

Frederick Law Olmsted Recounts Impressions of a Religious Meeting, 1856

In the mid-1850s, a northerner, Frederick Law Olmsted, ventured south to observe and report on the nature and characteristics of southerners. Among his many observations was his impression of a religious meeting in the woods of Georgia. Even in the backcountry, this document suggests, some of the principal ideas of the proslavery theologians found currency. (From Frederick Law Olmsted, *A Journey in the Seaboard Slave States, with Remarks on Their Economy* (New York: Dix and Edwards, 1856), pp. 454–8)

The religious service which I am about to describe, was held in a less than usually rude meeting-house, the boards by which it was inclosed being planed, the windows glazed, and the seats for the white people with backs. It stood in a small clearing of the woods, and there was no habitation within two miles of it . . . .

In the house were some fifty white people, generally dressed in home-spun, and of the class called "crackers," though I was told that some of them owned a good many negroes, and were by no means so poor as their appearance indicated. About one-third of the house, at the end opposite the desk, was covered by a gallery or cock-loft, under and in which, distinctly separated from the whites, was a dense body of negroes; the men on one side, the women on another. . . .

The preliminary devotional exercises – a Scripture reading, singing, and painfully irreverential and meaningless harangues nominally addressed to the Deity, but really to the audience – being concluded, the sermon was commenced by reading a text, with which, however, it had, so far as I could discover, no further association. Without often being violent in his manner, the speaker nearly all the time cried aloud at the utmost stretch of his voice, as if calling to some one a long distance off; as his discourse was extemporaneous, however, he some-times returned with curious effect to his natural conversational tone; and as he was gifted with a strong imagination, and possessed of a good deal of dramatic power, he kept the attention of the people very well. There was no argument upon any point that the congregation were likely to have much difference of opinion upon, nor any special connec-tion between one sentence and another; yet there was a constant, sly sectarian skirmishing, and a frequently recurring cannonade upon French infidelity and socialism, and several crushing charges upon Fourier, the Pope of Rome, Tom Paine, Voltaire, "Roosu," and Jo Smith. The audience were frequently reminded that the preacher did not want their attention, for any purpose of his own; but that he demanded a respectful hearing as "the Ambassador of Christ." He had the habit of frequently repeating a phrase, or of bringing forward the same idea in a slightly different form, a great many times. The following passage, of which I took notes, presents an example of this, followed by one of the best instances of his dramatic talent that occurred. He was leaning far over the desk, with his arm stretched forward, gesticulating violently, yelling at the highest key, and catching breath with an effort:

"A – ah! why don't you come to Christ? ah! what's the reason? ah! Is it because he was of *lowly birth*? ah! Is it because he was of a humble origin? ah! Is it because he was lowly born? a-ha! Is it because, ah! – is it because, ah! – because he was called a Nazarene? Is it because he was born in a stable? – or is it because – because he was of humble origin? Or is it – is it because" – He drew back, and after a moment's silence put his hand to his chin, and began walking up and down the platform of the pulpit, soliloquizing. "It can't be – it can't be –?" – then lifting his eyes and gradually turning towards the audience, while he continued to speak in a low, thoughtful tone: "Perhaps you don't like the messenger – is that the reason? I'm the Ambassador of the great and glorious King; it's his invitation, 'taint mine. You musn't mind me. I ain't no account. Suppose a ragged, insignificant little boy should come running in here and tell you, 'Mister, your house's a-fire!' would you mind the ragged, insigni-ficant little boy, and refuse to listen to him, because he didn't look respectable?"

At the end of the sermon he stepped down from the pulpit, and, crossing the house towards the negroes, said, quietly, as he walked, "I take great interest in the poor blacks; and this evening I am going to hold a meeting specifically for you." With this, he turned back, and without reentering the pulpit, by strolling up and down before it, read a hymn, at the conclusion of which, he laid his book down, and, speaking for a moment, with natural emphasis, said:

"I don't want to create a tumultuous scene, now; – that isn't my intention. I don't want to make an excitement, – that aint what I want, – but I feel that there's some here that I may never see again, ah! and, as I may never have another opportunity, I feel it my duty as an Ambassador of Jesus Christ, ah! before I go –" By this time he had returned to the high key and whining yell. Exactly what he felt it his duty to do, I did not understand; but evidently to employ some more powerful agency of awakening, than arguments and appeals to the understanding; and, before I could conjecture, in the least, of what sort this was to be, while he was yet speaking calmly, deprecating excitement, my attention was attracted to several men, who had previously appeared sleepy and indifferent, but who now suddenly began to sigh, raise their heads, and *shed tears* – some standing up, so that they might be observed in doing this by the whole congregation – the tears running down their noses without any interruption. . . .

It was immediately evident that a large part of the audience under-stood his wish to be the reverse of what he had declared, and considered themselves called upon to assist him; and it was astonishing to see with what readiness the faces of those who, up to the moment he gave the signal, had appeared drowsy and stupid, were made to express agonizing sentiment, sighing, groaning, and weeping.

James Henley Thornwell's Defense of Slavery, 1860

Here, one of the foremost thinkers of the Old South, James Henley Thornwell, Presbyterian minister, president of the South Carolina College, and editor of the *Southern Presbyterian Review*, offers some remarkable defenses of slavery. Thornwell's reasoning is based in both political economy and theology and he uses the braiding of the two to offer a stern warning to burgeoning liberal capitalist societies. Note too Thornwell's criticism of other proslavery ideologues (Josiah C. Nott, in particular) who defended slavery by arguing that black people were not simply inferior but biologically different than whites. Thornwell, as a man of scripture, rejects such reasoning as worryingly agnostic. (From James Henley Thornwell, *National Sins. A Fast-Day Sermon: Preached in the Presbyterian Church, Columbia, S.C., Wednesday, November 21, 1860* (Columbia, SC: Southern Guardian Steam-Power Press, 1860), pp. 33–7)

That the relation betwixt the slave and his master is not inconsistent with the word of God, we have long since settled. Our consciences are not troubled, and have no reason to be troubled, on this score. We do not hold our slaves in bondage from remorseless considerations of interest. If I know the character of our people, I think I can safely say, that if they were persuaded of the essential immorality of slavery, they would not be backward in adopting measures for the ultimate abatement of the evil. We cherish the institution not from avarice, but from principle. We look upon it as an element of strength, and not of weakness, and confidently anticipate the time when the nations that now revile us would gladly change places with us. In its last analysis, slavery is nothing but an organization of labor, and an organization by virtue of which labor and capital are made to coincide. Under this scheme, labor can never be without employment, and the wealth of the country is pledged to feed and clothe it. Where labor is free, and the laborer not a part of the capital of the country, there are two causes constantly at work, which, in the excessive contrasts they produce, must end in agrarian revolutions and intolerable distress. The first is the tendency of capital to accumulate. Where it does not include the laborer as a part, it will employ only that labor which will yield the largest returns. It looks to itself, and not to the interest of the laborer. The other is the tendency of population to outstrip the demands of employment. The multiplication of laborers not only reduces wages to the lowest point, but leaves multitudes wholly unemployed. While the capitalist is accumulating his hoards, rolling in affluence and splendor, thousands that would work if they had the opportunity are doomed to perish of hunger. The most astonishing contrasts of poverty and riches are constantly increasing. Society is divided between princes and beggars. If labor is left free, how is this condition of things to be obviated? The government must either make provision to support people in idleness, or it must arrest the law of population and keep them from being born, or it must organize labor. Human beings cannot be expected to starve. There is a point at which they will rise in desperation against a social order which dooms them to nakedness and famine, whilst their lordly neighbor is clothed in purple and fine linen, and faring sumptuously every day. They will scorn the logic which makes it their duty to perish in the midst of plenty. Bread they must have, and bread they will have, though all the distinctions of property have to be abolished to provide it. The government, therefore, must support them, or an agrarian revolution is inevitable. But shall it support them in idleness? Will the poor, who have to work for their living, consent to see others as stout and able as themselves clothed and fed like the lilies of the field, while they toil not, neither do they spin? Will not this be to give a premium to idleness? The government, then, must find them employment; but how shall this be done? On what principle shall labor be organized so as to make it certain that the laborer shall never be without employment, and employment adequate for his support? The only way in which it can be done, as a permanent arrangement, is by converting the laborer into capital; that is, by giving the employer a right of property in the labor employed; in other words, by slavery. The master must always find work for his slave, as well as food and raiment. The capital of the country, under this system, must always feed and clothe the country. There can be no pauperism, and no temptations to agrarianism. That non-slaveholding States will eventually have to organize labor, and to introduce something so like slavery that it will be impossible to discriminate between them, or to suffer from the most violent and disastrous insurrections against the system which creates and perpetuates their misery, seems to be as certain as the tendencies in the laws of capital and population to produce the extremes of poverty and wealth. We do not envy them their social condition. With sanctimonious complacency they may affect to despise us, and to shun our society as they would shun the infection of a plague. They may say to us, *Stand by — we are holier than thou*; but the day of reckoning must come. . . . We desire to see no such state of things among ourselves, and we accept as a good and merciful constitution the organization of labor which Providence has given us in slavery. Like every human arrangement, it is liable to abuse; but in its idea, and in its ultimate influence upon the social system, it is wise and beneficent. We see in it a security for the rights of property and a safeguard against pauperism and idleness, which our traducers may yet live to wish had been engrafted upon their own institutions. The idle declamation about degrading men to the condition of chattels, and treating them as cows, oxen, or swine; the idea that they are regarded as tools and instruments, and not as beings possessed of immortal souls, betray a gross ignorance of the real nature of the relation. Slavery gives one man the right of property in the labor of another. The property of man in man is only the property of man in human toil. The laborer becomes capital, not because he is a thing, but because he is the exponent of a presumed amount of labor. This is the radical notion of the system, and all legislation upon it should be regulated by this fundamental idea.

The question now arises, Have we, as a people and a State, discharged our duty to our slaves? Is there not reason to apprehend that in some cases we have given occasion to the calumnies of our adversaries, by putting the defence of slavery upon grounds which make the slave a different kind of being from his master? Depend upon it, it is no light matter to deny the common brotherhood of humanity. The consequences are much graver than flippant speculators about the diversity of races are aware of. If the African is not of the same blood with ourselves, he has no lot nor part in the Gospel. The redemption of Jesus Christ extends only to those who are partakers of the same flesh and blood with Himself. The ground of His right to redeem is the participation, not of a like, but of a common nature. Had the humanity of Jesus been miraculously created apart from connection with the human race, though it might in all respects have been precisely similar to ours, He could not, according to the Scriptures, have been our Redeemer. He must be able to call us brethren before He can impart to us His saving grace. No Christian man, therefore, can give any countenance to speculations which trace the negro to any other parent but Adam. If he is not descended from Adam, he has not the same flesh and blood with Jesus, and is therefore excluded from the possibility of salvation. Those who defend slavery upon the plea that the African is not of the same stock with ourselves, are aiming a fatal blow at the institution, by bringing it into conflict with the dearest doctrines of the gospel. . . . Our offence has been, that in some instances we have accepted and converted into a plea, the conclusions of this vain deceit. Let us see to it that we give our revilers no handle against us; above all, that we make not God our enemy.

Slavery Ordained of God

Elizabeth Fox-Genovese and Eugene D. Genovese

For the southern slaveholders any social order worthy of the name, and therefore its appropriate social relations, had to be grounded in divine sanction. In this conviction they did not depart radically from their contemporaries in the North and in Europe, or indeed from their pre-

From Elizabeth Fox-Genovese and Eugene D. Genovese, "The divine sanction of social order: Religious foundations of the southern slaveholders' world view," *Journal of the American Academy of Religion*, 55 (1987) pp. 211–33. Excerpt reprinted by permission of the authors and the *Journal of the American Academy of Religion*.

decessors and successors in the Western tradition, but they did differ significantly from others in their views of the appropriate relation of the human to the divine and of the legitimate relations among people. For, during the portentous century in which the western tradition as a whole was repudiating its own long-standing acceptance of unfree labor, especially slave labor, southern slaveholders not merely persisted in the defense of slavery, they purposefully raised it to an abstract model of necessary social order.

The slaveholders cohered as a ruling class on the basis of their own-ership of human beings. From an opportunistic reliance upon slaves as the most convenient laborers available during the seventeenth century, they progressed to a commitment to slavery as a social system. Their intellectual hegira led from the acceptance of slavery as a necessary evil to the defense of slavery as a positive good, which ultimately led to a defense of slavery in the abstract – to a defense of slavery as the best possible bulwark against the corrosive and un-Christian impact of indus-trial capitalism and its cruel and morally irresponsible market in human labor-power.

The slaveholders' insistence upon the legitimacy and charity of their own society took shape in tandem with the revolution in thought that attended and articulated the triumph of capitalism. This revolution, which resulted in the consolidation of bourgeois individualism, haunted the slaveholders at every turn. The proslavery argument never reduced to a reactionary celebration of the "ways of our mothers and fathers," much less to the celebration of feudalism or medievalism. Rather, it strove to fashion an alternate view of social order for modern times. But the slaveholders differed from their bourgeois contemporaries in the values they chose to promote and in their assessment of the social relations that could sustain decent and humane values, which to them meant Christian values.

The slaveholders' world view, like all world views, represented a complex mixture of old and new ideas. But, however modern their thinking in some respects, they decisively emphasized inherited prin-ciples over modern innovations. At the core of their thought lay a belief in hierarchy, particularism, and the necessarily unequal interdependence of society's members. . . .

Enough southerners believed in the justice of their cause to ensure four years of the bloodiest war this country has known. Many of them fought for narrower and more self-serving reasons: for the defense of their own households, for the prosperity of their own farms and planta-tions, for the protection of their own kin. Notwithstanding the diversity, complexity, and contradictions inherent in southern society, a specific vision of social order bound countless individuals to a larger sense of

human and divine order. For the slaveholders the place of divine sanction in the legitimation of social order weighed ever more heavily over
time. And however self-serving the slaveholders' vision of the particulars
of divine sanction, its general claims won broad acceptance among the
propertied but largely nonslaveholding majority of white southerners.
For southerners, more than their northern contemporaries, emphasized
a concrete or literal relation between signs of divine sanction and their
social referents. Southerners turned to the Bible – God's Word – to
justify their ways. And tellingly, their preferred language reversed matters. One after another, both secular and clerical proslavery writers,
invoking Milton, insisted that they were justifying the ways of God to
man.

At the heart of the conflict between antislavery and proslavery thought
lay contrasting visions of the relation of the individual to society. For
opponents of slavery, each individual must be free to dispose of his or her
person, including his or her labor-power. Ultimately, the individual –
understood as equal to and logically interchangeable with all other
individuals – constituted the only legitimate rationale for social institutions that in some ways necessarily hampered the exercise of the individual's innate right to freedom. Order depended upon freedom, to
which it was logically subordinated. Defenders of slavery reversed the
priorities. Freedom could be understood only as a function of order,
upon which it depended and to which it was logically subordinated.
Against opponents of slavery, who saw individual right as universal,
defenders of slavery preached individual right as particular. Individuals
were good not in the abstract, but only as representatives of their kind
and in their station. For southerners, slavery as a social system articulated and embodied this general principle.

In defending slavery as the foundation of social order, southerners
drew heavily upon a religious discourse that they shared in large measure
with their bourgeois opponents. Antebellum southern intellectuals have
largely been forgotten or have been dismissed by historians as an inferior
breed. This is nonsense. Their eclipse suggests nothing so much as the
common fate of those who back losing causes, especially causes judged
immoral. The southern intellectuals concerned themselves with modern
developments in science and epistemology, in social, political, and economic theory, and in theology. And in the South as in the North theology
and religious studies developed as inseparable from social thought. A
separation was indeed proceeding in the North but hardly at all in the
South. Still, innumerable common preoccupations bound southern
intellectuals to their northern counterparts. The issue in this instance,
as in so many others in the development of modern thought, lay not in
the separation between discourses but in the transformation within

discourses – specifically, not so much in the separation of the secular from the religious discourse but in the transformation of the religious discourse itself....

In the years following the Revolution North and South shared common concerns and faced common problems, notably disestablishment and rechristianization. Both also faced the countless problems of adapting a non-established Protestantism to a society increasingly shaped by market relations and defined by a secular polity. Both participated in the revolutionary transformation of Western thought that attended the accelerating developments in science, the emergence of what we now call social science, and the personalism of Romanticism....

Any religious discourse necessarily has to arrive at new accommodations with the ways and words of the world in which it exists. American Protestants began with an uneasy tension between the claims of the individual as soul and as actor in the world and the claims of God and His people. Evangelicalism infused this tension with a new spirit of personal adherence and enthusiasm. Yet, as the divergence between the Baptists and the Methodists makes clear, even this wave of feeling could coalesce around Calvinist or Arminian tendencies. In the decades between 1820 and 1860 this broad discourse of American Protestantism tended at an accelerating rate to crystalize around the central tendencies in northern and southern social relations. Thus, whereas northern Protestantism succumbed to a slow erosion of its claims to impose order in favor of a slow extension of its acceptance of individual conscience, southern Protestantism waged a determined struggle against individual claims in favor of a religiously legitimated social cohesion. By the 1840s, the churches were splitting along sectional lines, and the two branches were taking shape as rival discourses – rival interpretations of the place of religion in society as well as rival interpretations of the nature of religious discourse itself.

During 1830–1860 northern abolitionists took second place to none in their invocation of divine sanction for their hallowed cause, but they increasingly retreated to the swampy terrain of individual conscience. In so doing, they absorbed large doses of bourgeois individualism into the heart of their religious discourse. The individual conscience emerged in their thinking as the ultimate custodian of God's purpose. In this progress they radically reduced the social relations to which the Bible applied directly. They rested their case on the spirit of the Bible, not on its specific prescriptions. In so doing, they abstracted further and further from the Bible's words. Or they applied them to feelings of conscience, understood as somehow distinct from the governing principles of the real world. Their abstraction, which southerners considered a trivialization, inescapably if inadvertently eroded the place of religion in the ordering of human affairs. Southerners, by contrast, took great comfort in the Bible's demonstrable justification of slavery, which led them to attend carefully to the Bible's pronouncements on other matters as well, for the Word of God referred directly, not abstractly, to their society. . . .

In sum, southerners did not isolate themselves from the development of bourgeois thought but did insist on interpreting it with specific reference to their own social system. If this insistence led them to reject as pernicious the atomistic tendencies in bourgeois thought, it also led them to fashion their own world view in tension with bourgeois thought as whole. In the end, they came to rely heavily on religion to sanctify their preferred views, but in so doing they forged an original and distinctly modern view of the proper place of religion in the analysis and defense of the social order.

During the 1850s Frederick Law Olmsted published several influential accounts of his tours through the slave states. An antislavery moderate when he undertook his tours, Olmsted was, if not always fair, always an acute observer. In one memorable passage, he reported on a revival meeting among the poor to middling folk known as "Crackers" in Georgia. Appalled at what he heard and saw, he left us a long and vivid account of the performance of an ignorant, rough-hewn, but clearly effective, country preacher. Olmstead noted the forceful social message embedded in the wandering and emotional sermon. The preacher, Olmsted recalled, let loose "a frequently recurring cannonade upon French infidelity and socialism, and several crushing charges upon Fourier, the Pope of Rome, Tom Paine, Voltaire, 'Roosu,' and Jo Smith. The audience were frequently reminded that the preacher did not want their attention, for any purpose of his own; but that he demanded a respectful hearing as the 'Ambassador of Christ'." Olmsted's undisguised contempt for this social gospel of sorts appears to have been heightened by implicit doubts that the preacher had ever read Rousseau or any of the other worthies he was attacking. And certainly, neither Olmsted nor we could safely assume that many in the audience knew whom he was talking about, much less that any had read them. Olmsted, in short, put down the whole show as a striking illustration of the barbarism that enveloped southern slave society – the ignorance and bigotry, the demagogy and anti-democratic ideology, the insidious and all-too-effective appeals to a gullible folk to close their minds and hearts to the liberating voices of the Enlightenment and the emerging democratic world.

But was it? Or at least, was that all it was? Did Olmsted, intellectually and morally acute as he was, grasp the essentials of what he heard and saw? We have our doubts and would suggest that the preacher and his audience, however unlearned and prejudiced, were people who, for better or worse, knew who they were and what they were about; that they knew that their world – their chosen way of life and all it implied – was everywhere under fierce assault by those who would deny the essential sinfulness of man and would open the floodgates to the ravages of personal immorality and social disorder. At stake were their household-based, God-fearing communities; their sense of family order as well as personal and social order; their Christian values. And however imperfectly understood and primitively expressed, they knew what they were against.

Once we allow for great differences in style and learning, we may perceive that that preacher and those country people were closely bound to the South's most learned divines and their elite congregations – perceive that the highest levels of southern intellectual life and the *mentalité* of the humblest white citizens corresponded to each other much more closely than did their equivalents in northern and European bourgeois societies.

Consider, for example, the words of James Henley Thornwell, president of the immensely influential South Carolina College, editor of the *Southern Presbyterian Review*, unquestionably the greatest theologian in the South and, arguably, second to none in the United States. Thornwell had a first-rate mind, wide learning in history, political economy, and the sciences, as well as in theology and philosophy. A firm Old School Presbyterian who regarded slavery as ordained of God, he was a political moderate by the standards of South Carolina; that is, he had opposed Nullification and would oppose secession until the last moment. His uncompromising Calvinism led him to be skeptical of the claims of the state and to appreciate the essentially sinful nature of the best of men and therefore the fragility of the best of their institutions. Thornwell, who knew much of the world from his travels and practical experience as well as from his extensive reading, insisted upon empirical verification for all theories and hypotheses. Yet he expressed succinctly the common view held by the southern religious and secular leaders, from Methodist bishops and Presbyterian Elders down to Olmsted's country preacher. Referring to the deepening struggle of the South against abolitionism and the concentration of national power, he wrote in 1841 that abolitionism was only one form of the "madness," "fanaticism," and "great disease" that were convulsing both church and state.

In 1850 he denounced the European revolutions of 1848–1849 and "the mad speculations of philosophers, the excesses of unchecked democracy," and the "despotism of the masses." He asserted that the "parties in this conflict are not merely Abolitionists and Slaveholders; they are Atheists, Socialists, Communists, Red Republicans, Jacobins on the one side and the friends of order and regulated freedom on the other."

The South, then, stood as God's bastion against all the isms that were threatening Christian civilization. The South had a social order that hemmed in the evil inevitable in a world haunted by sin – a social order that imposed the discipline necessary to permit the flowering of the God-inspired good in man. For slavery provided the social, institutional, and political structures within which morally frail human beings could live together safely in a manner pleasing to God – with each given according as his work shall be, with each free to serve God in his or her proper station and thereby to prepare for salvation through Christ, if God through His grace willed it.

Thornwell had studied Rousseau and the great philosophers from Plato and Aristotle to Kant and Hegel. His social writings show over-whelming evidence of his learning in history and political economy, notably of his having studied Smith and Say, Ricardo and Malthus. And as a supporter of the Baconian inductive method in science, he accepted the laws of political economy as valid in their appropriate sphere. Hence, he viewed with foreboding the laws of diminishing returns in agriculture, of the falling rate of profit, and of the tendency of population geometrically to outstrip subsistence. For these laws, left to work themselves out in a society based upon freedom of labor, capital, and trade, must end by skewing society between rich and poor in a desperate class struggle.

In that struggle, the masses of mankind would inescapably be ground up if they did not rise with fearful violence to destroy the social classes that imposed such misery on them. Could anyone who called himself a Christian accept these alternatives? accept the immiseration of the masses by a cold-hearted bourgeoisie that refused responsibility for its laborers and left them to starve and, even worse, to plunge into a despair that would drive them from Christ and their own salvation? Conversely, could anyone who called himself a Christian support the revolutionary violence of those desparate souls? support the destruction of the very foundations of social hierarchy and order that God, in His mercy, had provided for a weak and sinful humanity after its Fall? To ask such questions was to answer them. Thornwell, ever the logician, did not hesitate. Social stratification under a ruling class that accepted the responsibility to be its brothers' keeper must prevail over siren calls to a false and oppressive freedom. Labor must be subordinated to capital and thereby disciplined, but it must also be protected and nourished. Slavery, in one form or another, must everywhere prevail over the cash nexus of the market – a slavery, to be sure, grounded in biblical princi-ples and regulated by Christian doctrine, a slavery at once humane and stern, compassionate and firm, paternalistic and demanding. Thus he declared on the eve of secession and war that the capitalist countries must everywhere institute slavery or everywhere disintegrate.

Thornwell and Olmsted's preacher shared more than a repugnance for the rhetoric of the "Roosus" of the world. They also shared a commitment to a positive model of Christian society as manifest in the South's distinctive institutions. For Thornwell, for Olmsted's preacher, and for southern slaveholders as a class, the question of social order assumed three analytically discrete yet systemically related forms: first, as order in the family, understood as the basic experience of social dependence; second, in the household, understood as the basic unit of the economy and community; and third, in the polity, understood as the community writ large as region and nation. The slaveholders took for granted that the families, households, and polity with which they were concerned were those of a Christian society that would stand or fall in accordance with its adherence to Christian principles. And those principles made God's will manifest in the legitimate authority that some, as members of specific groups, wielded over others.

The first of those Christian principles was the God-ordained power of men over women and the attendant duty of Christian women to submit to the authority of fathers and husbands. Almost all the scriptural defenses of slavery – and scriptural defenses probably accounted for a majority of all published defenses – and a great many of the secular defenses as well, rooted the subjection of slaves to masters and of blacks to whites in the prior subjection of women to men. Thus, superordination and subordination by gender constituted the foundation of God's ordination of hierarchy in social relations. Distinctions of class and race were similarly God-ordained as extensions of the principle of family order and male authority. In consequence, notwithstanding the slaveholders' commitment to individual liberty, to republicanism, and to the political equality of slaveholders and indeed of all white men, the individual was strictly defined as a social being. The state of nature was a mischievous myth. With Aristotle, they denied that the individual could exist outside society, and they made the family, considered as society in microcosm, the foundation not merely of civilization but of life itself.

In southern slave society the step from family to household was short; or rather, the one naturally articulated the other. The household provided the fundamental embodiment of God-ordained property, defined to include property in human beings. Property had arisen with human life itself. The slaveholders, in other words, viewed property as inherent in man's social nature and not as a creation of society, much less of the state. In this view, as in others, they betrayed their indebtedness to bourgeois thought and took their place with Locke and his followers against Filmer and Hobbes. Withal, they placed the emphasis differently than did Locke's northern successors. For they denied the theoretical right of all to that most basic form of property – property in one's own person and labor-power. For all the freedom attributed to that white male, the foundation of his freedom lay more in his social role as head of household than in his innate attributes as a laboring individual.

In the southern mind, family and household resisted disentangling. From our perspective it is tempting to view the two terms as different cognitive perspectives on a single system: For individual slaveholders, "family" designated a complex social, economic, affective, and political unit; for society as a whole, "household" designated the same unit. Society consisted in a network of households, the inhabitants of which were encouraged to view themselves as members of a family. The common expression "my family, white and black" was therefore no passing sentimentality or mere rationalization for the exercise of despotic power over labor. It laid bare the sense of a Christian community as an extended family within which the laborers were assimilated to an organic relation with their masters, whose duties included protection and succor as well as discipline and the imposition of order. Thus the vaunted individualism of the slaveholder, while real enough when properly understood, differed radically from that of the bourgeois, who faced his own laborer as a juridical equal – and indeed, as a fellow propertyholder since the laborer had property in his own person and was ostensibly free to sell his labor-power to the highest bidder in a marketplace world of autonomous individual units. The slaveholders had great sport with the idea and practice of bourgeois freedom. With Carlyle and the socialists, they noted that five-year old children were as free as adults to sell their labor-power each day for a meager return on fourteen hours of brutal labor – when, that is, they and their parents could find work and were not abandoned to starvation.

The household – the plantation, farm, urban workplace or even townhouse – constituted an organic community as captured in the depiction of it as a family. The social, economic, and political structure of the family grounded political and social order. Its propertied white male head, as husband, father, and master, presided over all, but not in the manner of some all-powerful Roman or even Filmerian patriarch. In these attitudes the slaveholders betrayed their immersion in the general discourses of their age. The masters' authority was juridically and even in practice far from absolute, and the human rights of women, children, and slaves were theoretically asserted and legally codified. The male heads of households exercised their power legitimately only when they exercised it in accordance with the Mosaic Law, the Sermon on the Mount, and the entire body of laws and commandments laid down in the Old and New Testaments. The "laws and customes" of their region granted husbands rather more power over wives than in the northern states, notably with respect to divorce, but only marginally and not uniformly from state to state. And the combination of explicit emphasis on biblical law and social hierarchy may even have granted married women somewhat higher status within their clearly defined station than that enjoyed by their northern counterparts. Southern legislatures that were generally remarkable for their conservative attitudes towards marriage pioneered in granting property rights to married women on the assumption that with marriages' being indissoluable a wife's ability to hold property in her own name could protect family assets from her husband's creditors.

The distinctive blending of Christian and bourgeois discourses also informed the southern view of the proper relations among propertied white men. Southerners took second place to none in their commitment to political democracy, but southerners did not rest their case for citizenship on secular notions alone. For men faced each other as Christian masters who represented the interests of the entire household – its wife, children, and slaves, each of whom constituted different kinds of dependents in a web of social dependencies. It remains difficult to evaluate the importance of these commitments among poor whites, but they clearly exercised considerable sway among the yeomen, who were, by definition, themselves heads of households and who remained, throughout the antebellum period, not merely occasional or potential slaveholders but necessarily dependent upon the labor of the members of their households.

We need not belabor the obvious: The reality ranged far from this ideal, and the crime against an enslaved black people constituted the greatest enormity in an age well marked by enormities. Here, we purpose to understand how a deeply committed Christian people could have viewed their world and their claims to power as they did and, in time, lay down their lives in terrible numbers to preserve their way of life. We ought, however, to note that religious leaders, as well as eminent jurists and other secular leaders, did rail against the evils – the abuses – of the system, did call for the legalization of slave marriage and slave literacy, and did demand that cruel masters be severely punished. Before the War, but especially during it, as Confederate losses piled up, they warned that if a proud and sinful southern people did not repent and reform, it would face the judgement of a God of Wrath. But to the bitter end, they denied that slavery was inherently sinful and argued that all human institutions lay open to abuse and injustice. Slavery as a social relation was ordained of God, who thereby charged the masters with a heavy responsibility toward those in their custody. It would be the fault of a sinful people, not of the social system, if those chosen to rule abused their privileges, failed in their Christian responsibilities, and provoked an angry God to withdraw His sanction.

No more than southern society itself did southern thought follow some preordained path. Like the society the values of which it articulated, southern thought developed in response to its internal logic, to countervailing voices within southern society, and to the pressures of the bourgeois world in which it was embedded. Southern social thought developed dramatically between 1820 and 1860. It passed from an apologetic defense of slavery as a necessary evil to a militant defense of slavery as a positive good for masters, slaves, and society as a whole. But the positive good argument itself underwent a fateful transformation during those very decades and especially during the 1840s and 1850s. In its early form, which persisted until the War side by side with more advanced forms, slavery raised savage and radically inferior Africans to Christianity, civilization, and useful labor. According to this view, even as slavery uplifted the black race, it freed the white race from drudgery and raised it to republican political and civil equality. Yet no sooner did this view begin to sweep the South and replace necessary-evil apologetics than it metamorphosed into a more general defense of slavery as the foundation for a safe and proper modern social order.

From the outset the racially grounded positive-good argument exhibited contradictions. Both biblical scholarship and social criticism drove the southerners toward a defense of slavery that abstracted from race to the structural principles of social order.

First, in a society that was witnessing a dramatic increase in the number of professing Christians, the Bible provided the natural grounding for the moral defense of slavery. Abolitionist critics tried to dismiss the purported biblical sanction for slavery as self-serving and hardly worthy of serious refutation, but they sorely underestimated the scholarship and learning of the southern clergy. The gyrations of abolitionist critics notwithstanding, the slaveholding theologians had little trouble in demonstrating that the Bible did sanction slavery and that, specifically, God had sanctioned slaveholding among His chosen people of Israel. The abolitionists lost the battle over the translation of Greek and Hebrew terms *doulos* and *ebed* and, more important, they lost the battle of scholarly inquiry into the nature of the Israelite social system. The slaveholders' version stood up during the antebellum debates and has been overwhelmingly confirmed by modern scholarship. The abolitionists found themselves driven to argue that slavery contradicted the spirit of the Bible, especially of the New Testament, even though Jesus and the Apostles, who denounced every possible sin, nowhere spoke against it. Religious leaders like William Ellery Channing, Francis Wayland, and Albert Barnes ended by insisting that if the Bible could be shown to sanction slavery, then the Bible would have to be discarded as an evil book. The southerners, preaching to people who knew their Bible well and who even in those days preferred to take it straight, responded that those who called themselves Christians had to accept the Bible as God's revealed truth and had to understand that God, not man, defined sin and virtue.

Some southerners, including clergymen, tried to reconcile the biblical sanction of slavery with racism by arguing that the Canaanite and other non Hebrew slaves of the Israelites had in fact been black Africans. But it took a northern clergyman, Josiah Priest, to elaborate a fantastic rereading of the curse of Ham that confused the color of Africans' skins with their purported sexual excesses, justifying slavery by a racism considered rabid even in the slaveholding South. His tack found few southern clerical followers. Some of those biblical slaves in fact had been Africans, but only some. The leading southern theologians easily rent this radical argument and insisted upon an honest reading. They saw clearly that the slavery sanctioned in the Bible had little to do with race. Hence, the scriptural defense of slavery decisively emerged as a question of social stratification and class power within which racially inferior Africans presented a special case of the general subjugation of labor. The scriptural defense of slavery thereby passed into a defense of what came to be called "slavery in the abstract."

Second, the southern defense of the slavery actually practiced in the South led to a wholesale assault on the free-labor system of the North and Western Europe – an assault on capitalism as a social system. The slaveholders never tired of saying that they treated their slaves better than capitalists treated free workers – that their slaves had better and immeasurably more secure living conditions than most of the world's proletarians and peasants. The slaveholders regularly received reports on the misery of the peasants of Eastern Europe and Asia and held up the cradle-to-grave security of their slaves in shining contrast. Now, if these comparisons were valid, as up to a point they were, did it not follow that a Christian ruling class had a duty to protect labor by assuming personal responsibility for the health and welfare of its laborers?

Third, the laws of political economy that were being developed by the followers of Adam Smith, most notably by Ricardo and Malthus, pointed not toward the amelioration of the condition of labor as the economy developed, but, to the contrary, toward growing immiseration. The division of society into a few rich and many poor would deepen over time, and the class struggle would become – indeed, was becoming – ever more violent and destructive. Many slaveholders warned of communist revolution and uttered a loud "We told you so" when the Parisian workers rose in insurrection during the bloody June Days of 1848. Unless the capitalist ruling classes came to their senses and instituted the kind of protection of labor that only some form of slavery could offer, the world would relapse into barbarism.

In these ways and others, southern writers transformed the proslavery argument into an argument for slavery as the solution to the Social Question for all countries that were being locked into a self-propelling economic development. By the 1840s the defense of slavery in the abstract had infected the southern intellectuals as a group and was sinking deep roots among the slaveholders as a class. In particular, the enormously influential southern theologians and ministers, from the sophisticated to the down-home, embraced the argument *con amore* and endowed it with biblical foundations.

No one should be surprised, for in the intensely religious South no social theory, and certainly not one as radical as this, could have gotten a hearing unless grounded in scripture. Even the secular proslavery theorists almost invariably began their treatises and addresses by assuring their audience that everything that they were about to say conformed to Christian teaching. And they knew enough to quote the Bible correctly, for they were talking to people who read it, even if many of them read little else, and who routinely judged their preachers by their ability to make a sermon actually elaborate its text. Indeed, diary-keeping shareholders were wont to identify a sermon by its text, noting specific arguments only if they departed from what would have been expected.

The secular social theorists proved revealing in several ways. If virtually all of them invoked scripture as a matter of course, some clearly lacked religious conviction and were accommodating their audiences. They knew, that is, that their audiences had to be accommodated by reference to religious discourse. Others, who invoked scripture but did not base their principal arguments on it, could be shown to have been genuinely religious men themselves. And if men overwhelmingly predominated among those theorists, intellectually accomplished southern women also raised their voices in defense of slavery as a social system explicitly grounded in a stratified male-dominated social order. Louisa Susanna McCord, to take the outstanding example, propounded the necessary subordination of slaves as laborers and the correlative subordination of women to men. McCord did not foreground the religious foundations for her arguments, preferring to emphasize the realities of social conflict and physical strength in a dangerous world. Yet she was a Presbyterian who belonged to the same tight Columbia, South Carolina, community as James Henley Thornwell and clearly took the claims of religion seriously.

Among the eminent male scientists and proslavery extremists, Thomas Cooper and Edmund Ruffin were thinly disguised skeptics, deists at best. Thomas Roderick Dew, the deeply learned and thoughtful president of the College of William and Mary and a major architect of the advanced proslavery argument, was a believer, but one who wore his Episcopalianism lightly. The powerful planter-politician James H. Hammond of South Carolina probably thought of himself as a believer – he was no stranger to self-deception – but he reeked with cynicism and led a life that only a God of infinite mercy and forbearance could pardon. Yet it is surely significant that even these men consciously spoke through a religious discourse. Ruffin privately admitted that he attended church as a social duty since he could not envision a safe and well-ordered society not based on religious institutions. These men, in any case, knew that they would never get a hearing in the countryside and in the villages – not even in the cities and large towns, not even in worldly Charleston – if they could not ground their special views in Christian doctrine.

And at that, such men were rare – and such women rarer, if they existed at all. The overwhelming majority of the South's secular leaders were believers who regarded Christian sanction as necessary to their peace of mind. And many of them were in fact well read in Christian doctrine and even in theology. John C. Calhoun told his friend Augustus Baldwin Longstreet that the Israelites of biblical times had created the purest government the world had ever seen. The deeply religious T. R. R. Cobb of Georgia, a secessionist and proslavery fire-eater, devoted careful attention to biblical history and scriptural sanction in his book on the law of slavery, which had no equal for erudition and scholarly power among proslavery juridical treatises. Examples could be multiplied many times over, but the most impressive evidence comes from the private letters and diaries of the luminaries of the southern ruling class and from the reports on how they tried to instruct their children. No one who reads those sources could fail to appreciate the subjective commitment to a Christian society that undergirded their public pronouncements on slavery.

In this connection it should be noted that the South did not undergo that "feminization" of religion that Ann Douglas has discerned in the North. Statistics for church membership and attendance remain partial, unreliable, and deceptive. But even were a complete picture to show that women joined churches in greater numbers than men among southern whites, and among slaveholders in particular, it would remain doubtful that they attended church more frequently than their men. More important yet, southern literature, broadly construed, does not reveal the same tendency as northern to marginalize, romanticize, or personalize religion. We are back to the internal transformation of discourses. Transcendentalism, to take a prime example, manifested a nostalgia for religious sensibility among northern intellectuals, but the emphasis should fall on the nostalgia and the sensibility rather than on the religion, at least as southerners understood religion. The transcendentalists had moved far down the road to religion as a matter of private conscience. The culture in which these ideas flourished proved eminently willing to leave the business of churches to women and ministers and the business of the real world to politicians and entrepreneurs, however acerbically it criticized them. The southerners, in contrast, insisted on holding the center intact. Religion, slavery, and social order stood or fell together and required the best efforts of the best men and women. The sciences, natural and social, should be explored as far as safety permitted, but in southern hands the Baconian mistrust of grand hypotheses took the specific form of abiding commitment to the Christian social standard against which any knowledge must eventually be tested. Within the discourse much was possible. Outside it all was lost. And, above all, the discourse must never be completely severed from its social foundations.

The Presbyterian divines, as might be expected, led the way, for they held pride of place as the best educated and most intellectually impressive of the denominational leaders. Their power and influence spread well beyond the number of their constituents in a society in which Presbyterians were heavily outnumbered by Methodists and Baptists. In particular the Presbyterian ministers wielded great influence over the educational system, from the old field schools through the academies or high schools right up to the colleges and universities. They exercised, for example, the single most powerful influence upon the state-supported College of South Carolina, the strongest and most prestigious institution of higher education in the Lower South. Within these schools they cooperated closely with the Methodists, Baptists, Episcopalians, and others to hammer out a nonsectarian Christian social ethos that accepted slavery or, more broadly, the subjugation of labor, as the firmest basis for a modern Christian social order. In these matters the Methodists, Presbyterians, and the Baptists differed little if at all in their basic social views.

The Methodist William G. Brownlow and the Presbyterian Frederick A. Ross provide a striking case in point. Before becoming pastor of the Presbyterian Church of Huntsville, Alabama, Ross had worked in East Tennessee, where Brownlow led the Methodists. They hated each other and regularly exchanged denunciations from the pulpit and in print that were foul enough to shame a bawdy house. Not only did they accuse each other of being heretics and demagogues, they added innumerable personal sins as well. No slander, no matter how filthy, escaped their vile and interminable polemics. Yet just compare the social theory espoused by Ross in his *Slavery Ordained of God* during the 1850s with that espoused by Brownlow shortly thereafter in his *Ought American Slavery to Be Perpetuated?* It is not even clear that Brownlow did not in fact crib freely from his old enemy's book. In any case, both extolled slavery as God-ordained and as the proper foundation of a Christian social order.

The common run of southern slaveholders followed their preachers. To be sure, the relation of congregation to ministry was no one-way street. The preachers knew their people and, in a sense, reversed matters and followed them on social questions. It had to be so in a religiously free society in which parishioners either directly controlled their church or could withdraw and join another. Thus the antislavery impulse within their church steadily waned during the late eighteenth and early nineteenth centuries. Antislavery ministers fell silent or left the South, with some exceptions in the largely nonslaveholding areas of the border slave states.

It would be a mistake and an injustice to interpret the proslavery stance of the ministers as a supine capitulation to Caesar and Mammon, for in countless ways a great many of them demonstrated impressive courage and selflessness. Rather, the great majority should be understood as having shared the values and attitudes of their congregations. Typically, the rural Baptist preacher supported himself by farming or in a trade, and, if he could, he acquired slaves. The Presbyterian minister, especially, often taught school for the children of slaveholders and owned, if not a plantation, some household slaves. Or like many of the Methodists, he might double as a lawyer and thereby become immersed in the civil and criminal problems of a slave society. A large if undetermined number of ministers came from slaveholding families or married into them. Indeed, the ministry, medicine, and the law constituted the principal roads to respectability – and to the ultimate "profession" of planting – in southern slave society.

Augustus Baldwin Longstreet may serve as an example. An outstanding humorist and one of the South's most widely read and appreciated literary figures, he owned a plantation from which he never did earn a living. He made his fortune by practicing law and won a considerable reputation as a judge. He also taught school and rose to become president of several southern colleges, including South Carolina College. And he was a Methodist preacher who played a modest but by no means trivial role in splitting the national communion in 1844 over the slavery question and in launching the Methodist Church, South. He and countless other ministers, from the most eminent to the humblest, accepted the slaveholding world they found around them and tried to make it correspond more closely to Mosaic law and to the Christian model of social relations.

Even by their own standards they failed, as their wartime jeremiads demonstrate. They had to fail, for however honest their purposes, slavery remained a massive injustice that poisoned the lives of all it affected. Yet up to a point they did remarkably well in their efforts to bring a Christian conscience to the slaveholding class. Whatever security and succor their slaves had, whatever decency and humanity they found in their masters, derived in no small part from the spread of Christian conscience among the slaveholders. To be sure, the high price of slaves occasioned by the closing of the African slave trade propelled the masters into more humane policies so as to guarantee reproduction of their labor force. But the correspondence of economic interest with depending religious sensibility does not render the latter mere rationalization or pretense. The evidence for that deepening religious sensibility and its positive social consequences may be found everywhere, most notably in the private diaries, journals, and letters of slaveholding men and women.

If we can understand the extent and depth of the effort to place slavery on Christian ground and to erect upon that very ground a God-ordained, class-stratified social order, then we can at least begin to understand the readiness of the southern white people as a whole to defend a social system so offensive, then as now, to most of the Western world. And that readiness appears nowhere so poignantly as in the diaries, journals, and letters of ordinary slaveholders. Thus the diaries and even the plantation day books that recorded business matters are dotted with prayers and cries for God's grace. One after another – but in no sense by formula or rote – the authors prayed from the depths of their souls for the strength to be good husbands and fathers, dutiful wives and mothers. But they also prayed for the strength to be kind and humane slave masters and mistresses. And they did so in words that, in one variation or another, we find uttered time and time again: "This we ask in Christ's name, and for His sake."

6

Proslavery, Gender, and the Southern Yeomen

James Henley Thornwell Associates Slavery and Gender Relations, 1852

How were white southerners who did not own slaves (or who owned very few) persuaded that slaveholding was, in fact, beneficial for all members of southern society? How, in other words, were nonslaveholders persuaded to join the proslavery cause? To understand part of this process, we should recall that proslavery arguments were often read and heard in public and in church. The following discourse – again by Thornwell – attempts to persuade slaveholders and nonslaveholders of the divinity of slavery. (From James Henley Thornwell, *Report on the Subject of Slavery, Presented to the Synod of South Carolina, at their Sessions in Winnsborough, November 6, 1851* (Columbia, SC: A. S. Johnston, 1852), pp. 3, 5–6)

It will be remembered that at the Session of this Synod in Columbia, in 1847, a series of resolutions was presented, setting forth the relations of the Church to slavery, and the duties respectively of masters and servants. After some discussion, it was deemed advisable to appoint a committee to take the whole subject into consideration, and submit a report, somewhat in the form of a circular letter to all the Churches of Jesus Christ throughout the earth, explaining the position of Southern Christians, and vindicating their right to the confidence, love and fellowship of all who everywhere call upon the name of our common Master. The design of appointing this committee was not to increase, but to ally agitation . . . . At that time the greatest danger immediately apprehended was a partial alienation, perhaps an external schism, among those who were as one in a common faith. But now, more portentous calamities are dreaded. The determined zeal, with which a policy founded, for the most part, in the conviction that slavery is a sin, is pressed upon the Federal Legislature, justifies the gloomiest forebodings in relation to the integrity of the Union and the stability of our free institutions.

.... has the Church any authority to declare slavery to be sinful? Or, in other words, has the Bible, anywhere, either directly or indirectly, condemned the relation of master and servant, as incompatible with the will of God?... Will any man say that he who applies to [the study of the Bible] with an honest and unprejudiced mind, and discusses their teachings upon the subject, simply as a question of language and interpretation, will rise from the pages with the sentiments or spirits of a modern abolitionist? Certain it is that no direct condemnation of it [slavery] can anywhere be found in the sacred volume.... The master is no where rebuked as a monster of cruelty and tyranny – the slave no where exhibited as the object of peculiar compassion and sympathy. The manner in which the relation itself is spoken of and its duties prescribed, the whole tone and air of the sacred writers convey the impression that they themselves had not the least suspicion that they were dealing with a subject full of abominations and outrages. We read their language – cool, dispassioned, didactic. We find masters exhorted in the same connection with husbands, parents, magistrates; slaves exhorted in the same connection with wives, children and subjects. The Prophet or Apostle gives no note of alarm – raises no signal of distress when he comes to the slave and his master, and the unwary reader is in serious danger of concluding that according to the Bible, it is not much more harm to be a master than a father – a slave than a child.... The Church was organized in the family of a slaveholder; it was divinely regulated among the chosen people of God, and the peculiar duties of the parties are inculcated under the Christian economy. These are facts which cannot be denied.

John L. Manning's Letter to his Wife, 1860

In their private correspondence to their wives, southern planters yoked abolitionism, fanaticism, and feminism. Here, with some sarcasm, South Carolina politician John L. Manning informs his wife of a debate in the Senate over the westward expansion of slave property. (From John L. Manning to his wife, May 29, 1860, Box V, folder 172, Williams-Chesnut-Manning Families Papers. Reproduced courtesy of the South Caroliniana Library, University of South Carolina, Columbia, SC)

Mr. Benjamin . . . *utterly* demolished Douglas upon his question of Squatter Sovereignty. . . . Beyond all question Mr. Benjamin is the ablest man in the Senate. Today his speech was admirable. He was followed by Pugh & Toombs & they by Wigfall. The Senate adjourned without taking a vote: but I regard it as opposed to our claim. Bayard of Del. speaks in our behalf tomorrow; and altho' the question is still in doubt I feel in my inmost mind that in this vulgar, radical, Agrarian Senate it will be lost. And whither will a fair and upright man turn in his dire distress, when right, justice, & law are thus rudely thrust aside in the highest tribunal of the land? Shall we go to Rhett, Yancey, and Jack Cunningham? God forbid. Let us rather go to the Black Republicans, to the Womens rights associations & to the Mormons for justice. And yet why do that for they have just overthrown their leader – their head and organization – their gifted and talented leader altho he is a demagogue. The man who gave their organization shape and effectiveness, the head as well as the soul of their party, and the most gentlemanly of their whole fraternity – rudely – without warning – in the most violent and remorseless manner, they set him aside because he was a gentleman. For let them say what they please about Mr Seward, he was the only respectable element that they combined among them. And all this because he said that if he was elected President that no one should touch the rights of the South with his Consent. And he had a will which would make his words good. In his place they have elected a wretched backwoodsman, who has cleverness indeed, but no cultivation, who is a fanatic in his political policy, and an agrarian in his practice. Nothing but ruin can follow in his track. I could write you all night long upon this topic, but as much as I have written makes me sick at heart, *for we have no southern men here to arrest the fatal downward tendency of political affairs.*

George Howe Justifies the Subordination of Women, 1850

Here, George Howe, Professor of Biblical Literature in the Theological Seminary at Columbia, South Carolina, outlines the "natural" and scriptural subordination of women. From Howe's perspective, women were entirely domestic creatures – never rulers, always ruled – whose submissiveness was to be encouraged and applauded. (From George Howe, *The Endowments, Position and Education of Woman. An Address Delivered Before the Hemans and Sigourney Societies of the Female High School at Limestone Springs, July 23, 1850* (Columbia, SC: I. C. Morgan, 1850), pp. 5, 9, 10–11)

The duties of life to all human beings are arduous, its objects are noble –
each stage of its progress is prepatory to some other stage, and the whole
a preparation to an interminable existence, upon which, in one sense, we
are hereafter to enter, and in another, have already entered. Others may
slightly regard the employments, trials and joys of the school girl. I am
disposed to put on them a higher value. Our wives, sisters, and our
mothers were in the same position yesterday. You will occupy a like
with them to-morrow. Whatever of virtue, of patient endurance, of
poignant suffering, of useful labor, of noble impulse, of generous endeavor, of influence exerted on society for its good, has been exhibited in
their example, in a few short years we shall see exhibited also in yours.
You will be exerting on society that influence which your own sex has
always exerted for good or for evil, and which the position in which
Providence has placed you, and the nature which the Creator has given
to us all, secure inevitably to you....

To woman,...there must be ascribed...acuteness in her powers of
perception,...instincts...and emotions. When these are powerfully
excited there is a wonderful vigor and determination of will, and a
ready discovery of expedients to accomplish her wishes. She has readier
sympathies, her fountain of tears is nearer the surface, but her emotions
may not be so constant and permanent as those of man. She has greater
readiness and tact, purer and more noble and unselfish desires and
impulses, and a higher degree of veneration for the virtuous and exalted,
and when she has found the way of truth, a heart more constant and
more susceptible to all those influences which come from above. To the
gentleness and quiet of her nature, to its affection and sympathy, that
religion which pronounces its benediction on the peace-makers and the
merciful, which recommends to them the ornament of a meek and quiet
spirit, which, in the sight of the Lord, is of a great price, addresses itself
with more force and greater attraction than it addresses man. Born to
lean upon others, rather than to stand independently by herself, and to
confide in an arm stronger than hers, her mind turns more readily to the
higher power which brought her into being....

Providence, then, and her own endowments mark out the proper
province of woman. In some cases she may strive for the mastery, but
to rule with the hand of power was never designed for her. When she
thus unsexes herself she is despised and detested by man and woman
alike. England's Queen at the present moment, if not more feared, is far
more beloved in the quiet of her domestic life, than Elizabeth was, the
most feared of her female Sovereigns....

When women go about haranguing promiscuous assemblies of men,
lecturing in public, either on infidelity or religion, on slavery, on war or
peace – when they meet together in conventions and pass resolutions on

grave questions of State – when they set themselves up to manufacture a public opinion for their own advantage and exaltation – when they meet together in organized bodies and pass resolutions about the "rights of woman," and claim for her a voice and a vote in the appointment of civil rulers, and in the government, whether of Church or State, she is stepping forth from her rightful sphere and becomes disgusting and unlovely, just in proportion as she assumes to be a man.

Proslavery, Gender, and the Southern Yeomen

Stephanie McCurry

The slave South was commonly represented as the last republic loyal to the principle of government by an exclusive citizen body of independent and equal men. However inadvertently, that portrait revealed the two faces of republicanism in the antebellum South. The first gazed outward on the public sphere and countenanced a purportedly egalitarian community of enfranchised men. This is the familiar face of slavery republicanism privileged by antebellum politicians and, for the most part, by historians. But to view the political edifice solely from that perspective is to remain captive to the designs of its proslavery architects. For southern men, like other republicans, established their independence and status as citizens in the public sphere through the command of dependents in their households. The modern slave republic was defined above all else, as its defenders never tired of saying, by the boundary that separated the independent and enfranchised minority from the majority of dependent and excluded others. Republicanism had another, more conservative face that gazed inward on the private sphere and countenanced inequality and relations of power between masters and their dependents: slaves, women, and children.

Any assessment of antebellum southern political culture, and especially of the yeoman–planter relations on which it hinged, must confront the republican edifice whole. This broader perspective is most pressing with respect to the politics of the yeoman majority. As independent proprietors, yeoman farmers were (and knew themselves to be)

From Stephanie McCurry, "The two faces of republicanism: Gender and proslavery politics in antebellum South Carolina," *Journal of American History*, 78 (1992), pp. 1245–64. Excerpt reprinted by permission of the author and the *Journal of American History*.

empowered by the exclusionary boundaries of the public sphere. Their republicanism, no less than that of the planters, was centrally configured around the politics of the household and around the public meaning of domestic dependencies.

The South Carolina low country, from which much of the material in this essay is drawn, provides a dramatic case in point. Nowhere did proslavery republicanism find more momentous expression; and nowhere was its social basis more starkly displayed in ways that confound a conventional focus on the public sphere in the interpretation of the yeomanry's politics. In that coastal region of vast rice and cotton plantations, where in 1860 more than seven of every ten people were black and enslaved, social and political inequality reached staggering proportions. Not only was the great majority of the population – slaves and women – propertyless and disenfranchised, and the political culture thereby defined primarily in terms of whom it excluded; but the concentration of wealth in land and slaves was so advanced (the top 10 percent of property holders owned more than 70 percent of the real wealth in one mainland parish) that it gave decisive shape to relations between yeomen and planters as well as between masters and slaves. Even in the aristocratic low country, yeomen farmers constituted the majority of the white population, and their relations with planters formed a crucial dimension of political life.

Social inequality was not comfortably confined to black and white and limited to the private sphere, as those who define slave society primarily in terms of race would argue. White society in the slave South was not a "herrenvolk" or racial "democracy," to use George Fredrickson's much-adopted term, that bound white, mostly propertied men in relations of rough equality.[1] Rather, inequality and relations of power took many forms in the South Carolina low country and indeed all over the black belt South where similar social patterns prevailed. They not only gave definitive shape to the public sphere but permeated its boundaries and infused its culture. To confront that pervasive inequality is to raise searching questions about such interpretations as those of Fredrickson and others that locate the yeomanry's politics and commitment to the slave regime in the purportedly egalitarian public sphere of the slave republic and the "democratic" culture and ideology it engendered. To confront the relations of power in yeoman households, including gender relations, and the political privileges to which they entitled male household heads is to reveal a yeoman republicanism rather more complicated and rather less distinctly egalitarian and "democratic." And it is to offer an interpretation that comports more with the manifest social and political inequality of the black belt South. Yeomen in the low country knew, better than their up-country peers, that the slave republic was defined by its exclusionary boundaries. But the patterns revealed in the low country speak nonetheless to a characteristic of republican political culture all over the South. To train our attention on it is to compel a quite different interpretation of republicanism in the antebellum South from the one that currently prevails. It might even compel another perspective on republicanism in all of its American variations.

Republican and proslavery politics already had a long and intimate relationship in South Carolina by the beginning of the antebellum period. Indeed, the vision of the slave republic around which sectional consciousness cohered in the early 1830s had been taking shape in political struggle within the state at least since the constitutional reforms of 1808, and, more alarmingly and visibly, in congressional debate over slavery in the Missouri controversy. But the crucial moment was the nullification crisis; then, in the midst of the state's greatest religious revival, South Carolina's antebellum political culture and ideology was forged.

As fire-eater politicians (not a few of whom were, like Robert Barnwell Rhett, newly born again) met the challenge of an unprecedented political mobilization, they embraced the language of evangelicalism, and with it the faith of its primarily yeomen congregants. Evangelicalism and popular politics were thereafter indissociable in South Carolina. As the ideological work of slavery took on new urgency in those years, so proslavery arguments, infused with evangelical references, acquired the discursive shape that they would maintain until the Civil War. While fire-eaters and moderates would continue to contest the particular political uses of proslavery ideology right down to the successful secession campaign of 1860, the representation of the Christian slave republic, forged in the fires of nullification, was beyond contestation. Proslavery republicanism had become the state religion. In 1852, in the tense aftermath of the first secession crisis, James Henley Thornwell, minister of the First Presbyterian Church of Columbia and the state's leading Presbyterian spokesman, looked back with satisfaction on the state's struggle for a self-conscious and self-confident sectional identity. The world's condemnation of slavery, he recalled, had forced southerners into a consideration of "the nature and organization of society" and "the origin and extent of the rights of man." But they had emerged from that philosophical essay, Thornwell concluded, "feeling justified in our own consciences" and confident "that we have been eminently conservative in our influence upon the spirit of the age." Proslavery ideology and republican politics were inextricably intertwined in antebellum South Carolina.

Evangelical ministers did the main work of the proslavery argument, contributing more than half of the tracts ever written on the subject in the United States and leaving their imprint clearly on the more secular remainder. Indeed, the Biblical defense of slavery was the centerpiece of an organic or familial ideology that encompassed far more than the relation of master and slave. Thornwell, among others, insisted that the central tenet of that conservative social theory, that "the relation of master and slave stands on the same foot with the other relations of life," was grounded in scriptural proof. "We find masters exhorted in the same connection with husbands, parents, magistrates," and "slaves exhorted in the same connection with wives, children and subjects." Such stitching together of all social relations into the seamless fabric of southern society became the mainstay of the proslavery argument, and it drew proslavery advocates inexorably into a struggle with abolitionists in which the stakes were no less than the nature of society and the republic itself. Thornwell characteristically minced no words: "The parties in this conflict are not merely abolitionists and slaveholders," he railed from the heated perspective of the 1850s. "They are atheists, socialists, communists, red republicans, Jacobins on the one side, and the friends of order and regulated freedom on the other." His view of the conflict was widely shared by ministers of every denomination and politicians of both radical and moderate stripe.

Throughout the antebellum period in South Carolina, ministers and politicians scored the philosophy of natural rights and universal equality as "well-sounding but unmeaning verbiage." "Is it not palpably nearer the truth to say that no man was ever born free and that no two men were ever born equal?" low-country politician William Harper asked in what became a famous contribution to proslavery literature. His answer was already, by 1838, a predictable one: "Wealth and poverty,... strength or weakness,... ease or labor, power or subjection, make the endless diversity in the condition of man."

Instead of natural rights and universal equality, Harper, Thornwell, and others offered an elaborate theory of providential relations and particularistic rights. As Charleston minister John B. Adger explained, all human beings did not have the same rights, but only the specific ones that attached to their role. In the Christian republic, wives did not have the rights of husbands, or slaves the rights of masters: a husband had "the rights of a husband ... a father the rights of a father; and a slave, only the rights of a slave." Slavery thus occupied no anomalous category in low-country social thought, and its defense became inseparable from that of Christian and conservative social order.

The real measure of the effectiveness of proslavery arguments, as politicians were acutely aware, was their social breadth. For the ideological work of slavery assumed the greatest significance precisely where it confronted the greatest challenge: in binding nonslaveholders and small slaveholders to planters within a common system of meanings and values. In reaching beyond masters and slaves to all relations of southern households, proslavery ideologues bid for the loyalties of all white male adults. They repeatedly reminded white southerners of all classes that slavery could not be disentangled from other relations of power and privilege and that it represented simply the most extreme and absolute form of the legal and customary dependencies that characterized the Old South – and their own households.

The conjoining of all domestic relations of domination and subordination enabled proslavery spokesmen to tap beliefs about the legitimacy of inequality that went and, sadly, still go so deep in the individual psyche and social structure that for most historians they are still unrecognizable as the subject of history. In the dual task of painting both the abolitionist image of social disorder and their own benevolent and peaceful social order, proslavery spokesmen returned repeatedly to gender relations, exploiting assumptions about the "natural" relations of men and women. On the common ground of gender they sought to ensure that every white man recognized his own investment in the struggle over slavery.

William Harper demonstrated the power of that approach, playing the trump card of gender inequality to give conclusive lie to the philosophy of the Declaration of Independence. "What is the foundation of the bold dogma so confidently announced?" he asked. "Females are human and rational beings. They may be found ... better qualified to exercise political privileges and to attain the distinctions of society than many men; yet who complains of the order of society by which they are excluded from them?" The transhistorical subordination of women was presented as incontestable proof that social and political inequality were natural.

In the lexicon of metaphors for slavery, marriage took pride of place, a discursive construction historians have rarely recognized. No other relation was more universally embraced as both natural and divine, and none so readily evoked the stake of enfranchised white men, yeomen and planters alike, in the defense of slave society. By equating the subordination of women and that of slaves, proslavery ideologues and politicians attempted to endow slavery with the legitimacy of the family and especially marriage and, not incidentally, to invest the defense of slavery with the survival of customary gender relations. In this sense, the subordination of women bore a great deal of the ideological weight of slavery, providing the most concrete example of how public and private distinctions were confounded in political discourse and culture.

Women's nature and appropriate social role became, perhaps as never before, a matter of political concern all over the country in the antebellum period. But they assumed added political significance in the South where their fate was shackled to that of slavery. While southern republican discourse, like its northern variants, had long depended on gendered language and images, the specific analogy of slaves with women, masters with husbands, and slavery with marriage appears, in the late 1830s, to have replaced an older emphasis on the family in general and fathers and children in particular. Perhaps the shift marked the need to put a more modern and benevolent face on familial authority (marriage was, after all, voluntary) as evangelical reformers urged masters to conform the institution to its Christian ideal; and it almost certainly reflected a new self-consciousness about gender relations and ideology that was provoked by the heated contestations of the antebellum period. But there can be no doubt that it reflected as well the need to put proslavery on the broadest possible social basis and the utility of the metaphor of marriage in that unceasing effort.

Although ministers continued to use the familial metaphor generally defined, insisting, for example, that "a Christian slave must be submissive, faithful, and obedient for reasons of the same authority with those which oblige husbands, wives, fathers, mothers, brothers, sisters, to fulfill the duties of those relations," they increasingly focused specifically on the relation of husbands and wives. For in the family, that "model state," Benjamin Morgan Palmer explained, "subjection to law" originated with the authority of man "as the head of the woman." By the time dutiful subjection was prescribed to the "servant," it had "already been exemplified to the child, not only in the headship of the husband, but in the wifely obedience which is its commentary."

The metaphor of marriage had much to recommend it to southern ideologues. But it was not without its problems, as they admitted; the most obvious was that the submission of wives was voluntary while that of slaves was not. Nevertheless, the problem of the analogy of husband and wife was more easily negotiated than that of parent and child. After all, male children grew up to lay claim in adulthood to the prerogatives of husbands, fathers, and masters. Female children, on the other hand, became wives; they remained, like slaves, as perpetual children, at least in relation to masters. Rice planter and one-time governor R. F. W. Allston literally inscribed this planter model of romantic love in letters to his wife by addressing them to "my dear child," while one plantation mistress, for her part, thanked the "Heavenly Father" for a husband who had "just such a master will as suits my woman's nature." Females thus provided the only constant point of reference for naturalizing subordination.

At another level, though, one cannot help but speculate that ideologues found a great deal more psychological satisfaction in likening slaves to women than to children. For the rebelliousness of women, like that of slaves, was a specter only summoned to be banished. By insisting that women *chose* to submit (a suspect formulation when one considers the options), men were, in effect, denying the personal power they knew women to have over them, however temporarily, in romantic and sexual love. Dependence on women was unmanly; manhood orbited around the display of independence. Hence, arguments about female submission not only naturalized slavery; they confirmed masculinity. Little wonder that proslavery ideologues went to such lengths to prove that women's subordination was grounded in nature and sanctioned by God. Their heart was surely in the job.

In their efforts to prove the "natural" subordination of women, ideologues faced no shortage of materials. Assumptions about "the different mental and moral organization of the sexes" infused southern society and culture and, as a result, it was not difficult to "prove" that the subordination of women followed nature's directives. Each sex "is the best in its place," Palmer reasoned. "The distinction of sex runs through the entire nature of both" and "forbids the comparison between the two." The question of equality was thereby answered in the usual particularistic fashion.

Notions about the different physiological, psychological, and moral constitution of the sexes were clearly not peculiar to the slave South; they had steadily gained currency throughout the Western world since at least the late eighteenth century. And while there is always reason for skepticism about separate-but-equal constructions, arguments about the complementarity of the sexes in the South put at best a transparent gloss on relations of domination. "Submission . . . will yield all that is incumbent upon the wife," Palmer insisted, as if to prove the point. "Dependence . . . is not her degradation but her glory," and man must learn to distinguish "betwixt subordination and inferiority." The distinction was a handy one for proslavery ideologues. As George Fitzhugh noted in characteristically direct fashion, "marriage is too much like slavery not to be involved in its fate."

Marriage did lend itself nicely to comparison with slavery, or rather the proslavery view of marriage did, and ideologues were quick to exploit it. God had ordained a position for slaves in the inevitable hierarchy of society, they argued, with particular rights and duties attached to it. Slaves, like women, were fitted by nature to conform comfortably to their place, and slavery, like marriage, was a relationship of "reciprocal interest" which ensured that a "due subordination is preserved between the classes which would otherwise be thrown into sharp antagonism." From their perspective, though not, perhaps, from that of white southern women, marriage was a benign metaphor for slavery. For while the metaphor enshrined male dominance and female subordination, it attempted to cast both in a benevolent light.

Yet the likeness of women and slaves, despite ideological claims, did not ultimately reside in the subjects' natural fitness for subordination, but rather in the masters' power to command it. "Is it not natural that a man should be attached to that which is his own?" William Harper queried, wresting benevolence from the self-interest that allegedly secured for women and slaves protection from their masters' brutality. "Do not men everywhere contract kind feelings to their dependents?" If women found this an imperfect protection, as Harper inadvertently admitted, slaves found it worse than none at all. But the striking feature of the analogy was their common status as "his," as "dependents" who lacked, as Harper said repeatedly, self-ownership. A "freeman" was one who was "master of his own time and action.... To submit to a blow would be degrading to a freeman," he wrote "because he is the protector of himself." But it was "not degrading to a slave – neither is it ... to a woman." Thus in proslavery discourse the metaphor of marriage worked in complex ways. It did not, in the last analysis, constrain the masters' boundless power; rather it confirmed that power by locating the only restraint on the exercise of it exclusively in the hands of masters themselves. The metaphor's multivalence, and particularly its manipulation of benevolence and power, explains its political efficacy.

In their efforts to impress on ordinary southerners the seamlessness of the social fabric, proslavery ideologues were afforded assistance from the most unlikely of quarters. In the 1830s, a handful of Garrisonian abolitionists also came to the conviction that the fate of dependents, slavery, and the subordination of women were inseparable, and that conventional gender relations were at stake in the national struggle over slavery. As that radical minority of abolitionists forged their own position in struggle and, indeed, in schism with the mainstream of the antislavery movement, they forever changed the meaning of the analogy of women and slaves by mounting a progressive challenge to its emergent reactionary proslavery construction. Abby Kelley, a committed Garrisonian and a leading figure in the antebellum women's rights movement, articulated the radical meaning most concretely in acknowledging a debt of gratitude to slaves: "In striving to strike his irons off, we found most surely that we were manacled ourselves." Garrisonians' yoking of the subordination of women and slaves and their public commitment to a dual emancipation proved a perfect foil for proslavery politicians.

If all men should have "equal rights," more than one South Carolinian worried, "then why not women?" That some northern women abolitionists, and some male ones too, asked the same question lent credibility to proslavery threats. The Garrisonians' radical actions in the late 1830s and 1840s lent new fervor and detail to standard comparisons of the natural, divine, and benevolent social order of the slave

South and the chaos of the revolutionary North, now embodied in the dual specter of abolitionism and feminism. No more dramatic illustration of the political significance of domestic, and especially gender, relations could have been imagined. South Carolinian politicians exploited it for all it was worth.

It was not difficult for ministers and politicians to convince low-country yeomen, among others, that abolitionists really threatened a violent end to Christian society as they knew it. By the late 1830s, the connection between Garrisonian abolitionism and women's rights had already found firm root in the American political imagination, planted there by the uncompromising actions of such women as Angelina Grimké. And if Grimké's appearance before a committee of the Massachusetts legislature in 1838 sent shock waves throughout the South, then the impression was nowhere so intense as in South Carolina, her native state. But the outraged and fearful response to Garrisonian feminism was not confined to South Carolina, nor even below the Mason-Dixon line; it was mirrored north of slavery, providing compelling evidence of how deeply gender undergirded conceptions of social and political order.

William Lloyd Garrison was no doubt right that "the proslavery heads and tails of society know not what to do when WOMAN stands forth to plead the cause of her degraded, chain-bound sex." His exultant tone, though, was surely misplaced; he soon discovered, if he did not already know, that similar resistance to female emancipation cut deeply into his political support in the North. Indeed there was a striking, even suspicious resemblance between some of the anti–women's rights, anti-Garrisonian formulations of conservative northern clergy and the proslavery southern versions. Resistance to Garrisonians was by no means limited to the ranks of conservative clergymen, though; in the early 1840s, conflict over the issue of women's rights provoked a split within the ranks of the broader antislavery movement as well. . . .

The radical and emancipatory analogy of women and slaves, the one embraced by Abby Kelley and her abolitionist–women's rights allies, is the one with which we are now most familiar, but it is perhaps the conservative power of the analogy, in its different northern and southern uses, that best captures antebellum meanings. In the South, where the household gave palpable form to the common dependency of women and slaves, the analogy buttressed an aggressive proslavery republicanism. In the North, by contrast, a commitment to customary gender relations did not sustain a proslavery politics, but it did work to conservative effect. The Free-Soil direction of mainstream antislavery activity in the 1850s appears to have been due, at least in part, to a social conservatism, particularly marked on matters of gender, and a general reluctance to envision the reconstruction of social relations according to liberal principles of equal rights as Garrisonians envisioned them. At the very least, the contestation over gender relations and ideology within even the progressive ranks of northern republicanism helps to explain the centrality of gender to proslavery republicanism.

It is not so surprising, then, that one of the most powerful and coherent proslavery tracts to come out of South Carolina, a virtual model of conservative reasoning, was written to meet the challenge of the woman suffrage movement. Louisa Susannah Cheves McCord argued in her 1852 article that "The Enfranchisement of Women" was "but a piece with negro emancipation." Advocates of women's rights such as Harriett Martineau ("the Wilberforce of women") do southerners a favor, McCord claimed, in standing "exactly where they should be, cheek by jowl with the abolitionists. We thank them, at least, for saving us the trouble of proving this position." Yet prove it she did attempt to do, and the evidence she adduced was an amalgam of by then classic proslavery positions. She began with the usual mocking references to natural rights: "Mounted on Cuffee's shoulders, in rides the Lady. The genius of communism bows them both in, mouthing over Mr. Jefferson's free and equal sentence"; and moved to the inevitable contrast of northern and southern society. Whereas southerners were "conservatives" who had accepted God-given "distinctions of sex and race" and sought reform by working with "Nature's Laws," northerners, she explained, held unnatural principles that inevitably produced unnatural spectacles. Here McCord took an old genre to new depths, calling suffragists those "petticoated despisers of their sex . . . would-be men . . . moral monsters . . . things which nature disclaims." Women on top, the world indeed turned upside down, McCord conjured up the most fundamental image of social disorder to demonstrate that reform threatened nothing less than revolution and to remind southerners that where all relations of power were connected, the assault on privilege would not stop short of anarchy or the threshold of their own households.

In the most literal sense, the subordination of women was at issue in the struggle over slavery; in another sense, however, the larger question was the social and political status of dependents, men and women alike, and thus the proper parameters of the republican polity. Although the debate was a national one, the conservative South clearly had more to gain than the North from the politicization of gender relations in the antebellum period.

Nationally the debate over women's emancipation strengthened conservative resolve on a whole range of social and political issues, the most important of which was slavery. In the North, however, it caused division within antislavery ranks, marking for the majority the limits of democratic republican commitment to the rights of man. But in the South, in the absence of any women's movement, ideas about the natural subordination of women contributed not a little to the ideological and political cohesion of the proslavery cause. . . .

Low-country yeoman farmers may never have read a sermon by Thornwell or a tract by Harper, but they almost certainly heard a sermon at their local Baptist church by the likes of Reverend Iveson Brookes or a speech at a July Fourth barbecue by a prominent politician such as Robert Barnwell Rhett. The gulf between high and low culture was just not that great; evangelical values played a central role in both. Moreover, despite the paucity of evidence testifying directly to their political ideology, there is little reason to assume that yeomen were an insurgent majority within plantation regions. To the contrary, in evangelical churches, whose extant records give us a rare glimpse of their communities, male yeomen demonstrated an unequivocal commitment to hierarchical social order and to conservative Christian republicanism. Unlike intellectuals and planter politicians, these low-country farmers articulated their world view piecemeal, in framing covenants to govern admission, fellowship, and representation and in the dispensation of gospel discipline. And they did so in the colloquial language of familialism. They represented Christian society most commonly as an extended family replete with paternal head and fixed ranks of dependents, a formulation that bore striking resemblance to the organic ideology of published proslavery ministers and politicians. In their Baptist, Methodist, and, less often, Presbyterian congregations, the yeoman majority, or rather its enfranchised male members, eschewed any attempt to interpret equality in social terms. Instead they assigned privileges and duties and meted out discipline according to secular rank, station, and status.

This should come as no surprise, despite historians' usual insistence on the egalitarian impulses of southern yeomen. In their churches as in their households, marketplaces, and electoral districts, black belt yeomen moved as independent and enfranchised men amid a sea of dependent and disenfranchised people. Whether slaveholders or not, yeoman household heads were, as they proudly claimed, masters themselves. Politicians acknowledged and confirmed this identity in representing the defense of slavery as the defense of all kinds of power and privilege, domestic and public. Masterhood is thereby revealed as a complex identity, literally engendered in all those independent "freeman" by virtue of personal domination over dependents in their own households. It was moreover ritually confirmed in the exercise of the political rights to which masterhood entitled them. Out of that same social matrix, located resolutely in the household and the private sphere, the yeomanry's commitment to slavery was similarly engendered. For the hidden assumptions and values that underlay their political choices were forged in the relations that engaged them most directly – with the few slaves they may have owned, but just as important, with the women they presumed it their natural right to rule. In the struggle over slavery, yeoman farmers understandably saw the struggle to perpetuate their privilege both at home and at the ballot box.

Viewed within a holistic social context rather than exclusively in relation to planters, yeoman farmers come into focus as part of a small minority in plantation districts privileged by the qualifications of republican citizenship. Little wonder that they exhibited a profound commitment to natural hierarchy and inequality even as they cherished equal rights as independent men. The political ideology of yeomen in plantation areas was thus a contradictory one that defies the common characterization of historians, liberal and left, as egalitarian in impulse. Yeomen did indeed press overweening planters for a greater share of power and resources, and they pressed them for recognition of their rights as masters. But they also found common cause with planters in maintaining and policing the class, gender, and racial boundaries of citizenship in the slave republic. Their commitment to the slave regime owed as much to its legitimation of dependence and inequality in the private sphere as to the much-lauded vitality of male independence and formal "democracy" in the public sphere. As good republicans, yeomen appreciated both of Columbia's faces.

It was a common trope of political tracts that the only true republic was a slave republic, for only a slave republic maintained the public sphere as a realm of perfect equality. But invariably in republican discourse, independence betrayed its intimacy with dependence, and equality with inequality. "No social state without slavery as its basis," Baptist minister Iveson Brookes offered, as if to make the point, "can permanently maintain a republican form of government." Yeoman farmers, like most enfranchised southerners, were aware of what republican independence entailed. . . .

Slavery everywhere exists in fact if not in name, Hammond reminded his fellow United States senators in an 1858 debate: "Your whole class of manual laborers and 'operatives' as you call them, are essentially slaves." To enfranchise slaves, as the free labor states were compelled to do, threatened a "fearful crisis in republican institutions" and invited revolution at the ballot box. Hammond sketched frightful portraits of the festering and explosive class politics of industrial England's cities, whose fate awaited, if it had not already visited, Boston, Philadelphia, and New York. The republic could not long survive such developments without the restraining conservative influence of the South. The genius of the southern system, Hammond insisted, was to have recognized the necessity of enslaving the poor and to have found a race of people "adapted to that purpose." Race was not, in his analysis, an essential but only a fortuitous characteristic of the slave labor system. It ensured that the South's dependent classes were confined within households under the governance of a master, where they could be deprived, as were women everywhere, of political rights. "Our slaves do not vote," Hammond pointed out. "In the slaveholding states... nearly one half of the whole population, and those the poorest and most ignorant, have no political influence whatever, because they are slaves." The half of the population who did vote were, as a result, if not rich, nonetheless part of a privileged class of independent men, "elevated far above the mass." Such men could be trusted, as they must be in a republic, to "preserve a stable and well-ordered government."

Slavery was above all else, in Hammond's account, a system of class and labor relations that had become, to the inestimable benefit of the South, a system of race relations as well. It was that convergence that made the South an exemplary republic, one committed to universal manhood suffrage yet able to restrict it to independent men – a herrenvolk democracy, if you will. "History presents no such combination for republican liberty," Rhett boasted, "than that which exists at the South. The African for the laborer – the Anglo-Saxon for the master and ruler." Slavery was the "cornerstone of the republican edifice." As Hammond, Thornwell, and numerous other South Carolina politicians and ministers agreed, the "primitive and patriarchal" social relations of the South prevented the republic from going down the French road of corruption (to use Thornwell's memorable phrase) from a "representative to a democratic government."

Such explicitly antidemocratic sentiments were not reserved, moreover, for the private communications of a handful of like-minded conservative extremists. On the contrary, editors, correspondents, and political candidates lauded the advantages of South Carolina's conservative republicanism on the stump and in the columns of local newspapers. In the midst of the Kansas crisis and the usual calls for unity within the state, the editor of the *Orangeburg Southron* rejected as "but a crude form of the wildest radicalism" an up-country editor's proposal to turn election of the state's presidential electors over to "the people." It was, he said, merely a ruse to reform the entire electoral system in the state. He aggressively defended the "compromises of our state constitution," and especially the restrictive franchise, as "those conservative elements of our polity, that constitute the bulwark of our strength and the barrier to radical and vulgar aggression." Even the pamphlets distributed by the 1860 Association, whose explicit mission was to galvanize popular support for secession, prominently employed the antidemocratic defense of slavery republicanism. At least in the coastal parishes and the middle districts of the state, politicians and aspirants to office asserted openly that the franchise was not the right of all men, but the privilege only of free and independent men. They were not loath, that is, to make a republican principle out of exclusion. And while it was always a potentially explosive issue, they articulated this view with some confidence that their largely yeoman constituencies responded as men empowered by the demarcation of such narrow boundaries to the political community.

The principle of exclusion was articulated, significantly, in the gendered language of republican discourse. Such terms as "manly independence" and "womanly weakness" served in political tracts and speeches to construct, legitimize, and patrol the boundaries of the republican community, excluding not just women but all those who bore the stigma of dependence. Robert Barnwell Rhett was a master of the genre and demonstrated his skill in regular calls to arms. In an early antitariff speech he wove gender, class, and politics into a republican tapestry in which unmanly men, guilty of "abject submission" to northern "tyranny," were not just rendered effeminate but "crushed and trampled slaves." Those, however, who left "despair . . . to the weak," those who "as freemen" would never consent to "lay the bones of a slave beside those of a free ancestry," only those were true republican men. Dependencies were deliberately conflated by the gendered language of republicanism; independence, by contrast, remained brilliantly distinct. As Rhett had put it in a speech the previous June to his constituents at Walterborough Court House, the seat of Colleton District, the tariff must be resisted as "an infringement on our privileges as men." "Impotent resistance" or "submissive patience" was a fit response only of women or slaves. It was in no small measure in defense of that conception of republicanism that southern citizens rallied in the name of republican manhood.

When a politician took the platform at a meeting, muster, or Fourth of July barbecue and claimed to speak "as a freeman," the salutation was not simply an invitation to his largely yeoman audiences to regard him as one among equals. It was that, but it was also an evocation of shared privilege, an invitation to see themselves as part of the elite: as freemen in a society in which the majority were not free. It was, moreover, a constant reminder of their stake in social hierarchy, political exclusivity, and slavery. "Slavery is with us a powerful element of conservatism," William Henry Trescot, a low-country planter and historian, wrote, because "the citizen with us belongs . . . to a privileged class." This was an argument with great appeal to yeomen.

The banner of "free men" was an emblem of the conservatism of "American republicanism," waved to distinguish it from "French democracy," or mobocracy, as so many low-country planters referred to the bastardized politics of the North. Thus the "MEN of the South," yeomen and planters, were challenged repeatedly to "set aside womanly fears of disunion" in favor of "manly and resolute action," not, as many historians have argued, of an egalitarian and democratic regime, but of a hierarchical and republican one. Their loyalties were secured to a regime in which the rights of citizens were awarded only to those few who were fully masters of themselves and their dependents.

Yeoman farmers were committed to the defense of social hierarchy and political privilege, including slavery, in large measure because of the relations of personal domination on which their own independence rested. But the prerogatives of power around which the public sphere was constructed could not be denied within. Thus the very values in which yeomen and planters found agreement also drew yeomen into a political culture and ideology in which planter prerogatives were difficult to resist. They were left, as a result, with few resources to represent effectively their specific interests as small farmers in a region of great planters, and they were over matched in every aspect of South Carolina politics. Empowered by a system that rewarded privilege, yeoman farmers found themselves overpowered by vastly more privileged planters.

Note

1 George Fredrickson, *The Black Image in the White Mind: The Debate on Afro-American Character and Destiny, 1817–1914* (New York: Harper and Row, 1971).

Study Questions and Further Reading for Part III

1 How, according to Fox-Genovese and Genovese, did proslavery thinkers use the Bible to justify slavery?
2 How did northern and southern religion differ with regard to the preservation of social order?
3 How did proslavery ideologues in South Carolina use gender to support slavery?
4 Compare and contrast the arguments of Fox-Genovese and Genovese and McCurry. What are the principal disagreements and agreements between the two interpretations?

Ashworth, John 1987: The relationship between capitalism and humanitarianism. *American Historical Review*, 92, 813–28.
Collins, Bruce 1985: *White Society in the Antebellum South*. London: Longman.
Davis, David Brion 1987: Reflection on abolitionism and ideological hegemony. *American Historical Review*, 92, 797–812.

Donald, David 1971: The proslavery argument reconsidered. *Journal of Southern History*, 37, 3–18.

Faust, Drew Gilpin 1977: *A Sacred Circle: The Dilemma of the Intellectual in the Old South, 1840–1860*. Baltimore, MD: Johns Hopkins University Press.

Faust, Drew Gilpin 1981: *The Ideology of Slavery: Proslavery Thought in the Antebellum South, 1830–1860*. Baton Rouge: Louisiana State University Press.

Faust, Drew Gilpin 1982: *James Henry Hammond and the Old South: A Design for Mastery*. Baton Rouge: Louisiana State University Press.

Ford, Lacy K. Jr 1988: *Origins of Southern Radicalism: The South Carolina Upcountry, 1800–1860*. New York: Oxford University Press.

Fox-Genovese, Elizabeth 1983: Antebellum southern households: A new perspective on a familiar question. *Review*, 7, 215–53.

Fredrickson, George M. 1971: *The Black Image in the White Mind: The Debate on Afro-American Character and Destiny, 1817–1914*. New York: Harper and Row.

Genovese, Eugene D. 1992: *The Slaveholders' Dilemma: Freedom and Progress in Southern Conservative Thought, 1820–1860*. Columbia: University of South Carolina Press.

Hahn, Steven 1983: *The Roots of Southern Populism: Yeoman Farmers and the Transformation of the Georgia Upcountry, 1850–1890*. New York: Oxford University Press.

Haskell, Thomas L. 1985: Capitalism and the origins of humanitarian sensibility, parts I and II. *American Historical Review*, 90, 339–61, 457–566.

Holifield, E. Brooks 1978: *The Gentlemen Theologians: American Theology in Southern Culture, 1779–1860*. Durham, NC: Duke University Press.

Jenkins, William S. 1935: *Proslavery Thought in the Old South*. Chapel Hill: University of North Carolina Press.

Kolchin, Peter 1980: In defense of servitude: American proslavery and Russian proserfdom arguments, 1760–1860. *American Historical Review*, 85, 809–27.

Loveland, Anne C. 1980: *Southern Evangelicals and the Social Order, 1800–1860*. Baton Rouge: Louisiana State University Press.

McCurry, Stephanie 1995: *Masters of Small Worlds: Yeomen Households, Gender Relations, and the Political Culture of the Antebellum South Carolina Lowcountry*. New York: Oxford University Press.

Maddex, Jack P. 1979: "The southern apostasy" revisited: The significance of proslavery Christianity. *Marxist Perspectives*, 2, 132–41.

Mathews, Donald G. 1977: *Religion in the Old South*. Chicago, IL: University of Chicago Press.

Snay, Mitchell 1997: *Gospel of Disunion: Religion and Separatism in the Antebellum South*. Chapel Hill: University of North Carolina Press.

Startup, Kenneth Moore 1997: *The Root of All Evil: The Protestant Clergy and the Economic Mind of the Old South*. Athens: University of Georgia Press.

Tise, Larry E. 1987: *Proslavery: A History of the Defense of Slavery in America, 1701–1840*. Athens: University of Georgia Press.

Wayne, Michael 1990: An Old South morality play: Reconsidering the social underpinnings of proslavery ideology. *Journal of American History*, 77, 838–63.

Part IV
Communities, Cultures, and Economies: Lives of the Enslaved

Introduction to Documents and Essays

One of the most important advances made by historians of slavery in the past two decades is their uncovering of slaves' independent economic activities – the acquisition and disposal of property by property. The following documents and essays explore this dynamic in detail. How did slaves acquire property? What did they do with it when they got it? And, most importantly, what does this acquisition and disposal of property by property mean for our understanding of slavery generally and the viability of the slave community in particular?

7

Benefits of the Lowcountry Slaves' Economy

Charles Manigault's Plantation Journal, 1844

There were limits to all planters' authority and nowhere were these limits more apparent than in the task system used principally in the rice growing districts of the lowcountry of South Carolina and Georgia. The task system defined work not so much according to time but, rather, to finishing a defined, preset job. Initially, planters, especially those involved in rice cultivation, defined what they thought constituted a reasonable task. The enslaved, however, often renegotiated the task. Certainly, they resisted any efforts to increase it. Here, we see Charles Manigault, a rice planter on Argyle Island in the Savannah River, bemoaning the fact that his slaves found ways to limit their workload, stick to what they considered a reasonable and fair day's task, and, in the process, finish their tasks early and gain more free time for themselves. The extracts are from Manigault's plantation journal for 1844. (From Charles Manigault's 1844 Plantation Journal, Manigault Family Papers, #484, in the Southern Historical Collection, Wilson Library, University of North Carolina at Chapel Hill, Chapel Hill, NC)

I have heard much discussion among Planters respecting the Quantity averaged in threshing with the flail stick. 12 Bushels are said to be the task while some planters say that one day with another they do not get more than 5 or 6 Bushels of cleaned winnowed rice. I have this day made a calculation with Mr. [A. R.] Bagshaw [Manigault's overseer at this time] & measured carefully. I have say 25 full hands on the floor 12 men who do 600 sheaves each 13 women & weak hands 500 each.

Mr. Bagshaw says the usual sized shaves should always give 2 bushels every hundred sometimes $2\frac{1}{2}$ bushels which latter would turn out 15 Bushels the 600 sheaves. But Negroes are cunning enough to remember that what they are harvesting they will have to thresh, & will tie as small sheaves as they can. Mr. B[agshaw] says at this last harvest he told them that he would give them 110 for every 100 if they went on tieing such small sheaves. Well, the last weeks threshing on an average each man & woman's threshing when winnowed out is ten Bushels. I told Mr. B[agshaw] that some planters went entirely by measure, & had a tub on the threshing floor which when full of the threshed rice just from under the flail mixed with the threshed particles of straw & tailings so as to come at a due estimation of their being what will produce when winnowed 12 Bushels. "Yes" said he, but the negro will then knock away so as to break up & intermix the greatest possible quantity of cut straw &c. with his days task & thus defeat justice by rendering things uncertain & unequal.

A South Carolina Rice Planter on the Slaves' Economy, 1858

Here, a South Carolina rice planter describes the slaves' economy on his plantation and outlines the benefits of the system for master and slave. (From James R. Sparkman to Benjamin Allston, March 10, 1858, from the collections of the South Carolina Historical Society, Charleston, SC)

The moral and social condition of the Slave population in this district has vastly improved within 20 years. The control, management and entire discipline has materially changed, crime and rebellion are much less frequent. They have learnt in many instances to govern themselves and to govern each other and throughout this section, "*Runaways*" are fewer and "*less lawless*." The improvements in Machinery has relieved them of a large portion of the heaviest work. Agriculture has improved too, labor is more judiciously and economically bestowed. Comforts have multiplied, and although the routine of duty on a Rice plantation *to day* is incomparably less arduous to the slave than at any period heretofore. As an illustration of the "indulgencies" which my own people enjoy, I have during the past year kept an item of their perquisites from the sale (to me) of Eggs, poultry, Provisions saved from their allowance, and the raising of hogs, and it amounts in Money to upwards of $130, and in Sugar, Molasses, Flour, Coffee, Handkerchiefs, Aprons,

Homespun and Calico, Pavilion Gause (Mosquito Nets), Tin Buckets, hats, pocket knives, seives etc. to the am't of $110 more. One man received $25, and another $27, for hogs of their own raising and I had the satisfaction of seeing most of these am'ts spent in comforts and presents to their families.

The question has frequently presented itself whether or not this habit of buying for my people articles which are ordinarily only to be obtained through shop keepers, and retailing to them in exchange for their poultry etc. etc. might not lead to some *abuse* and cause them to pilfer or speculate upon each other. Limiting this rule strictly to my own people I have found it to work well. They frequently ask me to become *Treasurer* of their little funds. I have become satisfied that they get better bargains than can be made by themselves with the shop keepers. I hold now in this way upwards of $70, which will be called for in dimes and quarters, through the current year. As a *system* this can not be carried out in detail *generally*, for only those who are *permanent residents*, can very well undertake it. But the custom prevails with most of my neighbors of supplying all reasonable demands by exchange as indicated, whilst some prefer paying in *Money* and allowing them to trade for themselves. The point established is that by reasonable industry and ordinary providence, our people all have it in their power to add materially to their comforts and indulgencies, and that their owners very wisely and humanely offer every encouragement to this effort.

Petition and Deposition of Former Slaves, 1873

After the Civil War, the federal government established the Southern Claims Commission in an effort to return and compensate freedpeople (as well as whites) for property unjustly taken from them during the war by Union forces. The various petitions that go to make up the claims are very useful for helping historians identify what slaves owned under slavery. Presented here is the petition and deposition of Jane Holmes, March 3, 1873, of Liberty County, Georgia. (From Case Files, Southern Claims Commission, Records of the Third Auditor, Records of the US General Accounting Office, Record Group 217, National Archives, Washington, DC)

PETITION

OF

Jane Holmes

TO THE COMMISSIONERS OF CLAIMS.

Residence of Claimant Liberty County, Georgia
Nature of Claim Stores for Genrl Shermans Army
Amount claimed, $492.00

No. of Item	NATURE OF CLAIM	AMOUNT CLAIMED Dollars	Cts	AMOUNT ALLOWED Dollars	Cts	AMOUNT DISALLOWED Dollars	Cts
1	One horse	150		90		60	
2	8 cows & calves	160		15		145	
3	5 hogs	40		15		25	
4	20 Bushels corn	20				20	
5	20 " rice	40				40	
6	20 fowls	5				5	
7	10 pairs ducks	5				5	
8	20 hives of honey	30				30	
9	One jar of butter	2	50			2	50
10	Kitchen furniture	30				30	
11	Bedding quilts &c	10				10	
		$492	50	$120		372	50

REMARKS

The claimant is a widow – was a slave & a field hand – she belonged to Joseph Bacon – Her husband was living during the war & was overseer for Rev. Dr. CC Jones.

This claim & many others filed by the colored people of Liberty Co. Ga – former slaves have been thoroughly investigated by agents of the commission – But few of these claims have been found meritorious. In this case we think the claimant had such a title to her property, taken by the Federal Army for supplies, as will justify a favorable report – We refer to the report of our agent Mr. Arny [?] & the testimony in the cases.

Most of the items of the claim are not army supplies and unfortunately the soldiers, as claimant testifies penned up her cattle with others & wantonly shot them down leaving the carcases for the buzzards – using but very little of the meat itself. It is doubtful whether the corn & rice was anything more than rations – We recommend the payment of $120. . . .

Testimony of Claimant

Interrogation by Special Commission.

1   My name is Jane Holmes. I was born in Liberty Co. Ga, a slave; became free when Sherman's Army came here. I think I am over 60 years old . . . I work in the field. I am the Claimant in this case.

2   I lived at Brier bay Liberty Co . . . I followed the Army to Savannah. . . .

29   I cooked for the soldiers after they came in here with the Army. I did anything else for them that they wanted me to do. . . .

43   At the beginning of the rebellion I was a slave & became free when the Union Army came through here. I went right to farming as soon as I became free. I came out of Savannah in July & went right at farming & been farming ever since. I labored for this property. I worked by tasks. My master gave us tasks & when we done we worked for ourselves. I raised chickens & hogs & got a cow & by raising & increasing I got my horse. For more than 30 years before the Army came here I was working & raising in this way. It is more than 30 years since I bought my first mare. I raised 9 horses from her, I sold one to Peter Harden, & sold one to my brother Denbo Bird, & one to Cato Holmes, & the Rebels stole one from me that makes 4. . . . My master would allow me to buy & sell & raise anything except cotton he wouldn't allow us to raise cotton. . . .

Testimony of Witness
Interrogation by Special Commissioners.
My name is Sampson Bacon. I was born in Liberty County, a slave and made free by the Yankees when they came into the County. I belonged to Joseph R Bacon, I am about 80 years of age. I live at Brier bay, I am a farmer, I know the claimant in this case. I am not related to her in any way. I have no beneficial interest in her claim & only came here to testify for her. I have known Mrs Holmes the claimant from a little girl & know she was a good Union Woman during the War I lived on the same Plantation with her, we belonged to the same Master. I was his driver for 40 or 50 years and when the Yankees came into the County. My Master worked all his hands by the task – a hand who was industrious could finish their task by 1, 2, & 3 Oclock PM. The balance of the time was their own – to do what they pleased Mrs Holmes was a good servant and industrious. I knew her husband he was a good servant and got along well. I know "Jane" owned the property charged in her account she had been raising horses for a long time and other things, Cattle, hogs, Poultry, and such like – her master always allowed her to raise and

own such things and any thing else she could time and money to pay for – he never interfered with his slaves property & know that because I was his driver and knew all about his business management &c. The property all belonged to her, her husband belonged to C. C. Jones and she belonged to Joseph R Bacon.

Benefits of the Lowcountry Slaves' Economy

Philip D. Morgan

Perhaps the most distinctive and central feature of slave life in the lowcountry region of South Carolina and Georgia was the task system. In Lewis C. Gray's words, "Under the task system the slave was assigned a certain amount of work for the day, and after completing the task he could use his time as he pleased." However, under the gang system, prevalent in most Anglo-American plantation societies, "slaves were worked in groups under the control of a driver or leader. . . . [and] the laborer was compelled to work the entire day. . . ."[1] The significance of this peculiar labor arrangement for those who operated it – particularly the use slaves made of "their time" to produce goods and gain access to property – has never before been systematically explored. This is the aim of the present essay.

The most obvious advantage of the task system to the slaves was the flexibility it permitted them in determining the length of the working day. The nearly universal lament that we hear whenever ex-slaves reminisce is that labor under slavery was "exhausting and unremitting." Working from sunup to sundown "was the pervasive reality." Ex-slaves from the low country recall a different reality. Listen to Richard Cummings, a former field hand: " . . . a good active industrious man would finish his task sometimes at 12, sometimes at 1 and 2 oclock and the rest of the time was his own to use as he pleased." Or to Scipio King, another former field hand: "I could save for myself sometimes a whole day if I could do 2 tasks in a day then I had the next day to myself. Some kind of work I could do 3 tasks in a day." Or to the ex-slave cooper who

From Philip D. Morgan, "The ownership of property by slaves in the mid-nineteenth-century low country," *Journal of Southern History*, 49 (1983), pp. 399–420. Copyright © 1983 by the Southern Historical Association. Excerpt reprinted by permission of the Managing Editor and the author.

remembered "hav[ing] from midday till night – sometimes from 3 o'clock and sometimes later" to work on his own behalf. Or, finally, to the former slave driver who recalled seeing men split two hundred rails a day, "and in that way have a day for themselves." . . .

Angrier voices occasionally make themselves heard above the swelling choruses of praise. One ex-slave voiced a criticism which, if general, would have undermined the main advantage of the system. Harry Porter, a former field slave, remembered that if the slaves on his plantation "got through early or half an hour before sundown . . . [their master] would give them more next day." During harvest time or other periods of comparable urgency the temptation to increase the work load must have been hard for planters to resist. And yet Frederick Law Olmsted identified one pertinent reason why few planters succumbed: "In nearly all ordinary work," Olmsted observed, "custom has settled the extent of the task, and it is difficult to increase it." If these customs were systematically ignored, Olmsted continued, the planter simply increased the likelihood "of a general stampede to the 'swamp'." Another complaint was less against the task system itself than against its incomplete application. One former slave remembered that slaves sometimes "had no task but worked by the day, then they worked till 5 oclock." Olmsted witnessed a group of low-country women "working by the day" rather than by task; and his observations once again explain its relative infrequency. The women, he noted, were "keeping steadily, and it seemed sullenly, on at their work," but they cleared only a quarter of the ground that would have been accomplished in task work. To work "steadily" was just not the low-country way. Indeed, more than one low-country ex-slave was unable to recall a single planter "who worked his hands from sun to sun."

A less tangible, but no less real, reason for the attachment of slaves to the tasking system was the sense of personal responsibility that it inculcated. Planters certainly tried to "create responsibility," as one put it, by offering the same task of ground to a slave throughout the season. In that way, "Where a negro knows that the task he is working is to be worked by him the next time he goes over the field, he is induced, in order to render the next working as light as possible, to work it well as [at] first." Olmsted was impressed by the results of this policy. The laborer under the task system, he noted, "works more rapidly, energetically, and, within narrow limits, with much greater use of discretion, or skill, than he is often found to do elsewhere." By assuming responsibility for his task, the slave had to be treated responsibly. He was not to be called away from his task: this would be tantamount to an invasion of his "customary privileges," one planter explained. Put another way, one former slave recalled how "his master used to come in the field, and tell the overseer not to balk we, if we got done soon to let us alone and do our own work as we pleased." This sense of personal responsibility, this quasi-proprietorial attitude that the system encouraged, may well explain one of the most distinctive responses of low-country slaves when confronted with freedom. It is graphically captured in the exchange that occurred in 1866 between a woman field hand and a plantation agent who had apparently overstepped his authority. She "ordered me out of her task," the agent reported, "saying if I come into her Task again she would put me in the ditch." An army officer who inspected another lowland plantation was "hooted at" and told by the freedmen that "they wanted nothing to do with white men." Without in any way suggesting that slavery was a beneficent school in which slaves gained a valuable education, perhaps a low-country master was close to the mark (closer than he realized) when he suggested that, under the task system, the slaves had "learnt in many instances to govern themselves and to govern each other...."

A sharply felt sense of personal responsibility was allied to a recognition of the merits of collective solidarity. A task system could conceivably encourage an individualistic, not to mention competitive, ethic; low-country slaves, on the other hand, seem on the whole to have valued the relative freedom it permitted for pooling resources when necessary. One planter recalled witnessing "with much pleasure the husband assisting the wife after he has finished his own task, and sometimes I have seen several members of a family in like manner, unite in aiding those who have been less fortunate than themselves in accomplishing their tasks." Speaking to the same point, but less romantically, James R. Sparkman reckoned "it is customary (and never objected to) for the more active and industrious hands to assist those who are slower and more tardy in finishing their daily task." Even less romantically, Richard Mack, an ex-slave interviewed in the 1930s, remembered that when he had "done all my task, and I help[ed] others with their task so they wouldn't get whipped...." The first few years of freedom could conceivably have seen an overthrow of any preexisting communal straitjacket. Instead, observers were astonished at the solid front presented by the low-country freedmen. "It is really wonderful," noted one army commander in January 1866, "how unanimous they are; communicating like magic, and now holding out, knowing the importance of every day in regard to the welfare of the next crop, thinking that the planters will be obliged to come to their terms."

The merits of collective solidarity could also be experienced in familial form. Once tasks were completed, slaves could work in groups of their own choosing. Many ex-slaves recall that family groups were by far the most preferred units. Susan Bennett, a former slave, remembered how she and her husband had worked "together on our own works after we got through our tasks"; George Gould and his wife, both former slaves, "put their labor together" after completing their tasks; Prince Wilson, an ex-slave from Chatham County, Georgia, recollected how his family of nine had "all worked together and all worked at task work and raised [their own] corn in that way." Toney Elliott had resided on a different plantation from his wife when he was a slave, but he recalled how "my wife and myself raised this corn and rice together. We both worked by task and when I had done my task I went over to her house and we both worked together." A neighbor added that Toney Elliott's son also helped his father; in fact, the neighbor noted with some surprise, the son worked only for his father and mother because he "had a master that didn't put his boys into the field until they were 15 or 16 years old." In other words, slave kin groups and families in the low country could function as significant *economic* units for at least a part of the working day.

Another facet of this collective solidarity can be detected in the reaction of the freedmen to their former drivers. Throughout the South the authority of the driver generally evaporated once freedom came. Many an ex-slave, interviewed in the 1930s, testified to the hatred felt by field hands towards these men. Although a loss of the driver's prestige occurred in the low country – Edward S. Philbrick reckoned that the driver's influence was reduced to "a cypher" – a more ambivalent response, traceable perhaps to the special role of the driver in a task system, can also be discerned. The special role of the driver in the low country stemmed from his role as "the second Master," as one former slave put it, whose function was not to wield a whip over a line of gang slaves but, rather, to allocate tasks, to ensure that they were satisfactorily performed, and to fulfill other managerial duties. Furthermore, in some respects, the driver was seen to be at a disadvantage for having, as one ex-slave put it, "no task-work and [having] no time of his own." By way of compensation, low-country drivers were entitled to receive a certain amount of help in tending their own crops.

The task system was, in other words, the yardstick by which most work in the low country was measured. It bound all slaves together. Thus, the unusual spectacle of field hands rallying behind their former drivers, which occurred in the low country in the immediate postemancipation years, becomes a little more explicable. When a white agent ordered a "Headman" to "take his hoe and work under the contract with the rest," he found himself facing the fury of a number of field hands; when he returned with a party of soldiers, he had to beat another hasty retreat under a barrage of blows from the women laborers. In one labor contract drawn up between a Georgia planter and thirty-four freedmen, the freedmen agreed to pay out of their share of the crop an extra cash sum to their foreman. This contract is a testimonial to the respect with which at least some foremen were held. . . .

The task system was characterized by, and indeed encouraged, a number of traits – an ability to lengthen or shorten the working day, a sense of personal responsibility, a commitment to and economic underpinning for the slave family, and attitudes of collective solidarity and communal worth. All these features manifested themselves, and in one sense reached their fullest expression, in the ability of low-country slaves to accumulate property. An investigation of this subject is the focus for the remainder of this essay.

Mid-nineteenth-century evidence exists by which it is possible to assess, however imprecisely, the scale and range of property-owning by slaves. It takes the form of depositions and supporting testimony submitted to the Southern Claims Commission from former slaves who could prove both their loyalty and their loss of property to Federal troops. Frank W. Klingberg, the author of the standard monograph on the work of the commission, may well have been correct, in general terms, when he stated that "A very small number of claims were filed by former slaves, for the obvious reason that during the war years they were virtually a propertyless class."[2] But this statement is inaccurate for the low-country region of South Carolina and Georgia. The settled or allowed claims from Liberty County, Georgia, amounted to ninety-two, of which eighty-nine were from ex-slaves. There were an additional sixty-one settled claims from ex-slaves in the neighboring counties of Chatham, Georgia, and Beaufort, South Carolina. As it is, the settled claims from the low-country region come overwhelmingly from ex-slaves; but if, as Klingberg suggests, most claims filed by former slaves were disallowed for lack of clear title, the disproportion between white and black claims would be greatly magnified.

Apart from the exaggeration virtually inherent in claims for loss of property (discussed below), a consideration of the background of these claims enhances, rather than diminishes, their historical value. First of all, only those areas where Federal troops officially took or were furnished quartermaster and commissary "stores and supplies" could produce claimants. In other words, the geographical origins of the claimants are bound to reveal a significant clustering, with some areas of the low country being totally unrepresented; moreover, the claims themselves probably do not represent all the property that the claimant owned. Second, although the total number of ex-slave claimants from the low country is small (a minute fraction of the number of slaves resident in their respective counties), they were not a privileged minority. Former field hands outnumber all other occupational groups, and while most claimants were mature adults when their property was taken, a significant number were under the age of thirty-five.

Finally, an awareness of the hurdles that had to be overcome before a claim could even be submitted, not to mention settled, makes the list of ex-slave claimants more impressive. To find a competent attorney and to be able to pay him (most freedmen had to employ a succession of attorneys) were major obstacles. Overcoming the ridicule and opposition of neighboring whites must have tested the determination of many an aspiring claimant. One ex-slave refused to call his former master as a witness in his claim "because he always was a great Rebel and now tries to cry down this claims business and tells people that they never will get nothing." Just being available when the commissioners came to the neighborhood was not necessarily a simple matter. One freedwoman, acting as a witness in another's claim, mentioned in passing that Federal troops had taken her buggy, potatoes, and poultry but that she had submitted no claim, for "when they were putting in claims, I had the rheumatism and couldn't go."

The historical value of these claims is enhanced because in them the authentic voice of the slave (or rather, the recently freed slave) can be heard, not recalling experiences some sixty or seventy years after the event but immediately and pointedly. These claim depositions are not simply matter-of-fact inventories of lost property but personal, moving statements. They combine a touching concern for detail (names of purchasers, prices paid, and dates of purchase); a dash of pride (one freedman referred to having raised stock "ever since I had sense"; another to having raised "fowls almost as soon as I could walk"; and a third claimed that "some slaves had more property than the crackers"); and an occasional display of emotion (Lydia Brown "cried when they took [my property]. I know I was foolish but I couldn't help it. I was very glad to see them come; but I didn't think they would take my things"); while the overall flavor was salty and direct (the appearance of William Tecumseh Sherman's troops was likened, among other things, to a pack of "ravenous wolves [that] didn't say howdy" and to "a flock of blackbirds only you could not scare them").

An analysis of these claims – and for this the Liberty County, Georgia, claims will serve as the sample – provides as detailed a survey as one can ever expect of the amount and variety of property owned by slaves on the eve of emancipation. Virtually all the Liberty County ex-slave claimants had apparently been deprived of a number of hogs and a substantial majority listed corn, rice, and fowls among their losses. In addition, a surprising number apparently possessed horses and cows, while buggies or wagons, beehives, peanuts, fodder, syrup, butter, sugar, and tea were, if these claims are to be believed, in the hands of at least some slaves.

The average cash value (in 1864 dollars) claimed by Liberty County former slaves was $357.43, with the highest claim totaling $2,290 and the lowest $49.

Before passing to a more detailed analysis of these claims, a pertinent question needs to be addressed. Can a person who is owned himself "own" property in any meaningful sense? A partial answer to this question is supplied by the claim process itself. Many ex-slaves were, after all, reimbursed for their loss of property, which constitutes one test of the validity of their titles. On average, the freedmen received 40 percent of the asserted value of their claims. But this, in turn, raises the question of why the commissioners discounted almost two-thirds of most freedmen's claims. The answer does not generally lie in exaggerated claims (although some undoubtedly were) or in disputed titles but, rather, in the construction put on the term "army supply." Virtually all claims for buggies, fowls, beehives, clothing, and crockery were automatically disregarded because these items were not considered to be legitimate army supplies. Though the commissioners and some planters often took issue with the values attached to the ex-slaves' property, rarely did they dispute the fact of possession. In fact, the testimony of whites is impressive in its support of the details of many freedmen's claims. Raymond Cay, Sr., a Liberty County planter, knew that slaves owned cattle on George Howe's plantation because he had himself purchased cattle from them; a slave's ownership of a buggy was proved when the county postmaster and his wife admitted to hiring it on Sundays; and one master even acknowledged paying taxes for one of his slaves who possessed horses, cattle, and a buggy.

While conceding that slaves in some sense possessed property, it may be argued that this property was held only on the sufferance of the master. In the final analysis, could not the master always expropriate all the property supposedly owned by the slave? Many ex-slaves addressed this question and, not surprisingly, showed a keen understanding of it. Some were exceedingly forthright and blunt about the matter: Hercules LeCount stressed that his master "did not own or even claim a cents worth of... [his property]"; Prince Wilson asserted that he was "the only one who has any legal right to the property"; and Henry Stephens "never heard of a master's claiming property that belonged to his slaves." When one witness was asked to address directly the proposition that a horse claimed by a slave in fact belonged to his master, he emphatically refuted the suggestion by stating "what was his'n [that is, the slave's] was his'n." One former bondsman, who, as a slave, was married to a free black woman, made the interesting claim that she "could own and hold property the same as slaves were allowed by their masters to hold property." Some slaves obviously believed that their titles to property were more, rather than less, secure because it was held, as one freedman put it, "by [the] master's protection." Others were prepared to admit the de facto nature of their property ownership, but this did little to diminish their assertiveness. . . .

If one accepts, then, that the property (or at least some of it) listed in these claims actually belonged to the slaves, what can this information tell us? Most conspicuous perhaps is the sheer amount of property claimed by some slaves. Paris James, a former slave driver, was described by a neighboring white planter as a "substantial man before the war [and] was more like a free man than any slave." James claimed, among other things, a horse, eight cows, sixteen sheep, twenty-six hogs, and a wagon. Another slave driver, according to one of his black witnesses, lived "just like a white man except his color. His credit was just as good as a white man's because he had the property to back it." Although the commissioners of claims were skeptical about his alleged loss of twenty cows (as they explained, "Twenty cows would make a good large dairy for a Northern farmer"), his two white and three black witnesses supported him in his claim. Other blacks were considered to be "more than usually prosperous," "pretty well off," and "hardworking and money-saving," unremarkable characterizations perhaps but surprising when the individuals were also slaves. Alexander Steele, a carpenter by trade and former house servant in Chatham County, Georgia, submitted a claim for $2,205 based on the loss of his four horses, mule, a silver watch, two cows, a wagon, and large quantities of fodder, hay, and corn. He had been able to acquire these possessions by "tradeing" for himself for thirty years; he had had "much time of . . . [his] own" because his master "always went north" in the summer months. He took "a fancy. . . [to] fine horses," a whim he was able to indulge when he purchased "a blooded mare," from which he raised three colts. He was resourceful enough to hide his livestock on Onslow Island when Sherman's army drew near, but the Federal troops secured boats and took off his prized possessions. Three white planters supported Steele in his claim; indeed, one of them recalled that before the war he had made an offer of $300 for one of Steele's colts, an offer that Steele refused.

The ownership of horses was not, however, confined to a privileged minority of slaves. Among the Liberty County claimants, almost as many ex-field hands claimed horses as did former drivers and skilled slaves. This evidence supplies a context for the exchange recorded by Frederick Law Olmsted when he was being shown around the plantation of Richard J. Arnold in Bryan County, Georgia. Olmsted noticed a horse drawing a wagon of "common fieldhand negroes" and asked his host if he usually let the slaves have horses to ride to church.

"Oh, no; that horse belongs to the old man."
"Belongs to him! Why, do they own horses?"
"Oh, yes; William (the House servant) owns two, and Robert, I believe,
    has three now; that was one of them he was riding."
"How do they get them?"
"Oh, they buy them."

Although a few freedmen recalled that former masters had either
prohibited horse ownership among slaves or confined the practice to
drivers, most placed the proportion of horse owners on any single
plantation at between 15 and 20 percent. A former slave of George
Washington Walthour reckoned that "In all my master's plantations
there were over 30 horses owned by slaves.... I think come to count
up there were as many as 45 that owned horses – he would let them
own any thing they could if they only did his work." Nedger Frazer, a
former slave of the Reverend Charles Colcock Jones, recalled that on one
of his master's plantations (obviously Arcadia, from Frazer's description) there were forty working hands, of whom five owned horses; and
on another (obviously Montevideo) there were another ten hands out of
fifty who owned horses. This, in turn, supplies a context for an interesting incident that occurred within the Jones "family" in 1856. In that year
Jones, after much soul-searching, sold one of his slave families, headed
by Cassius, a field hand. Jones, a man of integrity, then forwarded
Cassius the balance of his account, which amounted to $85, a sum
that included the proceeds from the sale of Cassius's horse. Perhaps
one freedman was not exaggerating when he observed in 1873 that
"there was more stock property owned by slaves before the war
than are owned now by both white and black people together in this
county."
The spectacular claims and the widespread horse ownership naturally
catch the eye, but even the most humdrum claim has its own story to tell.
Of particular interest for this essay, each contains a description of how
property was accumulated. The narrative of John Bacon can stand as
proxy for many such accounts: "I had a little crop to sell and bought
some chickens and then I bought a fine large sow and gave $10.00 for
her. This was about ten years before the war and then I raised hogs and
sold them till I bought a horse. This was about eight years before freedom. This was a breeding mare and from this mare I raised this horse
which the Yankees took from me." This was painstaking accumulation:
no wonder one freedman referred to his former property as his "labor-
ment." And yet, occasionally, the mode of procurement assumed a
slightly more sophisticated cast. Some slaves recalled purchasing horses
by installment; some hired additional labor to cultivate their crops; two

slaves (a mill engineer and a stockminder) went into partnership to raise livestock; and a driver lent out money at interest.

But whatever the mode of accumulation, the ultimate source, as identified by virtually all the ex-slaves, was the task system. Even slaves who had escaped field labor attributed their acquisition of property to this form of labor organization. Thus, a former wagoner was able to work on his own behalf, he recalled, because he was tasked; a waiting man explained that "if... [he] was given Morning work and... got thro' before 12 oclock... [he] was allowed to go" and produce for himself; and a dairy woman was able to acquire her possessions because she "worked and earned money outside her regular task work." For field hands, of course, this advantage was universally recognized. Provided a slave had "a mind to save the time," one former slave pointed out, he could take advantage of the task system to produce goods and acquire possessions. Joseph James, a former field hand, emphatically underlined the connection between tasking and property owning; all low-country slaves "worked by tasks," he noted, "and had a plenty of time to work for themselves and in that way all slaves who were industrious could get around them considerable property in a short time."

What all this suggests is that by the middle of the nineteenth century it is correct to speak of a significant internal economy operating within a more conventional low-country economy. According to the depositions of the freedmen this internal economy rested on two major planks. The first concerns the degree to which some slaves engaged in stock raising. One white planter, testifying on behalf of a freedman, recalled that "a good many" slaves owned a number of animals; he then checked himself, perhaps realizing the impression that he was creating, and guardedly stated that "What I mean was they were not allowed to go generally into stock raising." And yet some slaves seem to have been doing just that. One ex-slave spoke of raising "horses to sell"; another claimed to have raised fourteen horses over a period of twenty-five to thirty years, most of which he had sold; and one freedwoman named the purchasers, all of whom were slaves, of the nine horses that she had raised.

The other major foundation upon which this internal economy rested was the amount of crop production by slaves. Jeremiah Evarts observed that the slaves in Chatham County, Georgia, had "as much land as they can till for their own use." The freedmen's recollections from all over the low country support this statement. A number of ex-slaves reckoned that they had more than ten acres under cultivation, though four or five acres was the norm; and one freedman pointed out that low-country slaves "were allowed all the land they could tend without rent." The proprietorial attitude that this independent production encouraged is suggested in one freedman's passing comment that, when he was a slave, he used to work in his "own field" after completing his task.

Through the raising of stock and the production of provisions, together with the sale of produce from woodworking, basketmaking, hunting, and fishing, slaves were able to draw money into their internal economy. Some of these exchanges were regarded as legitimate, and their scale can occasionally be glimpsed. Robert Wilson Gibbes, for example, knew of an individual slave who received $120 from his master for his year's crop of corn and fodder; Richard J. Arnold owed his slaves $500 in 1853 when Olmsted visited him. Other exchanges were regarded as illegitimate, and the scale of these transactions remain clouded in obscurity. One freedman spoke of being about to sell the fruits of his three-acre crop "to a man in Tatnall County" when the plundering Federal troops dashed his hopes; another ex-slave spoke of taking his corn to Riceboro in exchange for tobacco. The recipients of such exchanges were, according to Richard Dennis Arnold, waxing fat on the proceeds. He noted that "These little shops [of Savannah] afford an ever ready market where the demand is always equal to the supply." As a result, he added, these shopkeepers "often acquire large fortunes." He cited one "man who commenced one of these negro shops with perhaps not fifty dollars of capital, some thirteen years [ago] . . . ," and in 1850 "bought at public outcry some wharf property for which he paid $19,000." Similarly, Daniel Elliott Huger Smith reckoned that "the keepers of the smaller grocery shops" in Charleston "made a good profit" from trading with slaves. Thus, while produce and livestock were constantly being bartered by slaves ("swapping" was rife, according to the freedmen) one observer of the mid-nineteenth-century low country was undoubtedly correct when he noted that "In a small way a good deal of money circulated among the negroes, both in the country and in the towns."

The autonomy of this internal economy is further indicated by the development of a highly significant practice. By the middle of the nineteenth century, if not before, slave property was not only being produced and exchanged but also inherited. The father of Joseph Bacon bequeathed him a mare and left all his other children $50 each. Samuel Elliott claimed a more substantial legacy. His father "had 20 head of cattle, about 70 head of hogs – Turkeys Geese Ducks and Chickens a Plenty – he was foreman for his master and had been raising such things for years. When he died the property was divided among his children and we continued to raise things just as he had been raising." Property was also bequeathed to less immediate kin. Two freedmen recalled receiving property from their grandfathers; another inherited a sow from his cousin; and William Drayton of Beaufort County, South Carolina, noted that when his father died he "left with his oldest brother, my uncle, the means or property he left for his children"; and Drayton bought a mule "by the advice of my uncle who had the means belonging to me." There were rules governing lines of descent: one woman claimant emphasized that she had not inherited any of her first husband's property because she had borne him no children; rather, the property went to his son by a former marriage. The ability to bequeath wealth and to link patrimony to genealogy serves to indicate the extent to which slaves created autonomy for themselves while they were still enslaved.

Slave property rights were recognized not only across generations but also across proprietorial boundaries. Some slaves employed guardians to facilitate the transfer of property from one plantation to another. Thus, when Nancy Bacon, belonging to John Baker, inherited cattle from her deceased husband, who had belonged to a Mr. Walthour, she employed her second cousin, Andrew Stacy, a slave on the Walthour plantation, to take charge of the cattle and drive them over to her plantation. According to Stacy, Mr. Walthour "didn't object to my taking them . . . [and] never claimed them." The way slaves took advantage of divided ownership is suggested by Diana Cummings of Chatham County, Georgia. Her husband's master, she explained, "allowed him to sell but mine didn't," so Diana marketed her crops and stock through her husband and received a part of the proceeds. On her husband's death she received all his property for, as she put it, her "entitle" (surname) was then the same as her husband's. She had since changed it through remarriage to Sydney Cummings, but, she noted, "He has no interest in [the] property [being claimed]."

By the middle of the nineteenth century the ownership of property by low-country slaves was relatively extensive and had assumed relatively sophisticated dimensions. By way of conclusion, the scale and significance of this phenomenon needs to be assessed as precisely as the evidence will admit. As far as scale is concerned, the proportion of slaves who possessed sizable amounts of property will, of course, never be known, although it is possible to report estimates of horse ownership on some plantations. Moreover, those freedmen who claimed property were not, on the face of it, an unrepresentative group. And yet, for a slave to take advantage of the opportunities inherent in a task system required consistent physical effort. Presumably, the young, the sick, and the aged were very largely excluded from these opportunities. Even those who were not excluded on these grounds may have been unwilling to endure or assume the attendant physical strains. William Gilmore suggests as much when he likened Raymond Cay's slaves to the "five wise and five foolish" and disparaged those who "slept and slumbered the time away."

Much more frequent, however, are the claims of ex-slaves that "almost all had property" or that "Every man on the place had property.... Our master allowed us everything except guns." White planters concurred in this view. One planter from Chatham County, Georgia, recollected that "people generally throughout the country permitted their servants to own hogs, and cattle, and other property to a certain extent. I knew a good many who had one, two, or even four cows. ...There may have been some plantations where the owners did not allow them to own property, but none such in my knowledge." But perhaps the best witnesses are the outsiders. R. B. Avery, the special agent investigating freedmen claims, reported that Somerset Stewart was "poor in slavery times" – not the sort of characterization one would expect of a slave. At the same time, Avery confirmed Stewart's claim to a horse, for which he was allowed $90. If a "poor" slave could own a horse, then property ownership must have been extensive indeed. Rufus Saxton's discovery in the early 1860s that low-country slaves "delight in accumulating" would appear fully justified.

The ownership of property by low-country slaves had a number of short-term consequences. First, the particular conjunction of task system and domestic economy that characterized the lives of low-country slaves afforded a measure of autonomy unusual in New World plantation societies. The low-country slaves worked without supervision in their private endeavors, and even their plantation work was loosely superintended. Second, the private economic activities of the slaves necessarily involved them in a whole range of decision-making, ranging from the planting of a crop to the purchase of an article of consumption. These calculations fed individual initiative and sponsored collective esteem. Third, when laboring in their own plots, slaves could work in cooperative units of their own choice, and these generally took the form of family groups. In addition, low-country slaves not only accumulated wealth in this way, they bequeathed it, which in turn strengthened the family unit. In these respects, low-country slaves resembled the proto-peasants found among Caribbean slaves.

Notes

1   Lewis C. Gray, *History of Agriculture in the Southern United States to 1860*, 2 vols (Washington, DC: The Carnegie Institute of Washington, 1933).
2   Frank W. Klingberg, *The Southern Claims Commission* (Berkeley and Los Angeles: University of California Press, 1955).

8

Ambiguities of the Upcountry Slaves' Economy

Former Slaves Recall Independent Production

Indications of the extent and nature of slaves' independent production on plantations can be gleaned from the testimony of former bondpeople who were interviewed in the 1930s about their experiences under slavery. The first of the two brief extracts is by Charlie Davis, who was 88 years old when interviewed in 1937. Charlie was, therefore, born in 1849 and was, like most of the ex-slaves interviewed in the 1930s, a child during bondage. The second extract echoes the first and is offered by Washington Dozier, who seems to have been born in 1847. Both men were slaves in South Carolina. (From George P. Rawick (ed.), *The American Slave: A Composite Autobiography* (Westport, CT: Greenwood Press, 1972), vol. 2, pt 1, pp. 245–7, 330–1)

Charlie Davis:

I can tell you a good deal bout what de people do in slavery time en how dey live den, ... I gwine tell you it just like I experience it in dem days. We chillun lived well en had plenty good ration to eat all de time cause my mammy cook for she Missus dere to de big house . . . . My Massa had a heap of other colored peoples dere besides we, . . . Dere been bout 80 of dem dat live up in de quarter just like you see dese people live to de sawmill dese days. Dey live mighty near like us, but didn' have no flour bread to eat en didn' get no milk en ham neither cause dey eat to dey own house. Didn' get nothin from de dairy but old clabber en dey been mighty thankful to get dat. Oh, dey had a pretty good house to live in dat was furnish wid dey own things dat dey make right dere. Den dey had a garden of dey own. My Massa give every one of he plantation family so much of land to plant for dey garden en den he give em every Saturday for dey time to tend dat garden. You see dey had to work for de white folks all de other week day en dey know when dey hear dat cow horn blow, dey had to do what de overseer say do ....

Didn' never know nothin bout doing no hard work in us chillun days. When I was a boy, I mind de crows out de field. Oh, crows was terrible bout pickin up peoples corn in times back dere. You see if dey let de crows eat de corn up, dey had to go to de trouble of planting it all over again en dat how-come dey send we chillun in de field to mind de crows off it.

Washington Dozier:

Dis heah sho' Washington Dozier. Dat is wha' de hard time left uv him.... Well, dey [slaves] ne'er hab so mucha sumptin, but I recollect dey make dey own produce den. Oh, dey libe very well. We call it good libin' at dat time.... Hadder do some sorta work in dem days lak hoe corn en re-plant and so on lak dat, but ne'er didn't do no man work. Waz jes uh half hand, dat is 'bout so. Dey gi'e us plenty sumptin to eat den, but ne'er pay us no money. Coase dey didn't 'low us no choice uv wha' we eat at dat time. Had plenty meat en corn bread en molasses mos' aw de time. Den dey le' us hab uh garden uv we own en we hunt possum many uh time en ketch fish too. Meat wuz de t'ing dat I lak mostly.

A Foreign Traveler Observes Wage-earning Slaves, 1860

Insights into southern life often came from foreign observers who traveled in the Old South and then reported on slavery. Laurence Oliphant was but one of many such travelers. In 1860, he reported briefly on the economic activities of whites, free blacks, and, in particular, slaves who, by his account, were embedded firmly in the market economy of the Old South. (From [Laurence Oliphant], "Rambles at random through the southern states," *Blackwood's Magazine*, 87 (January 1860), p. 114)

On the Alabama river especially, I have remained up nearly all night watching the bales of cotton chasing each other down steep slides from the top of a bank two hundred feet high, while uncouth figures, with huge flaring torches, light them on their headlong course .... As there is generally an opposition steamer just behind, despatch is the great object, and the workmen toil furiously: for this they are well paid; and I have seen free negroes and whites working together, and receiving wages at the rate of £120 a-year – a clear proof that at present, at all events, a negro who obtains his freedom need not be afraid of starving. This high rate of wage rather caused me to doubt the wisdom of what a negro once told me, who was on a remarkably well-managed plantation – viz. that slaves were fools if they wanted their liberty when they were under a good master. To be sure, he gave me to understand that a slave had in a great degree only himself to blame if he was not well off. "They'm poor ignorant critturs," he said, "don't know when 'em well off. Tink liberty make em happier – no, *sir*. More nor fifty people on our plantation wouldn't take dere liberty, 'spose you was to say to 'em, 'You free man, you go to debil.' Wife and I, we makes fifteen dollars a-month, one way and noder. 'Spose I say, 'Massa, I go away for a week,' massa darn't stop me; missis would fly at him – missis would – yes, *sir*. Massa more 'fraid of missis dan I am; dodges and hides from her jis like notting. Missis wery good to me, missis is."

Slaves on Trial, 1846

The following excerpts are from the trials of various slaves accused of fighting, resistance, and drunkenness in Anderson District, South Carolina, in 1846. All the accused were found guilty and were whipped. Attention should be directed to how the slaves' economy created conflict within the slave community. Note particularly the nature and perceived cause of the argument between Amos and Andrew, and Aaron's view of property and ownership. (From Pendleton/Anderson District, Court of Magistrates and Freeholders, Trial Papers, Case 185, *State v. Lossan, Bas, Joe, Andrew, Amos, Aaron, Lewis, Jesse*, July 31, 1846, South Carolina Department of Archives and History, Columbia, SC)

South Carolina
Anderson District

Personally appeared Richard Felton before me the subsiding Magistrate and made Oath that on Sabbath 28th June last past he has good reason to believe and does verily believe, that a short time after the close of religious service at Stopewell Church, that Certain negroe Slaves did then and there behave in a most disorderly manner (Viz.) Lossan belonging to Owen being drunk, also Irby's Bas and Duckworths Abe were both Quarrelling and Moorehead's Jesse was selling cakes Bas being stripped to fight, also S. Milliver's [?] Andrew and Doct. Webbs

Amos did there and then near the aforesaid church at or near the Spring and between the Spring and church fight each other and that at or near the same place on Sabbath 19th Inst. there being religious Service conducted by Ceasar a colored preacher a short time after the close of service that a certain fellow said to belong to own named Lewis who was then and there intoxicated, having a bottle and flask in his pockets misled the patrol, and that William Webbs Aaron uttered speeches calculated to excite to and encourage others against submitting to the operation of the laws. And also Lossan belonging to Owen was then and there drunk. Sworn to and subscribed before me this 21st July 1846.

R. Felton

South Carolina
Anderson District

Complaint having been made before me one of the Magistrates assigned to keep the peace in and for Sd. District by Richard Felton on Oath that Certain negroe slaves viz. Owen Lossan Irby's Bas, Duckworth's Joe, Millivers Andrew, Doct. Webbs Amos, Owens Lewis, Wm. Webbs Aaron Owens Lossan 2nd offence & Mooreheads' Jesse on Sabbath 28th June and Sabbath 19 July 1846 behave in a very disorderly manner in drunkenness and rioting fighting & Quarrelling and selling cakes at or near Stopewell Church about the close of worship or a short time afterwards contrary to all established order.

To any Lawful Office of Sd. District these are in the name of the state to authorize and Command you that you arrest all of the aforesaid negroes and bring them before me and a Jury of Free holders at W. L. Hammonds on Friday the 31st July Inst at 11 Oclock A.M. to be dealt with according to Law giving all their owners one days previous notice of the same in order that they may avail themselves of any evidence they may procure in their behalf. Herein fail not at your peril. Given under my hand and seal this 23rd July 1846.

Herbert Hammond

State vs Amos
Fighting at Church

Evidence on Trial
Duckworths Taney Examined

He was not there when they first began Quarrelling. He was at the Meeting house. Meeting had broke about half an hour before they were near the Spring. He saw them pass about two blows apiece. He got between them. He had some ginger cakes with him that day and he understood that he (Amos) and Andrew fell out about a debt contracted by Andrews having purchased some bread from him. Andrew struck the first blow.

Drayton Kermet Sworn

He was one of the patrol. They heard a noise Cursing and Quarrelling. They pursued in that direction and as they approached they run off. They followed them about a Quarter of a mile but could not overtake them. He thinks that Amos was one of them. This happened about half an hour after meeting broke. He saw one negroe have ginger bread and he gave it to another. He did not know either of them....

State vs Joe
Rioting at Church

Pleads not guilty
Evidence

George W. Hammond he saw some negroe stripped seemingly for a fight. They were about 180 yds from them. He heard them Quarreling but did not know who they were. Some of the negroes said that it was Joe and Bas that were about to fight.

Drayton Kermet heard cursing and swearing. He did not see the prisoner to identify him. He thought that there were two men engaged in cursing.

Wilsons Ben. He said Bas give Joe the Damned lie and Joe said it was no such thing that he was the one. He thinks they fell out about a woman. Bas had a stick. He struck a tree with it.

State vs Lewis
Charged with drunkenness and Resistance of Patrol
Evidence
Jesse Masters

He saw him passing about the meeting house spring. One of the patrol asked him where he got the bottle of liquor he saw in his pocket and he said he got down there meaning down the branch. He thinks that Drayton Kermet and Wm. Hammond had hold of him. They told him he had to give up his bottle and he refused to do it. He [wrestled?] loose from him and left his hat and umbrella and ran off....

State vs Aaron
Exciting to resist patrol   pleads not guilty
Jesse Masters in speaking of Lewis's Escape from the patrol and leaving his hat and umbrella he heard Aaron say that he would have taken his hat from him that way. This he said in company of six or eight negroes they all bursted out in a laugh and Aaron joined in the laugh.

Drayton Kermet

He heard him say that he would loose every drop of blood in him before he would give up his hat and that he would not shew his pass to a Master or Hammond because he was so well acquainted with them. Nor did he shew it and as to the rest of the patrol he did not regard.

State vs Jesse
Williams Examined. He saw him with the bread by the old Spring. He brought one piece of bread from him he said the bread was not his when he asked him for pay and when he reminded him of his owing him he consented to discount.

Ambiguities of the Upcountry Slaves' Economy

Lawrence T. McDonnell

Among the usual parade of farmers, planters, and mechanics who visited James Rogers's general store at Orange Hall plantation in 1825, a carpenter came. From the clerk he bought a padlock, a half pint of liquor, and some muslin. He paid less than a dollar for his purchases. Seemingly, it was a simple exchange of property by discrete individuals. One of the individuals, however, the carpenter, was himself property, the slave of Ephrahaim Liles of Union District, South Carolina. Other slaves preceded and followed his example at Orange Hall: skilled workers like Charles the blacksmith and George the mulatto shoemaker, women such as William Silby's servant Jenny, common field hands like those of Stepney Jenkins, Lewis Clark, and Isaac Hancock. Of their lives we know nothing except that by some means – gift, theft or labor – they acquired property, however slight, and chose to exchange it at market for other commodities – blankets, sugar, whiskey and the like.

Property holding by slaves, particularly those laboring under the task system, has drawn historians' attention of late, yet slave activity in the marketplace has gone virtually unconsidered. Such exchanges took place countless times throughout the antebellum South, yet their pervasiveness, complexity, and ritual importance remain unrecognized. Indeed, few incidents of slave life rivaled market relations for political and psychological meaning. Commodity exchange and property

---

Originally published as "Money knows no master: Market relations and the American slave community," by Lawrence T. McDonnell, in *Developing Dixie: Modernization in a Traditional Society*, edited by Winfred B. Moore, Jr, Joseph F. Tripp, and Lyon G. Tyler (Westport, CT: Greenwood Press, 1988), pp. 31–44. Reprinted with permission.

accumulation, however trivial, exposed and transformed real relations between master and slave and within the slave community itself. When slaves bought, sold and bartered, produced, accumulated, and consumed property they claimed as their own, central questions of power, community, and humanity arose. This [essay] sketches contours of slave commercial activity in one state, nineteenth-century South Carolina, to demonstrate the interplay of these questions. Commodity exchange was a subversive ceremony forcing participants and witnesses to confront dilemmas and contradictions slavery imposed on them. Viewed from the marketplace, an ambiguous, liminal sphere, both physical and mental, the "domestic institution" appears in a new light: fresh insights to political and psychological dynamics stand forth, shadows grow across slave familial, cultural, and community relations. Indeed, the necessity and orientation of a new history of slavery become more apparent.

In nineteenth-century South Carolina, slaves participated in a full range of market activity, licit and illicit, based on a broad spectrum of property holding. William J. Grayson boasted of the glories of black commerce in his proslavery poem, *The Hireling and the Slave*:

> Calm in his peaceful home the slave prepares
> His garden spot and plies his rustic cares;
> The comb and honey that his bees afford,
> The eggs in ample gourd compactly stored,
> The pig, the poultry with a chapman's art,
> He sells or barters at the village mart,
> Or at the master's mansion never fails
> An ampler price to find and readier sales.

As Grayson asserted, slaves sold a surprisingly wide range of items, grounding their trade in the garden plots masters allotted them to supplement bland diets of hog and hominy. Bondmen tilled gardens and kept livestock in all parts of the state in the antebellum period, not just those dominated by the task system. In many cases slaves dipped into their own weekly corn rations – not to mention master's corn crib – to feed chickens and pigs. Garden produce sometimes made the difference between hunger and malnutrition and an adequate diet. Slaves like Charlie Davis, however, worked their patches even though there was "plenty good ration to eat all de time." The point, the ex-slave made clear, was that "dey had a garden of dey own," and that master legitimized proprietary notions by allowing them Saturday to till crops.

Where planters refused slaves gardens, bondmen found other ways to enter the arena of exchange. In Columbia a slave named John earned monthly cash payments as caretaker for the First Baptist Church.

Barnwell District slaves sold timber to the South Carolina Railroad. George Briggs remembered how he "git money fer platting galluses and making boot string and other little things" up near the North Carolina border. Low-country slaves who exceeded their tasks also received cash payments. Others did day labor for cash, in the fields, carpentry and rail-splitting, sewing and weaving. In four coastal parishes the social statistics schedules of the 1850 census listed average day wages for slave labor only; they probably dominated other districts as well. As with egg and poultry production, by the late antebellum period slaves monopolized basketweaving and handicrafts. More lucrative but more dangerous, some slaves operated stills, sold provisions or passes to runaways, or committed prostitution. Wherever an opening presented itself, slaves moved swiftly to enter the marketplace.

A more well-traveled southern path enticed others: cotton production. The best antebellum records of slave cotton sales in South Carolina come from Darlington District, high on the Pee Dee. Leach Carrigan, merchant of Society Hill, purchased eight bales of ginned cotton and 10,809 pounds of seed cotton from slaves between 1837 and 1839, paying out $627.91 to fifty-three slave sellers. Their transactions comprised 9.3 percent of total sales, earning about 1.5 percent of all cash paid out. His account books show bondmen selling individually and collectively, in single lots and multiple sales. Both male and female slaves participated, receiving market prices for their produce. In many cases, it is worth noting, slaves sold larger bales, bigger crops, and received better prices than some whites coming to market on the same day. Carrigan's records for 1849–1860 list only one bale of cotton sold by a slave, and no purchases of seed cotton, but the accounts of Charles and Company in nearby Darlington and J. Eli Gregg and Sons at Mars Bluff suggest that slaves were not moving out of the cotton market, voluntarily or otherwise, during this period of white concentration. Cotton meant big money to South Carolina blacks: Cyrus Bacot's man Peter earned nearly $35.00 at one sale, and five other hands made $151.33 selling cotton to Charles and Company. In all, thirty-seven groups and individuals sold to the two firms over the period. Many more perhaps marketed crops under their masters' auspices. Church and court records show that slaves frequently produced their own cotton crops in all sections of the state, regardless of whether planters organized labor by task or gang. Along coastal areas unsuited to cotton, blacks cultivated rice patches in their free time. "Peoples would have found we colored people rich wid de money we made on de extra crop," Sylvia Cannon asserted, "if de slaves hadn' never been set free." Other ex-slaves claimed never to have seen money, but in her relatively remote area, "us had big rolls of money," which the Civil War consumed. "White folks didn' give de niggers no money no time," Sallie Paul stated, "but dey had money in slavery time much so as dey does now."

A tiny minority of slaves in the antebellum South did manage to a mass significant amounts of property – boats and carriages, horses and cattle, even real estate – while others, particularly those in the border states, managed to buy themselves or other kin from bondage. In South Carolina such instances were extremely rare. Through cash payments or barter, most blacks earned only small amounts, with no semblance of regularity, spending it as most working people have always done, on clothing, food, liquor, and other inexpensive creature comforts. Yet these purchases obtained real significance among slaves and whites alike. To understand the meaning of these exchanges we must shift our focus from property accumulation to market relations themselves.

Planters called their system "the domestic institution," promoting a paternalist ideology they were never able fully to implement. Both a strategy of social control and a moral ethos, paternalism sought to link masters and slaves in a web of material dependence, social deference, and psychological identification. It was difficult for slaves to resist this exploitative and dehumanizing logic, not only because of the potential violence which hung perpetually over their heads, but because of the intimate rituals planters contrived to manufacture mutuality. When masters doled out food and clothing, Christmas gifts, a dram of liquor or a blanket, when they named a child or blessed a union, seeds of identification sprouted, warmed not necessarily by affection, but rather by judicious respect for master's power. Seventy years after emancipation Solbert Butler remembered how "Massa'd come up to de Street every Monday morning with big trays of rations. He'd feed his colored people, den go on back" to a mansion called Paradise. Richard Jones recalled how his master would gather the hands on holidays. "Den he would throw money to 'em. De chillun git dimes, nickels, quarters, half-dollars and dollars. At Christmas he would throw ten dollar bills." "It is impossible but that human nature in such a situation . . . must feel himself lord of the earth," Jonathan Mason thought. It is impossible but that many slaves must have felt compelled to agree.

Commodity exchange provided slaves with a brilliant opportunity to actively deny the human chattel contradiction they labored under. It reveals incisively the ambivalence blacks felt toward both their masters and the slave community. The marketplace, economic analysts from Aristotle to Adam Smith to Karl Marx have agreed, is a neutral zone, a threshold between buyer and seller. "The market spells liberation," Fernand Braudel writes, "openness, access to another world."[1] Master and slave confronted each other at the moment of exchange as bearers of commodities, stripped of social dimensions. Exchange, in Aristotle's

words, "treats all parties as equals"; as Marx put it, the "social relationship between the two owners is that of *mutual alienation* ... each exists as
his own *surrogate* [equivalent] and as the surrogate of the other." In this
realm, each knew both perfect freedom and perfect dependence. When
Isaac sold Joseph Palmer "a hen, a capon, and four young fowls" in
1832, when Dorcas paid $2.32 for goods to Elisha Spencer in 1850,
when Louisa McCord's slaves bartered eggs and vegetables with the
translator of Bastiat at her library door, they showed themselves not
merely the dependent property of others but decisive individuals capable
of making important decisions about their own lives. For a slave picking
cotton for wages in free time, "it is a matter of indifference ... whether
his master gets his cotton all picked or not," Charles Ball claimed; "his
object is to get employment in a field where he can make the best
wages." Trading shad for bacon with a white boatman, he recalled the
sense of equity the market imposed: "he weighed the flitches with great
exactness ... and gave me good weight. When the business was
ended ... he told me, he hoped I was satisfied with him." In all future
dealings, the man promised, "I shall be honest with you." Isiah Jeffries
remembered too how wage labor brought a new sense of selfworth. "I
worked for [my master] to git my first money and he would give me a
quarter fer a whole day's work. Dat made me feel good and I thought I
was a man kaise I made a quarter." Henry Gladney remembered the
symbolic power of "de only money I ever have befo' freedom, a big
copper two-cent piece wid a hole in it." He wore it around his neck "and
felt rich all de time. Little niggers always wanted to see dat money and I
was proud to show it to them every time." Gable Locklier likewise
affirmed the importance of the dime he received for selling a book to a
white man. "Ma give me a needle en thread en little sack en I sew my
10¢ in it. Put in de rafter en it stay dere till next Christmas. Believe I took
it down en tote it a long time. ... " His money carried not only economic
value but conveyed human value and empowerment as well. His mode of
disposing of the precious dime is significant too: he bought a piece of
tobacco and gave it to his father. Charles Izard Manigault's slaves
demonstrated empowerment through exchange in less ambiguous fashion. When the slaveholder returned to his Beaufort District plantation
after Appomattox, he discovered that his slaves had defaced portraits of
his planter forebears, left them outside in the elements "as if to turn
them to ridicule," and even sold them to Union troops. Strutting blacks
selling objectified slaveholders to their own liberators here came as close
to an Aristotelian ideal of justice as any freedmen in that moment of
triumph.

As this example shows, the threshold of exchange linked black sellers
with white buyers, and hence with white society, not only by assertion of

black humanity but through white objectification. Slaves appeared here equally as purposeful as whites. Moreover, since buyer and seller confronted each other through their commodities, reduced, that is, to the level of things themselves, human chattel confronted each other momentarily on both sides of the exchange. In the marketplace, not only were blacks raised, but whites were lowered. A Marion District slave remembered the self-assertion of his first trip to market. "I ain' never been to de store fore den," he recalled, "but I go to de storekeeper en I say, Mr. King, half dis money mine en half Joes.' I thought it was his place to give me what I wanted...." Charles Ball similarly relished Sunday labor for wages because the overseer "paid each one the price he had a right to receive." The place of those who dealt with slaves warranted no high esteem among blacks or whites, conversely. When Askew called Jeter "a dam'd rascal" who had "been trading with negroes," the merchant had been doubly slandered. When Jim and Dick claimed, under the lash, that R. S. Smith had purchased wheat from them, Smith hauled them to Anderson District court in 1849 on charges of insolence to a white man.

Many whites deplored slave participation in the market, but their opposition showed few results. Some held that trading with blacks encouraged crime and gave illicit access to liquor. As early as 1795 white mechanics argued that competition with black products and labor depressed wages and debased talents. Such claims reached an angry crescendo in the decade before the Civil War. Planters and merchants feared slave collusion, not competition, with nonslaveholding whites. The Edgefield District grand jury in 1798 protested that "Negro slaves are allowed to Cultivate and trade in Tobacco – whereby they have Great Opportunities of Injuring their Masters Crops, Stealing and trading amongst each other and perhaps with unprincipled White men." Two decades later the Georgetown District grand jury opposed "the traffic carried on by negroes in boats upon our Rivers, under the protection of White men of no character," in defiance of the statute of 1712 forbidding slaves to possess watercraft of any sort. Some churches attempted to curb white trading with slaves by censuring and expelling members, with little effect. Municipal ordinances attempted deterrence, like Spartanburg's decision that citizens could buy "Baskets, Brooms, Mats and Bread trays," but not "Eggs, chickens, butter, fruit or any other article of trade" without "a written permit." Court dockets, however, suggest that such measures generated good revenue through fines, but little compliance. After 1834, the South Carolina General Assembly declared illegal the purchase of wheat, corn, rice, and cotton from slaves, whether or not the master assented to the sale, levying fines up to $1,000 and a year in jail. Nothing changed.

By the 1850s Vigilant Associations had formed in Edgefield, Barnwell, Sumter, Lancaster, Kershaw, and other districts, and informal networks operated elsewhere, to curb slave market relations through direct action. Immigrants and Yankee peddlers, perceived as agents of abolition, came in for special attention, but more stable merchants were pressured as well. In Darlington District in 1857, a vigilant society of farmers and planters warned A. Windham to stop trading with local slaves. When he persisted, they returned, seventy-five strong, burned his store and shot it out with the renegades. Six, including the storeowner, were killed, and eight more wounded. Groups like the Savannah River Anti-Slave Traffick Association, operating in Barnwell and Edgefield districts, feared not only the economic effects of slave crime abetted by trading, but the decay of proper subordination. Slaves had once been "essentially members of the family to which they belonged," but now, thanks to market involvement, "Masters and Slaves are beginning to look upon each other as natural enemies." Commerce made blacks "serpents gnawing at the vitals of plantation society"; they had to be restored to their proper status as "moral beings, holding a position in the framework of society." The slave had become "a kind of freeman on Sunday all over the southern country," Charles Ball admitted, well acquainted through trade with "the exercise of liberty on this day." "I am not talking of this matter as a pecuniary consideration," an anonymous farmer responded in 1857, "but alone to show the widespread ruin that awaits us unless ... our negroes are brought to chalk a line.... Make him feel his inferiority, and feel it too, in his pocket...." Fearful planters well recognized the threat to paternalism market relations; their solutions uniformly failed.

As a response to paternalism, slave relations with the market succeeded on an individual basis, providing an important avenue for self-assertion. Living standards and quality of life probably rose marginally in participant households, though it is impossible to say whether they became subsequently more or less satisfied with their lot. Negative consequences, however, emerged as well. If living conditions improved in some slave households, they remained stationary among those who did not participate. The young, the old, the weak and chronically ill, the overworked or rebellious – the most marginal figures in the slave community – had a lesser chance of market involvement. Division and conflict sometimes erupted between haves and have-nots. The British tutor John Davis complained that South Carolina slaves frequently "pilfered from each other" and that they had an "unconquerable propensity to steal." When Austin "lost some meat" in 1844, he confronted Florilla, the property of J. W. Norris, on her way to church, threatening to "Kick her Durned Brains" out if she did not confess. A riot ensued and three slaves went to the whipping post. Twenty years later in Anderson District, Tony turned on Dick and Sy, who had accused him of stealing "more leather than his back could pay for." Meeting Dick after church, he "struck him and knocked him down and stamped him severely hurting him very much," although the victim had boasted that "he had as many wepons as any one els." Sy came in for a similar treatment. Dissension and conflict of this sort, sometimes escalating to murder, seem common throughout South Carolina slave society.

In some communities slaves curbed theft among themselves by exposing, ostracizing, or privately punishing outlaws. Others, like the carpenter at Orange Hall plantation, purchased expensive, crude padlocks to protect possessions as best they could. Nothing better symbolized how insidiously private property and market exchange fractured slave society. Where preventive measures failed, violence flared. In 1846 a riot broke out among drunken slaves at the New Hope Baptist Church. The root cause which put eight slaves under the lash, the court learned, was that "Amos and Andrew fell out about a debt contracted by Andrew's having purchased some bread from him." Spartanburg District court records show slaves brought to the bar repeatedly in the antebellum period for similar offenses. More, probably most, conflicts, however, were resolved or died out on the plantation itself.

Unquestionably the worst violence between slaves occurred in the two-bit dram shops or "doggeries" where slaves could drink and gamble, often in the company of poor whites. Here they emulated manly white behavior, boasting, carrying weapons, carousing with white women, parading a desperate, overblown, paper-thin honor. It was a patent formula for conflict. In Pickens District in 1853, for example, Jess broke up a gambling party by accusing Wiley of stealing his tobacco. A white witness said that "if Wiley wold tak the like of that he was No-man attall," and a brawl began. Both went to the whipping post, Wiley minus an ear Jess had bitten off. In Spartanburg District a few months later, Willis, Dick, Charles, and Lon exchanged words over whiskey and wound up in court for drinking and fighting. Such incidents, as whites attested, were epidemic.

Even where conflict did not break into the open, fruits of market involvement created and confirmed differences in status or material well-being among slaves. Just as blacks defined whites as "quality" or "poor white trash" according to clothes, houses, lands, and slaves, so conspicuous consumption influenced how the slave community structured itself. At the moment of exchange, such abrogation was virtually inevitable: here, outside the bonds of the master and of the quarters, slaves interacted with free whites, and acted like free whites, if only insofar as they among all their fellows were trading with their oppressors.

Some slaves, however, worked to reinforce their newly acquired status by injecting the market into the slave community, purchasing the labor power of some, indebting others. Why should Lanham's Roger truck jugs of liquor to illicit sale at the church meeting when he could hire Daniel's Roger for the task for eighteen cents? Why should the powerful Ceasar risk stealing corn when cash could entice his underling Essex? Paternalism as a strategy of commanding labor seems, on occasion, to have worked as well for black overlords as for white.

The harmonious slave community that historians have so idealized probably bears little resemblance to reality. Soon after emancipation most quarters broke up as freedmen wandered roads, went to town, rented or cropped on subdivided plantations, or acquired a few acres for themselves. "Colored people just throwed 'bout all over de place," Heddie Davis recalled; "some of dey house was settin' side de road, some over in dat corner, some next de big house en so on like dat all over de place." Black involvement with the market may partially explain why ex-slaves so easily – almost joyously – gave up community life after emancipation, fighting to institute a system of land tenure based on nuclear families and household production. Community conflicts and strains engendered by market relations doubtless spurred this shift. Capitalist agriculture during Reconstruction was anathema to some blacks. Others actively, if hesitantly, embraced it. The much-studied Promised Land area of Abbeville County echoed the slave community's outward form in the postbellum period, but its dynamics were quite different. Black landowners hired black wage labor and took on black tenants. They showed no sign of retreat from the marketplace. As Elizabeth Bethel's evidence (though not her argument) shows, black landowners concentrated a higher proportion of acreage in cotton cultivation than tenants did.[2] Cotton production, thanks to better land or higher labor inputs, was also marginally higher for owners. At Marshlands plantation in the low country, Charles Manigault found that his former driver Frederick was anything but reluctant to plunge into staple production. "*He* immediately apportioned to ... *14 Negroes* a section of my farm to work *there on shares with him* – but without assisting them at all in their work, *he* being *Lord & Master* of *everything there*," the planter recorded. "He was to Receive half their Years Crop when Ripe & Harvested...." How typical such plans and choices were awaits future research, but some doubtless embraced the market as a rejection of their slave past, and in the best bourgeois spirit, for the opportunity it held out to some day wield the whip themselves over another's head.

For master and man alike the circulation of commodities was a process with implications they could fully neither understand nor control. Slave relations with the market corrupted the organic unity paternalist planters quested for, restructuring time and space. New conceptions of property and power stood forth, and behind it class antagonism gleamed. Black commercial activity opened deep fissures in white ranks, social divisions which loomed large on the eve of secession. Among slaves, market relations provided an important mode of resistance to paternalism, but self affirmation often weakened tragically the community as a whole. The commercial struggles and contradictions South Carolina slaves endured mirrored developments in every corner of the antebellum South.

The French proverb that Marx quoted fondly – "l'argent n'a pas de maître" (money knows no master) – defined the sources, directions and limits of slave resistance to paternalism in the marketplace. Exchange, he explained in *Capital*, is fundamentally "a relation between two wills," within a framework of power. That market relations forced whites to acknowledge the potency of black will was a remarkable achievement. Slaves were not finally human chattel, and the master–slave relation could never be finally perfected. But the individual slave's success too often proved the slave community's disaster. Black will under bondage had consequences and dynamics, both positive and negative, which few dreamed of, and none could control. Triumph and tragedy, struggle and victimization, will and power, here meshed in ways historians are only beginning to explore.

Notes

1 Fernand Braudel, *Civilization and Capitalism, 15th–18th Century*, vol. 2, *The Wheels of Commerce* (New York: Harper and Row, 1982).
2 Elizabeth Raul Bethel, *Promiseland: A Century of Life in a Negro Community* (Philadelphia: Temple University Press, 1981).

Study Questions and Further Reading for part IV

1 How did slaves in South Carolina acquire personal property?
2 How did masters and the state respond to the acquisition of property by property and why?
3 What are the chief areas of disagreement between Morgan and McDonnell? Can their interpretations be reconciled? If so, how?

Berlin, Ira and Morgan, Philip D. (eds) 1992: *Cultivation and Culture: Labor and the Shaping of Slave Life in the Americas*. Charlottesville: University Press of Virginia.

Blassingame, John W. 1979: *The Slave Community: Plantation Life in the Antebellum South*. New York: Oxford University Press.

Coclanis, Peter A. 1995: Slavery, African-American agency, and the world we have lost. *Georgia Historical Quarterly*, 79, 873–84.

Dew, Charles B. 1974: Disciplining slave ironworkers in the ante-bellum South: Coercion, conciliation, and accommodation. *American Historical Review*, 79, 393–418.

Dusinberre, William 1996: *Them Dark Days: Slavery in the American Rice Swamps*. New York: Oxford University Press.

Elkins, Stanley M. 1975: The slavery debate. *Commentary*, 60, 40–54.

Genovese, Eugene D. 1974: *Roll, Jordan, Roll: The World the Slaves Made*. New York: Vintage.

Gutman, Herbert 1976: *The Black Family in Slavery and Freedom*. New York: Pantheon.

Hudson, Larry E., Jr 1997: *To Have and To Hold: Slave Work and Family Life in Antebellum South Carolina*. Athens: University of Georgia Press.

Joyner, Charles 1984: *Down by the Riverside: A South Carolina Slave Community*. Urbana: University of Illinois Press.

Kolchin, Peter 1983: Reevaluating the antebellum slave community: A comparative perspective. *Journal of American History*, 70, 579–601.

Levine, Lawrence W. 1977: *Black Culture and Black Consciousness: Afro-American Folk Thought from Slavery to Freedom*. New York: Oxford University Press.

Lichtenstein, Alex 1988: "That disposition to theft, with which they have been branded": Moral economy, slave management, and the law. *Journal of Social History*, 21, 413–40.

McDonnell, Lawrence T. 1993: Work, culture, and society in the slave South. In Ted Ownby (ed.), *Black and White Cultural Interaction in the Antebellum South*. Jackson: University of Mississippi Press, 125–47.

Malone, Ann Patton 1992: *Sweet Chariot: Slave Family and Household Structure in Nineteenth-Century Louisiana*. Chapel Hill: University of North Carolina Press.

Morgan, Philip D. 1982: Work and culture: The task system and the world of lowcountry blacks, 1770–1880. *William and Mary Quarterly*, 39, 563–99.

Morris, Christopher 1998: The articulation of two worlds: the master–slave relationship reconsidered. *Journal of American History*, 85, 982–1007.

Penningroth, Dylan 1997: Slavery, freedom, and social claims to property among African Americans in Liberty County, Georgia, 1850–1880. *Journal of American History*, 84, 405–35.

Rawick, George P. 1972: *From Sundown to Sunup: The Making of the Black Community*. Westport, CT: Greenwood Press.

Stuckey, Sterling 1987: *Slave Culture: Nationalist Theory and the Foundation of Black America*. New York: Oxford University Press.

White, Shane and White, Graham 1995: Slave hair and African-American culture in the eighteenth and nineteenth centuries. *Journal of Southern History*, 61, 45–76.

Wood, Betty 1995: *Women's Work, Men's Work: The Informal Slave Economies of Lowcountry Georgia*. Athens: University of Georgia Press.

Part V
Selling Southern Bodies

Introduction to Documents and Essays

Following the ban on the importation of slaves from Africa after 1808, southern slavery was forced to reproduce its labor force. This, according to some interpretations, required slaveholders to encourage the formation of slave families and treat slaves with a sort of paternal kindness while still subjecting them to strict discipline. The slave trade that remained was, then, an internal one which sold slaves within the South. Who were the men who did the buying and selling? How did their businesses work? And how, precisely, did slave traders ascertain the market worth of the slave? Were their impressions formed solely by their knowledge of slaves or did slaves shape those impressions?

9

The Slave Trader in Image and Reality

A Boston Minister on Slave Traders, 1855

Not all non-southerners chastised masters and their peculiar institution. Following his tour of the South in 1854, a Boston minister, Nehemiah Adams, found benefits to slavery. But he was careful to distinguish between the good slaveholder and the wretched traders of humans and the legal system that facilitated their business. It was a distinction, according to Adams, made also by some masters. (From Nehemiah Adams, *A South-Side View of Slavery; Or, Three Months at the South, in 1854* (Boston: T. R. Martin, 1855), pp. 74–5, 77–8)

I walked with a gentleman, esteemed and honored by his fellow-citizens, and much interested with the settlement of estates. I knew that he would appreciate my feelings, and I disclosed them. I asked him if there were no other way of changing the relations of slaves in the process of law, except by exposing them, male and female, at auction, on the court-house steps.... I could not bear to see a fellow-being made a subject of sale, even in form; and I wondered that any one could look upon it with composure, or suffer it to be repeated without efforts to abolish it.

His reply was, for substance, that so far as he and the people of his town were concerned, no case of hardship in the disposal of a slave had ever occurred there, to his knowledge; that he had settled a large number of estates, and in every case had disposed of the servants in ways satisfactory to themselves; that he had prevented certain men from bidding upon them; that he had prevailed on others not to buy, because he and the servants were unwilling to have these men for their masters; and, therefore, that the question was practically reduced to the expediency of the form of transfer, viz., by public vendue.

He repeated what I have said of the desirableness that the sale or transfer should be public; whether in a room, or on steps, was unimportant, only that public outcry was ordained to be made at the court-house. He also said that the slaves, knowing that the sale was a mere form, and that they were already disposed of, did not in such cases suffer to the degree which strangers supposed. . . .

A southern physician described to me a scene in the domestic slave trade. He touched at a landing-place in a steamer, and immediately a slave coffle was marched on board. Men, women, and children, about forty in all, two by two, an ox chain passing through the double file, and a fastening reaching from the right and left hands of those on either side of the chain, composed what is called a *slave coffle*. Some colored people were on the wharf, who seemed to be relatives and friends of the gang. Such shrieks, such unearthly noises, as resounded above the escape of steam, my informant said can not be described. There were partings for life, and between what degrees of kindred the nature of the cries were probably a sign.

When the boat was on her way, my informant fell into conversation with a distinguished planter, with regard to the scene which they had just witnessed. They deplored it as one of the features of a system which they both mourned over, and wished to abolish, or at least correct, till no wrong, no pain, should be the fruit of it which is not incidental to every human lot.

While they were discussing the subject, the slave-dealer heard their talk, came up, and made advances to shake hands with the planter. The gentleman drew back, and said, "Sir, I consider you a disgrace to human nature." He poured scorn and indignation upon him.

He spoke the feeling of the south generally. Negro traders are the abhorrence of all flesh. Even their descendants, when they are known, and the property acquired in the traffic, have a blot upon them. I never knew a deeper aversion to any class of men; it is safe to say, that generally it is not surpassed by our feelings toward foreign slave traders.

They go into the States where the trade is not prohibited by law, find men who are in want of money, or a master who has a slave that is troublesome, and for the peace of the plantation that slave is sold, sometimes at great sacrifice; and there are many of whom, under pecuniary pressure, it is not always difficult to purchase.

There are some men whose diabolical natures are so gratified by this traffic – passionate, cruel, tyrannical men, seeking dominion in some form to gratify these instincts. The personal examinations which they make, and the written descriptions which they give, of slaves whom they buy, are sometimes disgusting in the extreme. It is beyond explanation that good men at the south do not clamor against this thing, till the transfer of every human being, if he must be a slave, is made with all the care attending the probate of a will.

The charge of vilely multiplying negroes in Virginia, is one of those exaggerations of which this subject is full, and is reduced to this – that Virginia, being an old State, fully stocked, the surplus black population naturally flows off where their numbers are less.

I heard this conversation at the breakfast house of a southern railroad. As several of us were warming ourselves at the fire, one of the passengers said to the keeper of the house, –

"Where is Alonzo now?"

"He is in Alabama."

"I thought he had come back."

"Well, he was to come back some time ago; but they keep sending him so many negroes to sell, he can't leave."

Alonzo is probably a negro trader of the better sort; a mere agent or factor. If slaves are to be sold, there must be men to negotiate with regard to them; these are not all of the vilest sort; yet their occupation is abhorred.

A Slaveholder Comments on Traders and Prices, 1846

In their attempts to distance themselves from the slave trader, self-styled paternalist masters demonized those involved directly in the trade. And, yet, even as they did so, masters kept a close eye on the prices and values of slaves whom they willingly traded with the putatively despised trader. These points are abundantly clear in the following letter from James Henry Hammond. (From James Henry Hammond, Silver Bluff, SC, to W. B. Hodgson, Nov. 16, 1846, James Henry Hammond Papers. Reproduced courtesy of the Rare Book, Manuscript, and Special Collections Library, Duke University, Durham, NC, 27708)

My Dear Hodgson,

I performed last week my long delayed trip to Thorn Island. I called at Dr Bailey's going & coming but he was absent. Mr Fraser was also in the Swamp & his wife at the "Pine Woods." His Brother did the honor . . . & reported 30 bales of Cotton & 1000 bushels of corn for the crop. . . . He also reported 90 head of cattle 75 of hogs – a few sheep – 8 mules & 3 horses & exhibited 59 negroes of all ages.

The crop is a very sorry one even for the season & the place & after paying expenses will I should suppose leave a *loss* unless you are a better economist than I am. Your force I estimated as equal to 20 *full* hands & ought to make such a year as this on tolerable land at least 75 bales & 2500 bushels corn. The land though very much worn was of good quality originally & susceptible of great improvement. There is I was told about 500 acres of upland & 1300 swamp. I speak of the upland – the swamp being low is of no value . . . . If the upland had two years of *absolute rest* & was then marled you might after two more with the proper management & manuring calculate on an average crop there with these hands of 100 bales & 3000 bushels corn. . . .

The negroes I examined carefully & was exceedingly surprised to find in your whole gang there but one prime fellow Sam. Isaac's leg make him a confirmed invalid & Lazarus tho' a likely boy is not a fellow. One fellow in 59 is what I never saw before. One fourth of my entire number of negroes are prime fellows between 20 & 40 years of age. At this rate you should have 14 in your gang at Thorn Island to rank it with mine. Only one seventh of my number are children too small for work; at Thorn Island there are *one half* under 10 years old . . . . In the gang of 22 which I bought of Roberts for $6000 there were 6 prime fellows & only one child. I must say however that yours are as likely a set of women & children, boys & girls as I ever saw to-gether & appear to have been well treated & moderately worked. They are therefore a valuable tho' not efficient gang . . . . I took a list of their names & ages, & valued each negro – that is all but Ailsie & Coomba whom I set down at 000. The 57 including Ventor, whose mother you have in town, I was rather surprised to find on adding up my figures came to only $14,275 – almost the amount of the appraisement I presume. I rated them at about 10 per cent under the negro trader's prices & at 10 per cent less than they would bring I think if sold separately as the trader sells. But this of course you would not think of doing nor would anyone who was not a monster – or a negro trader. In buying gangs one is obliged to take pensioners & invalids & many others that do not suit them & cannot therefore give as much for the best as if they could select such alone. Altogether, I think the lot worth $15,000, which not estimating the two pensioners at any thing & not including Ventor whom I presume you do not aim to sell as you have reserved his mother, would bring them to about $268 round. And the sum I would give you for them half cash & the balance within 12 months & interest. . . .

A Trader Notes Market Prices for Slaves, 1859

A slave's physical strength, versatility, and age were important considerations for buyers and sellers alike. Here, an agent for a Richmond, Virginia, slave trading company outlines the cost of slaves based on age and work capacity. (From Dickinson, Hill & Co., Richmond, to "Dear Sir," Dec. 24, 1859, William A. J. Finney Papers. Reproduced courtesy of the Rare Book, Manuscript, and Special Collections Library, Duke University, Durham, NC, 27708)

Dear Sir

There have been a large number of negroes selling in our market since our last, prices however are well sustained, and good No 1 are wanted. We quote below prices

No 1 Men	19 to 25 yrs old	1400 to 1500
1 Boys	15 ″ 18 ″	1350 ″ 1450
	10 ″ 14 ″	900 ″ 1300
1 Girls	16 ″ 22 ″	1200 ″ 1350
″	10 ″ 15 ″	900 ″ 1150

Women & children are also selling well.

The Slave Trader in Image and Reality
Michael Tadman

At the level of grand theory and sectional politics, the South had, with the trader, a problem of some delicacy. Inevitably, in northern minds the speculator was associated with the separation of families and with hard commercial exploitation – so that, whatever grass-roots opinions and practices were, it was difficult to give him a free run within the official theory of southern life. The official defense of slavery and much of the private rationalizing were essentially paternalistic, resting on notions that slavery benefitted the enslaved as well as the masters. In official theory, safety nets were available to protect slaves from virtually every

From Tadman, Michael, *Speculators and Slaves: Masters, Traders, and Slaves in the Old South* (Madison: University of Wisconsin Press, 1989, 1996), pp. 179–210. Copyright © 1989, 1996. Excerpt reprinted by permission of The University of Wisconsin Press.

conceivable abuse of arbitrary power, the white community supposedly rallying in almost every case to keep wouldbe slave exploiters in line and to maintain southern standards. Potentially, the link between paternalism and the supposed encouragement of stable institutions among blacks meant that, for the individual slaveholder and in sectional polemics, there existed a permanent tension over family separations (and the trader) as against wider southern values. This awkwardness led, in public print and more privately, to quite frequent southern condemnations of the trader. None of this should lead us to conclude either that traders were usually social outcasts, or that a permanent crisis of conscience on separation ran through the South. In practice, the nature of racism in the South seems largely to have preempted both of these outcomes.

Southern paternalism rested on profound racism, and racism, in turn, meant that whites should always judge what was best for blacks. It meant, too, that black families were not to be taken by owners as serious equivalents to those of whites. Blacks were seen as permanent children, or worse. They might have sometimes "excitable" attachments to family, but essentially such feelings were seen as short-lived. Whites "knew" that their general scheme of slaveholding and "race control" should not be broken by anxiety over "temporarily unsettling" and "discomforting" slaves. Owners could decide which traders and "brokers" to deal with, and the owners, too, could best order and determine the priorities of their plantation and its "people." In debate and less formal discussion, they would routinely observe that separations were not common and that the trader was not central to slavery. And from their perspective, such propositions need not trouble the conscience, because – so ran the argument – separations were not the purpose of slavery. Instead, its great goal was race control and the safe and fruitful employment of "less advanced" peoples. Racism was, of course, the heart of slavery, and, doubling as paternalism, could in the minds of its devotees cope with any inconsistency which the abolitionists could bring before them. In practice, then, "paternalism" was almost infinitely permissive toward speculation, while yielding for propaganda and internal purposes a convoluted literature and mythology on the role of the trader himself.

Uncle Robin and Uncle Tom

A sample of southern propaganda on the trade appears in that series of some fifteen or twenty proslavery novels which were speedily published in response to Harriet Beecher Stowe's *Uncle Tom's Cabin* (1852). In Stowe's own novel, the trade and family separation had been a crucial linking theme, so that those replying critically to her work faced the problem of whether or not to address the awkward matter of speculation. Most "replies" chose to avoid the trade, but in the several which gave it some consideration we find a considerable parade of improbable scape-goats. When the trader appeared in Randolph's *The Cabin and the Parlor* (1852) it was because "Messrs. Skin and Flint, factors and merchants of *New York*" [emphasis added] had, by charging excessive commissions and interest, forced their southern client, Mr. Courtney, to make a sale of his slaves. The feelings of southern communities on such occasions were, however represented as having been such that

> The slaves...were all purchased to remain in the district. Even among those planters who showed little concern for the ruined Courtneys there was a sentiment of honour on this point....A trader who had made his appearance was hustled away rather rudely by one or two present, so that, after making a few ineffectual bids, he thought it prudent to retire.

Again in J. W. Page's novel entitled, with consummate awkwardness, *Uncle Robin in his Cabin and Tom Without One in Boston* [1853], it was northern interference which threatened to bring disaster to the slave. Incited by visiting abolitionists, two bondsmen were persuaded to run away to the North and, in order to gain provisions for their journey, stole hams from a meathouse. As luck would have it, though, the theft was from an unreformed New Englander who, still with all of his "preju-dices," had recently settled in the South. In a desperate bid to frustrate this "evil" northerner's desire to have the slaves hung for theft, the gentle owner of the runaways hit upon the idea of selling them away to a trader. The latter, a certain Mr. Bosher, was not at all surprised to find that the slaves had "brought trouble upon themselves" by planning to run away. "Our trade," he explained to the good-hearted master,

> would be completely broken up...if t'want for runaway negroes; and I think sir, we have to thank the abolitionists for that; they entice them off, and we grab them flying. I know a *yankee* trader who gets whole lots that way. [emphasis added]

The plot of Page's novel suggested, too, that unlike their truly southern counterparts, northern-born slaveholders, interested only in brutal profit, frequently sold slaves without regard to their ties of family. Indeed, these Yankee planters were represented as providing the trader with the greater part of his stock. Moreover, according to Page, the traders themselves, more often than not, turned out to be Yankees! ...

Northerners and other outsiders could, then, sometimes read about the "outcast" trader in proslavery novels, and travellers to the South often heard the same sort of stories (and for the same propaganda reasons). In the 1850s, Nehemiah Adams, a Boston minister, visited the South and became much impressed with slavery. He reported meetings with Southerners who wanted to abolish the interregional trade "or at least correct [it], till no wrong, no pain, should be the fruit of it which is not incidental to every human lot." And "Negro traders," he found, "are the abhorrence of all flesh. Even their descendants, when they are known . . . have a blot upon them. I never knew a deeper aversion to any class of men." Traders, he seemed to have discovered, picked up only troublesome slaves or those of masters in extreme poverty; and the speculators tended to be "passionate, cruel, tyrannical men, seeking dominance in some form to gratify these instincts." As the historian Frederic Bancroft reported after reviewing a sample of contemporary works, the southern propaganda image of the trader was that of a brutal, ruthless sharper. "Imagine", he wrote,

> a compound of an unscrupulous horse-trader, a familiar old-time tavern keeper, a superficially complaisant and artful hard-drinking gambler and an ignorant, garrulous and low politician, and you will get a conception that resembles the southern ante-bellum notion of the "nigger trader".

Such an image, indeed, became part of the plantation legend and the tradition of southern history.

Perhaps the classic in the antebellum genre of trader stereotyping was Daniel Hundley's *Social Relations in our Southern States* (1860). Here we find the oily speculator in all his repellent features and with all of his characteristic vices. The trader, with his "grasping" instincts, was, he maintained, a "Yankee" and not a southerner in basic character. After listing a string of other southern outcasts, he resoundingly announced: "But the most utterly detestable of all southern Yankees is the Negro Trader – Speculator he delights to call himself in late years." The trader stood, according to Hundley, "pre-eminent in villainy and a greedy love of filthy lucre." He allowed that a few decent men might enter the trade, but soon even these became debauched, drunken, prematurely aged, gambling, ruthless swindlers.

> The natural result of their calling seems to be to corrupt them; for they have usually to deal with the most refractory and brutal of the slave population, since good and honest slaves are rarely permitted to fall into the unscrupulous clutches of the speculator.

In oaths and "downright blasphemy" the trader's only equals were "those infidel socialists, free-lovers, and abolitionists." As for honest dealing,

Ah! Messrs. Stock-brokers of Wall Street – you who are wont to cry up your rotten railroad, mining, steamboat, and other worthless stocks – for ingenious lying [even] you should take lessons from the southern Negro Trader!

Thus, of the mendacious speculator's stock, "nearly nine-tenths" were

vicious ones sold for crimes or misdemeanors, or otherwise diseased ones sold because of their worthlessness as property. These he purchases at about half what healthy and honest slaves would cost him; but he sells them as both honest and healthy, mark you.

And in classic proslavery fashion Hundley pronounced slavery as an institution to be sound – indeed, ordained by God. The problems of slavery were few, and the abuses brought about by the trader were perhaps chief among them. Indeed, he maintained, to argue against slavery

as a domestic institution simply because it is abused was like the socialists and free-lovers who argue against the marriage relation, because married people are always quarrelling, and running off to Indiana to be divorced. They have not the good sense to discriminate between the legitimate uses of an institution and the illegitimate abuses to which it can be subjected.

With Hundley, then, the speculator was turned from being an ideological embarrassment into being the lynch-pin of slavery's defense – the quintessential scapegoat, devoid of all honor in the South, and toward whom almost any awkward question could rhetorically be turned. . . .

Monsters and Negro Traders

In beguiling visitors to the South and impressionable northern readers, the "trader-as-monster" stereotype had obvious propaganda purposes. It is significant, however, that the same sort of stereotype can also be found in conversations *within* the antebellum South, and its appearance there raises another layer of questions about its purpose and about the position of the trader. A letter by J. H. Hammond, the South Carolina planter-politician and proslavery publicist, produced just such a reference. Having been approached by his neighbor W. R. Hodgson as the possible purchaser for Hodgson's gang of fifty-nine slaves, he made an offer of $15,000, and informed the neighbor:

I rated them at about 10 per cent under the negro trader's prices and at 10 per cent less than they would bring I think if sold separately as the trader

sells. But this of course you would not think of doing nor would anyone
who was not a monster – or a negro trader.

At first sight, we might see in Hammond's letter high principles and
genuine revulsion against the speculator. This, though, would clearly be
a mistake. From later correspondence, it is clear that the neighbor had
little difficulty in disposing of the gang – and at $4,000 more than
Hammond had bid. And in reality Hammond also made very numerous
and extensive purchases from traders. Surviving records clearly show
that the traders from whom he purchased included S. F. Slatter, Joseph
Woods, Ansley Davies, H. N. Templeman (as well as Templeman,
Omohundro & Co.), John W. Forward, Solomon Davis, J. Hull, Thomas
Ryan, and T. N. Gadsden. And, even worse, despite his avowed revulsion against selling "separately," at least half of Hammond's recorded
purchases from traders – being "separate" slaves aged from eight to
fourteen years – are likely to have involved forced family separations.
Indeed, as a recent biography indicates, over a thirty-year period Hammond bought 145 slaves "in gangs and as individuals from traders in
Charleston, Columbia, Augusta, and Hamburg, as well as from neighbors and friends."[1]

As Hammond's papers repeatedly show, he was a particularly astute
and persistent businessman. His association of traders with monsters was
no more than an attempt at blackmail for the purpose of gaining a price
advantage. The letters of traders do not suggest that there was in practice
any widespread problem of reluctance to deal with them. They complained of boredom, competition, bad weather, "bad" slaves, worries
over prices – but not of unwillingness to do business. Indeed, from all of
the traders' letters examined (running into many hundreds of items) only
two pieces have been found which indicate the possibility of particular
slaveholders being, for reasons [of] principle, unwilling to sell to speculators. Firstly, in the E. W. Ferguson Papers (a substantial collection of
trading correspondence) a colleague on one occasion reported to Ferguson: "I went out to the sale yesterday but they would not let a trader have
the negroes." Secondly, in the R. H. Dickinson Papers, a letter of H. M.
Nelson informed Dickinson, the prominent Richmond slave dealer, that,
having recently bought two slaves from a local citizen, he had sent one of
them to Dickinson for sale to the trade. "It has occurred to me, however," Nelson added, "that her master was possibly induced to sell her by
supposing she was to come to me and not to dealers." He therefore asked
that Dickinson should refrain from reselling the slave until the original
master's wishes had been ascertained.

At the same time, the fact that Hammond chose to use the trader-as-
monster device suggests that it had some sort of resonance in the South,

and that he might have had some hope at least of embarrassing his neighbor. The explanation seems to be that in order to be respectable one should not appear to be *too* willing to separate families. Slaveowners would often accept that separations brought some hardship to slaves. In the best society, therefore, one should not appear to be too willing to cause hardship. Along with this, and decisively taking precedence over it, however, went the rule that whites were the decision makers, and that they should in the end decide what needed to be done for themselves, their families, and their slaves. Although slaves might feel some hardship at separation, their distress was considered as in no way comparable to the sentiments and anxieties which whites could feel in their own family sphere. After all, black emotions, the proslavery argument ran, were merely temporary, excitable, or, at their more elevated, a doglike devotion to masters. Without great trouble to the conscience, then, slaveowners could square their condemnation of a set of traders with their extensive sales to the trade – the key being their "knowledge" that blacks would recover from "temporary hardships," together with their confidence that as owners they could best judge the interests of the slaveholding enterprise. From this perspective, of course, any sale was possible and open to legitimization. It helped, nevertheless, even within the South to have a notional class of outstandingly oily speculators who could be ritually condemned. And if buyers and sellers were to deal honorably with traders in practice, it helped too – in fact it was a necessity – that there also be honorable traders. The logic of slavery therefore demanded that there be stereotyping of vicious traders as a class, but also that a place be made for the trader.

The Trader as Citizen of Standing

If we sketch the careers of some of the traders...few if any pariahs emerge. Instead, the evidence seems clearly to be that traders, like almost any other successful businessmen, could become leaders of the local and even the wider community. The sample offered below is not scientifically selected and is not closely compared with a control group of other businessmen. It merely represents biographical information which could be gleaned for [a] sample of South Carolina traders...together with evidence from those manuscript collections of North Carolina and Virginia speculators which have been located. In this somewhat haphazard sample, however, the pattern is fairly consistent: trading, in itself, did not automatically lead to social ostracism, and a substantial section of the trading fraternity seems to have gained positions of real influence, respect, and leadership in the community.

A check through city ordinances and banking histories shows that several prominent Charleston (South Carolina) traders were aldermen in that city and directors of banks. Alexander McDonald, J. S. Riggs, Thomas Ryan, and Ziba Oakes (as well as A. J. Salinas, who sold large numbers of slaves and was probably a trader) were, for some part of the period 1845 to 1865, city aldermen. In addition, Ryan, Oakes, Thomas N. Gadsden, and McDonald were bank directors or vice-presidents. And whereas the banks concerned might perhaps have been partly the "pets" of traders, they were also the state's principal financial institutions. The career of McDonald, one of the speculators who served both as alderman and bank director, did, it is true, end in great confusion. This, however, had nothing to do with any question that trading was harmful to business or social standing. In a court case, Eliza Coldough testified that McDonald had enjoyed

> the confidence of the public and was reputed to be a man of large means and responsible for all his engagements . . . [but that] to the great surprise of everyone, about the year 184[5] he had suddenly and clandestinely left the state and went no-one knows where, leaving a large amount of debts and little or nothing out of which they could be satisfied.

Another witness, Samuel Mayrant, gave similar testimony, observing that "up to the time of his leaving his credit was very high – His leaving took everyone by surprise."

Of the other speculators just noted, T. N. Gadsden came from a family of particularly high repute. As the historian Frederic Bancroft wrote, in Charleston, "a community where old families of high character were numerous, few stood higher than the Gadsdens." The trader's close relatives included a bishop and a prominent lawyer, as well as James Gadsden, negotiator of the Gadsden Purchase, whose career combined the professions of soldier, planter, railroad president, and Minister to Mexico. Less is known of the trader Ziba Oakes's family, but there is no doubt that he became one of Charleston's most prominent citizens, highly influential too in South Carolina masonic circles. The Charleston City directory of 1855 shows that he was then an officer in the Most Worshipful Grand Lodge of Free Masons of South Carolina, serving on several committees, including the Charity Committee. In the same year, he was a Companion and the Grand Treasurer of the Grand Royal Arch Chapter of South Carolina Masons. Masonic connections have not always been universally popular in America and elsewhere, but in this case they do suggest, at least, acceptance within the Charleston business community. . . .

Of . . . fourteen Virginia and North Carolina traders cited earlier, quite detailed biographical evidence has been found on six, and limited evidence on four others. The careers of those concerned varied, but the very conspicuous success of some again indicates that trading *per se* was no bar to gaining social distinction. Several were planters as well as traders and several showed interest, during their careers, in a range of enterprises including turnpikes, merchandizing, ginning, and distilling.

Two Virginians, Francis Everod Rives and Floyd L. Whitehead, were particularly prominent in public life. From 1817 to 1820 (and possibly for considerably longer), Rives was fully and openly involved in buying and selling in the trade from Virginia to Natchez. This, clearly, did not hamper his political career, which from 1821 ran successfully for at least thirty years. He served as member of the Virginia House of Delegates (1821–31), member of Virginia Senate (1831–6, 1848–51), and member of the U.S. House of Representatives (1837–41), as well as serving as Mayor of Petersburg, Virginia (1847–8). In addition, he was engaged in planting, in the building and management of railroads in North Carolina and Virginia, and in the development of internal improvements in his state.

Whitehead, of Nelson County, Virginia, was, with his partner "Captain Loftuss," an active trader in the 1830s. Like Rives, he traded to Natchez and entered politics, though his political career was perhaps not quite so successful as that of Rives. In 1843 Richard Pollard urged that Whitehead, "acquainted with all of the voters of the county" should stand for office, and two years later a letter from Sterling Claiborne informed the trader:

> I have known you for a great length of time [in your capacities] as a citizen, as a merchant as a magistrate, as a sheriff, as a member of the legislature representing the county of Nelson in which I live, and ... at all times and under all circumstances the public opinion has been very favorable to you.

An undated memorandum signed by members of the legislature of Virginia and addressed to President Polk recommended Whitehead for "consideration in the appointment of officers in the public departments" and added:

> Mr. Whitehead is a gentleman of great intelligence, high minded and honorable. He possesses fine business qualities, an energetic character, persevering and laborious habits and great moral worth.

It is not clear whether this sort of recommendation was simply a standard piece of lobbying for the spoils of politics or a genuine personal recommendation. Clearly, however, a trading career did not prevent the development of the most influential connections, and in 1844 or 1845

Whitehead even had discussions with the nation's President and Vice President.

Another Virginia speculator, W. A. J. Finney, also appears to have been well respected and influential in local affairs. In 1865, a letter from A. H. McCleish asked him to use his influence in encouraging neighbors to contribute to the provisioning of troops; two years later the president of the Lynchburg and Danville Railroad asked Finney to join the railroad committee and so to encourage the taking out of subscriptions; and in 1876 Finney's neighbor G. C. Cabell, then a Representative in the United States Congress, urged him to use his influence to get a good delegate sent from their county to the state convention. Of the other Virginia traders less is known. James A. Mitchell, who, in the 1830s and early 1840s (and perhaps in later years), was an active trader to the west, by 1845 at least was producing tobacco in Virginia, and in the 1850s owned land in Texas. Like several other traders and extraders, he dabbled in franchising for agricultural inventions.

Of [a] sample of North Carolina traders, William Long seems to have had the most prominent public career. In the 1830s and 1840s Long was a very active slave trader, with planting interests as well. These latter, and perhaps his trading, continued into the 1850s, and in 1853 he headed a list of some sixty members of the local Caswell County Agricultural Society. In combination with his neighbor Abisha Slade, he is credited with inventing the process which produced "bright tobacco," a curing technique which seems greatly to have benefitted local planters. In the 1860s, he founded the Border Agricultural Society of Virginia and North Carolina. Not only was he a prominent local planter; his high profile in the community extended in the 1850s and 1860s to service first as state representative and then as state senator.

The North Carolina partners Tyre Glen and Isaac Jarratt, who took a great many coffles to Alabama and were fully involved in trading, were also active in planting and local politics. In 1852, the following note introduced Glen to U.S. Congressman James Brookes:

> I take this pleasure in introducing to your acquaintance Tyre Glen Esq. of this state – Tyre Glen is a gentleman of high standing among us, a genuine Whig . . . with good business habits. He visits your city upon a matter of business – and any civilities shown to him will be duly appreciated.

And in the same year a supporter of Sheppeard, a local Whig, sought Jarratt's assistance, telling Glen that

> with the aid of Jarratt we can give Sheppeard a start whether he wants the nomination or not. . . . I wish you would see Isaac [Jarratt] between now and court and see what can be done for Sheppeard.

A letter of 1858 refers to Glen as "a man having much influence in . . . [his] county and state"; and various letters of the 1850s and 1860s show that Glen was on close terms with John A. Gilmer, member of the North Carolina and later of the national legislature. In 1864, for example, in a letter concerning the entry of Glen's son into the Naval School, Gilmer informed the Secretary of the Confederate Navy that the youth was "a young gentleman of high character and very respectable parentage." Glen was a man of substantial property, with interests including flour milling, textile processing, and distilling; and in 1864 he had a plantation worked by forty-two slaves. In addition, he was, during the 1850s, a director of the Yadkin River Navigation Company. . . .

An Honest Calling to Support my Family

Judging by the extensive traders' correspondence which has been located, the speculator's self-image tended to be that of an energetic businessman pursuing the legitimate opportunities and rewards offered by a rapidly expanding economy and slave system. Some correspondence collections deal almost exclusively with business matters, and the emphasis, rather like that of a broker following the stock market, was upon catching market trends. Added to this, the disciplining of slaves formed a constant theme. And where letters were between relatives, one finds emphasis on sacrifices made for the support of the family, and sometimes upon the adventures of travel. Quite often, the traders gave an eye to wider speculative opportunities which might complement slaving. It is not surprising therefore that several Virginia and Carolinas traders became involved in a range of developing opportunities from ginning, franchising for mechanical inventions, transport improvements, to financial speculation. Some traders might have been ruthless sharpers, whereas others could appear to be insulted by occasional complaints from clients. After one such complaint, for example, the speculator McElveen reemphasized to his partner that on the health of slaves "I don't deceive no man if I am aware of the fact." Overall the impression is of men whose self-image was that of roving, practical businessmen, calculating the chance of high profits against the inconveniences of rough travel and hard work. One finds no indication of guilt or of a social ostracism which should be endured or kicked against.

While fully engaged in scattering black families to all corners of the South, the speculators could, without the slightest awkwardness, write affectionately to their own families back home and assure them that their every effort was for the benefit of their loved ones. Typical of many

affectionate letters from traders selling in the Lower South was a message from Obediah Field telling his wife:

> You may look for . . . [my return] between this [late November] and Christ-
> mas as it is out of my power to say in a day or two of the time, but my dear
> you may rest assured that it will be as soon as possible. Kiss my dear little
> children and tell them their Pap will soon be home. Give my complements
> to mother. . . . I am yours with all the affection in my breast till death.

A letter surviving from a selling trip of 1825 again shows Fields's tender-
ness toward his "dear loving wife" and toward his children; and in a
letter of 1834, the trader J. A. Mitchell told his children that they should
be "good boys and girls" and should "go to school and learn their
books" so that they would be able to "show Par how smart they have
been in his absence." Mitchell, like Fields, told his wife of his great
impatience to dispose of the remainder of his slave gang so that he could
get home to see her and the children.

The trader's double standards on the family again appeared when the
speculator Samuel Logan lamented the death of his wife. "In my family
sphere," he wrote, "I am utterly ruined as my children are to raise and
they cannot be raised as she would have done it." A paragraph or so
later, however, he could muster no sympathy at all for a slave family in
his possession and informed his partner:

> I have determined to send . . . [for sale in the Lower South] my woman
> Fan, about 30 years old, a daughter about 10, and a boy about 6, as they
> are so villaneous and triffling that I can't keep them.

But his own children would need looking after, and for that he planned
to buy two replacement slaves, "that is, a cook woman, and a girl that
can nurse your namesake and help to take care of my other little children." Another trader, the fledgeling speculator John D. Badgett, in
Georgia on a selling trip with his older brother, was keen to keep in
touch with his folks back home in Virginia, and asked his father to "give
my love to Mar, and all the family. Tell Mar that I want to see her very
bad and that I will come home as soon as I can."

Traders, it seems, might in their community take on the role of
pioneer, frontiersman, and even hero, enduring hardship, enjoying
adventures, and all in the end for the benefit of their families. Certainly
R. C. Puryear, writing to Isaac Jarratt, a trading friend, was envious that
"For you the task of writing a letter is quite easy – for new and interesting
scenes are constantly presenting themselves." It is true that even our
traders could stray from the paths of virtue in the family sphere, and
indeed Jarratt's partner Tyre Glen had been unable to join him on that

slaving trip of 1832, his ailment being a "great calamity" which "the fair
dame of Greensborough [not his wife!] had imparted to him." But the
theme of family crops up again and again in the Jarratt letters, as when
his "affectionate cousin" Betsy Ann wrote enthusiastically of his adventures and hoped that he would bring back nice presents, and later begged
him "pray to send us some beaux." Jarratt, however, feared that for his
cousin and his sister marriage

> is a long shot and a bad chance without a show of some negroes and beauty
> – both of which is lacking with Sarah [his sister] and unfortunately for you
> [Betsy Ann] you lack the negroes.

By 1834, Jarratt had married and his wife pressed him to forsake the
roving life of the speculator. "I'm afraid, my dear husband," she wrote,

> you and your friend Carson will keep up negro trading as long as you can
> get a negro to trade on, and when you cant get any thro the country you
> will carry of[f] all you can persuade at home, but one good thing Mr. C.
> has no wife to leave behind when he is gone.

Jarratt, though, assured her: "I have no disposition to negro trade and
hope to engage in something else by which I can accumulate a little and
remain with my family." Meanwhile, he wrote,

> Mr. Beverly Barksdale is here. He was married about ten days before he
> left home. He has some 50 negroes to sell and I have [only] 18. You
> complain of my absence. What do you think of the situation with Mrs.
> Barksdale. She cant expect him until April or May. We both [he explained]
> are toiling for our wives and their little ones.

Sometime in 1836 Jarratt did indeed retire to his home and farm,
although debt-collecting trips were still necessary, as in February 1837
when he wrote from Alabama to his wife:

> I was candid and never will make another negro trading trip without your
> approbation unless a kind Providence should frown upon my labors and
> make it actually necessary that I should leave home to make a support for
> my family. In that case [he concluded] I would resort to any Honest calling
> for the comfort of my family.

From his slave-selling trips, another North Carolina speculator, T. W.
Burton, frequently wrote of his restlessness to return home to his wife
and family; and in 1846 he made plans to take his family, when the
slaving season was over, on a vacation trip to Texas. A letter to his

trading partner explained his trading plans and, more generally, outlined his concept of duty to family. "I am quite willing," he wrote, to go on the Texas vacation trip,

> and think it my duty as it will be a great schooling for my children when young. My object is pleasure in this life and not riches as I know my incompetence to take care of property if I had it. I therefore wish to be content with a competency and [shall] let my children work for themselves and earn their living and then they will be better prepared to take care of . . . [property].

Traders, of course, showed the most settled complacency about the fact that their traffic was in people. This did not mean, however, that they did not feel more favorable to some slaves than to others. Indeed, a cardinal rule of slaving and of slaveholding racism seemed to be that – with the basic power foundation of racism and race hierarchy established – one could safely indulge in special favors to selected slaves, particularly to those who seemed to be especially cooperative. . . .

Profit and Prosperity

Although T. W. Burton suggested that his aim was to store away only "a competency," and several others, "toiling for their wives and little ones," might give an impression of being men of modest means, most specu-lators were probably wealthy or well on their way to accumulating considerable property. It seems, in fact, that the profit rates of the trade were high by antebellum standards, and data on real and personal estate suggest, furthermore, that traders were probably in the top few percent of southern and indeed of national property owners. . . .

[D]ata suggest fluctuations in profits over time, with net annual rates of 60 to 80 percent from 1817–19, 30 percent in the early 1820s, 30–50 percent in the early and mid 1830s, and 15–30 percent in the late 1840s and the 1850s. The exceptionally high profits of 1817–19 probably had much to do with the Lower South's especially rapid growth during those years, together with a brief lag in the trade's adjustment to supplying that surge in demand. The fact that the 1845–60 profit rates were generally lower than those of 1830–7 is probably, to an important extent, explained by the buoyancy of post-1844 tobacco prices in the Upper South and the consequent bidding up of that region's slave prices. What is particularly significant in understanding the position of the trader in the South, however, is not so much these absolute levels of profit but the comparison of traders' profits with those of other enterprises.

Profits from the trade were substantially higher than the 10 percent annual rate suggested by Robert Fogel and Stanley Engerman for slave agriculture from 1820–60.[2] At the same time, they were very close to the rates which Fred Bateman and Thomas Weiss calculated for a sample of some 2,000 southern industrial firms of 1850 and 1860.[3] The fact that rates of return seem to have been similar in slave trading and southern industry argues against any idea that there might have been a unique stigma attaching to the trade (a stigma discouraging recruitment to trading and bidding up the profits of those willing to become speculators). As Bateman and Weiss argued, there might have been some disinclination among planters to become involved in industry, an activity which probably carried less status than did planting. But they pointed also to the probability that poor information about opportunities and concern over the additional risks involved were strong discouragements against planters taking up industrial entrepreneurship. These practical factors, and several others, must go a long way to explaining the profit differential between trading and planting. Trading involved obvious financial risks, but also brought with it real physical dangers from discontented slaves; it involved much arduous travel in all weathers, and often meant that long periods had to be spent away from home. The stereotyping of some traders as "monsters" would probably have had some influence in raising profit rates; but it is clear that in practice the South found it possible to deal "honorably" with most traders. Most successful speculators, it seems, could easily combine slaving with the enjoyment of respect and influence within their own communities.

From scattered evidence in letters and from census information, it is clear that most traders would have been among the wealthiest men in their localities. In 1859, for example, Phillip Thomas informed his partner that "Robertson of the [slave trading] firm Smith & Robertson is dead . . . [and] has left Lewis Smith his fortune of $175,000." Thomas Williams, an important slave dealer based in the Washington, D.C., area, boasted that he had made $30,000 in a few months; and Franklin & Armfield are said to have made $33,000 in 1829. In the 1840s and 1850s, J. R. White several times achieved gross seasonal profits exceeding $20,000; and over a two-year period in the 1850s Bolton & Dickens received gross profits well in excess of $130,000.

More important than evidence of this sort, however, is the more systematic census data available for 1850 on real estate and for 1860 for both personal estate (including slaves) and real estate. . . . Several traders (Allen Vance, George Seaborn, Ziba Oakes, Benjamin Mordecai, E. S. Irvine, O. B. Irvine, J. W. Ford, and T. C. Weatherly) appear as owners of property valued at some $100,000 to $200,000, which would have meant that they were in the top 0.3 percent (for the South) (and the top 0.1 percent for the nation) of free adult males holding property. Not only that, but among the forty or so traders located in the South Carolina census of 1860 the statistically average trader would, in terms of real, personal, or total estate, have ranked in about the top 3 or 4 percent of free adult male holders of property in the South, and would have been in an even more conspicuously wealthy position compared with such men in the nation as a whole.

It is not clear whether the more common route was to enter the trade via an already established basis of family or personal capital, or to start from more modest beginnings and, through wealth gained in the trade, move toward the social and property-holding elite. Several traders appear in South Carolina's 1850 or 1860 censuses as apparently without property and, if they gave proper information to the census enumerators, might have been men starting at the bottom. Of those who did not declare any property, Charles Logan had been born in Ireland, was in 1850 listed as a shoemaker without property, but in 1860 was listed as "Negro Trader" and declared $26,000 of property. H. G. Burkett appeared as an overseer in 1850, and declared no property then or in 1860 when he described himself as a farmer. W. B. Ryan and T. B. Adkins appeared in 1850 as clerks to slave traders, and again declared no property. Perhaps Logan and Burkett were cases of men of humble origins, but Adkins and Ryan were in fact both members of successful family firms which traded in slaves. A somewhat similar case was E. M. Cobb, whose family had been dealing in slaves for perhaps two decades or more, and from that family connection Cobb would no doubt have gained access to substantial cash advantages. Leaving aside those traders who might have been linked to substantial family wealth, even though not yet directly sharing in its ownership, there are those traders who seem simply to have failed to declare substantial property which they did directly own. Several who did not declare property seem to have taken a generally lax attitude toward the census and also failed to declare their occupation or their place of birth. Furthermore, when checked in slave schedules of the census, several of those traders apparently without property appear as owners of slaves.

Uncertainties about some aspects of census evidence therefore complicate the task of establishing the economic status of our sample of traders, though there seems to be no reason why traders should have been any more or less lax than other citizens in assisting census enumerators with declarations of property. Although it is difficult to establish the case decisively, one suspects that most traders began their careers with a base of family wealth. Whatever the trader's origins, however, the census data on property do seem to be decisive: most traders were among the wealthiest in their community, many had planting interests (as the free and the slave schedules of the census show), and most probably had close involvement with the local elite. Their high levels of property holding help to explain the prominent role which many traders took in politics and the local community.

The Need for "Good" Traders and "Bad"

In fairly minor part, the hostile image of the trader which was so often found in southern prints and rhetoric stemmed from the fact that some speculators were, no doubt, thoroughly dishonest, vicious, and worthless by almost anyone's standards. And in part too it stemmed from regional differences of interest within the South. [I]n the case of Georgia, for example, old-established slaveholding sections of the state often felt alarm at slave importation into neighboring and less developed areas. Such importation brought fears of over-production of staples, overbalancing the state's race ratio, and bringing in dangerous slaves, as well as undermining the commitment of the Border South to the institution of slavery. Regional differences in attitudes to the trade and to the speculator himself no doubt to some extent existed. And, as particular areas passed from being net importers to net exporters of slaves, local changes in attitude would occur over time.

The slave Charles Ball pointed to this sort of regional difference in emphasis. In about 1805, Ball, with other members of his coffle, was taken by a speculator from Maryland to the then-frontier area of central South Carolina. There the speculator was greeted with delight by his host, a planter and innkeeper, who declared that

> any gentleman who brought such a stock of hands into the country was a public benefactor, and entitled to the respect and gratitude of every friend of the South. . . . It would be his [host's] chief business to introduce him to the gentlemen of the neighborhood, who would all be glad to become acquainted with a merchant of his respectability.

And, Ball continued,

> In the state of Maryland, my master had been called a negro buyer, or Georgia trader, sometimes a negro driver, but here, I found that he was elevated to the rank of merchant, and a merchant of the first order too, for it was very clear that in the opinion of the landlord, no branch of trade was more honorable than the traffic in us poor slaves.

There were then, to some extent, regional differences and variations over time. Low-country Georgia, when it sought to maintain control over the up-country, might be particularly sensitive to some practical (but not moral) implications of the trade. And the southern plantation legend, in slavery times and long after, tended strongly to marginalize the supposed role of the trader, to maintain that he was incidental and not fundamental to the aims of slavery. From this it was easy to create the myth that family separations were rare and the trader a mere detail within a broad, benign system. Such things could happen at the level of sectional propaganda and, just as important, could readily develop in lazy southern rationalizing and domestic myth-making. In practice, however, the antebellum South dealt with the trader daily. To have a scapegoat "evil" trader was a great convenience. But it was equally necessary, for practical purposes, that there be "respectable merchants" dealing in slaves. By making a place for such men in the life of the South – and, as we have seen, in southern society and politics at the highest local and regional level – slaveowners could readily cope with any "temporary hardships" of black family separations, and could get about the business of southern enterprise in their pursuit of personal and family advancement.

Notes

1 Drew Gilpin Faust, *James Henry Hammond and the Old South: A Design for Mastery* (Baton Rouge: Louisiana State University Press, 1982).
2 Robert Fogel and Stanley Engerman, *Time on the Cross: The Economics of American Negro Slavery*, 2 vols (Boston: Little, Brown and Company, 1974).
3 Fred Bateman and Thomas Weiss, *A Deplorable Scarcity: The Failure of Industrialization in the Slave Economy* (Chapel Hill: University of North Carolina Press, 1981).

10

Asking Questions, Reading Bodies

A Southern Physician on "Unsoundness in the Negro," 1858–1859

Since price was tied to physical integrity, ascertaining the health of a slave was critical to buyers. In their efforts to read slaves' bodies, buyers were aided by men of medical science who advised them what to look for when buying slaves. Moreover, doctors were often required to issue warrantees and certificates testifying to the soundness of the slave being sold. Extracted here is Juriah Harriss's article explaining "What constitutes unsoundness in the Negro?" Harriss was a Professor of Physiology at the Savannah Medical College, Georgia. (From *The Savannah Journal of Medicine*, I (September 1858), pp. 145–8; I (November 1858), pp. 217–18, 222; I (January 1859), pp. 291–3)

[What constitutes unsoundness in the Negro?] is a question of great import to the Southern physician and slave owner.... Physicians in the South are daily called upon to give medical evidence in court, in cases of prosecution for sale of an unsound negro, or by a citizen to pronounce upon the soundness of a negro slave, whom he proposes purchasing, or finally as medical examiner for insurance companies, to determine the condition of negroes as regards health .... There are some deformities which should constitute unsoundness. These may be congenital or accidental. Any deformity which materially diminishes the value of the negro, or disables him for the performance of such labor as is usual for him to perform, or prevents the execution of natural functions which are necessary to the preservation of health or life, should constitute unsoundness.

As instances of congenital deformities, I will only cite a few – an imperforate anus, or occlusion of the vagina, of such a character as to be irremediable by surgical interference, or if relieved, it is done at the great risk of the life of the patient. The latter comes under the head of congenital deformities, which prevent the performance of a *vital physiological function*, without which function, health cannot be secured, and life, when the subject reaches maturity, is in constant jeopardy. Even in cases where this deformity can be relieved by surgical aid, the vendee cannot reasonably be supposed to purchase a slave, and an expense of a surgical operation, to say nothing of the risk of life, which an operation may produce....

The loss of foot, leg, hand or arm, diminishes the value of a negro slave, incapacitates him for the usual duties of this class of persons, and constitutes unsoundness.... The negro slave with such deformities is both medically and legally *unsound*; but healthy. There might be no extra risk to an Insurance Company in giving a policy of life insurance for such an individual, yet he is to all intense and purposes unsound. The loss of portions of the hands, or deformities arising from burns, which prevent the dexterous handling of implements of labor, or the *feet*, which materially impede locomotion, should constitute unsoundness....

There are some fractures even when ununited, the non-medical man is unable to detect, and indeed their existence requires great care and considerable skill, on the part of the physician to determine. In illustration I might mention the fracture of the radius immediately above or below the tubercle. I have seen three or four cases of these fractures which had baffled the diagnostic skill of physicians. They had pronounced them strains or twists of the elbow. The existence of such a fracture, or a union consequent upon an improper treatment, produces serious difficulty in the use of the arm, and diminishes the value of the negro slave, though not increasing the risks to life....

Burns, after having been healed, leave a hard fibrous structure of little vitality, possessing a constant tendency to contract. When in the neighborhood of joints, often diminish the mobility of the limb, and in some cases prevent all motion in the joint. None can doubt but that such deformities should constitute unsoundness. Extensive scars upon the face diminish the value.... Example of simple deformity from burns; a negro boy about twelve years of age, from the effects of a burn, had his fingers completely flexed, and enveloping these a thick skin of normal color, as though the fist had been "doubled," and thrust into a bag. The fingers, could be partially moved, and distinctly felt beneath or within the cutaneous sac....

Tumors are multiplied in form and character. Some constitute permanent unsoundness, even after the tumors have been removed by surgical aid. Others during their existence do not diminish the value of the negro, and a larger number after extirpation never return. The benign or non-malignant do not usually cause permanent unsoundness, as when removed, are not liable to be redeveloped. Previous to this, however, they diminish the value of the negro slave....

In connection with the negro, the *cheloid* tumor which should be placed among the benign, is interesting and important. In the first place it is almost *peculiar* to the negro. I have seen but one case in the white. They are usually developed in the neighborhood of scars, particularly upon the face, chest, and often on the back. Another fact is that they almost invariably return. I indeed know of no exception, but unlike malignant tumors, they invariably return at the same point, or upon the old cicatrix. Being incurable, either by the knife or medication, and having a strong tendency to scrofulous ulceration, in persons of scrofulous diathesis, they usually constitute unsoundness. *Wens*, or pendulous sarcomatous growths, as a general rule do not seriously impair the value of the negro. They are exceedingly frequent in this race, and sometimes grow to an enormous size. But a few days since, I witnessed an interesting case. A negro woman with two large pendulous tumors hanging from the ears, like ear-rings, presenting a most singular appearance. Had it not been for a cheloid tumor in one of the temples, having a decided tendency to ulcerate, I should have considered her sound. The tumors could be easily removed without risk. The owners would not force her to have the operation performed. These tumors probably originated from wearing brass ear-rings, for which negresses have a great fondness. Indeed I do not know but that the remark might, with almost as much propriety, be extended to males.

A Trader Notes How Slaves Affect their Sales, 1856

The following letter from an agent, A. J. McElveen, to his slave broker employer in South Carolina, Z. B. Oakes, reveals much about the ways in which slaves manipulated their sales and the frustrations their behavior caused slave trading agents. (Reproduced by courtesy of the Trustees of the Boston Public Library)

I am here laying over a few days. I have had Some offers I have not Sold any thing up to this time. the Carpenter is out on trial for a few days. the Gentleman will See me on Saturday that will be the 24th, and will decide Dr Weatherly is here he lives in his tents he told me he Sold ten negroes last week at very fair prices. he is following the Counties Round attending Courts Mr Oakes James is cutting up. his Contrariness. I could Sell him like hot cakes if he would talk Right. you may blame me but I tell nothing on him but the fact and Dr Weatherly will tell the same. the Boy is trying to make himself *unsound*. he Says he wore a trust [truss] in charleston. I think it would be well to See his former master and Know the facts, and write me to Montgomery. I will be there next week also advise Mr Brown the course to persue.

S. N. Brown told me he would garantee any thing I done in the way of trading. By all means I will Give full warrantee by instructions you Give me So I hope the matter will not amount to much. I hope this will find you all well.

A Former Slave Notes Buyers Reading Bodies, 1855

Prospective buyers of slaves took advice concerning the soundness of bodies seriously, as the following brief account by Peter Randolph, a former Virginia slave emancipated upon the death of his master in 1844, attests. (From Peter Randolph, *Sketches of Slave Life: or, Illustrations of the "Peculiar Institution"* (Boston: Published for the Author, 1855), p. 52)

The auctioneer is crying the slave to the highest bidder. "Gentlemen, here is a very fine boy for sale. He is worth twelve hundred dollars. His name is Emanuel. He belongs to William Harrison, who wants to sell him because his overseer don't like him. How much, gentlemen, – how much for this boy? He's a fine, hearty nigger. Bid up, bid up, gentlemen; he must be sold." Some come up to look at him, pull open his mouth to examine his teeth, and see if they are good. Poor fellow! he is handled and examined like any piece of merchandize; but he must bear it. Neither tongue nor hand, nor any other member, is his own, – why should he attempt to use another's property?

Again, the bidding goes on: "I will give one thousand dollars for that boy." The auctioneer says, "Sir, he is worth twelve hundred at the lowest. Bid up, gentlemen, bid up; going, going – are you all done? – once, twice, three times – all done? – GONE!"

A Slave Reads a Buyer, 1858

Slaves were very sensitive to the gestures, sights, and sounds of slavery and, especially, the selling and buying of slaves. Charles Ball's account suggests this sensitivity and reveals how buyers read the bodies of the enslaved and how the enslaved managed to size up the character and moral worth of the buyers. (From Charles Ball, *Fifty Years in Chains; or, the Life of an American Slave* (New York: H. Dayton, 1858), pp. 36–8, 70–1)

Hitherto our master had not offered to sell any of us, and had even refused to stop to talk to any one on the subject of our sale, . . . but soon after we departed from this village [Lancaster, South Carolina], we were overtaken on the road by a man on horseback, who accosted our driver by asking him if his *niggars* were for sale. The latter replied, that he would not sell any yet, as he was on his way to Georgia, and cotton being now much in demand, he expected to obtain high prices for us from persons who were going to settle in the new purchase. He, however, contrary to his custom, ordered us to stop, and told the stranger he might look at us, and that he would find us as fine a lot of hands as were ever imported into the country – that we were all prime property, and he had no doubt would command his own prices in Georgia.

The stranger, who was a thin, weather-beaten, sun-burned fellow, then said, he wanted a couple of breeding wenches, and would give as much for them as they would bring in Georgia – that he had lately heard from Augusta, and that *niggers* were not higher there than in Columbia, and, as he had been in Columbia the week before, he knew what *niggers* were worth. He then walked our line, as we stood chained together, and looked at the whole of us – then turning to the women, asked the prices of the two pregnant ones. Our master replied, that these were two of the best breeding-wenches in all Maryland – that one was twenty-two, and the other only nineteen – that the first was already the mother of seven children, and the other four – that he had himself seen the children at the time he bought their mothers – and that such wenches would be cheap at a thousand dollars each; but as they were not able to keep up with the gang, he would take twelve hundred dollars for the two. The purchaser said this was too much, but that he would give nine hundred dollars for the pair. This price was promptly refused; but our master, after some consideration, said he was willing to sell a bargain in these wenches, and would take eleven hundred dollars for them, which was objected to on the other side; and many faults and failings were pointed out in the merchandise. After much bargaining, and many gross jests on the part of the stranger, he offered a thousand dollars for the two, and he said he would give no more. He then mounted his horse, and moved off; but after he had gone about one hundred yards, he was called back; and our master said, if he would go with him to the next blacksmith's shop on the road to Columbia, and pay for taking the irons off the rest of us, he might have the two women. . . .

One evening, when our master was with us, a thin, sallow-looking man rode up to the house, and alighting from his horse, came to us, and told him that he had come to buy a boy; that he wished to get a good field hand, and would pay a good price for him. I never saw a human countenance that expressed more of the evil passions of the heart than did that of this man, and his conversation corresponded with his physiognomy. Every sentence of his language was accompanied with an oath of the most vulgar profanity, and his eyes appeared to me to be the index of a soul as cruel as his visage was disgusting and repulsive.

After looking at us for some time, this wretch singled *me* out as the object of his choice, and coming up to me, asked how I would like him for a master. In my heart I detested him; but a slave is often afraid to speak the truth, and divulge all he feels; so with myself in this instance, as it was doubtful whether I might not fall into his hands, and be subject to the violence of his temper, I told him that if he was a good master, as every gentleman ought to be, I should be willing to live with him. He appeared satisfied with my answer, and turning to my master, said he would give a high price for me. "I can," said he, "by going to Charleston, buy as many Guinea negroes as I please for two hundred dollars each, but as I like this fellow, I will give you four hundred for him." This offer struck terror into my heart, for I knew it was as much as was generally given for the best and ablest slaves, and I expected that it would immediately be accepted as my price, and that I should be at once consigned to the hands of this man, of whom I had formed so abhorrent an opinion. To my surprise and satisfaction, however, my master made no reply to the proposition; but stood for a moment, with one hand raised to his face and his fore-finger on his nose, and then turning suddenly to me, said, "Go into the house; I shall not sell you to-day."

Asking Questions, Reading Bodies

Walter Johnson

When Richard Winfield went to the slave market to buy Elvira and Samuel Brown, he took James Calvitt, a more experienced slave buyer, along to help him see. As a witness remembered it, the sale went something like this: "The Negroes were called in and the girl was examined by Mr. Calvitt in the presence of Winfield. Winfield looked at the slaves. Calvitt asked the slaves some questions." Calvitt remembered the sale similarly. Winfield "looked" at Elvira and then Calvitt "put his hand where her breast ought to be and found nothing but rags." If he had been purchasing on his own behalf, Calvitt added "he would have made her pull her dress off." Soon after Winfield bought her, it became apparent that Elvira was mortally ill – the rags filled out a chest ravaged by consumption – and she died within a few weeks of the sale. Another witness to the sale drew a slaveholder's moral from the story: "Thinks Winfield a poor judge of slaves or he would not have purchased said girl. She is the first girl Winfield ever owned." The observers described the nonslaveholder's inexperience as a matter of insight: Winfield was a poor judge of slaves. Indeed, comparisons of the depth of slaveholder's insight with that of the nonslaveholders run through all of the descriptions of the sale: Calvitt "examined" while Winfield "looked"; Calvitt touched while Winfield stood by. Calvitt, by all accounts, could see things that Winfield could not.

Being able to see that way was a talent, and inexperienced buyers often took someone along with them when they went to the slave market. Friends, physicians, even other slave dealers went to the slave market "at the request" of uncertain buyers. These more experienced men examined the lots of slaves for sale in the market, reading their bodies aloud and helping buyers select the "likely" and the healthy from among them. The presence of these slave-pen guides hints at a masculine social world in which being a "good judge of slaves" was a noteworthy public identity, a world of manly one-upsmanship in which knowledge of slaves' bodies was bandied back and forth as white men cemented social ties and articulated a hierarchy among themselves. In the slave pens a white male public congealed through shared participation in the inspection and evaluation of black slaves. And as these white men watched one another examine and choose slaves, and as the slave-pen mentors helped inexpert buyers choose slaves, they daily reproduced and passed on the racial "knowledge" by which Southern slavery was justified and defended.

A savvy slave buyer knew enough to try to look past the fancy clothes, bright faces, and promising futures lined up against the walls of the slave pens. Mississippi planter John Knight was presumably passing on the opinion of the "old planters" upon whom he regularly relied for advice when he sent his slave-market wisdom to his father-in-law. "The fact is," Knight wrote, "as to the character and disposition of all of the slaves sold by the traders, we know nothing whatever, the traders themselves being generally such liars. Buyers therefore can only judge the *looks* of the Negroes." The effects of the traders' practice – the invisibility of slaves' origins and the obscurity of their histories – and their reputation for dishonesty limited buyers' options as they tried to see through to slaves' pasts and prospects. The conditions of the trade, the material context of the slave market, enforced a blinkered gaze upon the buyers: in the absence of reliable information about individuals' history or character as a slave, the buyers began with the physical coordinates of the people who stood before them in the pens.

The axes of physical comparison used by the buyers were pre-figured in the traders' practice. Slaves in the market were advertised by their sex, racial designation, age, and skill, and they were lined out for sale according to height. They were arrayed as physical specimens even as their origins, attitudes, and infirmities were covered over by the traders' arts. As is well known, buyers preferred darker to lighter people for work in their fields and lighter to darker people to do skilled and domestic labor; they generally preferred slaves of "prime age" (between fifteen and twenty-five), although skilled slaves reached their prime at a later age (around thirty-five); buyers favored men for work outdoors and women for domestic service; and they apparently paid higher prices for slaves based upon their height. As telling as they are, however, these broad correlations tell us very little about what buyers saw when they looked at slaves, about what was behind the "singular look" which so impressed Joseph Ingraham. What did skin color, or sex, or size mean to slaveholders?

Asked to explain what they looked for in a slave, most slave buyers would have responded with the word "likely." Today the word means probable, but as slave buyers used it was as much a description as it was a prediction. As they singled out the "likely" from among the many they saw in the pens, slave buyers made detailed inspections of people's bodies which went well beyond the traders' advertisements and the age, sex, and racial designation that were commonly recorded on an Act of Sale. The standard slave inspection, as one buyer described it, went like this: "my inspection was made in the usual manner: their coats being taken off and the breast, arms, teeth, and general form and appearance looked at." The whole process, according to another buyer, might take anywhere from a fifteen minutes to a half an hour. And the inspections, at least at the outset, were public. . . .

As the slaves were paraded before them, slave buyers began by reading the slaves' skin color, groping their way from visible sign to invisible essence. No doubt buyers were seeing skin color when they described a slave as "a Negro or griff boy," "a griff colored boy," "dark Griff color," or "not black nor Mulatto, but what I believe is usually called a griff color, that is a Brownish Black, or a bright Mulatto." But in describing the blurred spectrum they saw before them, buyers used descriptive language that was infused with the reassuring certitudes of race. The words they used stabilized the restless hybridity, the infinite variety of mixture that was visible all over the South, into measurable degrees of the binary opposition between black and white. They suggested that slaves' skin color could be read as a sign of a deeper, measurable set of racial qualities.

In the antebellum slave market, the buyers of field slaves boiled blackness down to a question of physical vitality. Slaveholders' broadest concern was with what they called "acclimation," and they endlessly expressed their preference for slaves who had survived the transition to the harsh conditions of lower-South slavery. John Knight looked to the swampy eastern shore of Maryland, which he thought would better prepare slaves for Louisiana slavery than the "more healthy" regions elsewhere in the upper South. Others would only buy slaves from Louisiana or Mississippi, the "Creole" slaves whom one slaveholder estimated were worth a full quarter more than slaves born elsewhere. In the absence of certain information about origins, however, skin color often served as a stand-in for acclimation. There are a litany of statements to the effect that the "blackest" slaves were the healthiest. From the published writing of Louisiana doctor and racial theorist Samuel Cartwright – "All Negroes are not equally black – the blacker the stronger" – to the slave-market wish list sent by John Knight to his father-in-law – "I must have if possible the *jet black* Negroes, [they] stand this climate the best" – white men in the antebellum South talked to one another as if they could see slaves' constitutions by looking at their complexions.

So far did slaveholders go in associating "blackness" and healthfulness, that they believed that slaves changed color when they got sick. "Cannot tell her color because she did not look sharp," remembered Maria Piaja of the dying Mary Louise. According to Dr. G. E. Barton dark-skinned slaves got whiter when they were ill. Barton bolstered his testimony that Elvira was consumptive at the time she was sold by referring to the observation which had led him to judge her unsound: "Her skin was of a whiter color than was natural from the ordinary complexion of the girl . . . a decided whiteness about the lips and lightness and paleness about the face . . . gums and eyes pale pearly white." This slave-market commonplace was built into a Law of Nature by Dr. Cartwright: "Deviation from the black color, in the pure race is a mark of feebleness or ill health." Blackness, then, was much more than a question of lineage. Indeed, blackness was much more than a question of color. . . .

Fully grown, the slaves at the top of the traders' buyer-tracking tables would look like Edward, a man whom slave dealer Louis Caretta called "One of the best slaves in the state." Edward was, according to a man who saw him sold, "Stout and low statured. He was black and looked fat...." And, according to one who worked with him, "a big, strong, athletic fellow." Similarly, "the likeliest girl" slave trader A. J. McElveen "ever saw" was "Black, 18 years old, very near as tall as I am, no Surplus flesh, fine form." McElveen, indeed, seems to have weighed and measured every slave he bought. "She weighs 173 lbs, 5 feet 10 and three quarters inches high," he proudly reported of the woman. The value of these slaves was outlined by their full physical presence, their size and their strength.

Buyers ran their hands over the bodies of the slaves who stood before them, rubbing their muscles, fingering their joints, and kneading their flesh. Nathan Brown described a fifteen-year-old boy as "very interesting" after he had seen the slave placed on a table and walked back-and-forth so that those present could examine him "by feeling his joints." Similarly, Solomon Northup remembered that Theophilus Freeman "would make us hold up our head, walk briskly back and forth while customers would feel of our hands and arms and bodies, turn us about." The buyers were searching for taut muscles and hidden problems – broken bones, ossified sprains, severed tendons, internal injuries and illnesses. Listen to Joseph Copes apologizing for a slave he wanted to hire to a friend: "small of stature, but wiry, strong, and tough." Copes realized that the man's size was against him, and he tried to answer the objection he had imagined with a list of compensatory adjectives describing how the man would feel beneath a buyer's fingers.

The buyers took slaves' fingers in their hands, working them back-and-forth to insure they were, as Charles Ball remembered, "capable of the quick motions necessary in picking cotton." In his slave-market primer, "What Constitutes Unsoundness in the Negro?," Georgia slave doctor Juriah Harriss spent paragraphs on hands, advising slaveholders to look out for slaves who had lost "portions" of their hands or had manual "deformities arising from burns," both of which prevented "the dexterous handling of implements of labor." Asked to remember their "hands," slaveholders sometimes came up with missing digits: three different witnesses remembered that Tom was missing his right forefinger, although they differed upon which joint had been severed, the first or the second. Asked to remember William both his seller and his overseer remembered his hands. "Short arms and hands," said one. "His arms were short, hands small, and short fingers," said the other. Quite literally, these men remembered William as a hand too small to pick cotton.

In an action which many observers connected with the practice of the horse trade, buyers thumbed their way into slaves' mouths to look at their gums and teeth. The whiteness of sick slaves first appeared, according to Southern medical science, in their mouths. Samuel Cartwright saw the signs of "Negro Consumption" in the whiteness "of the mucous surfaces lining the gums and the inside of the mouth, lips and cheeks: so white are the mucous surfaces that some overseers call it the paper-gum disease." Cartwright's description suggests that he thought it routine for a slaveholder to pull back slaves' cheeks and finger their lips. And, indeed, slave trader A. J. McElveen referred to teeth again and again in the letters he wrote to his boss: "Very badly whipped but good teeth"; "Likely except bad teeth"; "very likely, has good sense, fine teeth." McElveen may have been choosing slaves by a disquietingly revealing criterion (and one drawn from the horse trade): the ability to chew their food as they aged. Or, more simply, McElveen may have been looking because he knew that buyers would. The rote practice of the market could produce its own standards of comparison: teeth did not need to be a commonly accepted sign of anything in particular to be compared to one another. . . .

The spectrum of slaves lined out against the walls by the traders and investigated by the buyers ran in two directions: men on one side, women on the other. The bodies of those bought to work in the fields were comparable, but not entirely fungible. W. H. Yos compared the men and women he found in the market, found the men "more likely," and put off buying women for another year – in the short run he could compare men to women, in the long run he would have to have both. A similar perspective shows through John Knight's plantation plans, which stipulated that his slaves be "half men and half women . . . young say from 16 to 25, stout limbs, large deep chests, wide shoulders and hips, etc." Knight's list of body parts ran male and female attributes together, describing a body that was to be, like his slave force, half and half: men and women bought to work in the fields were comparable in any instance but they had to be sexed and balanced in aggregate. Having, like Knight, broken people down into parts, slaveholders could rebalance their attributes in the quest for slaves like those trader Samuel Browning called the "right sort" for the lower South. "Likely young fellows, stout girls the same and Black," was how Browning described the slaves who would sell best in Mississippi. Virginia trader Hector Davis similarly headed his slave-market tables with "Best young men" and "Best black girls." Likely young women were not the same as likely young men, but likely young black women might be. Being "black" made an enslaved woman look more like the men alongside whom she would work in the fields; in evaluating female slaves, the traders were imagining composite slaves, matching the vitality they attributed to blackness with vulnerability they expected from femaleness to make a better slave. As well as comparing women to men, however, the buyers compared them to one another.

Buyers palpated women's breasts and abdomens, searching for hernias and prolapsed organs, they tried to massage the enslaved women's bodies into revealing their reproductive history and capacity. In the probing gaze of the slave pens women passed through their period of "prime" interest to the slave traders at an earlier age than men. Among slaves over the age of nineteen in the slave trade, males predominated; below that age, females did. Behind the aggregates lie the assumptions that slaveholder[s] inscribed upon the bodies they bought. When Hector Davis set up his parallel categories of "Best" for young men and young women, the men included were those aged nineteen to twenty-four, the (black) women were those sixteen to nineteen. A. J. McElveen made the terms of comparison explicit in a letter describing two slaves he had bought. "A boy large enough to plow," he wrote, outlining the labor against which a boy's body was to be judged, and "a Girl large Enough to nurse." These sex-specific age categories reflected different evaluations of which capacities of the human body made a slave useful: production and reproduction. Putting it scientifically, one might say that slaveholders emphasized full physical growth for males and menarche for females.

Putting it like a slaveholder would, one might say that they were concerned that their female slaves be "breeders." Even without the eugenic implications it has taken on in the twentieth century the word is an ugly one. It contains within it a history of crass incentives to reproduction and occasional unwanted matchings to which many slaveholders subjected their female slaves. The apparent absence of evidence that a large number of slaveholders focused solely on breeding slaves especially for the market should not obscure the fact that in their evaluations of the women they bought to work in their fields slaveholders reduced consideration of gender difference to the medical consideration of generative capacity. The condensation of femininity into reproduction was ultimately embodied in the figure of the enslaved nurse and midwife. As described by John Knight, such a woman would be "a good, sound, intelligent, middle-aged woman of experience, not only for midwifery purposes, but as a constant nurse for [the children on] my plantation. That they may be properly taken care of and attended to regularly especially in absence of their mothers at work in the fields." As he built his plantation, Knight was building a composite Mother: one midwife and nurse evaluated according to age and experience who would take care of the children produced by many women whose own bodies would be evaluated solely according to their physical and reproductive capacity.

Repeatedly, in the parlance of the slave market, slaveholders "stripped" the slaves to the waist so that they might have a closer look: "stripped the girl and made a careful examination"; "examined the boy very particularly... stripped the boy and examined him... stripped all the boys... and this boy appeared to be the finest of the lot." Buyers and traders alike used the word "stripped" as if they had done it themselves, literally unbuttoned their slaves' clothes, and pulled them off: "I stripped the boy and examined him several times." Slave buyers began undressing their slaves by asking them to roll up the legs of their pants or lift up their skirts so that their legs might be examined for ulcers and varicose veins produced by incipient illness. As the slaves removed their coats and frocks and shirts, buyers inspected their naked bodies minutely, looking for what they called "clear" or "smooth" skin, skin unmarked by signs of illness or injury. Buyers avoided those whose bodies showed signs of diseases like scrofula – "the narrow chest, prominent shoulders... and relaxed muscular tissue" or evidence of the cupping and blistering used to cure a recent illness, like the "blister mark" discovered on the breast of a Virginia woman by a slave trader, or the marks on Dempsey's arm, "three scars of deep cuts which... had injured the arm and much weakened him."

More than anything, however, [buyers] were looking for scars from whipping. As Solomon Northup explained, "scars upon a slave's back were considered evidence of a rebellious or unruly spirit, and hurt his sale." As they worked their way from inflicted scars to essential character, buyers fixed slaves in a typology of character according to the frequency, intensity, and chronology of the whipping apparent on their backs: "not whiped"; "a little whipt"; "some scars upon her shoulders ... produced by the whip"; "considerably scarred by the whip"; "the back of the girl had been cut pretty severely"; "he had many old stripes and scars on his body and head"; "she is very Badly whipped [but] the whipping has been done long since"; "she had marks of the whip not perfectly healed but did not appear to have been severely whipped." Looking at the scars, slave buyers created whole stories for the people who stood stripped in front of them: perhaps if the scarring was very light the offense had been minor, perhaps if it was very old the vice had been whipped out of the slave. The buyers thought they could read slaves' backs as encodings of their history. ...

The daily routine of the slave pens – the preparations, the examinations, and the constant contingency of being for sale to anyone who cared to buy – alienated slaves from their own bodies. William Wells Brown conveyed this experience with the image of slaves forced to dance to a merry fiddle while "their cheeks were wet with tears." For Brown, those tears marked the distance between two selves, one outwardly presented by the traders and one inwardly preserved by the slaves. Other slaves recalled a similar doubleness when they described the experience of being sold. J. D. Green, whose narrative was entitled *Narrative of the Life of J. D. Green, a Runaway Slave from Kentucky, Containing an Account of his Three Escapes 1839, 1846, and 1848*, remembered his slave market self being described as "above all free from the disease of running away" with no small measure of irony. John Brown remembered "not being very well pleased to hear myself run down" as a buyer tried to knock a few dollars off his price. Henry Bibb so distanced himself from his own sale that he described the time he spent in the New Orleans slave pens in the third person: "They were exposed for sale . . . they had to be in trim . . . they were made to stand up straight . . . they had to answer as promptly as they could and try to induce the spectators to buy them." More than literal renderings of slaves' specific thoughts at the time of their sale, these memories should be read as accounts of their double consciousness. Each contains a recognition of what a slaveholder saw – a dancing body, a pliant slave, a run-down little boy, a well-disciplined lot of slaves – alongside a marker of the slave's separation from their buyers' evaluation. They describe the divided meanings of salable bodies – once from without, once from within. . . .

The daily business of the slave pens, of course, was manipulating buyers. All of the feeding, clothing, caring for, and preparing had that single goal in mind, and slaves in the market were carefully instructed about how to present themselves to buyers – about what would sell and what would not. As the traders pitched them to the buyers, the slaves learned more. Charles Ball, for instance, heard two traders evaluating his potential. He was, they said in his hearing, worth about a thousand dollars "to a man making a settlement, and clearing a plantation." Ball's bodily vitality would be what a buyer was looking for. Other slaves picked up hints from the way that they were dressed. John Parker guessed that he was to be sold as a house servant because his market clothes set him off from the other slaves in the pen: civility rather than strength would entice a likely buyer. And light-skinned Henry Bibb . . . was told by his seller to "act stupid in language and thought," to perform slave-market blackness in order to entice a buyer who might otherwise have been put off by his light skin. The traders' pitches, threats, and hectoring promises charged their slaves with enacting the slave buyers' fantasies. But they also provided slaves with a detailed account of buyers' system of signs, of how slave buyers read appearances. By the time the buyers entered the pens, the slaves knew a lot about them. . . .

As the buyers began to bargain, the slaves could learn more. Slave-holders negotiated by attaching reasons to offers, and often slaves stood by as sellers and buyers argued back and forth about the value of a slave, anchoring their opinions in accounts of the hidden failings or evident advantages of a given body. Dennis Donovan remembered that he was standing with a slave named Ben, "talking with the boy," when Benjamin Huntington walked up and started to talk to him about Ben, asking "if he was a good boy" and whether he was healthy. The discussions they had in front of the slaves revealed the buyers' criteria, but they also occasionally revealed the buyers themselves. The buyers, after all, were trying to match their needs with a slave, to match, that is, themselves with the person they bought. Charles Ball remembered watching a buyer announce himself and his intentions for the person he bought: "a thin sallow man" rode up to the house where Ball's coffle was staying and said "that he wished to get a good field hand, and would pay a good price for him." The information that Ball overheard could perhaps have been divined by another method, but the knowledge obtained by Solomon Northup as he listened in on a slave-pen bargain was more precious: "One old gentleman, who said he wanted a coachman, appeared to take a fancy to me. From his conversation with [the slave trader] Burch, I learned he was a resident in the city." To Northup that piece of information held a treasured hope.

The more minute the buyers' attention, the greater the opportunity for the slaves. John Brown remembered that the buyers who asked him questions ended up giving him answers: "I was careful, however, to draw out the buyers, in order to learn what they wanted me for; which I judged by the questions they put to me." The argument might be extended indefinitely: Can you drive a coach? Cook a bird? Wield an ax? Have you nimble fingers for picking cotton? Strong arms for cutting cane? Breasts for nursing a child? All of these questions, asked in conversation and examination, were also answers, accounts of a buyer's needs, their purposes, and their origins. Buyers in the slave pens were trading information about themselves for information about the slaves. . . .

When slaves looked at a particular buyer they could do so with an informed eye to their own future. Among the many poisoned outcomes faced by slaves in the pens, some were worse than others. As Charles Ball remembered it, the prospect that he would be sold to the rough looking man who was bargaining for his price, for instance, "struck terror" into his heart. Solomon Northup, by contrast, remembered hoping that the man who was examining him would seal the bargain. Northup had overheard that the man was from New Orleans and "very much desired that he would buy me for I conceived it would not be difficult to make my escape from New Orleans on some northern vessel." John Brown similarly wanted to be sold to a man from up the Mississippi River because upriver was the direction of freedom. And Henry Bibb wanted to be sold to an Indian because he thought it would be easier to escape from an Indian than a white man. Besides, the man "wanted me only for a kind of body servant to wait on him – and in this case I knew that I should fare better than I should in the field." Writing *Clotel*, William Wells Brown neatly summed both the signs of difference between buyers evident to slaves in the pens and the social character of the process of interpreting those signs. In the voice of Mrs. Devant, Brown described a slave's perspective on a buyer like this: "I observed a tall young man, with long black hair, eyeing me very closely, and then talking to the trader. I felt sure that my time had come, but the day closed without me being sold. I did not regret this, for I had heard that foreigners made the worst of master, and I felt confident that the man who eyed me was not American.". . .

Slaves were the information brokers in the slave market. Anonymous, they stood at the center of the slaveholders' bargains, between imperfectly known pasts and unpredictable futures, between traders who depended upon them to market their market selves and buyers who relied upon them to reveal their "real" ones. They knew what the traders wanted them to say and what the buyers wanted to hear. And they knew whether they fit the traders' representations and the buyers' expectations – whether they were sickly or skilled, whether they had thoughts of escape or revolt. Using these pieces of information, slaves could create themselves in the slave market, matching their self-representations to their own hoped–for outcomes. Sometimes, at enormous risk, they shaped a sale to suit themselves.

Their choices were hedged by violence on either side. Most slaves probably did not believe the traders' pledges to sell them to good masters if they were well behaved – they knew that prices meant more than promises in the slave market. But they also knew that they would be punished if the traders could tell that they were not representing themselves as they had been instructed. The traders' present threats, however, had to be balanced with the knowledge that dissatisfied buyers might hold slaves responsible for the answers they gave in the pens. Caught between the traders and the buyers, the slaves made tacit alliances that were both necessary and risky. Interviewed in 1892, L. M. Mills described his own slave-market dilemma in the third person: "When a Negro was put on the block he had to help sell himself by telling what he could do. If he refused to praise himself and acted sullen, he was sure to be stripped and given thirty lashes. Frequently a man was compelled to exaggerate his accomplishments, and when his buyer found out that he could not do what he said he could he would be beaten unmercifully. It was pretty sure a thrashing either way." Like Mills, slaves in the pens were interposed between bargainers – presented on the one hand and examined on the other – who made their expectations and intentions brutally clear. And like Mills, slaves in the market had to calculate their behavior: discouraging a sale might lead to an immediate beating, encouraging it too much might lead to violence down the road. L. M. Mills described shaping one's own sale as a dangerous necessity, a Hobson's choice – "a thrashing either way." And yet he also described a situation in which the business of slaveholders was *necessarily* done through the agency of their slaves, a situation of great danger, but also of opportunity. . . .

Small signs meant a lot in the slave market. Buyers, remember, were searching for vitality and responsiveness, and often used the words "lively" or "active" to describe the slaves they desired. To manipulate the buyers' minute attention, traders tried to discipline their slaves into postures of strength and readiness. Whether intentionally or not, the slaves sometimes undermined their efforts. As Henry Thomas explained about why he was so long in selling in New Orleans, "nobody there liked my countenance at all – no one would give a cent for me." Lucy, whose owner thought her "low spirited situation" responsible for his inability to sell her, was sent home from the slave market unsold. "Assure her," the owner wrote to the slave dealer, "that I will keep her myself or sell her in Falmo." Unwilling or unable to sell herself, Lucy was returned to the neighborhood where she would be happier and presumably more salable. Lucy's depression – her murdered soul – was a recognizable enough feature of the slave pens to be a commonplace explanation for difficulty in selling a slave. As John Brown remembered it, "A man or a woman may be well in every respect, yet their value be impaired by a sour look, or a dull vacant stare, or a general dullness of demeanor." . . .

At times, the slaves' role in undermining their own sales drove the traders to distraction. "I heard Coleman tell some men who were look-ing at him the reason his hair was out it was because he had been cupped. You must stop that. I forgot to tell you in Montgomery. I never was able to find the cup marks," wrote one exasperated Virginia trader to another in the 1850s. Similarly, from South Carolina in the same decade: "Mr. Oakes, James is cutting up . . . I could sell him like hot cakes if he would talk Right. You may blame me but I tell nothing on him but the fact and Dr. Weatherly will tell the same. The boy is trying to make himself unsound. He says he wore a truss in Charleston. I think it would be best to see his former master and know the facts." Or from New Orleans: "I have just got rid of your man Lawson . . . the hardest selling Negroe I ever sold and the worst talker he stuck out to the last that he was not healthy." Searching for signs of a disease they thought they might never find, these traders found themselves caught in the trap they had set for the buyers: unable to trust the slaves but uncertain about dismissing their answers.

Questions about skills and experience further involved slaves in determining the outcome of their sale. "The boy says he can make a panel door," gushed one expectant slave dealer about the self-proclaimed skill which he thought made Isaac salable. John Jones, apparently, was less forthcoming. "I was convinced that John Jones has been deceiving us with respect to his qualifications," wrote John Knight about his suspicion that the recently purchased Jones had under-represented himself in the slave market, and, he proudly continued, "one of the new hands just arrived . . . says he knew John well and that he has always been employed in shoeing horses, stamping plows & was a good hand at such work." Whether Jones lied because he had simply tired of being a blacksmith, wanted to reduce his value, or to avoid sale entirely, it was only the untimely appearance of a history he thought he had left behind that prevented him from living out his life in the role he had chosen in the slave market. . . .

Other slaves challenged the buyers to back their expressed concern for slaves' families with their behavior in the slave market. Joseph Ingraham overheard a slave in the Natchez market asking a buyer "would you be so good as to buy Jane?" and pointing out his wife so that the slaveholder could examine her for himself. Slaves' requests to be sold with their family members were often edged with desperation: "Please, master, buy Emily. I can never work anymore if she is taken from me; I will die," Solomon Northup remembered Eliza saying as she pleaded to be sold with her daughter; "Oh! master, master! buy me and my children with my poor husband – do, pray," J. D. Green remembered a woman calling from the auction stand where her husband, Reuben, had just been sold. This was not freedom: slaves like Eliza were forced to retail themselves according to one of the governing fictions of the slave market – that the buyers were there to rescue them from the traders. But it was hope: some, like the unnamed man in the Natchez market were saved from separation through their own intervention. Others, like Eliza and Emily, like Reuben and Sally, were beaten apart. . . .

The history of the antebellum South is the history of two million slave sales. But alongside the chronicle of oppressions must be set down a history of negotiations. To be sold with family members rather than apart from them, to be sold to a rich buyer rather than a poor one, to be sold into the anonymity of the city rather than the isolation of the country, for the house rather than the field – all of these were outcomes sought and obtained by the slaves in the pens. Placed on a scale between Slavery and Freedom or judged according to a theory which accepts revolution as the only useful goal of resistance, these slave-shaped sales do not look like much: as many comfortable skeptics have put it, "after all, they were still enslaved." But placed between subordination and resistance on the scale of daily life, these differences between possible sales had the salience of survival itself.

The antislavery of the slave pens, of those who opposed slavery where they met it, where distance or surveillance or attachment made escape impossible, where state power and a hopeless deficit of armed force made rebellion suicidal, transmits today an important reminder about the extent to which the histories of domination and resistance are inextricably intertwined. They are two sides of a single history. The worshipful admiration of the aesthetics of domination which has seethed through so much recent work in the humanities – the thrilling fear that the world is built out of the phantasmic dreams of the powerful, their language and categories and objectifying gaze – must be cooled with the recognition that dreams, even the dreams of powerful people, must be made material if they are to come true. And, in the slave market, slaveholders' dreams could not come true without slaves: without people who could look back, estimate, manipulate, and sometimes escape.

Study Questions and Further Reading for Part V

1 Did the image associated with slave traders accord with the reality? Why could masters simultaneously demonize and tacitly endorse the slave trader?
2 Why did slave traders do the job that they did?
3 At the point of sale, slave traders used a variety of techniques to assess the market worth of a slave. What were some of these devices and how were their decisions shaped by the slaves themselves?

Bancroft, Frederic 1931: *Slave Trading in the Old South*. Baltimore, MD: Furst.
Collins, Winfield H. 1904: *The Domestic Slave Trade of the Southern States*. New York: Broadway Publishing.
Drago, Edmund L. (ed.) 1991: *Broke by the War: Letters of a Slave Trader*. Columbia: University of South Carolina Press.
Inikori, Joseph E. and Engerman, Stanley L. (eds) 1992: *The Atlantic Slave Trade: Effects on Economies, Societies, and Peoples in Africa, the Americas, and Europe*. Durham, NC: Duke University Press.
Phillips, Ulrich Bonnell 1918: *American Negro Slavery: A Survey of the Supply, Employment, and Control of Negro Labor as Determined by the Plantation Regime*. New York: Appleton.

Russell, Thomas D. 1997: Slave auctions on the courthouse steps: Court sales of slaves in antebellum South Carolina. In Paul Finkelman (ed.), *Slavery and the Law*. Madison, WI: Madison House, 329–64.

Stephenson, Wendell Holmes 1938: *Isaac Franklin: Slave Trader and Planter of the Old South*. Baton Rouge: Louisiana State University Press.

Sweig, Donald M. 1980: Reassessing the human dimension of the interstate slave trade. 12 *Prologue* (Spring), 5–21.

Part VI
Womanhood in Black and White

Introduction to Documents and Essays

What choices did elite white women make in defining their motherhood? Sally McMillen's article answers this question by examining the breast-feeding patterns of elite white women in the Old South. She shows that they opted to breast feed their own children and details the sacrifices they made in so doing. While elite white women were not averse to using black wet nurses, McMillen's article and the accompanying documents show that they considered breast feeding important to their definitions of womanhood. Although black slave women enjoyed far fewer choices in how they constructed their womanhood, Brenda E. Stevenson shows that they not only defined themselves as women but that they did so against countervailing definitions offered by the slaveholding elite.

11

Breast Feeding and Elite White Womanhood

Southern Medical Opinions on Wet Nursing and Breast Feeding, 1850

The following is a review of two books. The first, *On the Diseases of Infants and Children*, was written by a northern physician, Fleetwood Churchill (honorary member of the Philadelphia Medical Society). The second, *A Practical Treatise on the Disease of Children*, was by D. Francis Condie, MD, also a member of the Philadelphia Medical Society. Both works were reviewed in South Carolina's *Charleston Medical Journal and Review* in 1850. The review is littered with references to other medical authorities and opinions on the practice of wet nursing and breast feeding. (From "Reviews. Art. VIII. – *On the Diseases of Infants and Children*. By Fleetwood Churchill, M.D.," *Charleston Medical Journal and Review*, 5 (March 1850), pp. 198, 199, 201, 203, 204, 205)

It has been said that the "Boy is parent to the Man," and that, "with his Mother's milk the young child drinketh education." If these apothegms be true with regard to the development of his mental and moral traits, they are equally so as respects that of his physical organization. Hence the importance attached to the consideration of the morbid conditions peculiar to infancy, and to those early periods of life at which are implanted the germs of future disease; and hence, the necessity of attending to and guiding, whatever modify or control, injurious tendencies so pervading and remote in their influences for evil. These reflections become invested with interest of a practical nature, when we observe the wonderful recuperative energies of the uninjured organism, in as much as they enable us, by a certain course, to ward off or destroy what is hostile to it. For nothing short of the extraordinary powers of endurance, implanted by a wise foresight of nature, could enable the infant and child to resist so successfully the various exciting causes of disease, engendered by imprudence, bad management, excess in diet, and general irregularity, at a period of life when the discretionary powers are not matured, and those of the mother or nurse are so often perverted by ignorance, bad precedent and worse advice. We must be excused for the remark, which from personal observation we hold to be true, that if we can bring an individual of ordinary constitution, without the maturation of these destructive tendencies, past the age of puberty, his life is almost ensured to him for several years. . . .

Among the men who have contributed towards the rescuing mankind from the dangers which encompass their early years, Dr. Churchill stands conspicuous . . . he treats of the infant "muling and puking in the nurse's arms." . . .

In *Part First* of Dr. Churchill's book "On the Management of Infancy and Childhood," the leading chapter embraces preliminary observations respecting the high degree of mortality which prevails among infants and children. . . . From the first report of the Registrar General of England, it appears that more than *one-third of the total deaths* in England and Wales, occur *under two years of age*; . . . From various sources, it is proved too, that the mortality depends upon external circumstances, and that it is in some measure under the control of good management. . . .

For some hours after birth, the child will not require food, the first necessity being warmth and sleep. At the end of about the third hour, when the secretion of milk has commenced, it becomes necessary to feed it. Here Dr. Churchill settles an important and much mooted question, by laying down the first canon, that milk is the article most serviceable for the infant, giving in it a little sweetened water, "as less likely to irritate the delicate mucous membranes of the stomach, than gruel or prepared barley, &c." . . .

In primaparae, where it sometimes happens that no milk is secreted for two or three days, to let the child suck frequently would not merely be useless, but positively injurious. A suggestion of Dr. Graves, Dr. C – has found very successful: "Order some 'milk powders,' a few grains of some innocuous or inert substance, . . . to be taken three times a day, and give the patient assurance that after *three or four days* the milk will be produced. The anxiety thus relieved or postponed, will allow nature fair play, and in the majority of cases your 'powders' will have the credit of success." For cracked or ulcerated nipples, which are often so troublesome, astringent lotions are advised, for some weeks before parturition. Dr. Dewees prefers the "application of a young but sufficiently strong puppy to the breast; this should be immediately after the seventh month of pregnancy." Nursing by the mother is preferable, but some circumstances forbid it, as 1st. Where the milk ceases; 2d. When there is incontinence, the milk escaping as fast as secreted. 3d. In women of a nervous, irritable temperament; the constitutional disturbance producing cough and sometimes simulating consumption. 4th. Women laboring under severe organic disease should abstain from nursing. 5th. Peculiarities in the mother, as when menstruation occurs during lactation. 6th. Circumstances may forbid the mother assuming the office of nurse. "Imperative (or imperial) duties, fashionable life makes such heavy demands upon the time, energies, and health of its votaries, that is fortunate for the child when mothers, who cannot give up their amusement, do not add to their folly by attempting to nurse." 7. Lastly, great mental emotion, two marked cases being mentioned by the Irish Accoucheur in which a fatal result occurred.

In the choice of a nurse, Dr. Merryman states that he much prefers nurses whose children are eight or ten weeks old, though most ladies are anxious to procure wet nurses who have not lain in more than a fortnight or three weeks. "Her catamenial discharge should be entirely suspended," adds Dr. Condie. In examining a nurse, the milk of the best quality, "when squeezed into a wine glass ought to be thin, clear, and of a bluish white color, very lipid, very sweet, and, if allowed to stand for a while, covered with cream."

Of course much care should be used in making a thorough examination.

Rosenstein mentions the case of a family in Stockholm, in which the father and mother, the children, the maid servants and the clerks were infected with venereal from the nurse. Dr. Churchill adds, "I saw very lately an infant who had been entrusted to a nurse for one day, and which was then transferred to another; by the first it was infected, and it again infected the new nurse." . . .

On the subject of weaning, between nine and twelve months is laid down as the usual time. In the United States, Condie recommends that the spring or autumn should, if possible, be invariably made choice of "and only under circumstances of imperious necessity, should it ever be attempted during the season of greatest heat, as cholera infantum almost invariably follows. The mother should even hasten the time of weaning in order to avoid this season."

Newspaper Advertisements for Wet Nurses, 1859

Should an elite white woman find herself unable to breast feed her child, she would often resort to hiring a wet nurse by advertising in local newspapers. Here are two such advertisements from South Carolina's Charleston *Daily Courier*, July 14 and July 27, 1859.

To HIRE, A COLORED WET NURSE,
with a healthy child. Apply at 1 Court House Square

To HIRE, A WET NURSE WITHOUT
a Child. Apply at the Northeast corner of East and Vernon streets

A Southern Mother on Child-rearing, 1844

Women found both pain and joy in rearing children and confided the details to friends in writing. Several of these themes are revealed in the following letter from Mary Ann Gwyn to Sarah Lenoir, in Wilkesboro, North Carolina, in 1844. Note the ways that motherhood created bonds of intimacy and affection not simply between mother and child but also between women in southern communities. (From Mary Ann Gwyn to Sarah Lenoir, Wilkesboro, NC, March 11, 1844, Lenoir Family Papers, #426, in the Southern Historical Collection, Wilson Library, University of North Carolina at Chapel Hill, Chapel Hill, NC)

My Dear Sister

I have been waiting for the last three weeks for Walter to pass through this place on his way to Hillsboro so that I could send some letters by him.... I expect you have been thinking hard of me and in fact I have been very lazy about writing since I got about. I have just been taking my ease any hour for the last few weeks for the baby is very little trouble and I have nothing to do but nurse it. Sally has got to running about again pretty well though she still limps very much and her lame leg is very stiff. Her poor little hand is still entirely useless, though her arm has become quite limber and she lets it hang down now, and can move it about as she pleases. The little thing tries very hard to make her sick hand hold her playthings, but she has no control over it at all.... Oh Sarah you dont know the agonies I have suffered since that child's sickness last fall. And even now my mind is always uneasy about her, and I believe if I were to give way to my feelings and allow my thoughts to dwell upon her situation now and what it will be thereafter if she should remain a cripple, I should go beside myself. . . . But I find I am writing altogether about Sally when no doubt you are anxious to hear a description of the stranger. Well she is a great *fat broad faced dutch-looking* thing – as greedy as a pig and grows about equal to your *Berkshire*. . . . I have plenty of milk for her and I count it a great blessing and privilege to be able to suckle my babe.

Oh me when I think of the trouble we had to raise my little Sally with the bottle I feel like . . . I should never be thankful enough for being so blest with this one. . . .

The ladies in town were very kind to me. Cousin Martha, Mrs Calloway and Mrs Clary were here at the birth of the child and Mrs Bouchelle stayed two days and a night with me. Cousin Sarah Brown stayed a night and a day and then my good and precious Jamie took charge of me and nursed me as good as any one could possibly do. We hired an old woman to come and nurse the baby, but she knew nothing about taking care of one. She slept with the baby at first and took very good care of it and was very kind and attentive to little Sally. . . .

Breast Feeding and Elite White Womanhood
Sally McMillen

"It will be a trial for me to wean him," wrote Rebecca Allen Turner of her eighteen-month-old son. "How am I to relinquish so sweet an office – that of giving nourishment to my darling? Are these foolish tears that dim my eyes when I think of the times, when he will no longer nestle in my bosom through the silent watches of the night?" Rebecca Turner's sentimental remarks express the commitment that middle- and upper-class southern women made to breast feeding and the joy that healthy mothers found in the task. Maternal nurturing was an accepted rite of motherhood and critically important, especially in an age of dramatic medical therapeutics and poor sanitation, for the physical needs of the

From Sally McMillen, "Mothers' sacred duty: Breast-feeding patterns among middle- and upper-class women in the antebellum South," *Journal of Southern History*, 51(3) (1985), pp. 333–56. Copyright © 1985 by the Southern Historical Association. Excerpt reprinted by permission of the Managing Editor and the author.

infant. Unfortunately, health problems, particularly those following childbirth, sometimes interfered with breast feeding, and other methods of feeding infants had to be found.

The South provides a particularly interesting region in which to examine the commitment of antebellum women to breast feeding. Long-established myths and misperceptions have prevented an accurate assessment of how southern mothers accepted this maternal responsibility. The presumed prevalence of black wet nurses and female domestic servants in the South has encouraged a belief that plantation women typically or often delegated breast feeding to slaves. A romantic view of the antebellum plantation mistress – slightly debilitated, crinoline-clothed, and eternally beautiful – adds to this misunderstanding.

Reminiscences of southern white childhood written after the Civil War often mentioned black wet nurses. Susan Dabney Smedes recalled that "The mistress had wet-nurses for her babies, chosen from among her Negro servants." Typical also was the description of a mammy's devotion to white children, perhaps surpassing the bond she felt toward her own offspring. Thomas Nelson Page, in his romanticized view of antebellum Virginia, remembered that "the careful and faithful" black nurse cared more for the master's children than for her own. Yet one must be cautious in interpreting these remarks. The writers, after living through the humiliation of the Civil War and Reconstruction, developed a sentimental view of antebellum days, when apparently devoted slaves seemed to serve kind masters. The devoted black mammy often became a symbol of a time when blacks allegedly knew their place. But some reminiscences, written with just as much conviction, state that white mothers rarely used black wet nurses. Susan B. Eppes noted that in her family of ten children and sixty-two first cousins, a black wet nurse suckled only one child. She declared that "Most Southern mothers nourished their babies at the breast" for "they had time for all domestic duties and the care and training of their children came first." These comments leave an ambiguous idea of nineteenth-century infant feeding practices in the South.

Adding to these misperceptions are travelers' accounts that often exaggerate the black nurses' role in feeding southern white babies. These accounts noted and sometimes emphasized black mammies' suckling white babies, which was not the practice in the North or in Britain – and which, in many cases, offended the racial sensitivity of travelers. Historians have used these accounts to prove that slaves often served as wet nurses. Frederick Law Olmsted, the most famous observer of antebellum southern society, was struck by the close association of blacks and whites and noted that black mammies often carried white infants in their arms. He did not, however, mention breast feeding, presumably because he either saw none or found the subject embarrassing. Frances Anne Kemble, an English actress who chronicled a visit to her husband's Georgia plantation, abhorred slavery. She found domestic servants lacking in basic cleanliness, yet she noted that "this very disagreeable peculiarity does not prevent Southern women from hanging their infants at the breasts of Negresses . . . ." Exactly how many white children "hung" from the breasts of slaves is not documented. One must use caution when quoting this outspoken abolitionist, for Mrs. Kemble was anything but a disinterested observer. Her own awareness of breast feeding can partially be explained by the fact that her two young children – one still suckling – and a white nurse accompanied her on her travels. Also, one should keep in mind that travelers often ignored habits familiar to them and commented on what they found unusual. Thus, writers would be unlikely to mention white mothers' suckling their own children, and, because it was usually done in private, breast feeding was probably not observed by visitors. Seeing even one white child at the breast of a slave would certainly have been cause for comment, particularly from an observer like Fanny Kemble who found black wet nurses to be far below her standards for domestic servants. One cannot ignore these observations, which confirm the existence of black wet nurses, but they do not accurately reflect typical practice in the antebellum South.

Personal narratives by former slaves add little support to the idea that nineteenth-century southern women delegated breast feeding to black wet nurses. In interviews gathered during the 1930s few slaves mentioned their role as wet nurses. This is not surprising since many of the slaves interviewed were only children or teenagers when emancipation occurred and therefore not old enough to suckle infants. Only in rare cases was it reported that a black mother "nu'sed de white babies f'om her own breas'" or "that my mother was always the wet nurse for my mistress." Perhaps slaves were reluctant to mention a task that they may have found distasteful. Perhaps this maternal duty was so natural to them that it received little comment. It is more likely that most white women breast-fed their own babies.

The best sources for understanding maternal behavior are the words of the women themselves and their families. This study is based on a variety of such sources. Hundreds of letters of southern families make it clear that mothers suckled their infants whenever possible, and careful examination of journals and letters written by southern women themselves between 1800 and 1860 shows that a large percentage of mothers breast-fed their newborn infants.

Unfortunately, this conclusion can be based only on the literate women who bothered to record their experiences. Nearly all of these mothers came from the middle and upper classes. Their husbands were usually planters, lawyers, physicians, ministers, educators, or merchants. Family income provided sufficient leisure for these women to write during their busy childrearing years. Thus, this study represents only southern mothers who had the time, energy, and education to leave a record of their maternal experiences.

The following data drawn from journals and letters indicates that most middle- and upper-class southern women in the sample breast-fed their babies. A count of every comment on infant feeding from the manuscripts consulted for this study suggests that more than 85 percent of these southern mothers nursed their own babies. Approximately 20 percent used a wet nurse, and 10 percent hand-fed their infants. Two or more methods of feeding were often necessary, such as a bottle and a wet nurse or a supplement for maternal milk, which explains the discrepancy in percentages. The relatively high status of their husbands – who represented a broad range of middle- and upper-class occupations – indicates that these families could have afforded a wet nurse. But these mothers breast-fed their children. Moreover, the data may actually be skewed toward recording feeding methods other than maternal breast feeding, for those women who found breast feeding difficult were usually the most articulate about infant nourishment. There is little in these letters to indicate that maternal habits altered significantly between 1800 and 1860, and for this period the letters studied show that most southern babies were suckled by their own mothers.

In most cases in which infants were fed by other means, the mothers' poor health, another pregnancy, or an insufficient supply of milk prevented breast feeding. Nourishing a baby was demanding and tiring, particularly for a woman whose health was poor. Mrs. De Rosset of Wilmington, North Carolina, noted that her cousin Eliza Ann "was sick and had to wean her baby." Anne Cameron wrote from Raleigh, North Carolina, that she could not nurse, for she had a painful abscess on one breast and admitted that "the operation of nursing dear little Mary drew tears almost every time." She finally consulted her physician who diagnosed a "stoppage of a milk vein" and recommended lancing. Eliza Middleton noted that a South Carolina friend who suffered a "rising" between her breasts had hired a "temporary substitute" because she could not nurse her infant, but she expected to resume soon. Medical advisers also cautioned women who were pregnant or menstruating not to breast-feed their babies. Whether doctors believed that suckling drew nourishment away from the fetus or that milk from menstruating or pregnant women was tainted is not clear, though there is more evidence for the latter idea. An Ohio physician, Dr. Alva Curtis, believed pregnancy decreased a lactating mother's milk supply, and Dr. Samuel Henry Dickson of the Medical College of South Carolina called the milk of pregnant women an "unwholesome secretion." Southern women often heeded such ideas and stopped breast feeding when they became pregnant.

Southern mothers had strong reasons for suckling their newborn, the most common of which was their acceptance of traditional patterns of childrearing. Widespread, almost silent, acceptance of tradition causes a lack of comment by writers of letters and journals, and with few exceptions, which included women who had difficulty lactating, most southern mothers wrote little on the subject. The only comment one might find after reading dozens of letters on infant rearing might be a cryptic reference or the brief comment, "weaned baby from breast." Mothers were far more eager to discuss their babies' uncertain state of health and their changing behavior, and they often wrote pages about infant antics.

Many southern mothers may have been influenced by medical and maternal advice books and by their own observations about infant health. Physicians and advisers, eager to define women's commitment to child care and family improvement, were unanimous in proclaiming a mother's duty to breast-feed her baby. A major theme in maternal advice books and medical guides written during the antebellum period was that mothers should assume the central role in childrearing. Lydia H. Sigourney and Lydia Maria Child, popular authors who promoted female domesticity, heralded the joys of infant care. As if she alone had discovered a new occupation for women, Mrs. Sigourney declared that through motherhood, women had now "taken a higher place in the scale of being." She urged mothers to create a "season of quietness" during lactation, foregoing their presumably gay social lives for the tranquil rewards of infant care.

Dr. William Potts Dewees, a nineteenth-century expert on child care, stated as one of his rules for mothers that they should breast-feed their newborn. He declared that only a small percentage of women were selfish enough to ignore their baby's needs and only a handful of men selfish enough to place the shapeliness of their wife's figure above the happiness of their child. Dewees added, unequivocally, that maternal breast feeding was superior to all other forms of nourishment: it benefited the mother because it prevented milk abscesses, headaches, nervousness, and even sore eyes; it was good for the baby's health and moral well-being; and it was preferable to a wet nurse's possibly indifferent care. He urged women to accept the task as God-given and as "a duty rendered sacred both by nature and by reason." John Eberle, an Ohio physician, also called breast feeding a woman's "sacred office" and declared that "the mother's breasts constitute the only genuine fountain from which this delicious and congenial nutriment is to be drawn."

Southern physicians waxed equally enthusiastic over the benefits of maternal feeding. A southern doctor writing for the *Charleston Medical Journal and Review* declared that "with his mother's milk, the young child drinketh education" and supported the encouragement that William Buchan, William Dewees, and Charles Delucena Meigs gave to the practice. "There is no period in a woman's life," wrote another adviser, presuming he had sufficient understanding to comment, "in which she has so great enjoyment, such perfect health, as when she is nursing the off-spring of her own blood." This southern writer decried the "fashion of transferring the duties of mother to the wet nurse." Almost without exception, antebellum advisers encouraged healthy mothers to breast-feed their newborns.

Doctors promoted maternal breast feeding primarily because maternal breast milk was the most healthful form of nourishment. A wet nurse might provide milk that was as nutritious as the mother's, but physicians often regarded substitute feeders with a wary eye. There was no guarantee, according to advice books, that the wet nurse was healthy, clean, and attentive to the baby's needs. Doctors cautioned mothers that a nurse's milk might be unwholesome, that she could resort to clandestine bottle feedings if she lacked sufficient milk, that a nurse often administered drugs to quiet a screaming infant, and that syphilis or other equally pernicious diseases might be transferred from nurse to suckling baby. Whether physicians had actual proof that wet nurses were inadequate or whether their reactions were overly dramatic to encourage the indecisive woman is not clear. Perhaps their advice to mothers was an attempt at professionalization, as doctors sought to establish themselves as experts about an activity that mothers had been performing for thousands of years. In any case, medical advice on the subject of breast feeding was not an attempt to change child-care practices but was rather a reflection of women's accepted behavior.

While discouraging the use of wet nurses, physicians recognized that mothers who were ill or lacked sufficient milk could not breast-feed their babies. In such instances a substitute was essential, and they urged women to exercise great care in selecting a wet nurse. A checklist of requirements included the proper moral and physical bearing of the nurse as well as the correct consistency and color of breast milk, which was to be observed in a wine glass or, better yet, under a microscope. According to doctors her habits should be temperate, and mothers should be wary of wet nurses who drank alcoholic beverages. The age of the nurse's baby must be considered, for doctors believed that a mother's milk altered as the infant matured. Dewees even cautioned against red-haired nurses, for he alleged that red hair indicated an unstable personality.

Despite precautions infant deaths remained alarmingly common throughout the antebellum period. Federal census data in the 1860 census show that in the entire country, nearly 17 percent of all deaths in 1850 were among infants under one year of age. That figure rose to nearly 21 percent by 1860. The 1848 Charleston census, which gathered population figures covering three decades, reveals similar statistics. In the 1820s, 20 percent of all the city's white children under five died; in the 1830s, the figure was 17 percent; and it rose to 26 percent in the 1840s. Despite an increasing number of medical schools and physicians, infant mortality remained high in the South at least until the Civil War.

One of the most troublesome and fatal illnesses experienced by antebellum southern infants and children was cholera infantum. The 1860 federal census reported the incidence of the disease to be $5\frac{1}{2}$ times greater in the South than in the North. This bacterial disease, now commonly referred to as summer diarrhea, is a severe intestinal disorder, particularly common from late spring through early autumn. Symptoms include severe diarrhea, vomiting, headache, dehydration, and debilitation. Southern mothers observed that youngsters between the ages of six months and two years were most susceptible to cholera infantum, and they commented on its being endemic to the South. Jean Syme noted of the Virginia county in which she lived, "this place is already getting sickly for infants, as many as six died in the course of this week, with bowel complaints." Jane Woodruff of Charleston wrote that she lost four of her young children to "the bowel complaint." Phoebe Elliott of Beaufort, South Carolina, remarked that the young children of three of their local doctors had all been sick with dysentery. Although doctors often linked the disease to urban areas, comments like these indicate that it was prevalent throughout the South.

If the number of journal articles on a subject provides an indication of general concern, cholera infantum apparently caused antebellum physicians much anxiety. It was endemic and virulent, and doctors tried, without success, to pinpoint its causes and discover effective remedies. So poorly understood was this illness that parents and physicians often blamed the disease on teething, since it usually occurred when a child was cutting its first teeth. From our present understanding of bacterial diseases, we know that the causes of cholera infantum were many, though the most common one, undoubtedly, was spoiled food and milk, particularly during the time when a child was being weaned. Mothers who breast-fed their infants had the greatest success in delaying, and occasionally preventing, the disease.

Mothers valued their maternal role and the enjoyment they derived from breast feeding. Motherhood and its attendant duties were highly prized during the antebellum years and touted as women's "sacred" occupation. Feminine pride was tied up with breast feeding, and when a woman could not perform this maternal task, she often felt guilty or inadequate. Just as it was assumed that most women could bear children, so was it assumed that most mothers could suckle their babies. Kate de Rosset Meares in 1854 had to supplement feedings because her milk supply was inadequate. She wrote her mother that she had accepted a slave's offer to help breast-feed her infant son but noted, "if I was certain that it was right, I would be delighted to have him well filled twice a day." Laura Norwood of Hillsboro, North Carolina, regretted her inability to breast-feed and wished that she could be a "good" mother – something she and her husband equated with an adequate supply of breast milk. Many men encouraged their wives to be competent nurturers and praised their ability to feed the newborn. In 1801 Daniel Anderson remarked to his brother-in-law that his infant son "has not had one hour's sickness" because his wife Mary "has aplenty for him." Breast feeding was a task that most people assumed mothers were well able to perform.

Mothers chose to breast-feed their newborns because they found the experience a rewarding one. As mothers and child-care experts now believe, special moments with the suckling infant can foster the development of a close bond between mother and child. Pregnancy, regarded as a "sickness" or "time of trouble," was often a debilitating experience. Parturition was the most painful event many women would experience and was often life-threatening. But a healthy infant was cause for joy, and its presence made the memory of previous trials wane. Mothers could forget past suffering as the blessed newborn lay at their breast. Eugenia Levy Phillips empathized with her daughter's emotions after the birth of her grandchild. "Thank God all is over and I picture your happiness, gazing on the little dough lump in your arms," she wrote. "There is no happiness equal to what you are now enjoying." Virginia Caroline Clay of Washington City, Alabama, echoed the feelings of many southern mothers. "Since the birth of my sweet babe it seems that my maternal instinct is so strong hope can never die again."

Personal comments in diaries and letters reveal mothers' joyful reactions to breast feeding their young. Rebecca Haywood Hall of North Carolina, whose mental and physical state deteriorated during her brief, unhappy marriage, nevertheless found a rare, blissful moment following the birth of her first child when she wrote to her absent husband, "Oh! would that you were here to see her at the breast suckling as she was on Sunday last when I received your letter." Mary Ann Gwyn of Wilkesboro, North Carolina, whose poor health necessitated hand feeding her first infant, expressed delight in nursing her second child. "I have plenty of milk for her," she wrote her sister, "and I count it a great blessing and privilege to be able to suckle my babe." Mothers experienced deep personal satisfaction, and it was assumed that infants preferred their mother's breast. Selina Lenoir believed that her granddaughter's taste buds explained her daughter's nursing after a year. "Her little ladyship has such a nice and delicate taste," she wrote. "She did not relish the nurse they hired for her and shewd symptoms of disgust whenever she took nourishment from her."

Many mothers found that weaning their children from the breast was difficult whether they breast-fed until the child was six months old, twelve months, or "till he gets his teeth." Some actually removed themselves from the infant's presence, sent the child away for several days, or covered their nipples with a bitter salve. Frances Moore (Webb) Bumpas of Raleigh, North Carolina, who was in poor health and also teaching school, had to cease feeding her daughter when the infant was only six months old. She sadly noted that it was "grievous to wean her." Poor health forced Caroline Olivia Laurens to wean her daughter prematurely. Missing those special moments alone with the infant, Caroline noted that she was "almost tempted to wake her and give her the breast one night." She escaped temptation by avoiding the baby at mealtimes so she would not reconsider her decision. An extreme example of maternal devotion was Mrs. Walter Lenoir of Boone County, Missouri, who probably carried her nurturing responsibilities beyond the limits of propriety. "My dear father and mother will be ready to scold me," she confessed to her sister, "when they have heard I have not yet weaned a boy that is large enough to talk of horse-racing, can make a fire, and feed calves." The youngster's age was not mentioned, but apparently he was either terribly precocious or far too old to be fed from the breast. An Alabama woman refused to consider weaning her infants, and a friend reported that this mother, who had both a newborn and a sixteen-month-old child, "suckles both of them, says she won't never wean either of them."

A number of women breast-fed despite pain or attendant physical problems. Nursing an infant was often difficult, particularly for women who were weak or ill from childbirth. Yet many mothers who were ill while lactating did not seek a wet nurse or rely on bottle feeding. Rebecca Holcombe, who had an abscess on one breast and a debilitating illness that kept her housebound for six months, fed her baby as frequently as possible. Mary Jeffreys Bethell broke out with measles the day she gave birth, experienced a relapse a month later, accompanied by chills, fever, cough, and stomach pains, yet she fed her infant until her milk ran dry. Lydia Turrentine, a North Carolina woman, and Ruth Berrien (Whitehead) Jones of Savannah, Georgia, nursed their babies despite the fact that each was on her deathbed. In most cases, mothers felt deep affection and concern for their newborn and freely accepted the duties associated with childrearing.

Mothers who breast-fed when ill aroused the concern of their husbands and relatives, who felt nursing under such conditions might adversely affect the new offspring. The nineteenth-century belief that breast milk contained the characteristics of the lactating woman explains their concern. Maternal advisers felt these traits could be transferred to the suckling infant. Thus, any woman who seemed deranged, over-excited, nervous, or ill was urged to cease feeding her infant. One may recall the prison scene in Nathaniel Hawthorne's *The Scarlet Letter* in which a physician was called to calm Hester Prynne, who was over-wrought and nervous, "not merely for Hester herself, but still more urgently for the child; who, drawing its sustenance from the maternal bosom, seemed to have drank in with it all the turmoil, the anguish, and despair, which pervaded the mother's system." We know now that lactating women in a tired or tense state often have less milk, but there is no evidence that the nourishment actually alters in form. Nevertheless, family members, and husbands in particular, worried about the new-born. Paul C. Cameron of Orange County, North Carolina, was anxious about his infant daughter's feedings. "Magey was more out of order than she has been since her birth," he observed, "doubtless caused by feeding on the feverish milk of the mother." Henry Watson, Jr., a Louisiana planter and merchant, took a deep interest in the well-being of his family despite his frequent absences. He was distressed to find his wife, Sophia Peck Watson, very ill following childbirth and inquired of their newborn, "will not the health, if not the life of the child, be endangered by letting it suck its sick mother?"

In neither case was there any mention of efforts to find a wet nurse, nor did the mothers cease breast feeding. It would appear from these examples that mothers often made the final decision about breast feeding. Those who wished to continue suckling their baby did so as long as they were able. In such cases, mothers perhaps ignored the concerns of husbands and physicians, continuing to do what seemed essential for the well-being of the child.

Family members also expressed concern that nursing might have a debilitating effect on the mother. North Carolina planter Thomas D. Bennehan worried that a sick woman on his plantation was nursing her baby, for it "must contribute to weaken her." William Elliott, upon hearing that his wife, Ann Hutchinson (Smith) Elliott, was seriously ill with fever, quickly diagnosed nursing as one cause. "From what you tell me of your sickness and nervous feeling," wrote the anxious husband, "I am persuaded that something must be attributed to your nursing so stout a girl as our daughter." One childless woman with no prior

first-hand experience in feeding a newborn baby nevertheless felt qualified to offer advice. She urged her sister, Adele Petigru Allston, to forgo
the pleasures of nursing and put her own health first. "Recollect your
health and strength is of much more importance to her future well
being," she cautioned, "than your nursing her can be, to nurse her
when you are not at all able would be a selfish gratification entirely."

Mothers, guided by prior first-hand experience with their own infants,
knew the demands nursing placed on their own daughters. Mary Hering
Middleton in 1842 suggested to her daughter Eliza that she not breast-
feed her baby at night. "I am sorry to find you allow the babies to disturb
your night's rest so much as to make you ill," wrote the anxious mother.
"As she grows older she will become more ravenous and you will I fear
suffer increasing fatigue." Mary encouraged Eliza to seek the assistance
of a nurse for these nightime feedings. In one case, it was noted that an
entire family opposed a mother's suckling her infant. A South Carolina
woman reported that the family of Eliza Ann Wright "dread her attempting to nurse – each time it has brought her to the grave." Despite the
difficulties – the fatigue, weakness, and demands of a newborn – most
southern women placed a commitment to the baby above their own
health. Those relatives and husbands most concerned about the lactating woman voiced their sentiments – as husbands and mothers tend to
do – but it is clear that most southern mothers did what they felt was
essential to insure the health and life of their infant, rarely relinquishing
their primary maternal duty. They placed the health of their newborn
above personal needs. . . .

Southern mothers may have favored breast feeding because they
understood that lactation delayed conception. How widely this idea
was known and used as a means of contraception is uncertain. In the
absence of other effective forms of birth control – except coitus inter-
ruptus, abstinence, and abortion – lactation may have been considered.
Current studies indicate that suckling an infant can limit birth to every
two years, depending on the frequency of breast feeding and the degree
of the infant's dependency on maternal milk. Lactation usually prolongs
the cessation of the menses following pregnancy, which would prevent
conception. In addition, nursing often implied that an infant slept with
its mother, perhaps curtailing coitus as well. Though most southern
women found motherhood a satisfying role, many must have agreed
with Ella Gertrude Clanton Thomas, who remarked during her third
pregnancy in as many years of marriage, "I would dislike to think I
would never have other children but then I would willingly have a
considerable lapse of time between them." The *Charleston Medical
Journal and Review* carried an article by Robert Barnes, a nineteenth-
century physician, analyzing the effectiveness of lactation as a method of

contraception. Based on his survey of one hundred English women, Barnes determined that "mammary activity" retarded uterine action. He concluded that mothers who breast-fed their infants had a lower rate of conception. Despite the appearance of this article in a well-respected southern journal, the topic of birth control was rarely discussed in medical advice books. Physicians must have been aware of the idea, though whether they privately encouraged the method is unknown. Southern men did not usually wish to limit family size, and many seemed to take pride in their large families. Southern women, however, may secretly have shared the knowledge that breast feeding delayed conception, but they seldom, if ever, discussed it in the privacy of their letters and journals. In the personal correspondence consulted for this study, no woman mentioned using breast feeding as a method of contraception.

When a mother could not breast-feed her baby, an alternative method had to be used. Hand feeding, or bottle feeding, was probably the least desirable. It was generally recognized that bottle-fed babies were not as healthy as breast-fed infants. It was also apparent, as noted earlier, that when babies were weaned from healthful breast milk to other liquids, they often became ill. Nineteenth-century doctors did not know that breast milk carried certain immunities to the infant – at least for the first six months – that helped the baby fight diseases. These natural immunities were absent from animal milk. Doctors were also unaware of bacteria and its presence in foods. Estimates made by an English doctor revealed that in the early nineteenth century seven out of eight hand-fed infants in London died. While Americans did not admit their situation to be as unhealthy, it was obvious, nevertheless, that bottle feeding often caused ill health. In an era of inadequate sanitation – without the benefit of pasteurization, refrigeration, and an understanding of bacteria – food was always a potential health hazard. There were few methods of properly cooling food, and during the long, hot summers, keeping food and milk fresh was difficult. Despite the hazards, doctors acknowledged that under certain conditions, mothers had to resort to hand feeding. If that were necessary, they recommended clean bottles and a milk substitute closely resembling maternal nourishment. Asses' milk received the highest recommendation. One very practical woman writer suggested that the ass be brought to the front door and milked six times daily to insure fresh milk. Yet a mixture of cow's milk, water, and brown sugar – or the same mixed with bread and called "pap" – was the most common breast-milk substitute in the antebellum South.

Bottle feeding proved to have few advantages. Southern women found it a nuisance and noted that it was often detrimental to the baby's health. In an age of poor sanitation, there was little guarantee that the bottle – of glass, metal, or bone – would be clean. Preparing a proper breast-milk substitute and insuring the milk's freshness were often difficult. No premixed canned formula or refrigerated bottles welcomed the weary mother at midnight feedings. Frances Brashear Lawrence of Louisiana, who had little breast milk to feed her infant, first used a wet nurse and then hand feeding. She found bottles a nuisance and related that one night she "took him down stairs and before they could get his milk ready he made such a fuss that Aunt took him." Mary Ann Gwyn found the contrast between bottle and breast feeding enormous. "When I think of the trouble we had to raise my little Sally with the bottle," she wrote, "I feel like I could never be thankful enough for being so blest with this one." Her sister Laura complained about the extra work involved in bottle feeding. "My time has been very much occupied with the children," she related, "as always must be the case with a fed child." Bottle feeding was inconvenient and often forced mothers to curtail other activities. Laura wished to show off her two-month-old daughter but decided that the long stagecoach ride to her mother's would be inadvisable. She declined the invitation because her baby was "obliged to be fed frequently through the day and I could not stop to get milk for her if I were in the stage – she could not depend on me for support, for I have not milk enough to keep a kitten from starving." From a mother's perspective, breast feeding was not only the most enjoyable and healthful but also the most convenient method of feeding the newborn.

Since bottle feeding had few supporters, the preferred alternative for mothers who could not breast-feed was a wet nurse. Finding a suitable nurse was often difficult, even in the South with its large slave population. The nurse probably had to be feeding her own infant and have enough milk to sustain two babies or have just lost a child whom she had been breast feeding. Yet there were instances when a satisfactory wet nurse was easily found. Ella Clanton Thomas of Georgia had lost her first child, suffered a subsequent miscarriage, and finally lost another infant when it was seven months old. Ella feared a similar fate for her newborn when she discovered that she did not have enough milk to keep the child healthy. Her mother convinced Ella that a wet nurse was necessary. "Ma concluded I had better have a wet nurse as I did not give nourishment enough," Ella wrote. "One of the women at the plantation had just lost a baby a week old, and Pa kindly offered us the use of her." Following the birth of her next child, Ella made a similar arrangement. Samuel Pickens of Alabama, who was distraught by his wife's death following childbirth, found solace in his sister's concern for the infant. "My sister Dorothy took it home as soon as she thought it could be safely removed," he wrote his mother, "and she fortunately had a woman who had a child about one month old .... The woman who suckles the child was a field hand." In each instance, it was unlikely that the families resorted to the precautions suggested by physicians and actually examined the woman's breast milk under a microscope. When an infant's life was threatened most families probably used whomever they could find to feed the baby. It would be interesting to know how slave women reacted to the nurturing duty imposed on them by their owners. Whether they resented feeding a white baby, particularly if their own had just died, or whether their maternal needs caused them to welcome the substitute baby is unknown.

Some families were able to find wet nurses fairly easily, but other family correspondence indicates that difficulties were not unusual. In rural areas most people probably relied on word of mouth among friends and neighbors. In cities like Charleston newspaper advertisements were used to find wet nurses. As the population increased, the city's papers carried a greater number of advertisements for nurses. . . .

Many of these advertisements ran for several days, possibly indicating some problem in filling the request. The requests also indicate that middle- and upper-class families considered both black and white nurses acceptable, perhaps depending on the type of domestic help they had become most accustomed to. It is also possible that a growing urban immigrant population made white help accessible. Of primary importance, though, was the life of the newborn, and however specific the advertisement's wording may appear, many families were probably willing to compromise to insure the health and life of the baby.

Southern mothers who used wet nurses were generally satisfied with those who fed their infant. While southern white women's reactions to domestic slaves ranged from dependence to annoyance, most mothers were surprisingly accepting of the substitute feeder. There is nothing to indicate that using a black wet nurse aroused a southern woman's racial sensibilities. It would have been understandable to be very demanding of a servant so intimately involved with one's child, but complaints were rare. Samuel Pickens was very complimentary of the black wet nurse found for his baby, and he described her as "a fine, healthy, careful negro woman." Laura Norwood attributed her third child's robust health and large size to her black nurse Eliza and commented that "Eliza is a great help to me, as she has plenty of milk for the baby." Three years later she complimented her slave for being "quite smart – has plenty of milk for her child and mine." Southern mothers were generally very grateful for help they received in insuring the life and health of their children. . . .

A majority of southern white mothers breast-fed their own infants. Yet when an alternate form of nourishment was needed and bottle feeding was rejected, southern women turned to whomever could provide a reliable milk supply. They did not routinely rely on black women to serve as wet nurses. As these examples demonstrate, families might actively seek a black or white wet nurse or find one of their slaves to serve in that capacity. But other families turned to a friend, a neighbor, or even a close relative for assistance. Available milk, not race, was the criterion. What was most important was locating a milk source to insure the survival of the newborn.

What may have been common but was rarely discussed in white women's personal correspondence was the breast feeding of a black infant by a southern white woman. Mary (Jones) Jones of Liberty County, Georgia, noted that her daughter, Mary Sharpe (Jones) Mallard, was feeding a slave child. "Your dear sister has such an abundance of nourishment," she wrote her son, "that she has had to nurse one of the little Negroes." Slaves may have been more likely to recall such interaction. Susan Dabney Smedes's published memoirs described Isaac, a slave, whose master's mother had nursed him. Isaac boasted that he even called this woman "ma," implying a special bond with the nurturing woman and with his own master. Robert Ellett, a Virginia slave, recalled seeing his younger brother and the master's infant both nursing from his mistress's breasts. These examples indicate that in the antebellum South, the sharing of maternal nourishment was not always limited by racial barriers nor confined to black women feeding white infants. Middle- and upper-class mothers occasionally fed slave infants. It was not necessary for them to do this to relieve the pressure from excessive breast milk, for milk could have been removed manually or with a breast pump. Economic motives could have encouraged such feeding. Whatever the motivation, a baby's life was at stake, and many mothers probably acted out of a desire to help keep any child alive and healthy, whether black or white. Sharing maternal nourishment between white women and black infants was one way some southern mothers rose above racial prejudice.

Southern mothers depended on close friends and neighbors for advice concerning breast feeding. Practical advice on breast feeding that mothers might have shared with one another is absent from women's correspondence. However natural the nurturing process may appear, questions and problems inevitably arose. Did these women turn to advice books and physicians for solutions, or did they rely on the wisdom and experience of other women close at hand, perhaps even domestic slaves? Medical advice books often included practical information, such as cures for dry and inverted nipples, breast abscesses, the correct formula until the mother's milk was ready, and proper preparation for nursing, including the suggestion that several weeks prior to childbirth, a puppy suckle the breasts. Yet immediate answers to other practical matters were often needed, and southern mothers, like their twentieth-century counterparts, probably turned to other women, perhaps crossing race and class barriers. Correspondence was too slow a process, and physicians could not provide the emotional understanding women needed from one another. Husbands and doctors ventured into the feminine arena with their advice and concerns, but it would appear that ultimately women acted according to their intuition and often turned to other women when necessary.

In these instances women relied on one another for assistance and support. When an infant's life seemed in danger, women could meet the nutritional requirement of the infant and provide the emotional support and practical information to help a worried mother. There are moments in all women's lives when only the knowledgeable assistance or sympathetic understanding of other women can meet a particular need. Carroll Smith-Rosenberg, in her important article on nineteenth-century female relationships, has noted that infant nursing allowed married women to become emotionally intimate. The critical moments surrounding breast feeding and infant care provide important examples of female bonding in the antebellum South, when shared concerns united women of all ages, and perhaps even both races. Even as the number of male doctors increased and their efforts in obstetrical matters intensified, other women remained the principal support system during this maternal experience. Through common activities and concerns, southern mothers shared their thoughts and fears and supported one another during difficult periods. The joys and problems that women shared during breast feeding enhanced female bonding and provided married women a sense of security and importance in their female world.[1]

This study has shown that antebellum southern women valued their role as infant nurturers and breast-fed their infants whenever possible. Outsiders often misinterpreted reality and our historical understanding of breast-feeding habits formerly based upon these misperceptions now deserves revision. Analyzing the actual words of mothers is critical for understanding their actions and how they perceived their role.

Imbued with the crucial importance of their maternal duties, southern women accepted breast feeding as an initial rite of motherhood. Perhaps the fact that slaves existed in the South and could have been used as wet nurses makes a southern woman's commitment to infant nurturing even stronger. Southern mothers believed that early contact with the newborn could influence a child's character. By observation, they recognized that maternal milk was conducive to an infant's health during its early months of life. Most exhibited great pride in their offspring and enjoyed the happy moments surrounding breast feeding. Some women even sacrificed their own health and well-being to insure their baby's future. Lactation as a method of contraception may also have encouraged maternal feeding. Slaves and white women sometimes served as wet nurses, and bottle feeding was used on occasion, but usually only when an emergency demanded an alternative method of feeding. Healthy middle- and upper-class women chose to breast-feed their young.

While breast feeding evoked the interest, concern, and advice of husbands, relatives, and physicians, women remained the principal participants and consultants. The ritual created an important bond among married women. Southern mothers could share their common concerns as well as the joys of motherhood. Childrearing for nearly all middle- and upper-class southern mothers became their sacred profession, and breast feeding was symbolic of women's commitment to that role. Southern women rarely abrogated that responsibility to others. For most mothers who could nurse, breast feeding became one of the most important gifts to bestow on the newborn: it implied a healthier future for the child and a closer relationship with the mother. The experience enhanced a woman's perception of herself, provided a significant arena for female bonding, and fostered a woman's understanding of her importance to her infant and to her family.

Note

1   Carroll Smith-Rosenberg, "The female world of love and ritual: Relations between women in nineteenth-century America," in *The American Family in Social-Historical Perspective*, ed. Michael Gordon (New York: St Martin's Press, 1978).

12

Slave Women and Definitions of Womanhood

Defining a "Good Wife" and "Good Woman," 1835

Womanhood in the antebellum period was constructed in part around the ideal of a good wife. Presented here is a typical depiction of what antebellum American men, North and South, considered the fundamental features of womanhood and a "good wife." But was it an ideal aspired to by slave women? If so, did they achieve it? The arguments advanced in this document should be kept in mind when reading the two documents which follow it. (From "A sermon of Rev. Dr. Bishop, in the *National Preacher*, 'A Good Wife,'" *American Ladies' Magazine*, 8 (April 1835), pp. 228–30)

1.   A good wife must possess a large share of what is called "common sense." She must know by a kind of instinct how to act on every emergency – catch as it were by inspiration, the leading features in the characters and dispositions of the individuals, old or young, friends or strangers, to whom she is introduced, and with whom she is to act statedly or occasionally. Without this, every other talent she may possess, and every attainment she may have acquired, will be of little use either to herself, or to her family.

2.   A good wife must be distinguished for self-command. A wife is the head of a little society, in which are all the elements of every kind of society. But all these elements are here in an unformed, and forming, and most fluctuating state. Hence the first and most important lesson to be studied and to be acquired by the individual who presides over a

society in this state is, that she have, on all occasions, the most perfect command of herself.

3.   Industry and economy form a third distinguishing feature in the character of a good wife. This is the leaving feature in the detail which is given us by the spirit of inspiration, Prov. xxxi. 10–end. It will be well for our country, and for our world when this passage of holy writ shall be fully understood by every mother and every daughter of our land.... The industry and economy of a wife, is particularly exhibited in having all the intervals of time, within the whole range of her government filled up with some necessary and profitable employment, and in taking special care of fragments of time and fragments of property.

4.   A good wife is an affectionate woman. The law of love and sincerity is written upon her heart; and in her tongue is the law of kindness. Every domestic, and every friend, and every stranger, and the friend of every distant friend and acquaintance, finds himself at home, while under her roof, and while partaking of her hospitality. Nor in all her intercourse with strangers or acquaintances, does she cherish a thought, or willingly utter a syllable with the design of injuring the feelings or the character of a single human being. She will not take up, much less will she give circulation to a reproach against her neighbor, though this reproach should be brought to her table or whispered to her in bedchamber.

5.   A good wife is of domestic habits, and of a domestic disposition. She enjoys herself nowhere so well as under her own roof, and while attending to her own private affairs. Her husband and her children, and the daily ordinary cares of the family occupy her chief earthly attention. She is a good neighbor, and can always enjoy a good neighbor, whether at home or abroad. But her own family is her peculiar and special province, and she has no desire to meddle with the domestic arrangements of any of her sister sovereigns. When she enters a neighboring family, it is to administer in some form to their friends, not to embarrass them with their friends....

One sinner destroys much good. One busy tattling woman, whether married or single, is enough to destroy all the social comforts of many families. And on the other hand, one prudent woman may be worth a thousand, in preserving all that is valuable in the social intercourse of a village, or city, or neighborhood....

6.   All these and similar qualifications in the good wife must be associated with the possession and the exercise of genuine and ardent piety. The description of a good wife in the Bible ... closes with these important words: "Favor is deceitful and beauty is vain, but a woman that feareth the Lord, she shall be praised."

Infidels themselves, with very few exceptions, acknowledge the importance and necessity of piety among females. Take a sense of Religion from a female, and she is an object of abhorrence even to those who are themselves polluted with every crime; and while many wicked fathers are by both precept and example initiating their own sons, and other young men, into all the elements of irreligion and debauchery, they shudder at the very thought of their wives and their daughters not being under the influence of Religion and the morality of the Bible.

Testimony of Three Former Virginia Female Slaves

The following testimony by three former Virginia slaves demonstrates, as the interview with Susan Broaddus shows, that female slaves (often by virtue of their access to information as house servants) were important for assisting other bondpeople and that, as Minnie Folkes suggests, slave women who were exposed to ruthless overseers resisted heroically. Lastly, May Satterfield shows that mothers under slavery would go to great lengths, including the transgression of their own sense of morality, to feed their children. (From Charles L. Perdue, Thomas E. Barden, and Robert K. Phillips (eds), *Weevils in the Wheat: Interviews with Virginia Ex-Slaves* (Charlottesville: University Press of Virginia, 1976), pp. 55–6, 93–6, 244–5. Reprinted with permission of the University Press of Virginia)

Susan Broaddus:

Was servin' gal fo' Missus. Used to have to stan' behin' her at de table an' reach her de salt an' syrup an' anything else she called fo'. Ole Marsa would spell out real fas' anything he don't want me to know 'bout. One day Marsa was fit to be tied, he was in setch a bad mood. Was ravin' 'bout de crops, an' taxes, an' de triflin' niggers he got to feed. "Gonna sell 'em, I swear fo' Christ, I gonna sell 'em," he says. Den old Missus ask which ones he gonna sell an' tell him quick to spell it. Den he spell out G-A-B-E, and R-U-F-U-S. 'Course I stood dere without battin' an eye, an' makin' believe I didn't even hear him, but I was packin' dem letters up in my haid all de time. An' soon's I finished dishes I rushed down to my father an' say 'em to him jus' like Marsa say 'em. Father say quiet-like: "Gabe and Rufus," an' tol' me to go on back to de house an' say I ain't been out. De next day Gabe and Rufus was gone – dey had run away. Marsa nearly died, got to cussin' an' ravin' so he took sick. Missus went to town an' tol' de sheriff, but dey never could fin' dose two slaves.

Was gone to free land. An' I spec' dey wondered many times how dem niggers knew dey was goin' to be sol'.

Minnie Folkes:

Honey, I don't like to talk 'bout dem times 'cause my mother did suffer misery. You know dar was an overseer who use to tie mother up in de barn wid a rope aroun' her arms up over her head, while she stood on a block. Soon as dey got her tied, di block was moved an' her feet dangled, you know, could' touch de flo'.

Dis ole man, now, would start beatin' her nekked 'til the blood run down her back to her heels. I took an' seed de whelps an' scars fer my own self wid dese two eyes. (This whip, she said, "was a whip like dey use to use on horses; it was a piece o' leather 'bout as wide as my han' f'om little finger to thumb.") After dey beat my mother all dey wanted, another overseer Lord, Lord, I hate white people and de flood waters gwine drown some mo'. Well honey, dis man would bathe her in salt an' water. Don' you know dem places was a hurtin'. Um! Um!

I asked mother, "what she done fer 'em to beat and do her so?" She said, "Nothin' tother t'dan 'fuse to be wife to dis man."

An' mother say, "If he didn't treat her dis way a dozen times, it wasn' nary one."

May Satterfield:

... I ain'y 'memberin' much but what ma mudder tole me [of slavery]. Po' critter, she in heaben now.

She tell me dat po' nigger had to steal back dar in slav'y eben to git 'nuf t'eat. White fo'ks so mean didn't eben want nigger t'eat. Do nothin' but work day and night. Done heard her say she been in de field 'long side de fence many day an' git creasy [cress] an' poke sallet an' bile it 'dout a speck o' greese an' give it to us chillun 'cause de rashon de white fo'ks lounce out fo' de week done give out.... Det waited till us chillun was sleep so dat ef de white fo'ks axe us 'bout it we wouldn't know nothin'. She say dey eben had to steal apples an' stuff lak dat as much as dey was on de place.

Now what do you think o' dat? White fo'ks allus talkin' 'bout nigger rougish, nigger rougish, an' ef it hadn't been fo' dem, nigger wouldn't know nothin' 'bout stealin'. Don't see whar dey gits dat f'om nohow.

Chile, nigger had to steal, an' I know ma mommer didn't tell no lie, fo' she was a good woman. Den too I knows dis is de truth 'cause I done heard mo' dan her say so.

Elizabeth Keckley Resists Bondage

In this document, Elizabeth Keckley (born 1818/1819) – a slave who later became seamstress and friend to Mary Todd Lincoln – describes some of her early experiences as a slave in Hillsboro, North Carolina. At age eighteen, Elizabeth moved from Virginia to North Carolina where her master, the Rev. Robert Burwell, "took charge of a church." Here, she encountered "Mr. Bingham, a hard, cruel man, the village schoolmaster" and a "frequent visitor to the parsonage." Specifically, she has just been beaten and now resists Bingham's and then Burwell's attempts to abuse her again. With the probable help of the writer James Redpath, Keckley wrote her memories of her enslavement and they were first published in 1868. (From Elizabeth Keckley, *Behind the Scenes or, Thirty Years a Slave, and Four Years in the White House* (New York: G. W. Carleton & Co., 1868), pp. 36–9)

It seems that Mr. Bingham had pledged himself to . . . subdue what he called my "stubborn pride." On Friday evening following the Saturday on which I was so savagely beaten, Mr. Bingham again directed me to come to his study. I went, but with the determination to offer resistance should he attempt to flog me again. On entering the room I found him prepared with a new rope and a new cowhide. I told him that I was ready to die, but that he could not conquer me. In struggling with him I bit his finger severely, when he seized a heavy stick and beat me with it in a shameful manner. Again I went home sore and bleeding, but with pride as strong and defiant as ever. The following Thursday Mr. Bingham again tried to conquer me, but in vain. We struggled, and he struck me many savage blows. As I stood bleeding before him, nearly exhausted with his efforts, he burst into tears, and declared that it would be a sin to beat me any more. My suffering at last subdued his hard heart; he asked my forgiveness, and afterwards was an altered man. He was never known to strike one of his servants from that day forward. Mr. Burwell, he who preached the love of Heaven, who glorified the precepts and examples of Christ, who expounded the Holy Scriptures after Sabbath from the pulpit, when Mr. Bingham refused to whip me any more, was urged by his wife to punish me himself. One morning he went to the wood-pile, took an oak broom, cut the handle off, and with this heavy handle attempted to conquer me. I fought him, but he proved the strongest. At the sight of my bleeding form, his wife fell upon her knees and begged him to desist. My distress even touched her cold, jealous heart. I was so badly bruised that I was unable to leave my bed for five days. . . . The Rev. Mr. Burwell was not yet satisfied. He resolved to make another attempt to subdue my proud, rebellious spirit – made the attempt and again failed, when he told me, with an air of penitence, that he should never strike me another blow; and faithfully kept his word....

The savage efforts to subdue my pride were not the only things that brought me suffering and deep mortification during my residence at Hillsboro'. I was regarded as fair-looking for one of my race, and for four years a white man – I spare the world his name – had base designs upon me. I do not care to dwell upon this subject, for it is one that is fraught with pain. Suffice it to say, that he persecuted me for four years, and I – I – became a mother. The child of which he was the father was the only child that I ever brought into the world. If my poor boy ever suffered any humiliating pangs on account of birth, he could not blame his mother, for God knows that she did not wish to give him life; he must blame the edicts of that society which deemed it no crime to undermine the virtue of girls in my then position.

Slave Women and Definitions of Womanhood

Brenda E. Stevenson

The autobiographical accounts, tales, and fantasies of Virginia slave women provide a wealth of information, collective and individual, existential and relational, about the private lives of bonded black females, their families, their overseers, their masters, and their mistresses. Fortunately, these accounts also entail much more. Through the vehicle of "autobiographical story," slave women were able to construct what, for them, was an operative, legitimate identity, a "counterimage" of black womanhood that flew provocatively in the face of popular contemporary images of black female degradation, promiscuity, and passivity. Slave women's image or images of themselves, more often than not, were overwhelmingly positive, even heroic. They also included notions of their principle and purpose as slave women. This essay explores some of the positive images that slave women drew of themselves and some of the practical (i.e., material, residential, occupational) conditions or variables which can be linked to the creation and perpetuation of these images.

From Brenda E. Stevenson, "Gender convention, ideals, and identity among antebellum Virginia slave women," in David Barry Gaspar and Darlene Clark Hine (eds), *More Than Chattel: Black Women and Slavery in the Americas* (Bloomington: Indiana University Press, 1996), pp. 169–90. Excerpt reprinted by permission of Indiana University Press.

Consider, for example, the following statement from the ex-slave woman Fannie Berry:

> There wuz an ol' lady patching a quilt an' de paddyrollers wuz looking fo' a slave named John. John wuz dar funnin' an' carrying on. All at once we herd a rap on de door. John took an' runned between Mamy Lou's legs. She hid him by spreading a quilt across her lap and kept on sewing an', do you kno', dem pattyrollers never found him?

Fannie Berry was born a slave in about 1841, the property of George Abbott of Appomattox County, Virginia. Her owner was a man of moderate means. In 1850, for example, Abbott and his wife, Sarah Ann, owned real estate valued at almost $2,000 and eleven slaves, seven of whom were female. But if the younger George was anything like his uncle and namesake, George Abbott, Senior, he probably had big plans. The elder Abbott also lived in Appomattox County in 1850, but he held real estate valued at $15,000 and owned thirty-two slaves, twelve males (8 prime hands), and twenty (nine prime hands, one elderly woman, and ten children) females.

Berry grew up in the work world prescribed by people like the Abbotts – in a small, rural county in which corn, tobacco, and cotton were the farmer's financial mainstay and land and slaves his most vital resources. She also grew up in a social and cultural community of slave women. They dominated her owner's work force and those of his closest relative. They, their life events, their ideas, and their morality dominated Fannie's memory of her time as a slave and her construction of slave female identity through her stories.

When interviewed during the 1930s, Berry was full of information about her life as a slave female and the other women whom she had known in Virginia's southern piedmont. Her account offers vibrant, stimulating images of morally driven, dynamic slave women (moral and dynamic at least in Berry's recollections and psyche). Fannie Berry's brief description of "Mamy Lou," a woman respected for both her age and occupation, pivots on the potent symbols Berry appropriates for black "womanhood" – Mamy Lou's quilt and "between her legs." In the culture of Fannie's owners these images traditionally signified the passive domestic world females occupied (the quilt) and female sexual surrender ("between her legs"). According to Berry, however, Mamy Lou used these black, "feminine" resources to a very different end – to save a vital, young slave man from the abuse of white patrollers.

Through her image of this one woman Fannie Berry is able to convey much about what many slave women expressed as their requisite concerns and responsibilities within the designs of their limited, oppressed social worlds. Read Fannie's description of Mamy Lou's actions carefully and you will find a basic premise of slave female morality and purpose – the protection and procreation of black life. Read even more carefully and you can detect the prerogative of slave female principle, the protection and procreation of black life in the face of white opposition. Clearly in her characterization of Mamy Lou, Fannie Berry is constructing a black female identity that is complex and oppositional.

Berry's "Mamy Lou," therefore, represents some of the attributes slave women believed were their most vital contributions to their families and communities. Mamy Lou is the embodiment of slave women's ability to give and nurture life. She also symbolizes their domestic productivity (her quilt) and their feminine sexuality ("between her legs"). Berry informs her audience, through the powerful image of Mamy Lou, that despite everything, slave women did not lose their female principle or moral purpose under slavery. Rather, they defined and redefined both in order to sustain domestic slave life and domesticity, often quite successfully.

Among the various ways black women chose to describe their lives and those of the other females with whom they came in contact, they especially were forthright in their appreciation of self-reliant, self-determined survivalists who had the wherewithal to protect themselves and theirs, confrontationally if need be. Of course, most women were not able to act on these traits openly for fear of severe retaliation. But it is clear that slave women held great pride and esteem for those who did. They overwhelmingly were the women whom slave females spoke most often about in "heroic" terms, attributing to them what seem like (and may have been) fantastical deeds and attitudes. While other southern residents might have believed that a woman's exhibition of such conduct was a profound suggestion of "defeminization," slave women often utilized this kind of behavior in order to survive. Some even offered embellished accounts in order to inspire others to act or at least think similarly, and of course to bolster self-esteem among them. According to them, to be such a woman helped them to maintain their most fundamental claims to womanhood; that is, their female sexuality and physicality, and their roles as mothers, nurturers, and wives.

True stories, for example, abound about slave female rape and physical abuse despite the belief commonly held by southern whites that black women could not be raped, since they were naturally promiscuous. Most slave women found no way to fight back (and win), except perhaps in the telling of their painful stories, which exonerated the images of their sexual morality. Those slave women who found a more direct manner to resist emerged in the lore and mythology of slave women both as models for black female conduct and symbols of resistance that were unique to the black female experience. Slave mothers, in fact, often told stories of these women to their daughters as part of their socialization and to engender a sense of group pride.

Virginia Hayes Shepherd, for example, spoke in glowing terms of three slave women whom she had known or her mother had told her about, who diligently protected their female selves from the ill-treatment of white, male authority figures: one successfully avoided the sexual pursuit of her owner, while the other two refused to be treated in the fields like men, that is to be worked beyond their physical endurance as women. Seventy years after her emancipation, Minnie Folkes still felt the pain associated with witnessing her mother being whipped mercilessly by her overseer. Yet her explanation of her mother's suffering (that she had refused "to be wife to dis man") and her description of how her mother had taught her to protect herself from sexual abuse ("muma had sed 'Don't let nobody bother yo principle; 'cause dat wuz all yo' had'") are tinged with pride and respect. The elder Folkes was determined to have control of the physical attributes of her womanhood even if it meant routinely withstanding brutal beatings. Her resistance was a powerful lesson to Minnie. (Decades after her freedom, she lamented the lack of resolve of young women of the early 1900s to resist their sexual exploitation, drawing on her own mother's stories to suggest the kind of resistance that these women should have mounted.)

Fannie Berry too had been the target of white male sexual abuse. But she had managed to escape without harm. Fannie boasted of her successful act of resistance or, to use her own word, her "rebellion." But she could barely manage to conceal her delight when she told the tale of another slave woman, Sukie Abbott, "a big strappin' nigger gal," who resisted both her owner's sexual abuse and the slave trader's physical violation, linking the two as equally dehumanizing and, therefore, necessary for her to oppose.

Sukie was the Abbott's cook, and Berry tells her audience that Mr. Abbott was always trying to "make his gal." One day while Sukie was in the kitchen making soap, Mr. Abbott tried to rape her. He pulled her dress down and tried to push her onto the floor. Then, according to Berry, "dat black gal got mad."

> She took an' punch ole Marsa an' made him break loose an' den she gave him a shove an' push his hindparts down in de hot pot o' soap. Soap was near to bilin', an' it burnt him near to death. He got up holdin' his hindparts an' ran from de kitchen, nor darin' to yell, 'cause he didn't want Miss Sarah Ann [his wife and Sukie's mistress] to know 'bout it.

A few days later, Mr. Abbott took Sukie down to the slave market. She again faced sexual abuse and physical invasion as potential buyers stared, poked, and pinched her and checked the soundness of her teeth. According to Fannie, Sukie got mad again. Standing on the block, "she pult her dress up an' tole those ole nigger traders to look an' see if dey could fin' any teef down dere. . . . Marsa never did bother slave gals no mo," Berry added with relish.

Many witnesses at the slave market in Petersburg that day no doubt thought Sukie vulgar and promiscuous. Not surprisingly, Fannie Berry, a woman who could attest to the kind of rage which emerged from the attempts to dehumanize slave women that Sukie had withstood, concluded something altogether different. According to Fannie, Sukie had exacted a high price from her master and the slave trader. True, she lost her slave community when Mr. Abbott sold her in retaliation for her resistance, but she still managed to deny her owner his supposed right to claim her "female principle." She also demanded that her new buyer see her for what she was, a woman (i.e., her physical reference to her sexual organs), not just a new work animal whose value could be assessed by looking at its teeth. And perhaps more important for the slave girls and women who came to know her story, Sukie lived on in lore as an example of slave female heroism and humanity, as the "nigger gal" whose acts of courageous defiance quelled Abbott's sexual abuse of his slave women and girls. (The fear of being "found out" by his wife, friends, and relations through a slave woman like Sukie whom he could not control seemed to have been too much for him.)

Certainly it is less difficult to discern slave female notions of acceptable, or even heroic, behavior than to comprehend the roots of these ideals which, at the very least, are patently riddled with complexity. It is clear, for example, that many variables had impact. Literate African-Americans who had access to periodicals and other literature could have been as little or as greatly affected by published lectures, sermons, and stories on this subject as were literate whites. Certainly at least a significant minority had to have had some introduction to Christian beliefs about female behavior through local ministers and biblical interpretations of slave preachers and exhorters.

Virginia's early female slaves also probably came into contact with several cultural models that included various prescriptions for gender-specific behavior. Most, for example, may have been familiar with broadly defined, Western European and West and Central African bodies of tradition which they could, at least theoretically, have drawn on while trying to design their own belief systems, practices, and ordered domestic world. Obviously, the cultural attributes which defined the proper behavior for slave women changed over time as slaves moved from membership in African cultural groups to the creation of an African-American culture and society intricately intertwined with those of southern whites. What resulted was influenced not only by the amount and kind of exposure that Virginia's blacks had to these cultural models and their advocates but also by their perceptions of the viability of certain aspects of each standard in relation to their individual and group needs, along with their own personal affinities.

Time and location, for example, were operable variables which helped to prescribe the cultural affinities of southern slaveholders and their slaves. So too did "class" and "ethnic" differences among slaveholders. Among the "master" class in Virginia, for example, there were many differences of class as well as ethnicity which not only may account for numerous differences in the idealized gender-specific behavior of southern European-Americans but also may have affected the kinds of idealized behavior that their slaves may have internalized from contact with them. "Class" and "ethnic" differences among the slaves themselves undoubtedly were even more influential.

Among Virginia slave women, "class" and even "ethnicity" often were associated with the kind of work that they performed because the spatial relationship, differential skill, and material reward levels of women with different occupations sometimes formed something of a social, cultural, and sometimes even moral barrier between them. To an important extent, for example, field "hands" and house "servants" constructed different identities. These boundaries often were reinforced when color (which also was a potent standard of slave female beauty and something of a prerequisite for some occupations) also fell along these occupational lines. Obviously much of this kind of class stratification can be attributed to the value impositions and needs of slaveholders who demanded that their "servant" women adopt their ideals of personal conduct, morality, marriage, and family.

At stake, as far as domestics were concerned, was their place in the plantation's occupational spectrum and the kind of rewards and privileges that place afforded juxtaposed against the morality, self-definitions, and culture of the majority of slaves who lived differently from them. The eventual range of response was great: while some still resisted, others acquiesced, and some even enjoyed their cultural assimilation and the behavioral standards it imposed. " 'We never went to a party in our lives,' " explained the supposedly "handsome and lady-like Custis house servant." " 'Mother would not let any of her children go to parties. We were as genteely [sic] brought up as white people.' " Clearly, this light-skinned, domestic female slave drew great distinction between her socialization and "identity" and those of field or less "genteely" bred slave women. She not only applauded her ability and desire to imitate the social graces, restraint, and morality of her mistress' class and culture but also believed that her doing so made her quite different from and superior to those slave women who acted otherwise.

Female field laborers, on the other hand, usually did not face the same kind of pressures from their masters and mistresses to conform. This is not to say that there were no agricultural workers who shared or purposefully adopted some of the gendered social ideals of southern whites Yet, more often than not, their standards were influenced by the needs, priorities, and opinion of the majority of slaves who, like themselves, lived and worked outside much of the influence of the "big house."

The field slave woman's "resistance" to this kind of control of her intimate and public life, along with the other pressures of slave life and the existence of a non-European cultural heritage within her community, created codes of morality and activity and a basis for identity that sometimes were remarkably close to those of slaveholders, but also could differ profoundly. Slave women of various statuses, for example, appreciated within each other demonstrations of kindness, generosity, warmth, piety, service, and selflessness – characteristics which southern society often applauded in the personalities of antebellum white women of all classes but especially expected of the elite. Yet most slave women, except those who felt particularly intimately or emotionally tied to their owners, also applauded indications of self-determination and resistance to white male authority in their behavior that most whites believed improper female conduct.

Service to one's family and community were significant commitments that slave females learned early in the quarters. Behavior indicative of selflessness, generosity, kindness, and warmth were part of the assistance or service that slave women gave their families and slave friends. These activities not only allowed slave women an opportunity to demonstrate their humanity and femininity but also were suggestive to other slaves that they recognized and respected the humanity and frailties of fellow slaves. Often the aid these women rendered was gender specific. Young slave females, for example, learned to share the domestic duties or "women's work" in their families, often caring for younger siblings, washing and making clothes for their kin, and helping to prepare meals. This sphere of labor, taught and supervised by women and performed almost exclusively by females, reinforced within these slave girls a sense of their "femaleness" and helped to maintain gender bonds and boundaries that the labor they performed outside of their homes threatened to blur.

Yet their mothers and socializing kin also taught their daughters other important sociopolitical behavioral skills that were not gender specific. Young male and female slaves learned a whole collection of dos and don'ts derived from communal concerns, such as not to abuse other slaves through lying and stealing, to keep the secrets of the quarters from whites, to protect and aid runaways, to help sick and disabled slaves by sharing their work loads, and to give covert aid to one another whenever possible. Obedience and reverence of slave elders was another important lesson, as was a general and genuine attitude of respect for other slaves.

The emphasis on gender-specific behavior within slave families became more important as children grew older. As slave girls reached adolescence, their mothers and other female kin prepared them to take on the most important commitments of their adult lives – marriage and motherhood. Indeed, whatever class or ethnic distinctions various occupations may have imposed on slave females, their roles as wives and mothers were universally important. "Master married me to one of the best colored men in the world," Marriah Hines told her interviewer. "I had five chillun by him." It was bad luck for a girl to walk around with one shoe off, another ex-slave said. "She'll stay single as many years as the number of steps she taken."

Hines's statement rightfully suggests that the significance of marriage and motherhood was intimately bound up in slave women's constructions of their identity. Yet motherhood in itself was singularly important to adult female identity and morality. Elizabeth Keckley's autobiography, for example, details the scabrous circumstances under which she, as a Virginia slave woman, gained a sense of her need to protect herself and have some control of her daily life as well as her future. Mrs. Keckley confirmed that she first learned a sense of self-reliance while acting as the surrogate mother to her mistress' child, noting that when she was only four years old she was given the burdensome task of caring for the newborn baby. Yet it was her own motherhood which compelled her to the realization that she had to be resilient, resourceful, and rebellious enough to protect, if not her own life, then certainly that of her son. The all-important roles of bearing and rearing one's own children caused many other Virginia slave women to conclude, and act, similarly.

Slave mothers viewed their youngsters both as extensions of their identities – a continuation of their kinship lines and proof of their existence – and as providers of future care and consolation. The importance of slave children as future bearers of their mothers' family heritage especially is suggested in the naming patterns evident among slave families. Often slave women, for example, named their daughters for themselves as well as other female relations. These same slave mothers also often spoke of their young as persons on whom they could depend for love, comfort, and service when they became older. "Tho I know From my heart that you and Mistress would never See me Suffer as long as my Body Lives and you Live," the slave woman Phillis wrote to Mr.

and Mrs. St. George Tucker during the 1820s, "I am going down very fast to my grave and . . . I would [like to] go and Live those other few dais with master Beverly and my Children." "My last child died two weeks ago," lamented a slave mother at Craney Island, Virginia. "She was amazing helpful. She could sew and knit. She could spin and weave and mind the chickens and tend the children." In spite of the oppressive and inevitably painful experiences of black women trying to rear their children as slaves, most respected and embraced their motherhood.

Even though child rearing was a task that slave mothers shared with other slave females in their families and quarters, they closely supervised the upbringing of their young. Many risked altercations with slaveholding men and women by merely asserting that they should have command over their children's lives. The bond that slave women felt with their youngsters caused many to make innumerable sacrifices – heroic sacrifices that they were proud to recount in their interviews and autobiographies. Some, like Mary Ann Wyatt of King and Queen County and Caroline Taylor of Norfolk, for example, worked incessantly in order to gain the right to "hire out" their "time" and that of their children. Others managed to escape to freedom with some of their young. Countless more refused opportunities to run away because they did not want to leave their youngsters behind.

The majority of slave mothers realistically were not able to secure their children from the most devastating consequences of slavery, such as brutal whippings and permanent separation from family and loved ones. Few slaves even expected that these women would risk further harm to themselves or their families by publicly criticizing slaveholding men and women who were responsible for such acts. After all, a mother's fundamental priority was to keep her family intact. More often than not, open defiance of her master or mistresses did more to threaten this hope than to promote it. Yet slave women did celebrate and "create" females who occasionally risked themselves (not their children or someone else) in order to make their feelings, as mothers, known.

Nancy Williams of Yanceville, Virginia, for example, recalled the story of "Ant Cissy," a slave woman who called their owner a "mean dirty nigger-trader" when he sold her daughter Lucy. When her son Hendley died some time later, Cissy refused to publicly acknowledge any grief for her son's death, preferring instead to again take the opportunity to voice her bitter feelings about Lucy's sale. "Ant Cissy ain't sorrored much" at the death of her child, Williams concluded. "She went straight up to ole Marsa' an' shouted in his face, 'Praise Gawd, praise Gawd! My little chile is gone to Jesus. That's one chile of mine you never gonna sell.' " In Williams's tale, Ant Cissy took tremendous risk when she criticized her master, not once but two times, for the power he exercised over her daughter's life. Through this image, however, Williams celebrates a woman who spoke for countless other slave women who suffered her pain and loss, sometimes repeatedly. If Nancy's story is completely accurate, Cissy's master probably wrote her off as a crazy old woman whose outburst posed little threat to his authority. Still the risk she took, and the cause she took on, made her a heroic image in the minds of young slave women like Nancy Williams.

And slave women did not just verbally criticize their owners for mistreatment of their children. Relying on their sense of responsibility as mothers, they rebelled against the poor material support that slaveholding men and women provided their families. Slave motherhood meant not hesitating to steal, lie, and cheat in order to guarantee the physical survival of their children and themselves. Their numerous stories of defiance in this regard again emphasized their determination to create self-images in which they had some control of their lives and used it to protect their children.

Perhaps two of the most significant variables which affected the lifestyles of slave women and their interpretation of it, given the importance of marriage and motherhood to slave female identity, were their domestic relations and the conditions of domesticity owners imposed upon them. The size and makeup of slave holdings, as well as the domestic structures these demographic characteristics in part inspired, undoubtedly exerted influence. Let us first consider the residential patterns of slave couples and families, and then some of the possible impact these patterns may have had on the behavioral standards, identity, and morality of the women involved.

Virginia's slaves were part of a variety of marriage, family, and household types – nuclear and extended family structures; monogamous, polygamous, and serial marriages; single and multiple generational households of various combinations of kin, friends, and sometimes strangers. This was so even when conditions theoretically seemed optimal for them to be part of nuclear households, such as a large slaveholding boasting equal numbers of men and women. Moreover, even that significant minority of slaves who lived in nuclear households did not experience the kind of family or domestic life that was synonymous with those who were free and middle class. Consider some characteristics of slave residential patterns in Virginia.

At least from the mid–eighteenth century through the antebellum era, slave women dominated small slaveholdings, living on farms and in households where there were few adult slave men. Matrifocality was the most common characteristic of their household and family styles. Their small slave communities and households, in fact, were those comprising largely single mothers, abroad wives, and their children.

Those who were married usually had monogamous, but not coresidential, and oftentimes short-term, or serial, relationships. The situation could, however, shift drastically for women who were part of larger holdings. Marriageable-aged men, for example, often dominated the population of moderate and large holdings (of ten or more). These findings are significant because they indicate that even when the general sex ratio was virtually even within the adult age cohorts within the large populations, most slaveholdings, whether large or small, did not have nearly equal numbers of men and women in childbearing, marriageable-age cohorts.

Moreover, while there tended to be greater numerical equality between men and women of marriageable age on holdings of twenty or more slaves, the men and women who were part of these holdings often were not married to one another. Instead of these holdings producing nuclear families and coresidential spouses, a variety of residential and family forms emerged, particularly large numbers of single men living together, and again single mothers and abroad wives living with their children and sometimes other kin, but not their children's fathers....

More often than not, Virginia slave women, even domestic and other privileged slave women, were single mothers and abroad wives who faced the challenge of rearing their children and addressing their families' needs without the daily attention or resources of their husbands or the fathers of their children. Those females who lived in small holdings, in particular, effectively were raised and later reared their own children in black female-dominated communities – there were few slave men of any relation (husband, blood relation, or friend) available to share daily care, socialization, or leadership tasks. Moreover, slave women faced the mounting threat of profound change even to these kinds of domestic arrangements, since more and more women and children left the state or their previous residence as part of the domestic slave trade and slave rental business over time. And keep in mind that most did not leave with their families intact.... Slave women in female-dominated households and communities, therefore, not only had to act practically as mother, father, and household head but also had to prepare themselves and their children to expect that one day they would have to survive even without the limited resources that they offered each other when they had the luxury of living together.

The kind of slave marital and familial diversity and instability prevalent among Virginia slaves had both practical and ideological influence on female gender convention, morality, and self-definition. Faced with profound challenges to their effectiveness or even permanence as wives, mothers, and community members, they appreciated oppositional and self-deterministic behavior. These ideals, after all, contextualized slave women's physical and psychological resistance to authority located outside of themselves and their communities.

Certainly the residential patterns and consequent marital and familial structures of slave women were not the only determinants of female slave behavior. The oppositional nature of slave culture and its origins, in general, and the nature of female identity among slave women, more than anything else, were responsible for the behavioral ideals and the ideology of heroic identities they constructed. Yet, in a society in which European-American female powerlessness and passivity, submission and secondhand citizenship emerged as by-products of a powerful patriarchy operating within the designs of coresidential nuclear family, it is not difficult to understand that without this patriarchy, their nuclear families and their male household head, white women's lives, to say nothing of their ideals, also would have been quite different. This kind of gendered dichotomy found in most white southern homes at the time was not a reality for slave men and women. It was not even a reality in the minority of slave families that comprised a resident father, mother, and children.

Slave husbands never provided the sole or most significant means of financial support for their wives and children. Husbands had no legal claim to their families and, accordingly, could not legitimately demand their economic resources or offer them protection from abuse or exploitation. The primary role of the slave mother, if compared with "mainstream" American gender convention, also was deeply compromised, for she never was able to give the needs of her husband and children greatest priority. Even though most slave children were part of matrifocal families, the slave woman's most important daily activities encompassed the labor that she performed for her owner, not for her family. This responsibility claimed so much of her time and energy that childbearing was limited, while child rearing necessarily was a task she shared with a number of females, within and outside of her blood and marriage-related family. These were the usual circumstances for slave life even when they were part of nuclear families. For that majority of men, women, and children who did not live as such, idealized notions of female passivity and helplessness were even more absurd. Most slave children grew up in households with their mothers but not their fathers present on a daily basis. It was their mothers who had to make the day-to-day decisions that fashioned their lives, their mothers and other members of their female communities who had to provide whatever protection and support they received. The male presence was so tenuous because of imposed residential isolation and frequent sale and hiring that women became the stabilizing forces in slave families and communities.

It comes as no surprise, then, that there are so many exemplary and heroic women found in the autobiographical stories of Virginia slave women. Heroism in the face of such austere social conditions became an especially important characteristic in slave women's self-identity.

The historical texts comprising the interviews that slave and ex-slave women like Fannie Berry gave, therefore, are important descriptive chronicles of southern society from the black female perspective. Criss-crossing the persons, events, and attitudes which were part of her life, Berry presents her audience not only with her own story but also with an array of narratives centered on the lives of other females whom she had come to know and sometimes to respect – the courageous and clever Mamy Lou; "Poor A'nt Nellie," who chose suicide rather than face another brutal beating; the much-loved Rachel, who managed to find her way back to her family after being illegally sold; the secretive Polly Monroe, who kept her free black husband hidden in her cabin's root cellar; the conflicted child Daphne, who finally chose to live with her master and mistress rather than her slave family; the indomitable Sukie, who fought her owner for control of her body; and, of course, Berry's consistently compromised slave mistress, Miss Sarah Ann.

Curiously, but not surprisingly given their lack of numbers at her place of residence, men rarely appear in Berry's long and detailed account of her life and the lives of the other women she spoke about. Her narrative is not unique in this regard. When men are present, they lack the complexity and moral presence of the women whose lives she so vividly recalls. The men are "stock figures," almost stereotypical in character. There are, for example, the sadistic, sexually depraved slave masters; the vicious, deceptive slave traders; and the fun-loving, emasculated, black male youths like Mamy Lou's John. Fannie rarely mentions her husband, a railroad man whom she sees only occasionally. She makes no mention of a father at all. Instead, the slave women she brings to life take on "typical" masculine characteristics: they are bold, active, courageous, aggressive and self-determined.

The identity that Fannie Berry and others constructed for themselves stood in stark contrast to their characterizations of white women. Calling planter women "hell cats" and "devils," slave girls and women implicated the immoral, indeed "unholy," behavior of slaveholding women who they believed abandoned their promise of "Christian" or moral female behavior when they forced black women to steal food, lie about slave activities, feign illness, and generally participate in all kinds of resistance behavior. Not surprisingly, slave females especially reacted strongly to those slaveholding women whose actions or attitudes had had some effect on their roles as wives and mothers or, generally, had some impact on slave family life. The fact that Liza Brown's mistress had Liza's mother stripped naked and beaten when she was pregnant, for example, seemed to incense Liza much more than the usual abuse this mistress meted out to other slaves who were not in that condition. Eliza Smith was accepting of her mistress' dishonesty and abuse until she refused to pay for the appropriate medical attention for Eliza's son. Cordelia Long put up with years of abuse from her mistress until this slaveholding woman sold Cordelia's two children.

On the other hand, Fannie Berry thought that her female owner was especially kind to attempt to keep slave couples and families united and to purchase the husbands of her slave women. Fannie also praised another slaveholding woman, Delia Mann, and other members of her family for the respect they demonstrated for her marriage – allowing the wedding to take place in their parlor and providing food for a reception. The one act of generosity that Mildred Graves described when speaking of her slave experience was that her mistress had given her a "cast off dress" in which she was married.

Slave women thus conspicuously constructed not only their own identities in their recollections but also the identities of their mistresses. Consider Fannie Berry's protrayal of her slave mistress, Sarah Ann Abbott. "Miss Sarah Ann was uh fine woman, even ef she was uh slave owner," Berry noted with a sense of finality to her description. The ex-slave obviously weighed carefully her good and bad memories of the white woman who had been such a large part of her life and that of her family and community of slave women before she rendered her concluding assessment. Miss Sarah Ann, according to Berry, was not of heroic character, but she "was very good to her slaves" and for that Berry was willing to give her credit. She took care of them when they were sick, allowed them to have a pet (a cat the slaves playfully named Tom Nippy Cat), tried to keep some slave couples united, and even dared to question a neighboring slave master's harsh treatment of his slave property.

Even while extolling the virtues of Sarah Ann, however, Fannie could not erase the relative quality of her description – "Miss Sarah Ann was uh fine woman, even ef she was uh slave owner." For Berry realized that regardless of what Abbott had done for her slaves, she had been a member of the slaveholding class who benefited from the oppression of Fannie and the other blacks whom she owned. Since Berry's code of morality and certainly her sense of female heroism were intricately tied to a fundamental quest for black survival, humanity, and freedom (of spirit if not body), she hardly could afford Mrs. Abbott an unambiguous character reference.

But Fannie did not view Sarah Ann as just another slaveholder with like-minded priorities. Mrs. Abbott also was a woman, and part of

Fannie Berry's judgment of Sarah Ann Abbott clearly was grounded in her convictions about female identity, the purposeful and privileged behavior of women, convictions that she derived from the experiences and ideals of slave women. Time and time again in her narration of her days as a slave, Berry juxtaposes her life and those of other slave women whom she had known with that of her mistress, provocatively suggesting the profound limitations (physical, emotional, situational, moral) that Mrs. Abbott, even as a white and a member of the elite, maintained in her interactions with her slaves. It was these limitations (or her unwillingness to make certain sacrifices in order to help her slaves), in Berry's judgment, that denied a basic heroic content in Mrs. Abbott's character that could have linked her, as a woman, to slave women.

While this mistress did not sanction the sale of slaves but rather hired them out, she seemingly could not keep her husband from selling those whom he found troublesome. Nor could Sarah Ann deter him from pursuing the sexual favors of her slave cook. She could not prevent her neighbor from whipping one of his slaves to death; nor did she feel able or compelled to report it to the local authorities after witnessing the brutal crime. The conditional quality of Berry's opinion of Sarah Ann Abbott, therefore, continuously begs the question of how a woman of such power (derived from her race and socioeconomic status) could feign such powerlessness in the aid of her slaves when women like Mamy Lou, who was poor, black, and merely the property of Abbott and her husband, found the wherewithal to do otherwise.

Indeed, it is certain that while Berry concluded that Abbott's intentions toward her slaves usually were good, she often depicted this slaveholding woman's ameliorative role in the lives of her blacks as a passive one, prodigiously hemmed in by her "place" as a woman and her economic concerns and sense of class allegiance as a slaveholder. These deep-seated qualities of this white woman's personality and lifestyle did not elude the sharp eye of Fannie Berry and figured prominently in her moral assessment. The choices that Berry believed that Mrs. Abbott – white, socially prominent, and with relatively substantial financial resources – made with regard to her slaves clearly were not the choices that she believed that she, as a slave woman, necessarily would have made.

Indeed, the combination of ideals incumbent in the self-images slave women actively created in their verbal and written texts – the one set which embraced a survivalist, self-determined philosophy and the other which emphasized service, honesty, selflessness, and good works – sometimes seemed at odds. Yet they were not conflicting value systems. Rather they comprised one system of morality, a morality whose benefits were exclusive to those who lived and acted within the community from which it derived, a morality founded on the perpetuation of black life, humanity, and femininity through good works and service within and opposition to those without who threatened this perpetuation....

Slave women imposed their ideas and ideals about female behavior not only on each other but also on the planter women with whom they came in contact. Their demonstrations of disregard for or disobedience of slaveholding women often were fundamental indictments of their disrespect for these elite women – disrespect grounded in slave women's beliefs about appropriate female behavior. Thus, while the southern antebellum patriarchy actively mythologized the elite white woman as the model of femininity for the world to emulate, slave women relied on their own standards. They created their own practical codes and a lofty mythology from their own reality and, in the wake, constructed viable, proud self-images that helped them evade dehumanization and defeminization.

Study Questions and Further Reading for Part VI

1 What were some of the advantages elite white women gained by breast feeding infants?
2 What were some of the problems elite white women encountered when breast feeding infants and how did they try to overcome these problems?
3 How did slave women's definitions of womanhood differ from those advanced by whites?
4 To what extent was there intimate interaction between black and white women in the Old South?

Bynum, Victoria 1992: *Unruly Women: The Politics of Social and Sexual Control in the Old South.* Chapel Hill: University of North Carolina Press.
Cashin, Joan E. 1991: *A Family Venture: Men and Women on the Southern Frontier.* New York: Oxford University Press.
Censer, Jane Turner 1984: *North Carolina Planters and their Children, 1800–1860.* Baton Rouge: Louisiana State University Press.
Clinton, Catherine 1982: *The Plantation Mistress: Woman's World in the Old South.* New York: Pantheon.
Fox-Genovese, Elizabeth 1988: *Within the Plantation Household: Black and White Women of the Old South.* Chapel Hill: University of North Carolina Press.
Friedman, Jean E. 1985: *The Enclosed Garden: Women and Community in the Evangelical South, 1830–1900.* Chapel Hill: University of North Carolina Press.
Jones, Jacqueline 1985: *Labor of Love, Labor of Sorrow: Black Women, Work, and the Family from Slavery to Freedom.* New York: Basic Books.

Lebsock, Suzanne 1984: *The Free Women of Petersburg: Status and Culture in a Southern Town, 1784–1860.* New York: Norton.

McMillen, Sally G. 1990: *Motherhood in the Old South: Pregnancy, Childbirth, and Infant Rearing.* Baton Rogue: Louisiana State University Press.

McMillen, Sally G. 1992: *Southern Women: Black and White in the Old South.* Arlington Heights, IL: Harlan Davidson.

Scott, Anne Firor 1970: *The Southern Lady: From Pedestal to Politics, 1830–1930.* Chicago, IL: University of Chicago Press.

Sommerville, Diane Miller 1995: The rape myth in the Old South reconsidered. *Journal of Southern History*, 71, 481–512.

Stevenson, Brenda E. 1996: *Life in Black and White: Family and Community in the Slave South.* New York: Oxford University Press.

Varon, Elizabeth R. 1998: *We Mean To Be Counted: White Women and Politics in Antebellum Virginia.* Chapel Hill: University of North Carolina Press.

White, Deborah Gray 1985: *Ar'n't I a Woman: Female Slaves in the Plantation South.* New York: Norton.

Index